The

Modern Cook's Manual

LYNDA BROWN

The
Modern
Cook's
Manual

All You Need to
Know About Cooking
with Over 200 Recipes

Michael Joseph
London

For Joanna,
fingers crossed

MICHAEL JOSEPH LTD
Published by the Penguin group
27 Wrights Lane, London W8 5TZ
Viking Penguin Inc., 375 Hudson Street, New York, New York 10014, USA
Penguin Books Australia Ltd, Ringwood, Victoria, Australia
Penguin Books Canada Ltd, 10 Alcorn Avenue, Toronto, Ontario, Canada M4V 3B2
Penguin Books (NZ) Ltd, 182–190 Wairau Road, Auckland 10, New Zealand

Penguin Books Ltd, Registered Offices: Harmondsworth, Middlesex, England

First published 1995
Copyright © Lynda Brown 1995
Illustrations copyright © Natalie Crouch

Typeset in Adobe Garamond by Selwood Systems, Midsomer Norton
Printed in England by Clays Ltd, St Ives plc

A CIP catalogue record for this book is available from the British Library

ISBN 0 7181 3815 5

Contents

Introduction

This is a book about modern cooking. It is not a traditional cookery manual nor does it make any attempt to rely on accepted views of what good cooking is. Starting from a blank canvas, I've tried to make sense of food and cooking as we want and need it today. Whether I've tackled an ingredient such as red peppers or saffron, how to deal with fresh fish or techniques such as how to barbecue or stir-fry, I have sought to answer one basic question only: 'What do you *really* need to know?' In short, it is a book about boiling things down to the basics.

In the past, we were led to believe that the more professional skills we acquired, the better and more accomplished cooks we became: we would start by learning how to boil an egg and count ourselves as having arrived when we could bone and stuff a duck and give a flawless dinner party for eight. But modern lifestyles and ideas demand food that is easy to prepare and easy to cook and this has not just revolutionised what we eat but made us reconsider our whole approach to cooking.

Good cooking today is simply being able to cook the food and dishes *you* like, the way *you* like them. Don't worry about what you can't cook, but cook to suit yourself and develop the confidence to know that this is all that counts and you are well on the way to being a good cook. After all, not even professional cooks are good at everything, and there is no reason why we should be either. Moreover, you don't need to have learnt how to poach an egg or make white sauce before you can risk grilling a chop or making a salsa: go ahead and grill the chop and make the salsa.

You might, for instance, be the kind of cook who likes pasta and who is content to learn what good pasta is and how to cook that well; you might take care to learn how to cook a steak exactly to your liking; take the time to buy potatoes with flavour; become a whizz kid at making instant pestos and opt for simple dressings made with decent olive oil rather than complicated sauces. Wanting maximum reward for minimum effort, not thinking twice about using a food processor and happily embracing anything new (or old) as long as it tastes good and is easy to do does not make you a second-rate cook; on the contrary, it will make you a mighty fine one.

How easy, then, is it to cook? Very. The big leap forward for modern cooks is not to compare the kind of cooking done at home with that of a restaurant, or to believe the *Masterchef* myth that the skills a chef has are necessary in order to be a good cook. This is not to say that all cooking is a doddle or that everyone can become a brilliant cook overnight, but that there is more than enough choice to suit everyone who wants to cook their own food without it once becoming boring or complicated. You could spend your life trying to make the perfect quiche and fail. Meanwhile, you could have had a lot of fun with pasta.

Modern cooking is about respecting your ingredients and letting their natural flavours shine through. This means anyone who cares about what they eat and has a native curiosity about food and cooking can cook modern food. The only skills you need are common sense, the ability to take note of what is happening in the pan and a little loving care. To cook well, you also need to cook the kind of dishes you enjoy eating. If you like eating salads, for example, you will make wonderful salads. If you don't, you won't. It is as simple as that. As long as you have genuine empathy with your ingredients and enjoy your food, I sincerely believe you can't – and won't – go far wrong.

At the heart of this book, then, lies the conviction that it is not so much the craft of cooking that is important these days as the craft of eating; that the quality of life is intimately bound up with what you eat; and that good cooking is about nourishment. You won't find in it how to make a mousse, or a quiche, or anything, in fact, that can't be prepared in less than 30 minutes and with minimum effort. Instead, I have tried hard to concentrate on what is relevant to the modern cook – how to buy, store and cook food in the best and simplest ways, how to judge when it is cooked and what are the important things you need to know to enable you to be your own cook. I have focused entirely on important basic food groups and currently popular ingredients and techniques and dealt with them in depth. Inevitably, this has meant some hard decisions and meant that subjects dear to my heart such as salads, bread and pizza will have to wait until another time. In the meantime, what I hope for most is that making sense of my experience will help whoever reads this book to make sense of theirs; and that, when you choose to cook, this book may help you enjoy your cooking more.

Happy cooking!

1

Cooking: Some Basics

This section of the book is about the 'How To' of cookery. Rather than concentrating on traditional know-how and techniques, it aims to provide a basic blueprint for when you shop and cook.

Cookery is like a three-legged stool: shopping, equipment and the act of cooking itself. The more familiar you are with your ingredients, the more comfortable you feel with your equipment and the more often you chop an onion (and work out the best way to do so), the sooner cooking becomes second nature.

Shopping

Writing this book has made it clearer to me than ever that the key to good cooking and good eating is buying good ingredients. The reason is very simple: the better your ingredients, the less you need to do to them and the more successful the finished dish will be.

That said, good quality and expensive food are often confused with each other, and it is important to distinguish between them. Expensive food is *not* necessarily the best. This is particularly true of fashionable ingredients (monkfish was once cheap, remember). Perhaps the most flagrant example of this is sun-dried tomatoes; always expensive, yet I suspect most that are for sale would be rejected on the spot in Italy. Food with impressive packaging is another category to be wary of. Nor is cheap food always inferior. Cheaper cuts of meat have more flavour, and fruit and vegetables are better and cheaper at the height of their season than they will ever be grown at other times, however expensive.

Good quality food speaks for itself, whatever the price. This is where learning to recognise what good quality food looks like will repay you many times over.

Equipment

You need very little equipment to cook; and not much more to cook well. Gadgets that are supposed to save you time rarely live up to expectations and tend to take up precious space. Nor do you need to buy the best. Domestic cooks are not professional cooks. We do not need the most impressive set of heavy duty knives, copper pans or a bottom drawer full of piping bags, interlocking soufflé dishes and dariole moulds.

- Build up your cooking equipment gradually as your cooking style develops.
- Be aware of the limitations of your cooking equipment. Where possible use the right equipment for the right job.
- When choosing equipment, think through its function. Handle it and get the feel of it as much as possible.
- Ask to see it work and ask as many questions as you can think of.
- Kitchens and equipment are personal: buy what you like.

Cheap and useful

Cake skewer For testing when vegetables are cooked, and to pierce chicken thighs and pork to see whether the juices are clear.

Hand grater This is simpler to use than a food processor and far easier to clean. For small quantities it is perfect. A square-shaped one, made out of stainless steel, has 4 grating surfaces – the fine grater is specially good for root ginger and onions as well as lemon zest – and lasts a lifetime.

18cm/7 inch serrated Kitchen Devil knife Light, lasts a lifetime and sharp. Useful for general slicing purposes.

Kitchen Devil knife sharpener Small, compact, award-winning knife sharpener, which sits on the work surface and sets the blade of the knife at the correct angle.

Tiny iron frying pan For toasting spices.

Potato masher Still the best and easiest way to mash potatoes, other root vegetables, dried cooked beans and to give instant texture to vegetable soups.

Muslin For straining yoghurt, stocks, etc. and for covering steamed rice or grains. J-cloths serve the same function but are not as nice to use.

Olive oil pourer A cork stopper with a thin metal tube in the centre that is inserted into the top of the olive oil bottle. Invaluable when making mayonnaise, as the oil comes out in a thin trickle instead of a gush. Very cheap.

If you cannot find one, you can easily make one by cutting a small groove either side of a cork that will fit into the top of the oil bottle.

Wooden/plastic pasta fork The best thing by far for scooping pasta out of boiling water. Make sure it has deep prongs.

Perforated spoon A large, very flat one is best. Invaluable for scooping out blanched vegetables, gnocchi, deep-fried food and for skimming stock and sauces.

Plastic-meshed sieves Light, do not rust and are easy to store. They make very good makeshift steamers for reheating or steaming rice. Being plastic, they are not particularly durable and melt if you put them too close to a naked flame.

Whisks The important thing about a whisk is to match its size to the amount of food or liquid you are whisking. Flat and spiral whisks are fine for liquids; balloon whisks are best for egg whites.

Wooden spoons The trick here is to have a variety of sizes. Use a size appropriate to the type or quantity of food you are mixing. Very large ones are necessary for mixing large amounts of food or dough. Small ones are useful for making mayonnaise.

Wooden and bristle washing up brush Comes complete with a hooked handle. Infinitely better than plastic ones. Nicer to look at, more pleasing to use and more efficient.

Zester This is invaluable for grating and cutting lemon and orange rind into julienne strips. Some, however, are sharper, more effective and easier to use than others – check with the shop first.

Others

Mushroom brush A small, soft brush available from specialist kitchen shops specifically for brushing dirt from and cleaning mushrooms.

Mouli If you make soups and home-made tomato sauces, this hand-operated sieve produces the best texture and is one of the few traditional pieces of equipment worth having. It is easy to use, though fiddly to clean. The medium mesh is the most useful.

Parmesan shaver For shaving fine slivers of Parmesan cheese. Again, you need to choose with care, as some cut the cheese into thin slices rather than shavings. Buy a proper Italian one if you can.

Pestle and mortar Though superseded by food processors for making pestos and large quantities of pastes or mayonnaise, nevertheless still invaluable for grinding up small amounts of spices, toasted sesame seeds, hazelnuts and walnuts, and for making small quantities of mayonnaise. Choose one with a pestle that has a broad rather than narrow base – the broader the base, the more effective and faster it will grind.

FOOD PROCESSORS

Food processors take the hard work out of chopping, mashing and pulverising food. I also use them for soups and to make pestos, though many cooks I know prefer a blender. They are fiddly to clean, take up space on the work surface and are noisy. Unless you cater for large quantities, the various slicing attachments are less useful than they seem: nine times out of ten, a hand grater is easier and quicker.

All are much more effective at processing medium quantities of food; no matter what manufacturers claim, processing very small amounts of food is tedious and fiddly. Some brands are much heavier than others – a small but important consideration if you need to keep it in a cupboard or move it about. If you only ever cook for one or two, a compact food processor will serve you better than a large one.

Cheap food processors are a false economy. Whether to buy one with variable speeds or one that automatically adjusts its speed according to the nature of the food in the bowl is a matter of preference; I find adjustable speeds are more versatile and make you feel more in control.

MEASURING SCALES

The most important feature of measuring scales is the bowl, which should be large and rest firmly on the base. Battery-operated digital scales are the modern equivalent of non-stick pans, are the easiest to use and store, light, take up the least amount of room and convert weights from British Imperial to metric at the press of a button. Not that it matters much, but no domestic scales are completely accurate. If you use digital scales, you will find that they have a margin of error somewhere between 5–10g/$\frac{1}{4}$oz, that is, will show the same reading whether you put exactly 30g/1oz of an ingredient on the scale or a bit more or less.

PANS

There is a certain amount of snobbery attached to pans, which it is wise to ignore. Pans tend to divide into those that are heavy and expensive; and those that are thin and cheap. Non-stick pans really do make life easy. It does not matter that they may not last a lifetime. See-through lids on pans are another worthwhile innovation, as are stay-cool handles.

Of the other popular materials, stainless steel looks good and is durable. Stainless steel is not a good conductor of heat, so make sure you buy ones with thick aluminium bases, which will conduct the heat efficiently and evenly. Cast iron is another material that is not a good conductor of heat; once heated, however, it retains its heat for a considerable period. Cast iron cookware is lovely but heavy – a small but important point when you are trying to get it out of the oven full of your dinner. Excellent for slow, steady cooking, it is far less suited for frying or top-of-the-stove cooking. Aluminium is light and second only to copper in its ability to conduct heat well but it reacts readily with acidic foods.

How many pans?

The number of pans you need depends on the kind of cooking you do, and how many you regularly cook for. A basic set – one small, medium and large pan – is essential, as is a frying pan. Buy a frying pan with a lid and it doubles up as an all-purpose pan in which to cook everything; choose non-stick.

- A tiny frying pan is invaluable for toasting spices, nuts, melting butter or frizzling herbs when making small amounts of pasta sauces. If you can't find one, any tiny deep-sided pan is similarly useful.
- Of specialist pans, a cast iron ridged grill pan or grillomat, which is used to char-grill meat, fish and vegetables, is invaluable. Choose one with a black matt enamel coating, which

prevents it from rusting and lasts a lifetime. Speaking personally, it is the one pan I covet. For full details, see p 263.

- The best all-purpose frying pan is a sauté pan. This has deep sides and a lid, and can be used as a frying pan and casserole dish when cooking on top of the stove.
- A fish kettle is only necessary if you are likely to cook whole large fish.
- If you make stock, a stainless steel stock pot is a good investment, and can double up as a preserving pan to make jams and preserves.
- If you pot roast meat or poultry, a large oval Le Creuset cocotte is a good investment.
- If you like to steam food, the most useful all-purpose steamers are those with a graded base which fits into various sizes of pans. To be effective, the lid must fit tightly and the steamer fit snugly into the pan.

Non-stick pans

Non-stick pans have revolutionised the way we cook; they may not have the kudos or feel-good factor of shiny stainless steel but they are tailor-made for modern cooking. They are easy to use and clean, take all the worry out of frying and enable you to cook with the minimum amount of fat. There are three types:

Cheap non-stick pans These are not worth buying. They have thin bases and thin non-stick coatings that scratch, blister and peel off easily.

Quality non-stick pans Good quality non-stick pans have heavier bases with bonded non-stick coatings, which do not peel or blister and last a reasonable time.

Titanium non-stick pans These are the latest, heaviest and most expensive type. Made from a rock-hard substance which is naturally non-stick, these last a lifetime.

To protect the non-stick coating, they should not be subjected to fierce heat or used with metal spoons, which scratch and damage the surface.

They should not be cleaned with abrasive scourers or cleaning material.

Non-stick pans burn easily; or rather all pans burn, but with non-stick pans the surface is irreparably damaged, whereas with other types of pans, as long as the burn is not severe, it is usually possible to scrub them clean.

Wok

The most versatile pan of all. For full details see p 267.

KNIVES

There is as much snobbery and confusing advice given about knives as pans. In addition to a bread knife, the only four you need are a chef's knife, a small vegetable knife, a serrated knife and a palette knife. Of the rest, a fish filleting knife is the most useful. If you roast meat, you will need a carving knife. Almost as important as the knives is a sharpener that is easy to use and effective.

Buying knives

Choose one which feels comfortable when you hold it, and which is strong enough for the job it has to do. For domestic purposes, good-quality mid-priced knives offer the best value.

- Knives divide into two groups: the traditional plain-edged knives which slice food; and modern stay-sharp knives, which have finely serrated edges and which saw through food rather than slicing it. Stay-sharp knives are fearfully sharp, and may even be too sharp for your needs.
- How good a knife is depends on the quality and hardness of the blade, and how the blade is fixed to the shaft. The best have blades that run throughout (or almost) the length of the knife; this makes the knife much stronger and better balanced. The rivets which hold handle and blade together should also go through the handle and not be merely cosmetic. Different brands of knives stay sharp longer than others.

- How comfortable a knife is to hold depends to a large extent on the shape and curve of the handle; some brands are much straighter than others and sit flat in the hand, others are noticeably curved. Wood feels better than plastic.

Storing knives

Knives should always be stored on a knife rack, in a wallet or knife block rather than kept loose in the cutlery drawer. This is safer and protects the knife blade and tip from accidental damage.

Knife sharpeners

A traditional butcher's steel needs skill to use properly, and is not necessarily as suitable for domestic purposes as modern compact sharpeners. The best mimic the traditional sharpening steel and are designed so that the knife blade is inserted at the correct angle, thereby making sure that the edge does not become distorted. For ease of use, choose one which sits flat on the work surface.

Sharpening knives

A new knife has a blade with a perfect edge. To keep this edge, it must be sharpened with a gentle action which does not strip away too much of the blade and at the correct angle; if not, in time the edge of the blade will warp and will not cut as effectively even though it is sharp. Knives should also be sharpened little and often.

If using a steel, the correct angle to position the knife is 15–20 degrees. To do this, hold the steel vertical, place the sharp edge of the blade against the steel and position the (blunt) edge of the blade 7mm/$\frac{1}{4}$ inch away from the steel. Sharpen the knife by moving it across the steel, first on one side of the steel, then the other.

The knife should be sharp enough for the job it has to do, but no more. In domestic kitchens, too sharp knives can be a nightmare – where children are around, for example – and are all too easy to cut yourself with: leave razor sharp knives to the professionals.

OVENS

Whether you cook for one or twenty, an oven offers convenience and freedom. Unlike cooking on top of the stove, you don't have to watch over food constantly. Nor is there anything to match the rich caramelising effect, which gives depth to any dish browned in the oven. An oven still remains at the heart of the kitchen, and brings its own emotional and psychological rewards. A wok says you have panache; an oven shows you care.

The traditional view of how to use an oven, however, saving it for roasts and packing in as much food as possible, is neither necessary nor fits in with the way most of us cook today. Contrary to popular mythology, ovens are not expensive to heat. To heat up and use an oven at high temperature costs less than 10p for 1 hour.

The main difference between gas and electric ovens is that gas ones work by direct heat, electric by radiant heat. What this means in practice is that gas ovens show more marked differences in temperatures zones within the oven. The quality of the heat is also different. Professional home economists who use both say that gas ovens have a 'moist' heat that tends to brown food more evenly and produce more open-textured cakes than the very 'dry' heat of an electric oven. Gas is also cheaper to use than electricity. Fan ovens distribute the heat evenly throughout, though whether or not this offers any real advantage is debatable. Whichever you choose, remember that an electric oven will behave differently from a gas oven, an Aga is a law unto itself and fan ovens are noisy.

Whether gas or electric, new or old, ovens are not the precise, impersonal heat machines that manufacturers would have us believe. To get the best out of any oven, you need to find out what it does and doesn't do well, and to learn to work with it. It requires exactly the same give and take as cooking on top of the stove, and taking note of how quickly a dish browns is just as crucial as learning to gauge a simmer on the hob so that the milk doesn't boil over in the morning.

Pre-heating ovens

This is unnecessary on most occasions. Bread, roast meat and any braised and baked dish can be put into a cold oven and then cooked just as successfully as if you had pre-heated the oven to the required temperature first. The only exceptions to this are temperature sensitive dishes such as pastry and biscuits which need to set immediately; pizza and Yorkshire pudding, which need high heat; or ready-made dishes (for these always follow the manufacturer's instructions). If the total cooking time is less than 15 minutes, then it is also usually better to pre-heat the oven first.

The majority of modern ovens, in fact, heat up quickly. Obviously, how much extra cooking time, if any, you need to allow depends on how quickly your oven heats up and how high a temperature it needs to reach. My own experience is that cooking times are not significantly altered. If putting the dishes straight into the oven without preheating it first:

- For dishes that cook in under 30 minutes, you may need to add an extra 5 minutes or so.
- For dishes that are cooked for longer than 30 minutes, I find cooking times are approximately the same.

Do whatever you prefer or suits you best. If you are the kind of cook who prefers fixed temperatures and cooking times, it is better to pre-heat the oven. If you prefer to cook in a flexible way, you will probably not want to bother. The real advantage of knowing you can cook from cold is the reassurance that your dishes will neither suffer nor fail. It saves hanging around waiting for the oven to heat up first – and saves panicking when you've forgotten.

Cooking times and temperatures

Given the variability of ovens, and that a cookery writer may have tested the recipe using a different kind of oven, cooking times given in recipes should always be taken as approximate rather than absolutely exact.

■ Cooking times depend on the size and shape of the food; the depth of the dish; the kind of dish the food is cooked in; if it is covered, how effective the seal is.

■ Allow 5–10 minutes either way for printed cooking times. For slow-cooked dishes (1 hour +), you may have to allow longer.

The extensive temperature range found on ovens is a fairly recent phenomenon. Convention now dictates that recipes are written to correspond to these, reinforcing the myth a dish needs X minutes at Y temperature. For most dishes, and for most of the time, all you really need to know is whether the recipe needs a low, moderate or hot oven. You can then make your own adjustments, juggling with shelves and the thermostat as necessary.

You should also remember that temperature conversions are not exact and vary slightly according to the source.

The Storecupboard

You don't need a well stocked cupboard to be able to cook well. Rather, keep the minimum and build your storecupboard contents around the kind of cooking you do and ingredients you use frequently.

Cans and packets, like us, are not immortal: check the date stamp, and try and use them sooner rather than later. The ingredients a modern cook is likely to use regularly are actually very few.

VINEGARS

Vinegars vary in quality as much as oils. The better the quality, the more mellow and flavourful the vinegar. Good quality wine vinegars are absolutely essential for salad dressings and piquant dishes and sauces. Ordinary white wine, cider or malt vinegars are fine for preserves and pickles.

Stored properly, somewhere cool and away from light, most vinegars keep more or less indefinitely. Nevertheless, as with oils, it is a good idea to use them within 12 months, particularly the more expensive kinds, which lose their nuances.

Though we tend to restrict the use of vinegars to salad dressings or preserves, they are a highly versatile flavouring that add zing and indefinable piquancy to many cooked dishes, soups and sauces.

Flavoured herb vinegars can be made simply at home by steeping branches of herbs in good quality wine vinegar. Flower and fruit vinegars can be made the same way: try elderflower, rose petal, lavender, raspberry and strawberry.

Two vinegars of particular note are balsamic and sherry. Both are dark, rich vinegars aged in wood. A few drops of either explode on the tongue and give a wonderful lift to just about anything. Both can be used extensively for salads or cooked dishes.

Balsamic vinegar

This is the sweeter of the two, and is the vinegar à la mode. The best, made in tiny quantities by traditional methods and aged for at least 10 years, is fabulously expensive. How much money it is worth paying is debatable; the majority of moderately priced balsamic vinegars, made commercially with added caramelised sugar and aged for much less time, are excellent for most cooking purposes and to use in salad dressings. It is important to read the label; balsamic vinegar that contains preservatives is below par, will taste thin and sugary and will be disappointing.

Balsamic vinegar can be used neat as a seasoning in countless ways: shaking a few drops on grilled or char-grilled meat, liver, fish and vegetables, for example, or over salads with shavings of Parmesan cheese. It can also be used in beef stews, or when roasting game and poultry. It is often sprinkled on fruit – especially strawberries and pears.

Sherry vinegar

This has a rich sherry flavour. The best is as mellow as balsamic vinegar but does not have the same sweetness. It is primarily used with olive or nut oil in salad dressings or in cooked meat dishes, with pork, beef or lamb. It goes particularly well with liver and kidneys, and is an ingredient of Spanish sauces – see Spanish Hazelnut and Pepper Sauce, p 186.
Rice Vinegar, see p 281.

OLIVE OILS

For many modern cooks, me included, olive oil has superseded butter as the cooking fat of choice. There are two essential things to know. First, olive oil is perishable, needs to be bought with care and stored properly. Second, olive oils vary in flavour and character enormously, depending on the country they come from and the type of olives used. The knack for anyone, particularly a newcomer to cooking with olive oil, is to find ones you like. Experiment and, like wine, olive oil can offer a lifetime's enjoyment and exploration.

Olive oils vary hugely in price. And though a good oil should never be judged by price alone, you cannot expect cheap olive oils, which frequently are blends from different countries, to sparkle. They are often coarse, one dimensional or very bland in flavour, and have a 'fatty', cloying feel.

The best oils, in contrast, have a rich, buttery, smooth unctuousness and a perfectly balanced, fruity yet complex flavour; these are not for cooking with but to use at the table where the warmth of the food brings out their inherent deliciousness to the full.

Between these two extremes are a wealth of medium-priced oils that have individuality and character, and offer the best of both worlds.

It can be worth having three different olive oils to use in the kitchen:

■ An everyday, not too strongly flavoured, reasonable quality olive oil. I only ever use extra virgin olive oils for cooking, many good brands of which are no more expensive than other types of olive oil.

■ A rustic, very fruity extra virgin oil for pasta, baked potatoes and gutsy dishes.

■ A 'best', fresh, aromatic, elegant, buttery extra virgin olive oil to use as a condiment for salads or grilled fish.

Buying olive oil

Olive oil is best up to 12–18 months after pressing. Whatever its price, the key to buying good olive oil is to find the freshest. And to read the labels.

■ Never buy olive oil that has been displayed in a shop window or under bright lights. Light causes oxidation, which makes the oil deteriorate, destroys its vitamins and will in time make it go rancid. Olive oil sold in dark green bottles or in tins is better protected from the light than olive oil in clear bottles. Check the date stamp, and where possible buy the latest vintage.

■ Bad olive oil is stale olive oil.

■ The character (and hence flavour) of olive oil changes with time, gradually losing its fresh fruitiness, eventually becoming tired and flat.

■ The colour of olive oil is not an indication of its quality, but depends on the type of olives used. The colour spectrum ranges from light golden to dark sea green.

■ The more information about the origins of the olive oil on the label the better. Vague descriptions, for example, 'Produce of Italy', mean it is a blend of oils, generally from different countries, which has been bottled in Italy.

■ Most olive oils these days are filtered to remove any residue of olive pulp so that the oil has a bright, crystal clear appearance. An unfiltered oil has an opaque appearance when first pressed and indicates that it has been pressed by traditional methods. In time, the residue settles to the bottom of the bottle as a film of dark sludge. It is perfectly harmless and can be reshaken into the bottle.

What is 'extra virgin' olive oil?

The nomenclature of olive oil can be misleading. For practical purposes, olive oil can be divided into two main categories, 'extra virgin' and 'pure'. Extra virgin olive oil is made from the first pressing of the olives, and is the only kind of olive oil worth buying. Pure olive oil is highly refined, made from inferior olive oil to which 30 per cent extra virgin olive oil has been added to give it flavour. Give it a miss.

Traditional, cold-pressed extra virgin olive oils These are milled in the traditional way in small quantities. Great care goes into the picking and handling of the olives. The olives come from the local area, and the oils vary from one year to the next, depending on the season. They include all olive oils grown and pressed by the same producer on the same estate, known as 'single estate olive oils', which are the equivalent of *cru* wines.

Commercially produced and blended extra virgin olive oils These are made at modern mills using olives sourced from various areas, including olives imported from another country. Many, including supermarket own-label and branded oils, are blended to ensure consistency of flavour. They have been likened to table wine and, like table wine, vary in quality. Good, commercially produced extra virgin olive oils represent excellent value.

Acidity rating of olive oils

The quality of olive oil is determined by the amount of oleic acid naturally present in the oil. This is what is meant by the acidity of olive oil and though you cannot taste it, the lower the natural acidity the better the quality, balance and finesse. To qualify as 'extra virgin', 'fine virgin' and 'ordinary virgin', oils must not exceed set acidity levels. Briefly:

■ The lower the acidity, the more stable the olive oil and the better its keeping qualities.
■ Extra virgin olive oil has an acidity of 0.5–1 per cent; fine virgin oil has an acidity of 1–1.5 per cent; ordinary virgin oil has an acidity of 1.5–3 per cent.

Unfortunately, it is now possible to treat an oil chemically to reduce its acidity, thereby allowing inferior olive oils to be called 'extra virgin'.

The character of olive oil

Four factors make up the character of any olive oil, and are worth knowing because it helps you judge the quality of the oil.

Style Whether the oil is sweet, mellow, pungent, etc.

Pepperiness A peppery feel at the back of the throat. This is present to a greater or lesser extent in all olive oil, and is a physical effect caused by compounds in the olive oil.

Fruitiness How much the flavour of the olive comes through. Whether it is fresh or lacks lustre.

Balance This refers to the overall feel of the olive oil in the mouth. Whether or not it is buttery and unctuous, clean or cloying, and if it has a lingering taste.

Olive oils from different countries

The main olive oil producing countries are Spain, Greece, Portugal, Italy and France, though olive oil is produced throughout the Mediterranean as well as in Australia and California.

Spain The largest olive oil producer, and the favourite oil of authority Ann Dolamore. The oils are generally high quality and very reasonably priced, making them excellent all-round value. They tend to be mellow, not peppery, of medium fruitiness and well balanced.
Uses A good choice for general cooking, fried foods, salads, mayonnaise and grilled food. For Spanish dishes.

Greece Greek oils vary in quality. Traditional ones tend to be heavy, strong tasting oils and feel 'fatty' in the mouth. Modern Greek olive oil is lighter and less assertive; much is excellent quality and very cheap, making them outstanding value for their price.
Uses A very good choice for gutsy and Mediterranean/Moroccan/Middle eastern-style meat, fish and vegetable dishes, for fried food,

for salads and barbecued/char-grilled fish. Greek cooking and Greek salads.

Portugal Though a major producer of olive oil, very few Portuguese olive oils are currently available in the UK. They tend to be similar to traditional Greek olive oil and are strong flavoured. The best Portuguese oils are lighter and more elegant.

Uses As for Greek oil. For Portuguese dishes, including potato and cabbage soups.

Italy Italy produces the widest and most divergent styles of olive oils from gentle, buttery, golden Ligurian to highly aromatic and peppery sea-green Tuscan ones: try oils from the various regions to see which style you like. They are never cheap but range from medium-priced to expensive, and are the best for pasta and risotto.

Italy also produces some of the best single estate olive oils in the world, of supreme elegance, balance and individuality. These can be glorious and are costly. They are best bought from wine merchants (wine estates often have their own olive groves) or from specialist suppliers.

At the other end of the scale, there are vast quantities of cheap inferior olive oil produced in Italy. For everyday use, Spanish and Greek olive oils represent much better value.

Uses Pasta, risotto, pestos. Mediterranean salads, green salads, dried bean salads and soups, marinated vegetables. Bread and bruschetta, seafood, grilled fish. Italian cooking.

France France is one of the smallest producers of olive oil. Most is produced in Provence and Southwest France. The oils tend to be sweet, golden or green and fruity with a rich buttery texture and are delicious on salads. Though some are excellent value, most are medium to highly priced.

Uses Mediterranean salads, green salads, dried bean salads, marinated vegetables and goat's cheese. Bread. Provençal fish soups and fish dishes, seafood, grilled fish. Mayonnaise, aïoli. French cooking.

Storing olive oil

How you store olive oil will affect its keeping quality. The best place to store it is a cool dark cupboard. The golden rule is to keep it out of direct sunlight. This applies to whichever bottle you may be using by the stove for general cooking purposes, and to any jugs of oil kept on the table.

In cold conditions, olive oil will solidify and turn cloudy. This is perfectly normal: leave the bottle in a warm place at room temperature, or in a jug of hot water, and it will become liquid again.

Cooking with olive oil

Olive oil is one of the best oils to cook with. It has a high melting point and remains stable at high temperatures, which makes it an excellent choice for frying. When food is fried in olive oil at the correct temperature, it absorbs less oil than if fried in other oils. Also:

- You don't need much olive oil. Once heated it becomes thinner and spreads: 1–2 tablespoons will impart flavour and is sufficient for most frying purposes.
- Warmth brings out the full flavour. The best way to add extra flavour to a dish is to pour over a little at the end of cooking. This will enhance the dish and bring out the savour of the oil far more than using plenty to start with.
- Never heat olive oil to smoking point. This will destroy many of its qualities and some of its flavour.
- Olive oil is a preservative. It is excellent for storing goat's cheese, olives, sun-dried tomatoes, mushrooms, etc.
- Flavoured olive oils – with herbs, lemon zest and chilli – are made by steeping herbs in the oil. These can be bought or easily made at home. The two best are lemon olive oil, which is wonderful for salads and fish, and chilli olive oil for spicing up pizza, pasta and vegetables.

NUT OILS

These are produced from crushed almonds, hazelnuts, pine kernels, pistachios and walnuts. The pulp is first 'roasted' to develop its flavour. The oil is run off, and the pulp pressed to yield more oil. The two oils are then mixed together, filtered and bottled. The quality varies depending on the nuts used and the care taken during processing – this is why, for example, some walnut oils taste stronger than others.

Nut oils have a certain snob appeal, specially the newer ones like pine kernel oil. Walnut and hazelnut are both delicious and still the best all-purpose nut oils. Buy them in small bottles and keep in the dark.

All nut oils are expensive. They can be used on their own or to flavour neutral oils and, because of their strong flavour, a little goes a long way. They all have a pronounced flavour of the nut from which they were made. Though you can cook with them, they are unstable when heated and are primarily used for salads, cold dishes or as a dressing for hot food, such as chicken livers. All oils, whether or not cold pressed, are best used within 12 months.

VEGETABLE OILS

For general cooking there is a wide range of processed and refined vegetable oils to choose from. All have a neutral flavour. They vary in their smoke points – the higher this is the more the oil can be heated before it degrades, and the better it is for frying. On both counts, grapeseed oil is the best one to opt for. It has the highest smoke point and is an excellent choice for salad dressings and mayonnaise.

Some varieties of vegetable oils are also available cold-pressed: though nutritionally superior, remember that all will taste of the seed from which they have been produced and that they are more unstable than their refined equivalents and therefore not as suitable for cooking.

ESSENTIAL MEDITERRANEAN FLAVOURINGS

Lemons

Lemons, closely followed by limes, are among the most useful ingredients. They vary in flavour and juiciness more than you would think. Buy the brightest, ripest-looking lemons that feel heavy for their size; the best and freshest are those that are still attached to their stalks, or on branches, imported from Sicily, which are now becoming more available; they also keep better. Thin-skinned lemons, which feel quite soft, inevitably contain the most juice. You will also get more juice out of a warm lemon than a cold one.

Lemons store best in a cool place for up to 3–4 weeks (there is no need to keep them in the fridge unless you want to store them for as long as possible); note that the skins gradually dry out and become tougher in a warm kitchen. Though technically lemons are not supposed to ripen further, decent ones kept out of the fridge do.

To replace the natural protective wax of the fruit, which is removed when the lemon is cleaned after harvesting, lemons are artificially coated with one of two natural edible waxes, beeswax or shellac. It is done to prevent moisture loss during transit, and the wax may be scrubbed off with hot water. To extend the shelf life further, lemons are also sprayed with permitted fungicide. This cannot be entirely scrubbed off by soap and water, but can be removed by Aloe Vera, an organic cleanser available from health food shops.

Unwaxed lemons These are often recommended for drinks or when the zest is required, but sound 'purer' than they are. Although they have not been artificially waxed, most have also been treated with permitted fungicides. The further the lemon has to travel, the more likely this is.

Organic lemons These have neither been sprayed with any chemicals nor waxed, and are available in large supermarkets most times of the year. Wherever possible, use these where the rind or zest is called for. Their shelf life is short, 1–2 weeks out of the fridge or 3–4 weeks in the fridge.

Preserved lemons

These are invaluable. Chopped finely, they add a bright note to salads and salsas, hot vinaigrettes and grilled fish, and they give stews and sauces a subtle edge. The salt softens the skins, mellows the flavour and lends a unique pickled taste. You only eat the skins, so buy the best and most fragrant lemons you can find. Limes can be preserved in the same way and are equally delicious.

---

3 organic lemons, washed and cut into quarters from top to bottom

85g/3oz sea salt

Pack the quartered lemons neatly into a 450g/1lb Kilner jar as tightly as you can – arrange them as an inverted 'V' with the skins uppermost and they will fit in easily, dredging them liberally with salt as you do so. Cover with a final layer of salt, seal, then leave, shaking the jar occasionally to distribute the salt and juice. The salt will eventually dissolve and form a brine.

The pickled lemons develop their full flavour in 3–4 weeks, though the peel softens sooner and can be used if you want. They keep for at least 6 months.

To use, take out however much peel you need. Scrape out the flesh and rinse thoroughly, then slice or chop as required.

■ If you can't get all the lemon quarters into the jar, fill the jar as described, then leave for an hour until the lemons begin to soften. They will then squash down easily, making room for the remaining quarters.

Olives

Olives vary enormously in quality, texture and flavour, and range in colour from green (unripe) through rose and violet to black (ripe). To a certain extent, the degree of ripeness determines the taste. Green olives contain little oil, have a firm flesh and tangy flavour. Black olives are full of oil, have a soft flesh and a rich, mellow flavour. Some, like the tiny Niçoise ones, are sweet. Olives are best bought loose; try before you buy. The less the olive appears bruised, the better the quality.

Olives should be bought in small quantities and used quickly. Exposed to air, they develop a white surface mould within a few days. To avoid this, gently shake the olives in a little olive oil so that all the surfaces are oily, and keep in the fridge. The only way to keep olives for any length of time is to store them in olive oil, when they stay plump, moist and juicy. The olives must be completely submerged in the oil, which can be flavoured with bay leaves, peppercorns etc.

When cooking with olives, remember that cheap astringent ones can all but ruin a dish. Unless you are sure of your olives, and particularly if they are for a braised dish or a sauce, it is better to be safe than sorry and add them only 10–15 minutes before the end of cooking.

Sun-dried tomatoes

Sun-dried tomatoes have their place, but not in everything. Usually you get what you pay for. If you can, buy them loose and insist on trying one – if you don't like it raw, think what it will do to your dish.

Good quality sun-dried tomatoes are soft, pliable and bright or magenta red in colour. The flavour is sweet and tomato-rich, tempered by a little saltiness. Poor sun-dried tomatoes are tough, leathery, dark and look more like shrivelled prunes. They have a strong, over-salty, rather unpleasant taste, reminiscent of overripe tomatoes on the verge of going mouldy.

Like dried mushrooms, a little of the rich, concentrated flavour of sun-dried tomatoes goes a long way. For this reason they should not be thought of as a substitute for fresh tomatoes, but as an ingredient in their own right.

They should be stored somewhere cool and dark. A good way is to keep them in a jar covered completely with olive oil. This makes them plump, juicy and soft. Stored like this, they will keep well for 6 months or longer, and are ready to eat as a snack on bread, or to add to pasta dishes, salads and salsas. The oil, meanwhile, takes on the flavour of the tomatoes, and can be used for cooking. They can also be bought ready bottled in ordinary olive oil, but these are more expensive, which is why it is better to do your own. Loose sun-dried tomatoes can be snipped with scissors and added directly to dishes, or rehydrated first in a little hot water. Use within 6 months.

See also Home-dried Tomatoes, p 118.

Anchovies

Anchovies are an age-old seasoning for all kinds of salads, sauces and relishes, as well as a main ingredient for pizza toppings and simple pasta sauces. Tinned anchovy fillets in olive oil mash easily to a pulp and dissolve into a grainy sauce over a gentle heat. Cooked anchovy fillets marinated in oil and flavourings can be bought loose from delicatessens. These have a fresher, less salty taste, are good in salads and can be substituted for tinned anchovy fillets in Salsa Verde (p 73). Salted whole anchovies can be bought in specialist food shops. These are strong, and should be soaked in water first; everything except the anchovy flesh should be discarded.

Anchovies are generally used with fish or vegetables, but it is worth remembering that they are an excellent seasoning for meat – add an anchovy fillet to meat stews, or pound and mix with butter to serve with steak. Anchovy butter is excellent, too, with fennel and spinach.

Dried wild mushrooms

Dried wild mushrooms are one of the most useful storecupboard ingredients. They have a rich, concentrated flavour and totally different character from fresh mushrooms. The best are porcini (ceps): Chanterelles, loofah-like morels, and the tiny dark brown *trompettes de mort*, are the other dried mushrooms commonly used in European cooking, while shiitake mushrooms are used in Asian.

Dried mushrooms vary in quality because perfect specimens are rare in the wild. Where possible, buy them loose so you can inspect and smell them first.

Ceps are large mushrooms and dried ones are sold in wafer-thin slices; other dried mushrooms are sold whole. Look for clean mushrooms with an appealing appearance as usually the more knarled, dark, dusty, or broken up the pieces, the more inferior the quality. Their smell is another reliable indicator. Good dried mushrooms have a fresh earthy aroma.

Each variety of dried mushroom has a distinctive character. Chanterelles, for example, are buttery and delicate, morels and ceps rich and strong. All add a 'meaty' flavour to dishes. They can be used in a variety of ways, but are best in mushroom soups, pasta dishes, risotto, with polenta, and wild rice and earthy grain pilafs. Dried morels are generally served whole, and are excellent with celeriac, beef and lamb. Although they are expensive, you need very small amounts; 1–2 pieces of cep will add depth to a mushroom soup, for example, while 3–4 slices will flavour a risotto.

All dried mushrooms inevitably contain particles of dirt: if you feel badly about this, rinse them briefly first. It is usual to rehydrate them first in a little hot water for a few minutes. The soaking liquid has a strong mushroom flavour and should be added to whatever dish you are cooking: pour it in gently, leaving behind any particles of dirt in the bottom of the bowl. They may also be rehydrated in sherry, vermouth or wine, if appropriate.

Dried mushrooms can also be added direct to any dish which is moist or contains liquid, without prior soaking: check the pieces are clean, and either add whole, or tear or crumble by hand.

Twice-cooked mushrooms

To give extra depth and flavour to fried mushrooms, add a few soaked and finely chopped cooked dried mushrooms.

Soak 2–3 pieces of dried mushroom in a little hot water. Squeeze out the excess moisture (reserve), chop finely and cook gently in a knob of butter for 3–4 minutes. In a separate pan, slice and toss cultivated mushrooms over a high heat in butter or olive oil for 3–4 minutes until just done. Add the dried mushroom mixture, and their soaking liquid, stir around and serve.

Variation Just before serving, add 1–2 tablespoons of Marsala wine to the mushrooms in the pan; or add cream for a cream sauce; or add chopped chives, finely chopped parsley or tarragon.

SPICES

Spices should be stored in airtight containers in a cool, dark place as light dries out the essential oils that contain all the flavour.

Stored properly, whole spices have an indefinite shelf life. Ground spices can keep their flavour for up to two years; as it is impossible to tell by looking how old a ground spice is, it is best not to buy them loose out of large jars or in packets that do not have a date stamp. If a ground spice, or spice mixture, smells or tastes musty, or has hardly any flavour, replace it.

Spice mixtures other than the familiar curry powder or garam masala can now be bought by mail order, including Indonesian and oriental ones.

Whenever possible spices should be bought whole and ground as you use them. Grinding releases the full fragrance of the spice, and makes an enormous difference to the dish. A coffee grinder kept specially for spices grinds them in seconds. Dry-frying cumin, coriander, mustard and sesame seeds in a small pan for 3–5 minutes over a gentle heat until lightly toasted heightens their flavour and makes them easy to grind by hand in a pestle and mortar.

Ready-made Indian Spice Pastes I am not easily converted to anything that comes out of a jar but I make an exception for these. Apart from their role in Indian cooking, they can be used to flavour a range of soups, sauces, salads and cooked dishes. They are preferable by far to stale ground spices. Stirred into rice or other cooked grains, they produce instant, hard-to-better results.

The brand I use is Patak's. Once opened the pastes will keep for 12 months in the fridge.

It is not necessary to have a full complement of spice pastes. Patak's garam masala paste, a mixture of warm spices, less overtly Indian than some, imparts a general spicy flavour that hovers somewhere between India and the Middle East. Their Balti and Korma are two mild, distinctive pastes, also suited to general cooking.

Harissa

This is a fiery red, warmly-spiced chilli paste available in tubes or small cans. Imported from Tunisia, it is used for Moroccan meat and vegetable stews (tagines). Made from chillies and garlic and spiced with cumin, it is also very useful for fish stews, to stir into grains and rice and is excellent with chickpeas. A tube is most convenient and can be used like tomato purée, only in smaller quantities, by the teaspoon. Keep it in the fridge once opened. If you buy a can, transfer the harissa to a small glass jar and pour over a film of olive oil to exclude the air. It will then keep for 1 month.

Root ginger

Fresh ginger dries out fairly quickly and is better bought in small quantities. Buy fat, smooth-looking pieces of bulb; these will be nice and juicy. Shrivelled ones will be dry, tough and difficult to deal with. In a warm kitchen ginger dries out within a couple of weeks or so. To keep it juicy, store in the salad drawer of the fridge where it will keep for 3–4 weeks or longer. Use a potato peeler to take off the skin, which comes away easily.

Because of its fibrous nature, fresh ginger is not that easy to chop finely by hand. Much easier is to grate a peeled knob of ginger on the fine holes of a hand grater. For ginger juice, press a knob of peeled ginger through a garlic press. Its flavour is powerful. Like garlic, the finer you chop it the more the flavour will disperse throughout the dish. It is used in very small amounts, and $\frac{1}{2}$–1 teaspoon is sufficient to flavour most dishes. Though it tastes quite hot and pungent raw, this dissipates when cooked, with the flavour of ginger remaining.

Excellent with meat, fish, shellfish, stir-fried vegetables, with roasted carrots, parsnip and pumpkin, fresh ginger can also be used in sweet-sour salad dressings, or cut into julienne strips, or fried in oil for a few seconds until crisp and used as a garnish.

SAFFRON

A time-honoured ingredient of Mediterranean, Middle Eastern and Indian cuisines, this most majestic of spices can be used to impart its exotic flavour and colour to food in countless different ways and will turn any dish into a feast. Apart from its use in classic rice pilafs, paellas and risottos, it is superb with fish and shellfish, chicken, veal, with pasta and vegetables such as peppers, fennel, peas and potatoes and in soups and sauces. You can also use it in desserts and baking, to flavour mayonnaise or in salad dressings. Nor do you need to save saffron for high days and holidays. The best way to enjoy it is in simple dishes made with everyday ingredients, where its special qualities can be appreciated most.

Saffron comprises the dried stigmas of the tiny crocus, *crocus sativus*. Referred to as saffron 'strands', 'filaments' or sometimes 'threads', they are intensely pungent and highly aromatic. They have a faintly bitter flavour and give a glorious golden yellow colour to all dishes.

As it is bought in tiny quantities and costs considerably more than other spices, saffron is universally perceived to be expensive. In fact, saffron is tremendous value. Because it is so potent the amount you need to use is negligible. A 1g box of saffron strands is easily enough for 20–30 dishes, each good pinch (20–30 strands) costing only 12–30p, depending on the price you have paid for it.

Buying and storing saffron

Saffron varies in quality and price and is available as strands or powdered. It is a good idea to have both. Poor quality saffron will colour your food but has no aroma and very little flavour. Good quality saffron will be bright rather than dull and always has a powerful aroma. The best is Mancha Superior saffron from Spain. Buy through mail order (p 282) or buy a recognised brand such as Safinter. Look on the label for '1st category', which is the highest quality.

Saffron stores extremely well. It should be stored in a tin in a cool, dry and dark place and will easily remain in good condition for 6–12 months.

Saffron strands A good way to buy these is in small transparent boxes, so you can see how many of the strands are whole or broken into bits. Safinter saffron is also available in small 1g/0.025oz clear plastic packs; note these are difficult to open (snip along the top with a pair of scissors) and impractical to store saffron in.

Though they often break into single threads, a complete stigma has three red filaments joined at the base to a white/yellowish stalk. In the box, Spanish saffron will appear red streaked with white or yellow. Both have the same amount of aroma and flavour but only the red filaments colour the food. Saffron from other countries may not contain the white parts and will appear dark red throughout.

Saffron strands have an aesthetic appeal; many people prefer them because you can also judge the quality more easily. They are convenient when you want just a few strands to flavour a soup or when you might like to see whole strands in a dish.

Powdered saffron Powdered saffron releases its colour and flavour instantly, is stronger and can be added direct to dishes, so is easier and more convenient to use. It appears to be more expensive than saffron strands (though it is better value), and is available only in small sachets weighing 0.125g/0.0044oz. It is deep red in colour, with specks of white and yellow, if Spanish. Despite what you may have heard, adulteration of powdered saffron is extremely rare, and powdered saffron is *not* inferior to saffron strands.

Powdered saffron varies in quality, with some brands having greater strength than others: good powdered saffron has the same powerful aroma as strands; when fresh you can smell it through the packet. The label must say saffron; if it doesn't and you open it up and it is bright orange, it is colouring, not saffron. Spanish powdered saffron is usually better than Italian.

Toasting and crumbling saffron strands

To get the most out of saffron strands it is usual to dry them for a few seconds first over a very low heat in a tiny pan so that they become more brittle. This is called 'toasting' – though don't take the term literally: the strands should do no more than warm through or they may burn. After toasting they will now crumble easily. Pound in a tiny pestle and mortar or put them in a ramekin dish and use the handle of a teaspoon to crush the strands – be careful as the fragments tend to fly out of the bowl. This takes a few seconds only. Crush them as finely as you can and infuse as suggested below.

You can, if you like, pound the toasted saffron strands with a few grains of sugar or salt, which enable you to crush the saffron more finely as they act as an abrasive. Note, though, if you are making an infusion and want to taste the liquid to test its strength, the sugar or salt slightly masks the pure flavour of the saffron.

How to use saffron

Whether strands or powdered, the best and simplest way to use saffron for most dishes is to make an infusion first by dissolving the saffron in a little liquid, either water, milk, wine, wine vinegar or citrus juice as appropriate. This enables the saffron's flavour and colour compounds to be released thoroughly and to diffuse through the dish quickly and effectively. Second, and most important, it also helps you to judge how much saffron to add, because you can add it a little at a time until the flavour seems right. Saffron strands need to be 'toasted' first; saffron powder can be stirred directly into the liquid.

- How much infusion to make depends on the dish, but a good standard infusion for substantial or main courses is to use a large pinch of (20–30) strands or $\frac{1}{2}$–1 sachet of powdered saffron in 1 tablespoon of hot water or other liquid.

- This preliminary soaking is much more important for saffron strands. Powdered saffron is so finely ground it releases its compounds very quickly, needs less soaking time, and will be almost as effective when added direct. However, as it takes a few seconds only to do and you can control the amount to add better, I recommend making an infusion.

- The longer you leave saffron to infuse, the more the flavour and colour will be released. Infuse for 30 minutes or longer if you can.

- If you have some infusion left over it stores well for a week or so in the fridge (and will become stronger). Keep covered with clingfilm.

- Saffron will release its colour and flavour faster in wine, wine vinegar or citrus juice than in water.

- You don't have to make an infusion for all dishes. You can, for example, crumble saffron strands directly into soups. Similarly, powdered saffron can be used to flavour cold sauces, to make saffron mash or saffron pasta etc.

Substituting strands for powdered saffron

Saffron strands or powdered saffron can be substituted for each other in any recipe. Because the intensity of both varies, it is impossible to give exact equivalents. By my reckoning, a pinch of whole saffron strands (15–20) is roughly equivalent to half a packet of good quality powdered saffron. If the recipe says saffron strands and you are using powdered saffron, make an infusion, and add until the flavour seems right. Finally, a tip well worth knowing is that if you have added too little, a pinch of powdered saffron stirred into the dish at the end will improve matters.

How much saffron?

You need to use enough for the flavour to come through. Taste a single strand or a few grains of powdered saffron and the flavour will fill your mouth; this is what to aim for. The colour of the dish is one of the best guides: the more golden it is, the more it will taste of saffron. You will also find dishes which soak up liquid, for example, rice, will take more saffron than others. Saffron is potent. If you add too much the flavour will become overpowering, and start tasting 'medicinal', so as soon as the flavour seems right, don't add any more.

Recipes will tell you how much saffron to use for that particular dish. The problem here is that often they indicate 'a pinch', which may mean anything from, say, 10–40 or more strands depending on the size of your pinches. Whatever the recipe says, the answer is to use the amount of saffron which tastes right to you and to be prepared to add a little less or more. When using saffron without a recipe as a rough rule of thumb:

- A pinch of saffron is reckoned to be about 15–20 individual strands.
- $\frac{1}{2}$ a pinch of saffron strands will flavour a fish soup: a big pinch (20–30) saffron strands will flavour a risotto or paella for 4–8 people.
- $\frac{1}{4}$ packet of powdered saffron is sufficient to flavour a pasta sauce; $\frac{1}{2}$–1 packet will flavour a risotto for 4–8 people.

Remember, all this depends on individual taste, the size of your pinches, and the potency of the saffron. If your saffron contains a high percentage of broken filaments, counting out strands or measuring by pinches is irrelevant. A quick check is to taste the saffron liquid: if it taste like faintly flavoured water, add more saffron.

When to add saffron

The foolproof way to use saffron in any cooked dish is to make an infusion and add half when you start cooking and the remainder just before the end. This will give you the best of both worlds because:

- The longer you cook saffron, the more it will colour the dish. To get the full colouring effect, add half of the saffron at the beginning.
- Though saffron permeates the whole dish if added at the beginning, the flavour dulls with time. For a full saffron fragrance, keep back half of the saffron liquid, and stir it in just before the end of cooking, adding it to taste until the flavour seems right.

If using powdered saffron direct, do the same, adding most at the beginning and a touch at the end of cooking the dish.

Cooking : Theory

RECIPES

Understanding recipes – or rather learning to recognise which are and are not likely to suit your style of cooking and eating – is fundamental to being able to cook well. The simplest way to ensure success is to be discriminating from the outset. The same is true of cookery authors and cookery books: some suit and some do not.

A good recipe is one that has been well thought out and has taken ingredients and combined them in such a way that the sum is greater than its parts; a bad one is more an ill-conceived hotchpotch which sounds good on paper but falls flat on its face in the pan. It is not necessarily true the more detailed the recipe the better it is. A good recipe will have clear instructions but will also *explain* them, giving you the details that count to enable you to understand the fundamentals of the dish, and highlighting any pitfalls or giving you a sense of 'what happens if'.

The way recipes are written, with precise quantities and instructions, suggests that they are tablets of stone, and that if you follow the recipe exactly, you will get exactly the same result as the author of the recipe. There is an expectation, too, that a recipe will produce the same results over and over again. In practice, recipes are an interaction between ingredients and cook. This makes them fluid, elastic and flexible, which is why the best recipes for domestic cooks are often those with a certain amount of give and take. No matter how thoroughly a recipe may have been tested, it can turn out slightly differently in another pair of hands. Nothing is the same, neither the ingredients, the equipment, nor the cook. Even the size of the pan can make a significant difference. How you are feeling also influences how you cook. You can cook the same recipe over and over again, and it will be better some days than others.

- The fewer the ingredients, the easier the recipe, but the more the quality of ingredients becomes crucial, influencing the final flavour.
- There is a logic to good recipes. Recipes with a few well thought-out ingredients that complement, contrast or harmonise with each other are more likely to succeed than those with long lists of ingredients that have no apparent affinity with each other.
- Never feel a recipe has to be inventive. Tried and tested combinations with the occasional reinterpretation often work best.
- When reading a recipe through for the first time, it is a good idea to tick off the ingredients as you go along and try and form a mental picture of what the dish is likely to taste like and whether you can manage it comfortably in the time available.
- Always allow for your own taste. Wholesale changes to a recipe are likely to end up as a disaster but a little fine tuning will not.
- Remember, too, printed recipes are not infallible, and mistakes and misprints occasionally occur.

Finally, never be discouraged by the occasional disaster. You learn more about the fundamentals of the recipe, what makes it work, and how to cook it correctly, when it goes wrong than when it goes right. Should you have a failure (we all do) or the recipe doesn't work out exactly how you anticipated, try and assess why so you can make the right adjustments next time.

TASTE AND TASTING

A basic appreciation of the importance of taste and learning how to develop your palate is as helpful in understanding how to cook as the mechanics of cooking – indeed, it is one of the most important cooking skills I can think of.

The ability to taste depends on individual likes and dislikes, experience and habit. The more you like a particular flavouring, for example, lemon zest, the more you will want to use, and the more you can use before the flavour becomes overpowering. Conversely, the less you like a flavouring, the more sensitive you are to its presence.

Each person's perception of what a particular food tastes like depends, in turn, on their own taste bank of experience or terms of reference. This is the all-important yardstick. If you have only ever eaten supermarket tomatoes, your view of what a 'good' tomato tastes like will be very different from someone who grows their own and knows how rich, sweet and truly 'tomatoey' they can be. Similarly, the wider the range of foods you taste, the broader your personal taste bank becomes.

This is what is meant by developing or 'educating' your palate. At the stove, your palate acts like an aide-memoire; the more experienced it is, the more it will help you make better judgments every time you cook.

Apart from the quality of the ingredients, taste and flavour are influenced by how hungry you are, whether the food matches your mood, and what you eat with what. Hunger, ironically, is the best seasoning of all – almost anything tastes wonderful when you are truly hungry. Though it sounds trite, this is why half the success of being a good cook is, literally, knowing that eating a little bit of what you fancy will always be a greater success than something more extravagant you do not.

Tastebuds quickly become blunted. Though tasting a dish as it cooks provides a useful check (I do it all the time), the more often you do so, the less you are able to tell what changes, if any, are going on. It is better to taste a dish towards the end of cooking. If you want an objective opinion, ask someone else to taste it for you.

Cooking: Practice

The elementary skills you need to cook are very few and can be divided into how to prepare ingredients and how to handle them as they cook. For preparing ingredients you need sharp knives – it is hopeless trying to cut anything with less. As for cooking, the two single most important factors are choosing the right pan and controlling the heat. Do this, and you are well on the way to cooking every dish successfully.

Thick or thin?

The size and shape of an ingredient has a profound bearing on the outcome of a dish. The obvious example of how important this can be is stir-fried food, but it applies to anything you cook. Bother to chop or slice an onion finely so that it melds into a sauce, for example, and you will produce a dish that 'eats' better.

A decent recipe should tell you what size ingredients should be; if it doesn't.

- The thinner the slice or dice, the more quickly an ingredient will cook, obviously.
- The more finely flavouring ingredients or seasonings, such as garlic, ginger, citrus zest and herbs, are chopped or grated, the more the flavour will disperse and blend throughout the whole of the dish. Conversely, coarsely chopped or grated flavouring ingredients will be more noticeable as independent flavours within a dish.
- If the dish is to be braised slowly, vegetables should be left whole or cut into large chunks.
- Meat should be sliced across the grain.
- 'Bite size' means just that; the size and shape that is comfortable to eat in one go.
- For vinaigrettes or salsas, it is better to chop the ingredients separately and then combine them. See Salsas, pp 70–3.

Chopping and Slicing

How fast or proficient you become at chopping and slicing is immaterial, so long as you do the job properly. To chop vegetables or herbs finely, to make a gremolata (p 246), or hash of ingredients, or to chop cooked meat finely, you need a large cook's knife. With one hand on the handle, hold the tip of the knife down with the other so that it doesn't move from its spot, move the knife backwards and forwards in an arc over the ingredients with quick chopping movements: it doesn't take long to get the hang of it – see the diagram right.

- To slice or chop hard vegetables and meat you need a plain sharp knife of whichever size you feel comfortable with – a 10cm/4 inch blade or larger.
- For softer vegetables like tomatoes and for chopping onions and shredding leafy vegetables such as cabbage or lettuce, a finely serrated knife is easier and makes a better job than a vegetable or chef's knife.
- A fish filleting knife is essential to fillet fish; but if you do not have one, a plain vegetable knife is the best substitute.
- For slicing meat, cheese or hard-boiled eggs you need a plain knife.
- The simple way to snip herbs and dice bacon is to use a pair of kitchen scissors.

Grating

The same remarks about cutting and slicing apply to how food is grated. Finely grated root vegetables tend to be both softer and sweeter than when coarsely grated, whereas coarsely grated vegetables are necessary for rösti, and are best for frittatas, fried vegetable patties and for dishes where you want to retain some of the texture.

Another example of how the way you grate food affects its flavour and eating quality is Par-mesan cheese. Very finely grated Parmesan has a soft, downy texture, which melts like snowflakes when added to hot pasta and forms the finest crust when used to gratinée food under the grill or the oven. In contrast, wafer thin shavings of Parmesan have a pleasant gritty texture that is perfect for salads, but is not as suitable for gratins as it forms thin sheets of cheese rather than a crust. Note that if Parmesan or any other cheese is to be combined in a sauce, it doesn't matter how you grate it.

Be specially careful about citrus zest. This has a very powerful flavour and surprisingly hard texture to bite into. Depending on the recipe, it is usually best either very finely grated, cut into hair-like strands or diced into small specks.

Crushing and grinding

Not many ingredients are crushed. The quickest way to crush a clove of garlic or bruise whole spices is to lay a large chef's knife on top and press down smartly with the heel of your hand. To crush toasted nuts, pound them briefly in a pestle and mortar or roll a rolling pin over them. The best way to grind spices or nuts finely is to use a coffee grinder kept just for the purpose.

SIZING UP THE PANS

The size, weight and, to a lesser extent, the shape of a pan have a critical bearing on how a dish will cook. Cook the same food in two different sized pans and you immediately see how the cooking of each progresses at a slightly variable rate, how the food cooks more quickly in one, and how you need to adjust the heat in both pans differently. Such small and apparently insignificant factors affect the final flavour of a dish, and, equally importantly, the amount of effort and care you will need in order to get the dish right.

The golden rule is to choose a pan that will take all the ingredients comfortably. Too small a pan and ingredients will steam rather than fry; too large and they will burn more easily and you will need to use more fat to fry the food successfully. The larger the pan, the larger the surface area and the faster liquids will evaporate. The smaller the pan, the more you run the risk of liquids boiling over. For soups and other dishes, never have the pan much more than half full.

A heavy-based pan takes longer to heat up, holds its heat better and distributes the heat evenly. A thin-based pan heats up more quickly, develops 'hot spots' in the areas where it comes in direct contact with the heat source, and therefore burns food more easily. This is why knowing your pan, being aware of its strengths and limitations, is fundamental to being able to cook: if you know what you are in for, you are less likely to make mistakes.

Always put pans to soak immediately you have finished cooking with them; this makes them far easier to clean when you come to do the washing up.

CONTROLLING THE HEAT

Controlling the heat, be it on the hob, under the grill, or in the oven, is one of the secrets of learning to cook well and simply means adjusting the temperature as and when necessary to maintain the cooking on an even keel – be it the slowest of simmers or a stir-fry. Good recipes will stipulate how high or low the heat should be, but often this is left to your discretion.

- Irrespective of what the recipe says, monitor the heat regularly, adjusting it according to how quickly or slowly food is being cooked.
- The heat required will depend on how much food there is in the pan and what kind is being cooked. Vegetables with a high percentage of water, for example, such as sliced courgettes or chopped tomatoes, create steam and lower the heat in the cooking pan more quickly than those which have a dense texture such as potatoes.
- The various cooking methods depend on maintaining different levels of heat, deep-frying requiring the most and poaching the least. The visible signs associated with each cooking method (see over) are the best guide to whether the food is being cooked at the correct temperature.
- When grilling or barbecuing, move the food nearer or further away from the heat source, as necessary.
- Gas burners can be turned up or down instantly. Electric hobs take time to adjust. Much depends on the efficiency of your electric ring; if yours is slow, and food is cooking too quickly, move the pan off the heat until the food is cooking the way you want it.
- The most difficult cooking process to control on top of the stove is a simmer: here, a heat diffuser may help.

BASIC COOKING METHODS

Frying

Frying, that is, using a frying pan or similar shallow pan to cook food with added fat on a moderate–high heat, is about as convenient a method of cooking there is. Easier to control than grilling, none of the cooking juices is wasted. It is suitable for any tender piece of meat, for fish, eggs and vegetables. Because you can see, smell and touch the food, and adjust the heat promptly, it is one of the easiest methods of cooking to get right.

To say 'fry' these days, however, is somewhat misleading. The modern way to 'fry' foods is in effect to 'dry-sauté' them. In practice, you can fry foods successfully in very little fat.

- The easy and thoroughly modern way to 'fry' foods is to use a non-stick pan.
- A very hot pan will burn fat and food instantly. Two simple ways to tell if the pan is hot enough to begin frying are:

Hold your hand about 2.5cm/1 inch above the pan: it should feel hot. Or splash a few drops of water or put a small piece of food into the pan: if they sizzle, the pan is hot enough.

- It is better to heat a frying pan over a moderate–moderately hot heat; this only takes 2–3 minutes for most pans. Remember that heavy-based pans take longer to heat up than thin-based ones; and that a thin-based pan is pretty useless for frying food anyway. Should you have overheated the pan, let it cool a little before adding the food.
- Although you can 'fry' in a non-stick pan without any fat, there seems little point. A little fat or oil helps to lubricate the food and adds its own flavour. Either add to the pan and swill it around to coat the base, or brush the food lightly with oil first. Foods already rich in fats or oils will require none – their own fat will provide more than enough.

- Frying pans made from materials other than non-stick will need more fat. Use enough to coat the base of the pan lightly, adding extra as needed.
- Damp foods stick to the pan (not a problem with non-stick) and steam rather than fry. A way of overcoming this with soft foods such as liver or scallops is to brush them lightly with oil before adding them to the pan.

Food should be fried at what can best be described as a gentle–lively sizzle. Too much splattering and hissing indicates the temperature is too high; too little sizzle or pools of liquid seeping out of the food indicate the temperature is too low. If you are using more than the minimum amount of fat, food will also be far more greasy if fried too slowly. Otherwise:

- Thin slices of tender food are cooked briskly over a constant highish heat.
- Thicker pieces of tender food are sealed over a high heat, then cooked more gently until the cooking is complete.
- It is not essential to brown foods first: turning up the heat once vegetables have softened, for example, will brown them just the same.

Searing and turning

Searing makes food look more appetising and produces flavour-enhancing compounds, which help it taste better. The food is browned in a hot pan to form a crust or seal and it takes very little time, anything from 30 seconds for slices of scallop to 2–3 minutes for cubes of meat. Once the food is seared, the heat should be lowered to complete the cooking. Though searing temporarily drives meat juices inwards, it does not 'seal' in the juices for any length of time. For more notes on this see p 234.

Often, if you try and turn char-grilled meat, fish and vegetables, specially pan-fried or char-grilled slices of polenta, fishcakes, hamburgers, and rissoles made from vegetables or dried pulses, too quickly, they will stick to the pan or fall apart. You need to wait a little longer until the crust has formed properly, when they can be turned easily.

Deep-frying

Deep-frying, the opposite of shallow frying, is when food is cooked very rapidly in a deep pan half full of hot oil. A specialised form of frying, it is generally done in a deep-fat fryer. However, the method can be successfully adapted for small quantities of food:

Take a small, heavy saucepan, and pour in about 1.25cm/$\frac{1}{2}$ inch of oil – use half groundnut and half olive oil. Heat until the oil is very hot but not smoking. To test, drop a cube of bread in to the pan: it should turn brown and become crisp in 20–30 seconds. Add the prepared food, though only as much as the pan will comfortably accommodate in a single layer. The food should sizzle immediately. Cook for the required time, turning over the pieces half way through. Remove and drain thoroughly on kitchen paper. Cook the rest of the food in batches in the same way.

When deep-frying, the oil should bubble up and around the food vigorously and the food sizzle loudly throughout. If the food turns dark brown instantly, the oil is too hot. If the oil only bubbles gently, it is not sufficiently hot enough, and the food will be greasy.

It is also important to wipe the food dry of any moisture before putting it into the hot oil; to help prevent moisture seeping into the oil during the cooking, the food is often coated first, which then forms a crisp crust.

Grilling

Grilling food is an excellent way of cooking whole fish and char-grilled vegetables, getting bacon really crisp, melting cheese toppings and browning dishes. Otherwise, a frying pan is more convenient and easier to wash up.

Except for anything which needs to brown fast, for example, crème brûlée, you do not need to pre-heat the grill. Any food that is likely to curl up – fat around the chop, fish tails – should be nicked with a knife. A good safe distance to position most food is so that the top is 10cm/4 inches from the heat surface. Closer than this and the outside of food begins to burn too quickly; further away and it stews rather than grills. Anything that is flat, thin, and needs quickly browning can go slightly nearer, 8cm/3 inches from the heat surface.

Grilled food should sizzle in a steady and appetising way, and brown gradually. Moisture will bubble on the surface, as will the skin of fish. If the food is grilling too quickly, the surface will burn rather than brown. If the food is grilling too slowly, it will sweat and steam rather than grill, and more moisture will be lost. For full details on Barbecuing and Char-grilling, see pp 251–65.

Roasting

Roasting – cooking food in a hot or moderately hot oven – is suitable for all tender joints of meat, fish and vegetables. The main difference between roasting and other forms of cooking in the oven is that the food is not cooked in any liquid and is left uncovered so that the surface browns and becomes crisp.

The addition of olive oil, butter or appropriate animal fat to baste the food while it roasts is critical, and an important key to succulent, crisp and flavourful roasts. Though you can roast food with a minimum of fat, the results are never as good.

Roasting food is generally more flexible and well-tempered than frying or grilling. The sounds of food roasting are more measured, and have a more melodic quality. The higher the temperature, the more vigorous the sounds and the more the fat spatters as the juices progressively seep out of the food. How quickly food browns depends on the roasting temperature; given enough time, meat will even brown at low temperatures.

Braising, casseroling and stewing

For full details on slow-cooked meat dishes, see pp 232–47; for braised vegetables see p 84.

Poaching and simmering

Poaching is the gentlest method of cooking and is used for meat, fish, eggs and various soft mixtures such as gnocchi and quenelles. Food is immersed completely in water or stock and cooked over the gentlest heat possible until ready. It is usually done on top of the stove, but can be done in the oven.

Poaching is not the easiest of methods to get right for success depends on regulating the heat very carefully. The liquid should never boil or simmer, but rather tremble. All you should see are the occasional wisps of steam. Soft mixtures and eggs should always be put into very hot or gently simmering water, so that the outsides set quickly. For more details, see poaching fish, p 175.

When simmering the liquid should be maintained at a steady, but barely, boil. You will need to adjust the heat frequently, using anything from a very low to a fairly moderate heat.

Steaming

Steaming is the purest form of cooking. Food is cooked gently in an enclosed pan surrounded only by steam: if cooked without any additional flavourings, the food will have the most natural flavour possible. It is commonly used for vegetables and fish, though tender meat such as chicken can be steamed. Grains such as rice and couscous are also excellent cooked in this way.

Steaming is not a particularly fast method of cooking; nor are steamed vegetables necessarily superior. If you particularly like steaming, an electric steamer is probably a good idea; otherwise any simple or makeshift steamer will do.

The water used to create the steam should never come into contact with the food while it is being cooked. It should boil gently and evenly. The lid should fit tightly so that little steam escapes, and the water in the bottom pan should be checked regularly to see if it needs replenishing. If you are using stacked steamers, food in the top steamer will take longer to cook than that in the bottom so whatever is going to take the longest to cook should be placed in the bottom steamer. A full basket of food will also take longer to steam than one containing less.

LIQUIDS

Liquid measurements rarely need to be exact, specially in savoury cooking. How much to add is largely a question of experience and depends partly on the size of the pan (which is why instructions which say 'cover the base of the pan' can sometimes be more useful) and how high the heat is. As it is simpler to add a little extra liquid than to have to compensate because you have added too much, unless you are cooking dishes that require lengthy cooking, it is always a good idea to stop slightly short of the amount stipulated in a recipe, just in case you don't need it. The same goes when you are adding liquid or oil/butter to hot or cold egg-based sauces such as hollandaise or mayonnaise.

Lids

Lids are as significant in regulating the heat of the dish as the heat of the hob or the temperature of the oven. Whether they are on, off or ajar can mean the difference between the gentlest of simmers or a furious boil so they need to be checked and adjusted frequently.

The other thing to watch for is how effective a seal the lid, aluminium foil or whatever other cover you have makes for dishes cooked in the oven. The usual reason why braised dishes dry up unexpectedly is because the lid was not as watertight as you'd imagined. The tighter the cover, the less liquid will evaporate but the more difficult it is to maintain a gentle simmer so it's best to turn down the oven. If the dish has ample liquid and is bubbling too fast, leave the lid slightly ajar.

It's an obvious point, but an uncovered pan of liquid will take twice as long to come to the boil as a covered one.

Reducing

Reducing is a most useful technique of boiling down liquids to concentrate their flavour. Any sauce, soup or stock that tastes thin or watery can usually be rescued by simply reducing it until the flavours come through to your liking. A liquid or sauce will reduce much faster in a wide shallow pan than in a saucepan.

Though liquids can be, and often are, reduced by fast boiling, it is usually better to let them reduce gently. This allows impurities or fat to collect on the surface (instead of emulsifying with the liquid), which can then be skimmed off and will help keep them clear.

THICKENING SAUCES

It is useful to know how to thicken a sauce should you want to. The simplest ways are set out below. Remember that no thickener should ever be added to very hot or boiling liquid or it will form a hard lump and be unable to disperse and thicken the sauce.

Simple reduction This works for all liquids that can be boiled. The disadvantage is that you may end up with very little sauce. Be careful when reducing any meat or fish juices derived from gelatinous cuts of meat, or gelatinous or strong-tasting fish; if you reduce them too much they become unpleasantly strong and gluey. Reduce until the liquid tastes well-flavoured, then stop.

If it still needs thickening, use a butter and flour paste, or potato flour as described below.

Butter and flour paste (*Beurre manié*) This is the instant way to thicken a sauce without using a *roux*, or cooked butter and flour mixture, and is used primarily for meat and fish sauces. Blend 15g/½oz soft butter and a level tablespoon of plain flour to a homogeneous paste with a fork. Drop it in small balls into the hot liquid one at a time, whisking it in gently until the mixture becomes as thick as you want. Once the paste has dissolved the liquid can be boiled without any risk of lumps forming. Cook for a minute so that the flour is cooked, and the sauce is ready to serve. This amount will thicken up to 600ml/1 pint of liquid and produces a 'traditional' tasting thickened sauce.

For meat stews, you can add the paste direct to the stew, shaking the pan gently until it has melted and formed a liaison. For fish dishes, remove the fish first (otherwise it will overcook), thicken the sauce and put back the fish.

Potato flour (*fécule*) This admirable thickener is made from pure potato starch, is tasteless, easy to use, thickens instantly and requires no cooking. It can be bought from delicatessens and health food shops.

To use, mix it first with a little water. Stir well and then add, a teaspoon at a time, to hot but not boiling liquid, stirring thoroughly until the desired thickness is achieved. Be careful not to boil the thickened liquid vigorously, or the potato flour will change texture and become gluey. A generous teaspoon of potato flour mixed into 1–2 tablespoons of cold water will thicken up to 300ml/½ pint liquid.

Cornflour I do not find this a good thickener, except in Chinese cooking where it is used frequently. It produces a cloudy, gluey sauce and needs to be cooked through, otherwise you will be able to taste it. Use as potato flour.

SEASONING

Salt and pepper

Salt and pepper are not obligatory: many foods and dishes require neither. Unless they specifically enhance the dish they have not been included in the recipe instructions but left to the discretion of the cook. Season at the end of cooking, not at the beginning. Remember, too, that salt, while bringing out the flavour of some foods, tends to mask the natural sweetness of many others and that black pepper is a ferocious seasoning best employed, I find, as you would other spices, as a distinct flavouring for particular dishes.

The quality of salt matters. Different salts have different flavours, some are stronger and saltier, others sweeter and milder, and it is worth trying various brands to find the one you like. Sea salt is infinitely preferable to table salt. Pepper should be freshly ground. For stockists of both, see p 282.

Quick guide to using salt

Our liking for salt is largely a question of habit. The more you use it, the more your tastebuds become acclimatised and crave its special flavour. Conversely, start using less and familiar foods and dishes containing salt quickly start tasting unpleasantly salty.

Salt brings out and improves the flavour of certain types of food. These include dried pulses and most grains; fried foods; bread; oil-based sauces and dressings such as mayonnaise and vinaigrettes; pork; and fish and shellfish. Dishes which contain salty foods or seasonings such as bacon, smoked fish, soy sauce and other Eastern sauces will require none. It is well to remember the amount of salt a recipe stipulates is based only on its author's taste, and can be either increased, reduced or left out if you prefer.

Finally, you do not need to salt the cooking water of vegetables. But you should use salted water to cook pasta or to poach fish.

Sugar as a seasoning

Sugar makes a very good seasoning. A pinch of sugar can bring out the sweetness and flavour of root vegetables, onions and garlic. It is used as a general seasoning in Thai food. A light sprinkling can be used to help grilled and roasted vegetables caramelise.

Other seasonings

Seasonings and powerful flavourings like lemon zest, chilli and ginger need to be approached differently from other ingredients. Small variations can make a profound difference to the flavour of a dish. A few tips:

- If you know you are particularly sensitive to a flavouring, use half the amount to begin with, adding the rest if necessary.
- If you particularly like a flavouring, you can add extra, but do so very cautiously and in quantities proportional to the original amount given in the recipe.
- If you are using any seasoning or flavouring for the first time, taste it first to see how much you like it and to gauge its strength, so you can judge how much to add.
- If you do not like salted food, be particularly wary about the amount of salt in a recipe. Leave it out until the end of the dish.

COOKING WITH WINE

One of the significant changes in recent years is that cooking with wine has become commonplace. Wine adds a certain fullness and body to a dish as well as adding its own flavour. But the common perception that any dish is improved by wine is not true. Good cooking does not depend on wine. In *French Provincial Cooking*, Elizabeth David made two essential points about cooking with wine: do not overdo it, as more wine doesn't make a better dish; and the best reason to use wine is because you like the taste it gives to the finished dish. Obvious but true. Teetotallers need read no further.

It is largely a myth that the better quality the wine the better the dish. Once heated, the nuances that give a fine wine its character (and hefty price tag) are destroyed so, within reason, it doesn't matter that much what you use.

You should, however, always use a wine of reasonable quality you would be happy to drink. Cheap and nasty wine will do nothing for your cooking or your hangover. All you get is more chemicals in your dish than you bargained for. Similarly, avoid anything labelled 'cooking wine'.

The style and weight of the wine required for the dish – whether it is a robust country red wine for a meat daube or a dry white wine for fish – are more important than its name or which country it comes from. The reason, I suspect, traditional dishes specify a particular wine is because it is local and readily available. So long as the wine is similar in character the dish will not suffer if you substitute one wine for another.

Medium-bodied wines suit most purposes. A little red or white wine is useful to add to rich tomato and ragù sauces and other minced meat dishes. Though red wine is not customarily used with fish, simple red wine and butter sauces go well with salmon and meaty fish like tuna. Soft, rich red wines and aromatic, sweet white wines are best for desserts. Sweet white wines can also be used to very good effect in savoury dishes where the sugar imparts a subtle richness. Try them with fish, chicken or slow-cooked garlic cloves in the oven. If a dish calls for sweet wine, and none is available, sweeten whichever full-flavoured white wine you have with a little sugar.

How to add wine

Wine is a strong flavouring and should never be added willy-nilly but with due care and attention.

- To ensure the flavour is completely harmonised in cooked dishes, add the wine all at once.

- For savoury dishes and sauces, add the wine before any other liquid and boil it down for a few minutes until reduced by half, or the amount specified in the recipe. This removes its raw taste (and the alcohol), leaving the flavour-enhancing residues behind. It is these, and not the alcohol, which help give a sauce its structure, and the dish its savour and balance. Wine that has not been sufficiently 'cooked out' may make the dish taste obviously winey.

- In braised meat dishes, or any dish which involves lengthy cooking, it is enough to bring the wine to the boil as the alcohol will evaporate naturally.

- Occasionally, the flavour of the wine is part of the recipe, for example, Lentils Cooked in Wine, p 166, and is added last. Here, use a wine with a rounded flavour, or a sweeter wine; a wine which is noticeably acidic or tannic is not suitable and may introduce an unwelcome harsh note to the dish. Except in these cases, don't add wine at the end of the dish as its raw flavour can easily dominate.

- When using wine that will not be cooked, for example, in dressings and desserts, select one that is not too tannic, acidic or thin flavoured.

How to store wine

Once opened, a bottle of wine keeps only 1–2 days. Thereafter it loses its flavour, becoming flat and uninteresting, and oxidises, eventually (within 1–3 weeks) turning to vinegar.

As you almost never need a whole bottle (or even half a bottle) to cook with, the best idea is to decant wine into small glass or plastic bottles ranging in size from miniature bottles to one-third bottle capacity. Screw on the top tightly and the wine will keep satisfactorily for a couple of weeks (white wine will keep longer in the fridge). Otherwise, use a few tablespoons of whichever wine you're drinking.

Small bottles of wine handed out on planes are perfect for cooking with. They contain decent wine and hold just the right amount for most dishes.

Flaming with brandy

This is rarely used in modern cooking, but setting light to the brandy serves the same purpose as boiling wine first and removes the alcohol. If you are using brandy or another spirit in dishes that require lengthy cooking, flaming is not necessary.

USING FATS, CREAM AND YOGHURT

Natural fats and oils – butter, cream, meat fats, cold pressed olive and nut oils – add flavour to a dish and are vital for health. The modern and sensible way to use them is in moderation.

■ A little olive oil or butter added at the end of cooking will round out the flavour and give a richness to the dish far more than using more to cook with in the first place.

■ As a general guide, use the minimum to fry or cook foods. In practice, this means enough to coat the base of a pan. For a medium-sized pan, for most purposes, this works out at about $7–10g/\frac{1}{4}$oz butter or 1 scant tablespoon of olive oil. This is what I intend in the recipes when I refer to a small amount of butter or a little olive oil. A large knob of butter means $10–15g/\frac{1}{3}–\frac{1}{2}$oz.

For notes on Meat Fat, see p 217.

Cream is both voluptuous and very rich. If you prefer to use less than the recipe states, you can cut back on the amount, adding it to taste, without sacrificing flavour. Even as little as a couple of tablespoons is enough to give body and a creamy feel to most dishes. When I refer to a little or dribble of cream, this means anything between 1–3 teaspoons per person. Some important points about using cream:

■ Single cream can be substituted for double. As long as you use them carefully, neither will curdle or split when you boil them. Whipping cream, which is a mixture of single and double, is best for whipping.

■ Never add cream to a large amount of boiling liquid. Take a little of the hot liquid and mix with the cream first, then add the cream gently, off the heat. Once the cream has been incorporated, the liquid can be boiled safely. When adding cream to juices in the frying pan to make a sauce, gradually stir in the cream off the heat, then bring to the boil.

To prevent eggs from curdling, dishes which contain eggs and cream need to be cooked over a very gentle heat, or in a bowl set over simmering water (a *bain-marie*).

If you do not want to use cream but want a creamy taste and texture, use either plain sheep's or Greek-style cow's milk yoghurt. Low fat yoghurts are not good substitutes. Drain off any watery liquid from the yoghurt first as it has a more acidic taste. If you need to make yoghurt thicker for dips, drain it first in a sieve lined with muslin set over a bowl to catch the drips and leave for a couple of hours.

Heating fats and oils

All fats and oils 'degrade' or break down when heated to high temperatures. This has various serious deleterious effects and taints and sometimes ruins the flavour of food as well as ruining the fat or oil. It is therefore important not to heat fats or oils too fiercely, and to choose the right one for the right job. Fat or oil in a deep-fat fryer should be changed after it has been used two or three times – every time you heat it, it decomposes more.

If you overheat a fat or oil it begins to smoke. This is known as the 'smoke point' and varies with each fat or oil: the higher the smoke point, the higher the temperature the fat or oil can be heated before it starts to break down and vaporise. Use oils with a high smoke point such as grapeseed oil for stir-fry or deep-frying.

If overheated too much fats and oils will ignite spontaneously. This is very rare, except when barbecuing food. In the unlikely event that your pan of oil catches fire, throw a blanket or thick towel over it immediately to smother the flames. Flames from fats and oils produce toxic compounds. For a brief note on this, see p 253.

Clarifying butter

The milky solids in butter burn easily and for frying it helps if you remove them by clarifying the butter first. This is easy to do. Melt the butter in the smallest pan you have, until a white scum appears on top. Pour through a wire-meshed tea strainer into the frying pan, leaving the milky solids behind.

Mopping up fat

Fat gives flavour to food and lubricates it while cooking. Once the dish has been cooked, its job is done and the excess should be removed. There are four easy ways to do this. Use whichever best suits the dish.

For the flavour-enhancing properties of fat, see p 217.

The simplest is to blot up excess fat with kitchen paper. This is effective for both very small amounts or 'spots', and for larger films that cover the entire surface of the dish. Lay the kitchen paper gently over the top of the fat: the fat immediately soaks into the paper. Remove and repeat with fresh kitchen paper until all the fat has been mopped up. For 'spots', use a small piece or corner of kitchen paper.

It is important to remove the kitchen paper immediately the fat has seeped into it and before it starts to take up the liquid underneath the fat.

If cooking a braised meat dish to be served later, or the next day, allow the dish to cool, then refrigerate. The fat will solidify on the top of the dish and can be picked off by hand.

If there is only a small amount of meat juices which you want to save from the roasting tin, tilt the tin so that the fat and juices collect in the corner. The fat will sit on the surface and can be removed with a spoon, leaving the meat residues behind.

If simmering liquids gently to concentrate their flavour, move one corner of the dish off the heat source. The fat will collect in this corner – tip up the dish, and remove with a spoon or blot with kitchen paper. You will also find that fat collects in the web of clear 'scum' that rises to the surface. Remove this at intervals with a spoon.

Stocks

MEAT STOCK

Stock costs virtually nothing to make, is easy to do and stores well in the freezer for up to 12 months.

There are many misconceptions about making stock. For everyday purposes, all you need is leftover carcasses/bones and water. A piece of pork rind – which can be cut from pork chops, leg or shoulder of pork and then kept in the freezer – or a split pig's trotter enriches and jellifies meat stocks. Anything else – wine, herbs, spices, chopped root vegetables – is purely optional. A few basic guidelines:

■ You can make meat stock from any leftover carcass, cooked or uncooked, any bones or a mixture. If using bones, add some raw minced meat for extra flavour.

■ You can use any pan, but if you are going to make stock regularly, a stock pan is a good idea.

■ You do *not* need to add extra flavourings to stock. In fact, meat stock keeps better if made with only meat and meat bones.

■ Veal and marrow bones (which can be bought very cheaply) and chicken wings are rich in gelatine and make excellent stock. Bacon rind adds flavour and is good to use with game stocks.

■ The flavour of the stock depends on the quantity of bones, etc. you use.

■ You do not have to make large quantities of stock or use large quantities of bones. Just use whatever you have.

■ You can brown the bones first or not. Browning adds colour and flavour. The best way to brown bones is to roast them in a moderate–hot oven.

WHICH STOCK?

Chicken stock is the most useful all-purpose stock to make. It is essential for risotto, makes delicious broths, gives body to soups and can be used to enrich meat juices to make a simple sauce when pan-frying meat, etc. It can also be used to cook fish.

You can make it with either a raw chicken carcass (which you can occasionally buy very cheaply) or the remains of a cooked chicken. Follow the basic method opposite, simmering very gently for 2–3 hours.

Beef stock This can be used for beef dishes, game, mushroom soups and gravy, and to enrich meat juices to make a simple sauce when pan-frying beef, lamb, pork and game.

Veal stock A naturally gelatinous stock with a mild, meaty flavour. Excellent for risotto, poultry and game, for meat sauces and gravy, and for enriching meat juices when pan-frying pork, beef, lamb, chicken and game. It can also be used to cook fish.

Lamb stock This is too strong for general cooking, but can be used for lamb dishes or to make spiced parsnip soup.

Pork stock This is not usually made. Pork bones and belly pork, however, are good to add to chicken stocks for extra richness.

Basic meat stock

1 Put the bones, carcass, etc. into a stock pot or pan. If you want to brown the bones, either do so in the pan over a gentle heat or roast them in the oven first.

2 Add any flavourings, a piece of pork rind or a chicken wing if available, and enough water to cover the bones completely. Set over a gentle heat, bring to boiling point and remove any scum.

3 Simmer very gently for 2–3 hours, or until it suits. Alternatively, bring the liquid to simmering point and transfer to a very low oven, around 130°C/250°F/Gas Mark $\frac{1}{2}$. Leave for 6–8 hours or longer.

4 Strain the stock, remove the fat and reduce until well flavoured.

5 Cool and store as required.

Flavourings These are the common flavourings for meat stock. Use whatever you have. Small quantities are sufficient.

■ Vegetables – a carrot, celery stick, leek, onion, whole tomato.

■ Herbs – bay leaf, parsley, celery leaf, a little thyme.

■ Spices – 3–4 whole peppercorns.

Basic vegetable stock

Vegetable stock can be used for cooking fish, rice, grains and pulses and to add that little extra to vegetarian dishes. Have the vegetables chopped finely (this takes a few seconds in a food processor) as the stock does not cook for long.

110g/4oz each carrots, onions or leeks, and celery, finely chopped
a few parsley stalks
bay leaf

Cover the vegetables with water (about 600ml/1 pint) and simmer for 30 minutes. Strain, pressing through all the juices. Reduce to concentrate if necessary and use as required.

Some do's and don'ts for perfect stocks

■ Never add salt to a stock. Save any seasoning until you come to use it in a sauce, soup or whatever.

■ If making a brown stock, be careful not to overbrown the ingredients first: burnt bones produce burnt stock.

■ Stock should *never* boil but should simmer very gently: the liquid should barely shimmer. This is the secret of a clean-tasting, clear stock. Meat stocks can be simmered for at least 2–3 hours and even longer. If you use a low oven, this saves the kitchen becoming steamy.

■ Never cover the pan.

■ A few pots of well-flavoured stock in the freezer are much better than lots of faintly flavoured water. Reduce as necessary.

■ Do not, however, reduce an already rich meat stock too far, as it will become gluey and unpleasantly strong.

■ Cooked onion sours quickly, so a meat stock made with onion can be kept only for 2–3 days in the fridge. If you want to keep it longer, reboil the stock. Clear meat stock made from only meat and bones will keep longer, up to 4–5 days.

FISH STOCK

Making fish stock is easy. It is not necessary for the majority of fish recipes but it does make the world of difference to Mediterranean-type fish stews and soups. Nor do you need to worry about buying fish heads or a bag of additional bones, adding wine or making a fine delicate stock, unless it is for a special recipe. Virtually any fish bones and trimmings, raw or cooked, plus water to cover will produce a serviceable stock.

A few useful ground rules:

- Fish stock tastes of the type of fish you use: a delicate-tasting fish will produce a delicate stock, a robust-flavoured fish a robust one. Dover sole, lemon sole, turbot, brill and John Dory all make excellent stock.
- Gelatinous fish such as halibut, Dover sole, turbot and skate produce rich stocks that set to a jelly when cold.
- Oily fish are not suitable for stock and make it taste unpleasantly oily. The exception to this is salmon, which produces a rich, slightly sweet, jellied stock that is useful for soups. If you are using salmon to make stock it is best on its own, rather than combined with other fish.
- Never throw away prawn shells or other shellfish debris. Shellfish make sweet-tasting stock, excellent for Mediterranean fish stews and soups and simple crab, lobster or shellfish bisques. If you eat them in restaurants, ask to bring the carcass home.
- You don't necessarily need raw fish trimmings; cooked debris from whole baked fish makes good stock.
- There is no point making pints of faintly flavoured water which then takes extra work to boil down; use just enough water to cover the fish bones.
- You do not need to cook fish stock for long; 15–20 minutes is usually adequate. Long simmering can produce unpleasantly strong-tasting stock.

- Never boil fish stock. Always simmer it very gently on the lowest possible heat. If you want to concentrate the flavour, strain the stock, then reduce it by more gentle simmering.
- Never season stocks. If the stock ends up salty you cannot correct it and it may spoil the sauce. Leave the seasoning until you use the stock to cook the fish or make the sauce.
- Fish stock freezes well and will keep for 2–3 months. Reduce it first until well flavoured, then taste before freezing and label accordingly: light and delicate stocks are suitable for poaching and baking fish or making sauces, while robust stocks are good for stews and soups.

Basic fish stock

It doesn't matter what quantity of fish trimmings you have; less just makes less stock. Besides, only chefs need panfuls of stock. For domestic cooks, 600ml/1 pint is ample for most purposes. Similarly, flavourings such as herbs, lemon zest, bay leaves, peppercorns, etc., are all optional. This recipe produces a clean-tasting clear stock. If you don't have any other vegetables to hand, make do with a piece of onion or celery.

---

assorted fish trimmings, bones etc., as available

Plus any of the following

finely chopped onion, leek (the tops are good for stock), carrot, celery, celeriac, fennel

Optional flavourings

parsley stalks, bay leaves, peppercorns

Wash the fish trimmings in a bowl of water and remove any blood (this will taint the stock). Put the chopped vegetables and any other flavourings in a roomy pan. Put the fish trimmings on top, cover with water and bring slowly to the boil. Skim off any scum.

As soon as the stock comes to the boil, turn the heat right down and simmer very gently for 15–20 minutes. Take the pan off the heat, leave to cool and then strain. If the stock tastes watery, reduce it further until well flavoured.

Cooked fish stock

The debris from whole baked fish or whole grilled fish with warm vinaigrette (p 189) will make a decent stock for fish soups and stews, as long as you omit any burnt or charred bits of skin or bones. Scrape the debris into a pan, cover with water and cook as for Basic Fish Stock (opposite).

Basic shellfish stock

One of the best fish stocks. Use for shellfish risottos and Mediterranean fish soups and stews.

prawn or langoustine shells and legs, or crab/lobster carcasses as available
1 small onion/leek, carrot, celery stick, all finely diced
1 clove garlic, crushed
1 small ripe tomato or 1 dessertspoon tomato purée
sprig of basil or parsley
olive oil

Check the shells – langoustine, crab and lobster shells are often muddy in the crevices – and scrub lightly with a brush if dirty.

Gently sweat the shells, diced vegetables and garlic in a little olive oil in a covered pan for 5 minutes. Add the tomato or tomato purée, herbs and water to cover, then simmer for 30–40 minutes.

Pick out the large pieces of shell, then strain everything else through a sieve, pressing hard with a wooden spoon to extract all the juices. Pour into a clean pan and simmer gently to reduce, until well flavoured.

Basic Mediterranean fish broth or bisque

This is the best fish soup I know, and comes out a thinnish red-brown broth. Serve it with croutes spread with some leftover aïli and you could almost be on the seafront in Cassis. The exact flavour will depend on the type and quantity of shellfish you use. Be prepared to reduce it right down to get the flavour you want, and to adjust the proportions of the flavouring ingredients if necessary.

SERVES 2–4

ingredients for Basic Shellfish Stock (left)
300ml/$\frac{1}{2}$ pint fish stock
1 small wineglass of dry white wine (about 100ml/$3\frac{1}{2}$fl oz)
$\frac{1}{2}$ teaspoon ground anise or a pinch of dried chilli
a good pinch (about $\frac{1}{8}$ packet) of powdered saffron, or a few whole saffron strands

Clean the shells and sweat them with the vegetables as for Basic Shellfish Stock. Pour in the white wine and cook until almost evaporated. Add the tomato, herbs and spices, together with the fish stock and water to cover.

Simmer and strain as for Basic Shellfish Stock. Reduce until well flavoured, adding extra tomato purée if necessary. Check the seasoning, then serve with croutes of dry baked bread rubbed with garlic, and a dollop of rouille or aïoli.

Variation For a crab or lobster bisque, add 2 tablespoons of brandy, letting it evaporate before adding the wine. Save a little shellfish meat and add at the end.

WEIGHTS AND MEASURES

Cookery books still list ingredients in both metric and British Imperial, giving the cook the choice: use whichever you think in and feel comfortable with.

As 1oz actually equals 28.35g, measurements are rounded up or down, taking either 30g or 25g as the working equivalent to 1oz, and multiplying the rest accordingly. Except when the ingredients are extremely light, for example dried yeast and thickeners, and for some cakes and pastries, it doesn't matter which conversion rate is used, recipes will work just as well. Because I have been brought up with Imperial, this is the system I have opted for in developing and testing the recipes, checking the metric equivalents on digital scales.

Whether conversions are based on 30g or 25g, it is often stated that in order for recipes to work you must adhere to one set of measurements throughout. This is not so. Apart from the exceptions above, conversions are sufficiently accurate that there is no need to panic if you get the occasional weights mixed up.

Ratios

Although I have adhered to convention and given precise amounts, it cannot be stressed enough that weights and measures for the vast majority of modern recipes do not need to be that accurate and that your recipes will not fail if you do not use the exact weight stipulated. Learning to judge by eye and to get a feel for the proportions of ingredients to use is just as valuable, if not more so, in helping you to cook.

It is also worth remembering that for certain foods, ratios are simpler to use and help you understand the nature of ingredients and how they react with each other better than exact weights. The amount of liquid rice and grains will absorb is a good example.

Spoon measurements

Spoons are handier than weights and are useful for measuring out small quantities of liquids, chopped fresh herbs, oils and many dry ingredients. Remember that sizes of spoons vary slightly from one brand of cutlery to the next (and are not necessarily the same as standard spoon measurements). Accurate sets of plastic measuring spoons can be bought but are awkwardly shaped and not as convenient to use as your favourite kitchen spoons. A much better idea is to check out how much your own spoons hold, weighing out spoonfuls of ingredients you are likely to use frequently, which you can then use to measure all the time, checking them against the standard spoon equivalents below.

The following standard spoon measurements are useful to know.

2 teaspoons = 1 dessertspoon
3 teaspoons = 1 tablespoon
1 teaspoon = 5ml
1 tablespoon = 15ml
2 tablespoons = 30ml/1fl oz
1 tablespoon butter = $15g/\frac{1}{2}oz$
1 tablespoon oil = $15ml/\frac{1}{2}$ fl oz
2 tablespoons = 30g/1oz rice or raisins
2 tablespoons = 40g/generous 1oz sugar or salt
3 tablespoons = 30g/1oz flour or ground almonds

Level and heaped spoons

A level spoonful means what it says: the ingredients should be levelled by running a knife or your finger across the spoon. A heaped spoonful should have as much of the ingredient above the edge of the spoon as below it. There is twice as much in a heaped spoon as there is in a level one. A mean or scant teaspoon or tablespoon should be somewhere between $\frac{1}{2}$ and a level spoonful. A generous tablespoon should be somewhere between 1 and 2 tablespoons.

Whether or not your spoon is exactly level rarely matters. In this book, if it does, it will say so in the recipe.

2

Pasta

Pasta is the great success story of recent years. Its two great attributes are its ability to satisfy and its chameleon-like character. Almost any ingredient you can think of, whether cheap or expensive, can be served with pasta. The same goes for sauces, be they creamy or delicate, vibrant or rough and ready.

Most pasta is made from wheat, and is available either dried or fresh. People who are allergic to wheat can obtain other types of dried pasta from health-food shops. Home-made pasta can also be made with different flours – see pp 59–60.

DRIED PASTA

Plain

This is the pasta we have all been brought up with. It is the most common form of dried pasta and is made from hard durum wheat and water. All the well-known pasta shapes – spaghetti, fusilli, shells, bows, cartwheels and so on – are made this way. The quality varies, depending on the quality of the wheat and the method of manufacture, and this is why some dried pasta is more expensive than others. It is worth paying extra for the best brands, which are usually Italian.

Egg

Egg pasta consists of soft flour, durum wheat, eggs and water. It is made by a slightly different process from plain pasta and has a richer flavour and smoother, silkier texture; this translates to a flabbier texture when cooked, though unless you are a pasta cognoscente you probably won't notice that much. It costs approximately 50 per cent more than ordinary dried pasta and is most commonly available in long coiled strands.

Coloured: green, red, black

Egg pasta coloured with spinach, tomato or squid ink has no extra flavour that I can detect.

Dried pasta flavoured with bizarre ingredients is now available imported from the USA. For home-made flavoured pastas, see p 62.

Wholewheat

This is made from wholewheat durum flour and water and has a nutty, wholesome taste. It suits robust sauces and is good in thick, minestrone-type vegetable soups, or with chickpeas and spinach or Swiss chard. Organic wholewheat pasta is the best; indeed, the only kind I would recommend.

Buckwheat

Pasta made from buckwheat flour is an earthy, chocolate-brown colour. Its dusky flavour goes particularly well with mushrooms, poppy seeds, soured cream, soft cheeses and smoked fish such as salmon and eel. Japanese soba noodles are also made from buckwheat flour.

Wholewheat spelt

This is a new form of dried pasta made from an ancient variety of wheat. It has a sweet flavour and mushy texture and is not to be rec-ommended unless you are allergic to ordinary wheat pasta, in which case you may be able to tolerate spelt.

FRESH PASTA

Fresh pasta is not the simple product it appears:

Most commercial fresh pasta is made from varying proportions of durum wheat semolina, flour, eggs and water. Because it contains flour and eggs, it is inherently softer than dried durum wheat pasta. The quality of commercial fresh pasta varies enormously. Cheaper (and inferior) fresh pasta tends to be made with more water and as few eggs as possible, resulting in a taste-less, bland, pappy product. This is why it is not worth buying cheap fresh pasta – better to stay with good-quality dried. Supermarket pasta is similarly variable; Marks & Spencer's is very good.

■ Fresh pasta bought from high quality Italian delicatessens or other specialists who make their own pasta on the premises is usually extremely good.

HOME-MADE PASTA

Home-made pasta is superior to most bought pasta. Supplementing it with good-quality dried pasta gives you the best of both worlds. It is also far cheaper to make your own fresh pasta than to buy it – and much quicker than you might think. With the aid of a food processor and a hand-cranked pasta machine to roll out the dough, it takes 30 seconds to mix and a few minutes to roll out. And you can't get faster pasta than that. For details see p 59.

STORING PASTA

Bought fresh pasta needs to be consumed as soon as possible. It will keep for 2–3 days in the fridge and, surprisingly, it also freezes well for 1–3 months. Alternatively, it can be dried and stored for a few weeks in a cool cupboard – see p 62. Dried pasta keeps for 12 months or longer if stored in a cool place.

HOW MUCH PASTA SHOULD YOU SERVE?

The simple answer is as much or as little as you want. As a general rule, allow 55–110g/2–4oz dried pasta or 110–225g/4–8oz fresh pasta per person. But rather than go by weight, a better yardstick is to go by eye, and judge the volume of pasta that seems right, be it for a starter or main course.

■ Dried pasta swells in volume and weighs approximately twice as much once cooked. Fresh pasta does not increase in volume.

■ If you are serving pasta with a rich cream sauce or meat, you will need considerably less than if you are serving it plain or with a simple tomato or vegetable sauce.

■ Pasta is not particularly high in calories and will not make you fat; but in a pool of cream or olive oil, or with cheese added, it is and it will.

■ You will unfailingly eat more home-made pasta than dried.

■ Leftover cooked pasta makes excellent salads. Keep it in the fridge and use within 2–3 days. As a precaution, if you want, toss in a little olive oil first to prevent it sticking.

HOW TO COOK PASTA

How you cook pasta is crucial; what you cook it in, the size of your pan and the amount of water are not. A few important points:

■ Fresh pasta takes next to no time to cook; anything from 30 seconds to a couple of minutes.

■ Depending on the shape and brand, dried pasta takes 2–3 times longer than fresh; stuffed pasta may take longer still.

■ Pasta should never be overcooked. The commonly used expression, *al dente*, or 'firm to the teeth', describes it best. Whether you prefer it on the soft side of *al dente* or distinctly toothsome is up to you. One way to test pasta is to break a piece in half; if you can still see a fine, hairlike thread of uncooked pasta running through the centre, then it is ready.

■ Manufacturers' recommended cooking times for both dried and fresh pasta are generally far too long; cut the cooking time by half and start testing from that.

■ Overcooked pasta is soggy, unpleasant to eat and will not hold or absorb the sauce as well.

■ Pasta continues to cook in its own heat and in the heat of the dish. This is why you should stop cooking it the second it is ready and drain it immediately.

Every cookbook states that, irrespective of the quantity, pasta should be cooked in the largest pan possible and in volumes of boiling water. This is not necessary:

■ Pasta cooks perfectly well in any saucepan as long as it has room to move around. Choose a pan size appropriate to the amount of pasta being cooked.

■ Pasta cooks perfectly in enough boiling water to cover it by about 5–8cm/2–3 inches. It does not stick together, and is no different from pasta cooked in large amounts of water.

■ The water should be salted, as this improves the flavour of the pasta. Be wary of adding too much, though, for the pasta can begin to taste unpleasantly salty, especially if you are cooking it in smaller quantities of water. As a rough guide, allow 1 teaspoon of salt per 1 litre/$1\frac{3}{4}$ pints water.

■ The water must be boiling before you add the pasta. You do not need to add oil to prevent the pasta sticking; pasta only starts to stick together when it is cooked.

■ Once you have added the pasta to the water it is important to stir it to separate the strands. A pasta spoon with prongs is the best thing to use for stirring or extracting pasta. Remember that the water will boil much faster if you cover the pan. If you are cooking a fair amount of pasta, re-cover the pan until it comes back to the boil; as soon as it boils, remove the lid, or the water will boil over.

1 Bring the water to the boil in a pan over a high heat. Add salt.
2 Add the pasta all at once, stirring to ensure the strands are separate.
3 Bring back to the boil and cook briskly until the pasta is *al dente*.
4 Drain, though not too thoroughly. There is no need to pour fresh boiling water over the cooked pasta to separate it. Add the sauce and serve immediately.

Pre-cooking dried pasta

Dried pasta can be cooked ahead – hardly necessary but useful to know if ever you need to feed 5,000 pasta addicts. Keep it firmly undercooked, then drain and set aside. To reheat, dunk it into boiling water until thoroughly hot, drain and serve.

SERVING PASTA

Pasta should be served the minute it is cooked; if you do not toss it immediately in a sauce – or lubricate it with olive oil or a little of the cooking water – it is now that it will start sticking. This is why pasta should never be drained too thoroughly – the water acts as a lubricant and helps the strands remain separate.

There is much unnecessary mystique about the correct way to toss pasta. Here are some tips:

- To toss the pasta in a sauce, either put the pasta into a hot, roomy serving bowl, add the sauce and toss lightly, or add the pasta to the pan containing the sauce – whichever is easier.

- If, once tossed, the sauce is too thick, add a few spoonfuls of the pasta cooking liquid.
- If serving plain pasta, put a couple of tablespoonfuls of cooking water or olive oil into the serving dish. Add the pasta and toss lightly, handing round extra olive oil at the table. If using butter, add as much as you like to the hot dish so that it melts, then add the pasta, and toss as before. Add any extra seasoning now if you want.
- Pasta loses its heat quickly. Hot serving bowls are essential, for nothing is worse than serving pasta on to cold plates. Pasta bowls or deep soup plates, which allow you to toss and swirl the pasta around, make the best serving dishes.

Cooking with Pasta

Although one might occasionally spend a couple of hours lovingly putting together a lasagne, most of the time modern cooks want pasta dishes to be instant. This is precisely where pasta comes into its own, for there is no other food that allows you to do so much with so little. Flicking through books of pasta recipes reveals a reassuring pattern of ingredients and themes. There is an inbuilt harmony and logic to pasta sauces, which gives you the confidence to put together a few ingredients in the knowledge that the dish will taste fine. In short, go for a balanced combination of ingredients you like, and the recipe will take care of itself.

Good things that go with pasta

Vegetables Fennel, leeks, onion, garlic, tomatoes, peppers, aubergines, spinach, broad beans, chicory, broccoli, cauliflower, peas, asparagus, globe artichoke hearts, courgettes, mushrooms (fresh and dried).
Fish Squid, mussels, prawns, scallops, clams, sardines, tuna, smoked salmon.
Meat Ham, bacon, Parma ham, pancetta, salami, beef, pork, veal, rabbit, liver (chicken and calf's), hare.
Cheese Mozzarella, ricotta, Parmesan, pecorino, Gorgonzola, fontina, mild goat's cheese.

Flavourings Olives, capers, anchovies, chilli, saffron, dried tomatoes, nutmeg, lemon zest, bay leaves, peppercorns, poppy seeds.
Fresh herbs Parsley, basil, rosemary, sage, thyme, oregano, mint.
Oils and fats Olive oil, butter, cream, crème fraîche, thick, creamy plain yoghurt.
Dried beans Chickpeas, white beans, borlotti beans.
Nuts Pine kernels, walnuts, almonds, hazelnuts.

WHICH SHAPE FOR WHICH SAUCE?

There are said to be over 300 different pasta shapes – a testimony to the Italian love of design and individuality. The shape and thickness of pasta are significant. They are an integral part of its texture, which affects the way it combines with the sauce – an important element in the enjoyment of pasta. However, there are no hard and fast rules about this. Most pasta works with most sauces. A general guideline is to match the weight and substance of the sauce to the thickness of the pasta, as follows:

■ Fresh pasta is thought to suit delicate cream sauces better than dried pasta does (though there are many exceptions).

■ Long thin pasta, for example, spaghettini, linguine and spaghetti, is considered best with simple sauces based on olive oil. The oil serves to lubricate the strands, keeping them separate. Long thin pasta also goes well with sauces that contain finely chopped ingredients, rather than ones with discernible chunks of meat or vegetables.

■ Long thick pasta such as bucatini and spaghetti, flat pasta ribbons, including fettuccine and tagliatelle, and coiled pasta such as fusilli, go well with both cream and olive oil sauces, and with sauces containing small chunks of meat, fish or vegetables.

■ Wide pasta such as pappardelle, tubular pasta such as penne and large pasta shapes such as conchiglie are usually paired with robust meat sauces or vegetables, or used in baked dishes.

■ Spaghetti is sturdy enough to go with a wide variety of sauces; tagliatelle is the traditional pasta for bolognese sauce.

■ Very small shapes – pastina – such as orzi and stellini, are used for soups.

PASTA SAUCES

Tomato

This is the classic pasta sauce. It can be made from uncooked tomatoes or from canned, cooked in olive oil or butter. Hundreds of variations exist and it suits every kind and shape of pasta. Cooked tomato sauce is always served with grated Parmesan.

Tomato Sauces – see p 117.
Tomato, Caper and Mint Sauce – see p 51.
Pasta with Anchovies and Breadcrumbs, Sicilian-style – see p 51.

Pesto, herbs and other chopped things

Pesto is the other classic sauce to serve with pasta. There are many variations, although most of these are modern inventions. Innumerable simple sauces, including many classic Italian ones, are also made from chopped herbs and a few aromatic ingredients such as garlic, anchovies, capers, chilli and olives. They all suit just about every type of pasta and are usually served with grated Parmesan.

Pesto and other herb pestos – see pp 65–9.
Pasta and Herbs – see p 54.
Pasta with Fried Breadcrumbs – p 53.

Vegetables

These offer the widest choice and are often used for pasta shapes. See pp 55–6.

Ragùs and other meats

Ragù, or bolognese sauce, is the best-known pasta sauce and is usually served with spaghetti or tagliatelle. Any richly flavoured braised beef dish, including oxtail, makes an excellent sauce for pasta, as does hare. Tagliatelle or pappardelle are a good choice for these.

Basic Ragù – see p 58.
Daube of Beef – see p 244.

Fish and shellfish

There are fewer fish than meat sauces for pasta, though anchovies are a favourite ingredient in many sauces. Shellfish and squid are best. Pasta and fresh sardines or canned tuna are two other popular combinations. They are generally served with long pasta such as spaghettini.

Stir-fried Squid, Roasted Red Pepper and Coriander – see p 278.

Pasta with Smoked Salmon, Crème Fraîche and Nutmeg – see p 52.

Cheese, cream and yoghurt

Pasta dressed only with the best olive oil and freshly grated Parmesan or pecorino cheese is still one of the world's greatest pasta dishes. The other two cheeses most suitable for instant pasta sauces are creamy blue cheeses and ricotta. Mild, soft goat's cheese and a runny Brie are also good. Pasta with butter, cream and Parmesan is a classic combination, as are simple cream sauces containing cooked mushrooms or choice tender summer vegetables such as peas, asparagus and artichoke hearts. Yoghurt sauces are a modern creation, with thick creamy yoghurt frequently used to replace cream.

Gorgonzola sauce – see p 51.

Ricotta Sauces – see pp 52–3.

Lemon Cream Sauce with Basil and Broad Beans – see p 56.

Storecupboard

Dried mushrooms, canned or dried beans, canned fish and jars of Mediterranean vegetables in oil are the great standbys – see Faster Pasta pp 51–2.

New wave

These are modern recipes that combine pasta with Eastern flavours or currently fashionable ingredients. Be more wary of them as they can sometimes be disappointing compared with traditional combinations.

Using Parmesan and pecorino

Like olive oil, Parmesan (or pecorino) cheese has a central role in pasta dishes. Very often it provides the 'meat' of the dish, as well as adding its creamy, salty savour. This is why it is important to buy good-quality cheese – taste before you buy. There are some rules about which pasta dishes to serve cheese with but working them out can be a nightmare. It is pretty good with most things. I have a partner who insists on using it whatever the sauce; don't fight it.

■ Parmesan is considered the cheese *par excellence* for pasta. Commercially made pecorino has a milder, creamier taste and texture and is just as good.

■ To accompany pasta sauces, Parmesan and pecorino should be grated as finely as breadcrumbs, so that they melt into the sauce on contact with the hot pasta. If serving pasta plain or with something very simple like fried mushrooms or asparagus spears, shavings of either cheese work well; it's a question of personal taste.

Faster pasta

Most recipe ideas in this section – pasta with fried breadcrumbs, pasta and herbs, ricotta sauces – qualify as faster pasta. Here are a few extra ideas to start with to make from the storecupboard or fridge or which require no cooking to speak of.

Pasta with anchovies and breadcrumbs, Sicilian-style

Anchovies have a remarkable effect on tomato sauces, both thickening and enriching them. If you have never tried them in a sauce before, this old Sicilian recipe, adapted from a recipe in *Sicilian Food* by Mary Taylor Simeti, is a good place to start.

SERVES 4

300ml/$\frac{1}{2}$ pint smooth tomato sauce – home-made, bottled *Sugocasa* or passata

6–8 anchovy fillets, soaked in water for 15 minutes

$\frac{1}{4}$ teaspoon ground cinnamon

good pinch of ground cloves

1 tablespoon olive oil

about 55g/2oz fried breadcrumbs, to serve

Melt the anchovies in the olive oil in a small pan over a low heat; stir and prod them gently and you will find they dissolve into a creamy sauce in 4–5 minutes. Stir in the tomato sauce, cinnamon and cloves. Taste – there should be a recognisable hint of spice, so add another pinch if necessary. Simmer for 10 minutes, then toss with pasta and serve, handing round the breadcrumbs separately.

If you have no ready-ground spices, or want a really fragrant sauce, grind a 1.25cm/$\frac{1}{2}$ inch piece of cinnamon stick and 1 clove in a spice grinder. Add to taste.

Tomato, caper and mint sauce

Another idea from Mary Taylor Simeti, which is useful to jazz up bottled sauces.

SERVES 2–4

300ml/$\frac{1}{2}$ pint smooth tomato sauce – home-made, bottled *Sugocasa* or passata

2 garlic cloves, finely chopped

2 tablespoons capers, rinsed and finely chopped

small handful of mint leaves (1 large sprig), finely chopped

freshly grated Parmesan cheese, to serve

Heat the tomato sauce, add the garlic, capers and mint and simmer for 5 minutes. Toss with pasta and serve with grated Parmesan.

Gorgonzola sauce

Blue cheese sauces with pasta are a real find. This version, the best I've come across, is from Claudia Roden's book *The Food of Italy* and takes only a minute to make. You can use other creamy blue cheeses in the same way. This recipe scales down easily to a single portion, so if you have a bit of blue cheese going spare you've got yourself a dinner.

SERVES 4

200g/7oz Gorgonzola cheese

200ml/7fl oz milk

15g/$\frac{1}{2}$ oz butter

freshly ground black pepper

freshly grated nutmeg

Start by melting the butter in a small pan. Add the cheese and milk and stir over a low heat until smooth and creamy, then season with freshly ground black pepper, if you like it, and a touch of nutmeg. Toss with freshly cooked pasta and serve immediately.

Variation Add a handful of cooked broccoli florets, cut into bite-sized pieces, to the pasta bowl and toss with the sauce.

Pasta with smoked salmon, crème fraîche and nutmeg

The marriage of smoked salmon and pasta is a modern one. It works well, as long as you cut the smoked salmon into thick strips and don't heat it.

PER PERSON

55–85g/2–3oz smoked salmon
2–3 tablespoons crème fraîche
freshly grated nutmeg

Cut the smoked salmon into bite-sized thick fingers. Mix the crème fraîche to a thin cream with a spot of the pasta cooking water. Drain the pasta and put it in a hot serving dish. Spoon over the crème fraîche, scatter with the strips of smoked salmon, and grate lots of nutmeg over the top. Serve immediately.

Pasta with creamed tapenade

Tapenade is a zesty paste from Provence, made of olives, capers and anchovies pounded with olive oil, lemon juice and herbs. It can be bought in small jars from high-quality food shops. Once opened, it will last for ages if you cover the surface with a film of olive oil to exclude the air, and keep it in the fridge. One jar will serve 2–4 people. Mix tapenade with thick cream, Greek-style yoghurt or crème fraîche to taste and stir it into hot pasta. Olive paste can be treated in the same way.

Pasta e ceci

Pasta and chickpeas is simple soul food at its best. All you need is some dried pasta (wholewheat is a good choice here) and a can of chickpeas.

The usual proportion is half chickpeas to half cooked pasta – but suit yourself depending on your addiction to chickpeas. Simply mix together the pasta and chickpeas and serve with olive oil, adding grated Parmesan if you want. You could also serve with a tomato sauce; fry the chickpeas first with chopped garlic and parsley; add a dried chilli to flavour the oil; add a couple of chopped tomatoes if you have them handy; stir in some pesto.

Pasta with shredded chicory

Pasta and chicory is another excellent combination. The chicory keeps its texture and provides a crunchy foil and slightly bitter edge to the softness of the pasta.

You can use any kind of chicory – white, red radicchio or frilly endive – adding as much or as little as you like. Shred the chicory and mix with the hot pasta. Dress with olive oil and shavings of Parmesan cheese.

Variations Add toasted and chopped walnuts; small cubes of soft goat's cheese; stoned and chopped olives; finely chopped fillets of anchovy.

RICOTTA SAUCES

Ricotta cheese is most often used for stuffed pasta dishes but it is also good for dreamy, delicate, creamy pasta sauces. For each serving, mix about 55g/2oz ricotta with 4–5 tablespoons milk or pasta cooking water and beat to make a smooth sauce. Heat gently, if you like; it won't curdle.

Ricotta, basil and nutmeg sauce

Smoked salmon, cut into strips, turns this into a luxurious dish.

PER PERSON

55g/2oz ricotta cheese
freshly grated nutmeg
chopped basil

Add enough milk or pasta cooking water to the ricotta to form a sauce, then toss with the pasta. Grate nutmeg generously over the top and scatter with chopped basil to taste.

Ricotta, honey and oregano sauce

The idea for this comes from *A Taste of Tuscany* by John Dore Meis. You can use finely chopped fresh oregano if you prefer.

PER PERSON

55g/2oz ricotta cheese
about $\frac{1}{2}$ teaspoon chestnut honey or other strong, rich-flavoured honey
good pinch of dried oregano

Mix enough pasta cooking water into the ricotta to form a sauce. Stir in honey and oregano to taste. Toss the sauce with the pasta and serve.

Ricotta and toasted walnut sauce

One of the best ricotta sauces.

PER PERSON

15g/$\frac{1}{2}$oz walnuts, toasted under the grill
55g/2oz ricotta cheese
4–5 tablespoons milk

Rub the skins off the walnuts: no need to be fussy, but remove as much as you can, as the skins have an unpleasant bitter taste. Process the ricotta and walnuts in a food processor or blender with sufficient milk to make a smooth sauce. Heat through gently in a pan, pour on to pasta, toss and serve. If you don't want to use a food processor, chop the walnuts finely by hand, then heat everything through in a pan.

Ricotta, saffron and basil sauce

PER PERSON

55g/2oz ricotta cheese
4–5 tablespoons milk
1–2 pinches of powdered saffron
chopped basil

Mix the ricotta with enough milk to form a sauce. Stir in a pinch (or more) of powdered saffron, until the colour and taste seem right. Toss with the pasta, and strew chopped basil on top.

Variation Add 55g/2oz cooked peas.

PASTA WITH FRIED BREADCRUMBS

This is one of the great combinations. Use fried breadcrumbs with tomato or vegetable sauces or (best of all) on their own, dressing the pasta first with olive oil. Serve the breadcrumbs in a separate bowl or toss them with the pasta and vegetables at the last moment. Allow 15g/$\frac{1}{2}$oz breadcrumbs per person. A few ideas:

- Grated pecorino, fried breadcrumbs and extra virgin olive oil.
- Sautéed asparagus spears, fried breadcrumbs mixed with chopped parsley, finely grated lemon rind and olive oil or melted butter.
- Courgette, fried breadcrumbs, chopped mint and olive oil. Cut the courgette into strips and toss over a high heat for a minute or so.
- Cooked broad beans, chopped hard-boiled egg, fried breadcrumbs and olive oil.
- Cooked peas, Parma ham, cream and fried breadcrumbs. Cut the ham into little strips.

Pasta and Herbs

Pasta and chopped fresh herbs go together uncommonly well. Use them as if you were making a salsa, chopping a good handful of herbs with perhaps a little red onion or spring onion, garlic (if you like it), chopped fennel or celery, or chopped fresh chilli and mix with olive oil. Chopped watercress makes an excellent padding and gives these uncooked mixtures a fresh, peppery taste.

■ Almost any combination of herbs can be used. Basil and parsley are the classics but dill, tarragon, sorrel, mint, chives, celery leaf, fresh garlic shoots and coriander also work well. Thyme, rosemary, sage and oregano are more pungent. Addicts, like me, will use them liberally but if you are not so keen, add them with a little more caution.

■ You can approach these impromptu sauces in two ways. Either chop the herbs and any other flavourings and stir them directly into the hot pasta, or fry them first in a little hot olive oil for 1–2 minutes until they frizzle. This enhances their flavour and makes them deliciously crispy.

■ Add cream, crème fraîche, fromage frais, ricotta or thick, Greek-style plain yoghurt and you have another set of instant pasta sauces. Process herbs with nuts, garlic, finely grated Parmesan or pecorino and a splash of olive oil and you have pesto.

Frizzled parsley and anchovy sauce

Heat 2 tablespoons of olive oil in a small pan with 2 whole dried hot chillies/pinch of chilli powder/toasted chilli flakes or a chopped fresh chilli. Add a chopped clove of garlic and cook for 30 seconds or so until it releases its aroma. Throw in a handful of chopped parsley (about 2–3 tablespoons). Cook for a minute, turning up the heat if necessary, until the parsley shrivels and turns bright green. Remove from the heat, add 2 mashed anchovy fillets or 1 teaspoon of bottled Italian anchovy paste and enough olive oil to make a sauce. You can also add a chopped ripe tomato. Toss the pasta in the sauce or put it in a small bowl to serve on the table, with a separate bowl of fried breadcrumbs if you have them. Discard the dried chillies. Serves 2.

Frizzled rosemary, walnut and lemon sauce

Heat a knob of butter in a small pan, add a crushed clove of garlic and cook for 30 seconds or so until it releases its aroma. Add a generous tablespoon of finely chopped rosemary and the zest of 1 small lemon, shaved into hair-thin strands with a zester. Fry for a minute or so until crisp, then stir in 30g/1oz finely chopped walnuts. Cook for another 2–3 minutes and then stir in lemon juice to taste. Toss the pasta in the sauce and serve with grated Parmesan cheese if you like. Serves 2.

You can use hazelnuts instead of walnuts.

Pasta and Vegetables

Pasta and vegetables are a marriage made in heaven. I have yet to find any popular vegetable that you can't serve with pasta for a tasty meal. It is a very flexible combination which lends itself to impromptu cooking rather than having to rely on specific recipes all the time. Precise quantities are not important and can be judged by eye and appetite. Generally speaking:

■ You can use any proportion of vegetables to pasta up to half and half.

■ More vegetables than pasta changes the dish into a vegetable rather than a pasta one.

■ Pasta shells, bows, spirals, tubes, hoops and good old macaroni tend to be the best types of dried pasta to use. But don't feel hidebound by this.

If you wanted to devise a formula for pasta and vegetable cookery the essentials would be:

Diced vegetables + / – aromatics,
softened in olive oil/butter,

+ fresh herbs, tossed with pasta

= success

Add to this:

■ cream or tomato sauce/passata/tomato purée and (if you like):

■ grated pecorino/Parmesan cheese or fried/toasted breadcrumbs, served in a separate bowl and handed round at the table.

■ *For non-creamy mixtures, pad out with*:

■ cooked beans (tinned are fine), such as haricot/flageolet/borlotti/chickpeas/cannellini.

Leek/onion, parsnip, potato, carrots, celery, broad beans, peas. Plus smoked pancetta, slivers of sun-dried tomato and chopped thyme. To finish, olive oil and freshly grated Parmesan.

A tasty winter combination. The smoked pancetta gives the vegetables an attractive smoky flavour – you could use chorizo, salami or any continental smoked bacon instead.

Use one large leek (or finely sliced onion or red onion), roughly equal quantities of winter vegetables and a hefty shake of frozen broad beans and peas (there is no need to thaw or cook them first). Make sure you dice or slice the vegetables into bite-sized pieces. You can use unpeeled potatoes if you prefer.

The smoked pancetta should be cut into strips about $7mm/\frac{1}{4}$ inch thick and 2.5cm/1 inch long. Ditto the sun-dried tomatoes, which should be snipped into neat shreds with kitchen scissors.

In a roomy pan, fry the pancetta in a little olive oil until it starts to sizzle. Add all the vegetables except the frozen beans and peas and cook gently for about 20 minutes until soft and slightly browned, turning them regularly. Add the frozen broad beans, peas, slivers of sun-dried tomato and fresh thyme. Cook for another 5–10 minutes until the flavours have melded, toss with pasta and serve with extra olive oil and grated cheese.

Courgettes with pine kernels, caraway or cumin seeds, and mint or basil. Plus fried breadcrumbs to finish. Slice the courgettes into thin chips. Fry quickly in a little hot olive oil for 1–2 minutes: they should be slightly browned but still crisp. If you are using caraway or cumin seeds, fry these with the courgettes. Toast or fry the pine kernels separately as these burn easily. Toss with the pasta and chopped fresh herbs. Hand the breadcrumbs round at the table.

Leek, green olive and mushroom pasta

A richly flavoured pasta dish for winter. There is no need to soak the dried mushroom pieces first.

PER PERSON

1 leek, trimmed
3–4 large green olives, stoned and chopped
55g/2oz mushrooms, fairly finely chopped
1 large or 2 small pieces dried porcini (ceps), torn into small pieces
1 teaspoon chopped thyme
a little olive oil
freshly grated Parmesan cheese, to serve

Slice the leek down the centre, then shred it across. Moisten the chopped leek and olives with a little olive oil in a bowl, mixing well; the leek will cook better if well coated in oil. Fry gently in a shallow pan for about 10 minutes, until the leek is soft but not coloured. Add all the rest of the ingredients, cover and cook over a low heat for about 15 minutes until the flavours have mingled, removing the lid for the last 5 minutes. Pile the sauce on to cooked pasta and serve with finely grated Parmesan and extra olive oil.

Broad beans with ham, mint and watercress

SERVES 2 AS A MAIN COURSE, 4 AS A STARTER

225g/8oz fresh or frozen shelled broad beans
55g/2oz lean ham, cut into strips
$\frac{1}{4}$ bulb of fennel
$\frac{1}{2}$ bunch of watercress, tops only
2 sprigs of mint
a little olive oil

Simmer the broad beans in a little water in a covered pan until soft (frozen beans will only take 2–3 minutes). Drain, put them back in the pan with a little olive oil and a sprig of mint, then cover and cook gently for 10–15 minutes. Meanwhile, chop the fennel, watercress and second sprig of mint fairly finely. Stir them into the beans with the ham, heat through and toss with hot pasta.

Lemon cream sauce with basil and broad beans

A lovely summer dish. The sauce is Frances Bissell's, from her *Book of Vegetarian Cookery*, the topping mine. Don't omit to skin the broad beans or half the pleasure of eating the dish will be lost. You can, of course, serve the sauce without the topping. The buttery strips of lemon rind, which curl up, can be eaten as well.

SERVES 2

1 large organic lemon
30g/1oz unsalted butter
4–6 tablespoons single, double or whipping cream

FOR THE TOPPING:

110–170g/4–6oz broad beans, cooked and skinned
good handful of basil, shredded
butter

Peel away half the lemon zest in long strips; finely grate the rest. Squeeze the juice. Put the strips of lemon zest and the butter into the smallest pan you have, set over a low heat and leave to infuse for 5–10 minutes: the butter should just melt and should not brown. Remove the lemon zest; add the cream and the finely grated zest to the pan. Cook very gently for 4–5 minutes until well flavoured. Meanwhile, in a separate pan heat the cooked broad beans in a little butter, letting them crisp a little. Tip some cooked pasta, not too thoroughly drained, into a hot serving dish. Working quickly, pour over the cream sauce and the lemon juice. Toss lightly, top with the broad beans and shower with shredded basil. Serve immediately, in hot pasta bowls.

Variation Substitute cooked fresh peas, asparagus spears or sliced artichoke hearts for the broad beans.

Pasta Salads

Pasta salads are as flexible as pasta sauces, and can be made from the same wide range of ingredients – see Good Things to Go with Pasta, p 48. A little leftover cooked pasta, mixed with whatever tasty morsels happen to be in the fridge and set on a bed of salad leaves, makes a fool-proof impromptu first course. A few guidelines:

■ Pasta shapes make better salads than long pasta; if using leftover spaghetti/tagliatelle etc., cut it into short lengths.
■ Home-made flavoured pastas (p 62) add an extra dimension to salads. Choose complementary flavourings such as slices of orange and chicory with Scented Orange Pasta, celeriac with Chestnut Pasta, scallops with Saffron Pasta, crushed hazelnuts with Hazelnut and Cardamom Pasta, etc.
■ Cut ingredients into bite-sized pieces.
■ Pasta salads are best served at room temperature, not fridge-cold.
■ If using freshly cooked pasta, dress it while hot to allow it to absorb the flavours.

Pasta salads can be dressed in a variety of ways:

Olive oil, lemon oil and nut oils; vinaigrettes
These suit all kinds of pasta salads.

Mayonnaise
This suits salads containing tuna, chicken and soft, cooked vegetables, such as broad beans, carrots, artichoke hearts, potatoes and cauli-flower. It is also good with chicory and walnut pasta salad. For crunch, add finely diced celery or fennel. Thin the mayonnaise with hot water before mixing it with the pasta. You can also use a mixture of mayonnaise and thick yoghurt, or flavour the mayonnaise with mild curry powder.

Pestos
These suit pasta salads made with Mediterranean ingredients and vegetables. Thin the pesto with olive oil before mixing it with the pasta.

Frizzled herb dressings
Frizzled herbs (p 54) make good dressings for pasta salads. For a simple salad, add chopped tomatoes and a few stoned and halved olives.

Sardine and parsley salad
This is equally good hot or cold and can be scaled up or down easily to feed just yourself or hordes of people. Fresh sardines are messy, but worth the trouble if you can be bothered. If you have no fennel use celery, taking it from the tender heart. Allow 110–170g/4–6 oz cooked pasta of your choice.

SERVES 1 AS A MAIN DISH OR 2–3 AS A SALAD

2 large fresh sardines, gutted and cleaned, or 1 small can of sardine fillets in oil
2 tablespoons pine kernels
2 tablespoons finely chopped fennel bulb
2 tablespoons raisins
$\frac{1}{2}$ small, fresh, mildish chilli, or to taste
2–3 tablespoons chopped parsley
1–2 ripe tomatoes, chopped (optional)
olive oil
lemon juice

If using fresh sardines, lay them in a shallow dish lined with aluminium foil, pop under a hot grill and cook for about 4–5 minutes or until just tender. Cool. Remove the skin – it will come away easily with a fork – then pick off the flesh. If using tinned sardine fillets, just chop the flesh into bite-sized pieces.

Fry the pine kernels, fennel, raisins and chilli in a little olive oil for 1–2 minutes. Stir in the parsley and set aside. Lightly toss hot, drained pasta with the parsley mixture, sardines and tomatoes, if using. Dress with good olive oil and lemon juice to taste. Season. If serving hot, add lemon juice at the table, passing round lemon quarters for people to add their own. As a salad it may be kept for 24 hours. Keep in the fridge, but serve at room temperature.

BASIC RAGÙ

Ragù is meat sauce, made with pork, veal, beef or lamb. Depending on the proportions it can be either a meat-flavoured tomato sauce or a tomato-flavoured meat sauce. This is a basic (and therefore adaptable) recipe, which works just as well for leftover roast meat as for uncooked meat. It can be frozen but if you do so, use it within a month, or leave out the garlic, which develops off flavours in the freezer quicker than you might think. The other good thing about this recipe is that, whichever way you make it, it never fails to produce a tasty result.

Leftover roast meat is excellent, and is what I generally use myself. If using raw meat, only buy the best quality, or buy it in a piece and mince it yourself, or buy extra when you get a joint and save some for this dish. If you haven't tried it, for choice, I would recommend pie veal, which can be bought from some large supermarkets ready minced. You can use canned tomatoes but bottled tomato sauces are better and produce a smoother sauce.

This is the meaty version, but you can use less meat if necessary.

Variation For extra bite, add a little chilli. You can use a finely chopped mild–medium hot fresh chilli, a small dried chilli, a pinch of chilli powder or $\frac{1}{2}$ teaspoon toasted chilli flakes to taste. The ragù should not be hot but *piccante*. If using a dried chilli, remove it when the ragù has the amount of bite you like.

SERVES 4–6

340g/12oz lean meat, minced

generous 600–750ml/1–1$\frac{1}{4}$ pints tomato sauce, such as passata, bottled *Sugocasa*, home-made tomato sauce, or 2 × 400g/14oz cans tomatoes, chopped

110g/4oz vegetable base (see below), consisting of
1 small onion
$\frac{1}{2}$ celery stick
1 small carrot

1–2 tablespoons tomato purée

olive oil

OPTIONAL FLAVOURINGS:

wine glass (100ml/3$\frac{1}{2}$fl oz) of red or dry white wine

1 clove garlic, crushed

bay leaf

chopped parsley or oregano

1 Make the vegetable base by cutting the onion, celery and carrot into large pieces and whizzing them to a hash in a food processor. Alternatively chop them very finely by hand.
2 Soften the vegetable base in a little olive oil over a fairly low heat until it begins to colour. Add the meat, stir it around until it becomes crumbly, and continue to cook for about 5 minutes or until it starts to brown, turning up the heat a little if necessary.
3 Pour in the wine if using, cook until evaporated, then add the tomato sauce, tomato purée, and the garlic and bay leaf, if you are using them. Simmer steadily for 15–20 minutes for cooked meat or about 35–40 minutes for raw meat, adding a little extra water if the sauce begins to dry up too much. Check the seasoning and stir in chopped herbs at the end.

HOME-MADE PASTA

Home-made pasta tastes better than most pasta you can buy and is extremely satisfying to make – easier than pastry and much more fun. You can cut it into wide or narrow strips, roll it into thin sheets to make ravioli or lasagne, vary the flours, and add herbs, spices etc., for exotic or unusual pasta that you could not otherwise buy.

■ To make home-made pasta you need only two ingredients, flour and eggs.

■ You can use any size eggs – the smaller the egg, the less flour will be absorbed and the smaller the final quantity of pasta.

■ Pasta dough freezes well. Freeze it in a ball, thaw out when required, and roll and cut in the usual way – see p 61.

■ With a food processor you can mix excellent pasta in a matter of seconds. If you like making pasta you should also invest in a small, hand-cranked pasta machine which makes light work of rolling out the dough.

■ Contrary to accepted wisdom, there is no need to rest pasta dough before rolling it, and it is not even absolutely essential to rest it after cutting. This means you can, if you want, make and serve home-made pasta in 10 minutes or less.

Like bread, good pasta is a matter of texture and flavour. Briefly:

■ The texture depends firstly on the quality and type of flour and secondly on the consistency of the dough. A stiff dough will produce a denser, more toothsome pasta. A soft dough will produce a soft, silky pasta.

■ The flavour comes partly from the flour but also from the eggs. The richer the yolk, the richer the flavour. This is why it is important to use the best-quality free range eggs you can buy. The deeper the colour of the yolk, the more golden the pasta.

■ You do not need to use special flour to make pasta – see below.

■ It is not necessary to add water or oil to pasta dough. Water especially dilutes the texture and flavour of home-made pasta.

■ It is not true that the thinner you roll the pasta, the better it will be. A slightly thicker pasta, about the same thickness as dried pasta, is easier to handle, easier to cook and more satisfying to eat.

Flour

Unbleached plain flour, unbleached bread flour, Italian pasta flour, finely ground semolina or a combination of semolina and flour are all suitable for making pasta. Each results in a slightly different texture.

Unbleached plain flour This is made from soft wheat and results in a soft pasta – the dough will feel malleable and is very easy to stretch. Buy a good-quality household flour.

Unbleached bread flour This is made from hard wheat and makes a slightly firmer dough. The flavour will be the same as pasta made with plain flour.

Ground semolina This is made from hard durum wheat. It gives added texture, a deeper colour and, I find, a better flavour. If you like a toothsome rather than a soft, silky pasta, you will like pasta made from this. Substitute it for whatever proportion of flour you like. You can make pasta using just semolina; this forms a much harder dough but, once rolled, it is easier to cut and the strands do not stick together. For plain pasta, I use 25 per cent or more ground semolina. Ordinary packet semolina, used for making semolina pudding, is fine.

Italian pasta flours These are often recommended for making pasta and can be bought from Italian and Polish delicatessens. They are worth trying but do not necessarily make better pasta than good-quality plain or bread flour. There is no difference in flavour that I can detect and they produce silky-feeling doughs. Use the '00' grade.

- A large egg absorbs 85–110g/3–4oz flour.
- A two-egg dough makes about 340g/12oz pasta. This is sufficient for two main-course servings or four small servings.
- A three-egg dough makes around 500g/generous 1lb pasta. This is sufficient for three to four main-course servings or up to six smaller servings.

Making the pasta

Making good pasta is largely a question of practice. Read through the method and tips for success and be prepared to have a couple of trial runs. The knack is learning to judge the feel of the dough. Remember, too, that each time you make pasta it is bound to come out a little differently.

3 large fresh free range eggs
285–340g/10–12oz flour
extra flour for dusting

1 Break the eggs into a food processor and process briefly to mix, about 15 seconds.
2 Add the flour and process until the dough has formed a single ball, about 30–60 seconds. Don't worry if it takes a little longer, it won't harm the pasta.
3 Remove the dough and briefly knead by hand on a floured work surface: using the palm of your hand and starting from the centre, push the dough away from you to stretch it. Fold the stretched portion back to the centre, turn and repeat a few times for 1–2 minutes until the dough is smooth. If the dough is still sticky, work in a little extra flour as you knead it.
4 The dough is now ready. It should be smooth, firm and malleable, neither too hard nor too soft, and not sticky. You can roll it out and use it straight away or store it in a plastic bag in the fridge for up to 24 hours.

········ **Tips for success** ········

- It is easier to add more flour to a dough that is too soft than to correct a dough that is too stiff. For this reason, do not add all the flour at once but keep back about 30g/1oz, adding the rest through the funnel as necessary if the dough feels too soft or sticky.
- A soft dough is easier to stretch but tends to stick when cut into strands, takes longer to dry and is more difficult to handle. A stiff dough is difficult to knead and to roll, and may crumble when you put it through the pasta machine. The right texture is between the two, but slightly more firm than soft.
- If the mixture becomes crumbly and will not cohere into a ball in the food processor, it means you have added too much flour and the dough will be too stiff. To correct this, add just enough water or olive oil to make the dough stick together (about 1–2 tablespoons). Sprinkle it into the mixture and process again briefly until it forms a ball.
- If making pasta with all semolina, do not try and incorporate more by hand if the dough is too sticky; add flour instead.
- A good pasta dough should feel elastic. If necessary, knead a little longer.

Rolling out the pasta

A pasta machine is a simple hand mangle which stretches the dough to the required thinness. It comes with a cutting attachment. A three-egg pasta will take about 5 minutes to feed through the machine and cut.

An important point: at the side of the machine are six notches. These set the rollers closer or further apart, and the closer the rollers, the thinner the pasta. It is customary to feed the dough through all six settings, moving down a notch at a time. If you want to save time, feed the dough through the first, third and fifth notches only. This is what I always do.

Finally, should the pasta start to stick at any time dust the sheets very lightly with flour, making sure you brush off all the excess.

1 Divide the dough into 4–6 portions and flatten each with the palm of your hand.

2 Set the machine on its widest setting. Feed the first portion of dough through. Fold into three, give it half a turn and feed it through the machine again. Repeat this a few times until the dough feels smooth and silky. Repeat with all the other pieces of dough.

3 Turn the setting down a notch. Feed through each sheet of pasta and set aside as before. Each time you feed the dough through it gets progressively longer and thinner. Repeat until you get to the last but one notch, feeding the pasta through for one final time.

4 The pasta needs to dry a little before it can be cut. Hang the sheets of pasta over a chair back or an open cupboard door, or lay it out on a towel. Leave until it feels dry to the touch and starts to look slightly leathery but is still pliable; this will take around 30 minutes, though it can be left for up to an hour. Soft pasta will take longer to dry out than hard pasta.

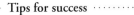
········· **Tips for success** ·········

■ The final notch on the pasta machine produces an impossibly thin sheet of pasta for tagliatelle.

■ Never stack sheets of fresh pasta on top of each other; they will stick.

■ If the pasta gets very long, cut it in half – long sheets have a habit of breaking when you hang them over a chair; if this happens, press the crumpled sheet into a flattened ball and start again, feeding the pasta through the machine as before.

■ If the pasta feels very soft when you start to roll it, leave the sheets to dry for 30 minutes or so and then re-roll. This is a good trick if you like toothsome pasta.

■ Drying the pasta out first makes it easier to cut and helps prevent the strands sticking together; you can cut the pasta without leaving it to dry as long as you cook it immediately, before the strands have time to stick together.

■ Never let the pasta dry out so much that it becomes brittle; it will break up into fragments as soon as you try to cut it.

Rolling pasta by hand

Divide the dough into 4–6 portions and roll them out using a rolling pin. Work on a small section of each piece of dough at a time, swiftly moving the rolling pin backwards and forwards with a fair amount of elbow grease to coax the dough into a fine even sheet of pasta.

Cutting the pasta

Either feed the pasta sheets through the large cutters on the machine or, taking each sheet in turn, run a sharp knife down the sheet, making the strands as thick or thin as you want.

- You do not need to curl up the pasta sheets to cut them. If the sheets are sufficiently dry, you can stack two or three on top of each other without fear of the strands sticking while you cut them.
- Once cut, keep the strands separate: hang them over the back of a chair or lay them out on a towel or work surface.
- The pasta is ready to cook whenever you are ready to eat. The longer you leave it the more it dries out, which means it will take slightly longer to cook.
- To dry the pasta out completely, leave it overnight. It can be stored in a bag in a cool cupboard for a few weeks. Dried home-made pasta is much more brittle than bought dried pasta.

Flavoured Pasta

Flavoured pasta is very straightforward to make – just add the flavouring ingredients with the flour to the food processor and make in the same way.

- Flavoured pasta made with dry ingredients such as ground spices is the easiest to handle; it will feel exactly the same as plain pasta.
- Flavoured pasta made with moister ingredients, such as chopped herbs, is softer and needs extra flour to soak up the moisture.
- Coloured pasta is primarily just that, and rarely tastes of the vegetable it is made from, be it spinach, beetroot or tomato (the same is true of the dramatically coloured squid ink pasta). Consequently it is not really worth bothering with at home.

There are four broad types of pasta flavourings. Quantities given below are intended as a guideline only.

FLOURS

White flour can be replaced in part by wholewheat semolina or buckwheat, chickpea or chestnut flour to make a range of pastas with distinctive nutty flavours. You can buy these flours from wholefood shops or specialist food shops and delicatessens. Wholewheat semolina produces a gritty, nutty-flavoured pasta, while other flours produce soft pasta because they contain no gluten.

For a three-egg pasta, use about 225g/8oz white flour, preferably white bread flour, and no more than 110g/4oz other flour of your choice (with non-gluten flours if you increase the quantity the dough becomes too soft to make successful pasta). Make the dough in the same way as ordinary pasta, kneading in extra white flour by hand if necessary.

To appreciate the flavour and texture of buckwheat, chickpea and chestnut pastas, serve them with simple sauces, dressed in oil or butter, or as an accompaniment.

Buckwheat pasta

A distinctive smoky-flavoured pasta. Serve with smoked fish (especially smoked salmon), game, fried mushrooms, mushroom and ricotta sauces.

Chickpea pasta

A smooth and silky pasta, with a suave flavour and satisfying texture. Serve with plain olive oil or olive oil flavoured with toasted chilli flakes, garlic or rosemary. It can also be served instead of couscous with Moroccan vegetable and meat tagines; spicy tomato sauce; fried courgettes and breadcrumbs; or fish, chicken or lamb.

Chestnut pasta

An unusual pasta that can be served in both savoury and sweet dishes. It is excellent with game. To preserve the natural sweetness of the pasta, salt the cooking water very lightly or not at all. Serve with olive oil; olive oil and chopped rosemary; olive oil and chopped toasted walnuts or walnut sauce; game; mushrooms; or Ricotta, Honey and Oregano Sauce (p 53).

Wholewheat semolina pasta

Serve as for dried wholewheat pasta.

. . . .

FRESH HERBS

Fresh herbs produce bright-green, speckled pasta with a good flavour. For a three-egg pasta, put 2–3 tablespoons of finely chopped herbs in the food processor with the eggs, whizz briefly, and make the pasta in the usual way.

■ You can use a mixture of herbs or make single-herb pasta. Choose aromatic herbs with soft leaves: parsley, dill, fennel, tarragon, chervil, oregano, mint, chives and coriander. Tougher-leaved herbs such as rosemary, sage and thyme are less successful.
■ Try to include a little tarragon. This gives the pasta a strong aromatic base and blends in well with other fresh herbs.
■ Basil and sorrel are moist, fleshy herbs and will need extra flour to compensate. Alternatively, mix them with equal quantities of parsley. Allow 30g/1oz herbs per three-egg pasta.
■ Serve mixed-herb pasta with butter and Parmesan; butter and cream; Fresh Tomato sauces; ricotta sauces; or young tender summer vegetables such as asparagus, peas, broad beans, globe artichokes and fennel.
■ Serve sorrel pasta with salmon and other fish; tarragon pasta with chicken; basil pasta with summer vegetables or chopped ripe tomatoes.

VEGETABLE PURÉES

These are more work. You need to cook and purée the vegetables first, and it is more difficult to get the balance of flour right. For this reason I do not really recommend them.

Spring onion pasta

This lovely, zingy and unusual pasta is easier to make than other vegetable pastas and is adapted from a recipe by Lyn Hall, published in *Taste* magazine. Like all vegetable pastas, the spring onions add a great deal of moisture so you will need to add extra flour.

SERVES 4

1 bunch of spring onions
3 eggs
340g/12oz fine semolina
55–110g/2–4oz white flour

Trim the bases and any fading leaves from the spring onions. Chop both white and green parts and process to a rough purée. Add the eggs and whizz for a few seconds to blend with the spring onions. Add the semolina and process to a ball of dough. Remove the lid and feel the dough; add enough extra flour to form a firm dough. Knead, then roll and cut in the usual way.

SPICES, NUTS AND AROMATICS

There are potentially as many different pastas in this group as you have imagination to make. A few ideas:

Saffron pasta

The ultimate pasta, and what a colour! For a three-egg pasta, steep 1 sachet of powdered saffron in a scant tablespoon of boiling water for 30 minutes or longer. Add it to the eggs in the food processor and make the dough in the usual way. Rub a small piece of dough around the bowl in which the saffron has been steeped to get out the last precious drops. Knead, roll and cut in the usual way.

Serve with scallops, squid, tender young peas, mangetout, asparagus or spinach tossed with butter; fresh tomato coulis; or buttery chanterelle mushrooms, finished with cream.

Hazelnut and cardamom pasta

A wonderfully aromatic pasta. For a three-egg pasta, use about 55g/2oz roughly crushed hazelnuts, the seeds from 1 dessertspoon of green cardamom pods (about 15–18 pods), and 285–340g/10–12oz plain flour. Grind the hazelnuts and cardamom seeds to fine speckles in a spice grinder. Scrape out and add to the eggs in the food processor. Whizz briefly, add the flour and make the pasta in the usual way.

Serve on its own tossed with butter; with chicken, salmon or trout, lobster or large prawns; or mushrooms, broccoli, peas, aubergines or asparagus.

Scented orange pasta

An Arabian-inspired recipe. For a three-egg pasta, use the finely grated zest of 1 medium well-scrubbed orange and 1 scant tablespoon of orange flower water (available from Turkish and Iranian shops, good delicatessens and large supermarkets). Add to the eggs in the food processor, whizz briefly, then add the flour and make the pasta in the usual way. When in season, make with Seville oranges, or tangerines or clementines.

Serve on its own with butter; slivers of unblanched almonds that have been fried in butter or toasted under the grill; grilled chicken; lightly cooked mussels; cooked spinach; or shredded chicory and chopped walnuts. For Scented Orange Pasta salad, mix with slices of orange, slivers of onion, black olives, olive oil and a squeeze of orange juice to taste.

Chocolate pasta

An old favourite, this is excellent with strong game. For a three-egg pasta, sift 30g/1oz cocoa powder with the flour and make the dough in the usual way. Serve with venison, hare, wild duck and pigeon; ricotta sauces; or as a dessert, with honey, cream, a little finely grated bitter chocolate and a pinch of cinnamon.

3

Pestos and Salsas

Pesto is pizzazz. The ultimate sauce for pasta, modern cooking could not exist without it. As the *grande dame* of Italian cooking, Marcella Hazan, put it in *The Classic Italian Cookbook*, every spoonful comes loaded with the magic fragrances of the Riviera. So popular has it become that these days you find it in everything, including bread. Many bottled versions exist but none can compare with the real thing, which can be made in seconds in a food processor and costs far less than any you can buy.

Classic pesto is made from basil, garlic, olive oil and pecorino or Parmesan cheese. However, it can be made with other herbs and can even be adapted to Far Eastern flavours (p 69).

Here are general points about making classic pesto, which also hold true for other types.

- You do not need to make pesto in a pestle and mortar or to chop everything by hand. A blender or food processor does the job perfectly, and takes 30 seconds or so.
- Unless you have a mini-bowl, you will not be able to make small amounts of pesto (that is, with less than 30g/1oz herbs) in a food processor; use a blender instead.
- To make good pesto you need good fresh garlic, the fresher the better. So that the garlic permeates throughout, if you can be bothered, crush it to a pulp with a few grains of salt and chop finely before processing it with the other ingredients.
- You can use either Parmesan or pecorino cheese. Both must be finely grated.
- Pesto that contains garlic does not freeze well and will develop off flavours. Minus garlic it freezes well for up to 6 months, and the garlic can be added after defrosting.
- Pesto should be a creamy paste with the consistency of softened butter.

Nuts

Nuts are a classic and important ingredient for pesto:

- With their mild, milky flavour, creamy texture and unique softness, pine kernels are the best nuts to use. The snag is they are expensive and go rancid quickly, so buy them with care.
- Though none has the same soft quality as pine kernels, other mild, naturally creamy nuts that make good pestos are blanched almonds, pistachios and cashew nuts.
- Hazelnuts and walnuts make excellent pestos but give them a more gritty texture and have a distinctive taste. They produce better pestos if you can be bothered to skin them first. Roasting them briefly – just until pale brown – freshens them, brings out their flavour and makes skinning easier. If you cannot find good-quality walnuts, buy pecans, which are milder and sweeter.
- Pestos made with half walnuts or hazelnuts and half pine kernels are also successful (and cheaper than using all pine kernels).

Cheese

The two traditional cheeses used in pesto are Parmesan, a cow's milk cheese, and pecorino, a sheep's milk cheese. You can use either, or a mixture of the two, but the important thing is that it should be freshly grated. Each gives pesto a slightly different flavour.

Parmesan This is the stronger flavoured of the two and slightly gritty, producing a marginally more assertive, less creamy pesto.

Pecorino Pecorino is the generic Italian term for sheep's milk cheese and it is made throughout central and southern Italy, Sardinia and Sicily. The best-known varieties are Romano, Toscano,

Sardo and Siciliano. Traditional pecorino is a white cheese, which has a sharp, salty taste when mature but is also eaten very young and fresh, when it is much milder and softer. It is available from good Italian shops and delicatessens. For pestos, you need the hard kind, like Romano, which is used for grating. Factory-made pecorino is made either from a mixture of sheep and cow's milk or from cow's milk. The kind I buy, Sardo pecorino, is readily available. It is pale yellow with a yellow waxed ribbed rind and has a creamier texture and milder flavour than Parmesan. Cheaper than either Parmesan or traditional pecorino, it is the cheese I prefer for pesto and use most of the time for pasta and risotto.

CLASSIC PESTO

The ingredients for classic basil pesto are always the same. It is the proportions that matter: different proportions produce different-tasting pestos. This is the one I have settled on as the best, and the proportions, 2:1:1, are simple to remember. Don't worry if you don't have quite enough basil; you can make up the amount with parsley.

SERVES 3–4

55g/2oz basil leaves, stripped from their stalks
30g/1oz pine kernels
30g/1oz pecorino cheese, freshly grated
1 fat clove garlic, crushed and chopped
4–5 tablespoons olive oil, preferably Tuscan

1 Put the basil, pine kernels, cheese and garlic in the food processor, then add the oil through the feed tube with the motor running and process to a smooth creamy paste.

2 Stop the machine and scrape the ingredients back into the base of the bowl if you need to; add extra oil if the pesto is too thick. Transfer to a small bowl and serve.

To keep for a few days Smooth the top, pour over a thin layer of olive oil and store in the fridge. Stir in the olive oil from the surface just before serving.

To freeze Omit the garlic and mix in fresh garlic, mashed and finely chopped, when you come to use the pesto.

Additions Some modern recipes include 1–2 tablespoons of butter, Greek yoghurt or thick cream. These mellow the fragrant, fresh sharpness of classic pesto, making it more suave (butter) or milder and creamier (yoghurt or cream). They should be mixed in at the end and the quantity of olive oil reduced accordingly.

You can also add a little ricotta, which makes pesto both sweeter and milder. See also Goat's Cheese Pesto, p 69.

Thin pesto sauce

A neat idea from The Seafood Restaurant in Padstow: instead of serving pesto thick, whizz a small amount with enough fruity olive oil to make a thin green sauce. Delicious with fish.

Basil and tomato pesto

The addition of fresh ripe tomato to classic pesto gives it another dimension and is indescribably good. You can add either a grilled tomato, which is the way Joyce Molyneux makes pesto at The Carved Angel in Dartmouth, or a peeled very ripe fresh tomato.

Tomato, basil and almond pesto

A delicious pesto from Sicily. This is Sophie Grigson's version, from *Travels à la Carte*. I have given the recipe in half quantities, which is ample for two. If you have no blanched almonds you can make do with flaked or ground almonds.

170g/6oz ripe tomatoes (4 small/2 medium), skinned, seeded and roughly chopped

20g/$\frac{3}{4}$oz basil leaves, stripped from their stalks

55g/2oz blanched almonds, roughly chopped

30g/1oz pecorino or Parmesan cheese, finely grated

1 fat clove garlic, crushed and chopped

4 tablespoons fruity olive oil

1–2 teaspoons tomato purée (optional)

$\frac{1}{2}$ teaspoon sugar (optional)

Process the ingredients in a food processor to a smooth sauce. Taste and add the tomato purée and/or sugar if the tomatoes need help, and salt and pepper if you want. Serve with pasta or grilled fish.

USES FOR PESTO

Classic pesto has innumerable uses. Although you can use it for baked meat, fish and vegetable dishes I prefer not to cook it, as this blurs the flavours and changes its essential character. Stirring it into hot dishes at the end of cooking is fine.

Soups

Pesto goes very well with minestrone-type soups, bean soups (fresh and dried), tomato and red pepper soups, pumpkin soup, gazpachos, and cold cucumber, tomato and avocado soups.

Rice and other grains

Pesto stirred into hot rice is delicious. It is also good stirred into couscous and bulgar, or tabbouleh salads.

Bread

Spread pesto on bread and layer it with mozzarella, feta cheese, tomatoes, avocado, chicken, etc. for sandwiches. Add pesto to bread dough for a green, aromatic herb bread.

Potatoes

Pesto goes extremely well with potatoes. Toss new potatoes in pesto, use it to flavour rösti or as a filling for baked potatoes, or serve it with potato gnocchi.

With soft cheeses and dairy produce

Stir pesto into soured cream, crème fraîche or thick plain yoghurt for instant sauces. Mix it with ricotta and other soft cheeses for instant dips or pasta stuffings.

With vegetables

Mix extra olive oil into pesto and drizzle it over grilled or roasted vegetables.

Omelettes and frittatas

Use pesto as a filling for omelettes, adding it just before you fold the omelette, or mix it with the beaten eggs and vegetables when making a flat omelette or frittata.

Fish

Serve pesto as a sauce for grilled or baked fish, or with salmon, scallops or mussels.

OTHER HERB PESTOS

These are made in exactly the same way as classic basil pesto. A few points:

■ Not all herbs make successful pesto. The most suitable tend to be fresh-tasting ones with succulent or tender leaves, such as dill, parsley, sorrel, etc., rather than pungent or tougher herbs such as sage and rosemary.

■ After basil, parsley is the second most popular herb for pesto, deservedly so, and is often used in conjunction with other herbs, including basil, either to bulk up an insufficient quantity of herb or to temper the flavour of stronger herbs. Rocket makes a vivid green and pleasing pesto.

■ All herb pestos can be used in the same way as basil pesto. Both parsley and rocket pesto go with pasta a treat. Other herb pestos tend to go with fish, meat or vegetables better.

Parsley and sun-dried tomato pesto

Sun-dried tomatoes in olive oil are best for this; if you only have dried tomatoes, soak them first in hot water until they are pliable.

SERVES 3–4

| 55g/2oz parsley leaves |
| 4 slices of soft sun-dried tomato, chopped |
| 30g/1oz pine kernels, blanched almonds or skinned pistachios |
| 30g/1oz pecorino or Parmesan cheese, freshly grated |
| 1 fat clove garlic, crushed and chopped |
| 3–4 tablespoons fruity olive oil |

Make as for Classic Pesto, adding the sun-dried tomato with the cheese, garlic, etc.

Rocket and pecan pesto

Serve this lovely pesto with potatoes, beans or pasta. Follow the recipe for Classic Pesto, substituting rocket leaves for basil and pecan nuts for pine kernels.

Lemon and parsley pesto

Serve this with grilled or barbecued fish of any description. It is also good stirred into cooked white beans, potatoes, or other cooked vegetables such as French beans, courgettes, peppers and aubergines, and served as a salad.

SERVES 3–4

| 55g/2oz parsley, chopped |
| 3–4 thinly peeled strips of washed lemon zest (use organic lemons) |
| 30g/1oz pine kernels |
| 1 fat clove garlic, crushed and chopped |
| 3–4 tablespoons fruity extra-virgin olive oil |
| juice of $\frac{1}{2}$ lemon, or more to taste |

Make as for Classic Pesto, adding lemon juice to taste at the end. Season with salt, transfer to a small bowl and serve.

RED PEPPER PESTO

Red peppers make vibrant orange-red pestos. Balance their natural sweetness with something sharp, such as sun-dried tomatoes, anchovies or capers. To compensate for their moistness, use extra cheese and nuts. Parsley and red pepper pesto is extremely good, as is red pepper and goat's cheese pesto.

SERVES 2–3

| 1 large ripe red pepper, seeded and cut into chunks |
| 45–55g/1$\frac{1}{2}$–2oz pine kernels or ground almonds |
| 45–55g/1$\frac{1}{2}$oz–2oz pecorino or Parmesan cheese, finely grated |
| 2–3 pieces of sun-dried tomato in oil, or 2–3 anchovy fillets, or 2–3 tablespoons capers |
| 1 fat clove garlic, crushed and chopped |
| 4–5 tablespoons fruity olive oil |

Make as for Classic Pesto and process in the usual way to a smooth, thick sauce. For a richer, sweeter flavour, use a grilled and skinned red pepper (p 102).

EXOTIC PESTOS

Pesto is brilliantly adaptable. Follow the formula for classic pesto but change the ingredients and the many different possibilities rapidly become apparent. General points worth bearing in mind are:

- The distinguishing characteristic of any pesto is its creamy, full-bodied texture; without this it is simply herb sauce or salsa.
- Garlic is an essential ingredient and without it, the sauce is no longer a pesto.
- Pesto owes its distinctive texture to nuts and cheese. Either or both are essential. If you don't include cheese, double the quantity of nuts.
- Pesto made with Parmesan or pecorino cheese does not usually require additional seasoning with salt. Those without cheese definitely do.
- New-wave pestos that don't contain cheese can be sharpened with lemon or lime juice.
- Non-traditional pestos often need fine tuning. Be prepared to add extra cheese, nuts, olive oil, etc., to get the flavour you want.
- Adding extra olive oil and lemon or lime juice produces a looser consistency, which turns the pesto into a sauce.

Coriander, cashew nut and ginger pesto

For fish and chicken, and especially good with Cod in a Polenta Crust (p 193). You can use blanched, flaked or ground almonds instead of cashews.

SERVES 2–3

30g/1oz coriander leaves
30g/1oz cashew nuts
1 tablespoon finely grated fresh ginger
1 fat clove garlic, crushed and chopped
4–6 tablespoons olive oil
juice of $\frac{1}{2}$ lemon or lime, or to taste

Make as for Classic Pesto. Season with salt to taste.

Lemon grass, coconut and chilli pesto

A cool-looking, Thai-style pesto with a citrus kick. Serve with fish and chicken, cold soups or prawns.

SERVES 2–3

3–4 sticks of lemon grass
55g/2oz coconut, freshly grated (see p 276)
2 fresh, mild fleshy chillies such as Caribe, seeded and chopped
1 fat clove garlic, crushed and chopped
juice of 1 lime or lemon
3–4 tablespoons olive oil

Peel away the outer stalks of the lemon grass (save for flavouring soups, etc.) until you get to the tender heart. Slice finely and process with the rest of the ingredients in a food processor in the usual way to form a thick white sauce. Season to taste with salt.

GOAT'S CHEESE PESTO

Goat's cheese pesto is a find, and makes excellent dips and sauces. Instead of Parmesan or pecorino, use double the quantity of rindless soft goat's cheese. The flavour of the goat's cheese comes through, producing a distinctive mild, creamy pesto.

Salsas

Salsas have changed the face of modern cooking and are the most exciting thing to have happened in recent years. All you need to make them is a knife, a chopping board and a little imagination.

The reason for this is that they offer a real alternative to traditional cooked sauces and conventional dips and dressings. In this respect, they liberate the cook from what can often be one of the most daunting and problematic areas of cookery. In short, if you don't have the time, the inclination or the confidence to make a conventional sauce, try salsas instead.

The word salsa means sauce. Many are uncooked – salsa fresca – and are no more than stunningly chunky, fresh-tasting dips. They are made predominantly with tomatoes and mixed with chopped onion, fresh chilli, herbs and spices. Salsas may be made with other vegetables and fruit: avocado, cucumber, peppers, banana, tomatillo, pineapple, melon and, most heavenly of all, mango. With all of these, freshness is the key: salsa fresca is meant for immediate eating. Cooked salsas are variations of tomato sauce and usually contain chilli and spices.

Modern salsas take their inspiration from Mexico. Authentic Mexican salsas are essentially chilli dips, comprising chopped fresh chillies of all kinds and, usually, tomatoes (but also avocado, tomatillo or soft fruit such as banana). These are mixed with chopped onion, garlic, fresh herbs (coriander or oregano) and spices (cumin, cloves and allspice) and sharpened with lemon or lime juice. They can be mild or fiery, cooked or uncooked, and are usually made fresh every day.

. . . .

MAKING SUCCESSFUL SALSAS

Salsas do not depend on strict recipes but are meant to be made in a spontaneous way to suit each and every occasion. The fundamental thing is to add ingredients to suit your taste. Success depends on three things:

■ The most important is to cut the ingredients carefully, using a sharp knife, without bruising or squashing them. This is what distinguishes salsa from any other kind of sauce or dip. Mix the ingredients together lightly, just enough to distribute the flavours.

■ Each ingredient should be cut to a size appropriate to its nature – whether it is juicy or firm, used as the main ingredient or a secondary ingredient, and so on. The stronger the flavour, the more finely it should be cut. Soft-fleshed, juicy ingredients should be larger – 7mm–1.25cm/$\frac{1}{4}$–$\frac{1}{2}$ inch dice.

■ The flavours should be balanced. As cookery writer Geraldene Holt wrote, 'The most pleasing fresh salsas depend upon a counterpoint of flavours and textures which tastes pungent yet sweetly acidic.' Remember that and you've cracked salsas.

USING SALSAS

Salsas can be used any way you want – as a dip, a side salad, an accompaniment or a sauce:

■ Tomato salsas are a godsend for the modern cook. You can use them as a relish, a salad dressing for green salads, an instant sauce to serve with grilled fish and meat, and to pile on top of things to be baked in the oven.

■ Salsas go best with grains, pulses, bread, vegetables, green salads and grilled meats and fish.

■ Uncooked salsas are made to be eaten fresh. Serve them immediately or soon after making.

Simple salsas

You can build your own salsas using the following formula.

Base:

■ chopped vegetables or fruit

plus flavourings:

■ onion/garlic
■ fresh herbs/spices/chilli/salt

plus liquid to moisten:

■ lemon or lime juice; wine vinegar
■ tomato juice
■ olive oil

FRESH TOMATO SALSAS

Tomato salsas are the easiest and most adaptable of all. The basic formula is simple: chop some good, ripe tomatoes (the juicier the better), stir in various piquant additions and some fresh herbs, then season with a few drops of the best vinegar and a little olive oil, plus salt and pepper if you want, and it is ready. The only thing to remember is to make more than you think you will need. Tomato salsas disappear fast, and are very good eaten on their own, with bread.

Here are some suggestions for making fresh tomato salsas. As a rough guide, 225–340g/8–12oz chopped tomato base should provide enough salsa for 2–4 side servings.

Piquant additions
■ Finely chopped fennel, celery, spring onions, garlic, finely sliced red onions, mild Spanish onions, diced cucumber
■ Chopped raw or roasted red pepper
■ Chopped avocado
■ Chopped anchovies, olives, capers, chillies
■ Lemon or lime zest, finely diced preserved lemon (p 21)

Herbs Chopped basil, parsley, fennel, tarragon, coriander, mint

Dressings Balsamic vinegar, sherry vinegar, good-quality wine vinegar and lemon or lime juice, fruity olive oil or lemon olive oil.

········ **Tips** ········
■ Vary the salsa according to the ingredients you have handy and how you plan to serve it.
■ A little piquancy goes a long way – a good tomato salsa should have just enough to provide contrast and added zip, so don't overdo the other ingredients. Taste as you go along, adding extra a little at a time if needed.
■ Balsamic vinegar works very well in these salsas, as does lemon olive oil, especially with fish.
■ Roasted red peppers make any tomato salsa irresistible. Another good idea is to pour hot water over the onion to soften its texture and flavour. Leave until cool, drain well and add to the salsa.

See also Caribe Salsa, p 95.

MANGO SALSAS

Anything made with ripe fresh mango is bound to taste divine and mango salsas are no exception. They are especially good with grilled prawns, chicken or crab but can easily be eaten by the bowlful with most salads you can think of.

Like any fruit, a mango must be ripe to be worth eating. It is one of the most devilishly messy fruits to prepare. The simplest way to get at its precious flesh is not to try and cut it in half but to slice down either side of the flat stone. This gives you two thick cheeks and a central stone surrounded by flesh. Peel away the skin, slice and dice. Suck the stone: cook's perk.

Mango, red onion and coriander salsa

You can use chopped spring onion instead of red onion if you wish, and sharp the salsa with lime juice.

SERVES 2–4

1 large ripe mango, cut into 1.25cm/$\frac{1}{2}$ inch dice

2–3 tablespoons finely sliced and chopped red onion

1–2 tablespoons chopped coriander

Tabasco sauce

Mix everything together lightly in a small bowl, adding the onion and coriander to taste and seasoning with Tabasco (cautiously – a few drops works wonders). Serve immediately or soon after making.

OTHER FRUIT SALSAS

So long as it is luscious, any fruit will make good salsa. Pears, peaches and apricots are three winners.

Two-pear and red pepper salsa

This is everything you could want a salsa to be: juicy, soft, crunchy, hot and cooling. Serve with salads or on its own. It is worth seeking out toasted chilli flakes (p 94) for this and other salsas.

SERVES 2–4

1 large ripe avocado, peeled and stoned

1 large ripe pear, peeled and cored

$\frac{1}{2}$ large roasted red pepper (see p 103), skinned

Plus – all to taste

2 mild, fleshy fresh chillies such as Caribe, seeded and sliced into small slivers

2–3 tablespoons finely sliced spring onion

1 teaspoon toasted chilli flakes

juice of 1 large lime

1–2 tablespoons shredded mint leaves or coriander

a few shakes of Tabasco or Jamaican hot pepper sauce

Cut the avocado, pear and red pepper into 7mm/$\frac{1}{4}$ inch dice. Mix lightly in a bowl, then add the other ingredients, tasting as you go along and blending the flavours as you see fit.

Note The sweetness of roasted red pepper complements the two pears nicely. If you prefer a crunchier version, use a raw ripe red pepper.

SALSA VERDE

Salsa verde is not a Mexican-inspired salsa but the classic uncooked green Italian sauce. It is made with lots of parsley, plus garlic, anchovies and capers, and is served with *bollito misto* – mixed boiled meats – or fish. This recipe is from Simon Hopkinson and Lindsey Bareham's book, *Roast Chicken and Other Stories*, and is the best I have found. I think it is the mustard that does it. It also works well as a parsley and mustard sauce without the garlic, or with mint and tarragon instead of basil, and is excellent served with asparagus or grilled vegetables. I like to use fresh brined anchovies, available in tubs.

SERVES 4–6

1 bunch of parsley, leaves only
10 basil leaves
15 mint leaves
2 cloves garlic, crushed
1 tablespoon Dijon mustard
6 anchovy fillets
1 tablespoon capers, drained
150ml/$\frac{1}{4}$ pint fruity olive oil

Put all the ingredients in a food processor, using only a few tablespoons of the olive oil, and process to a smooth paste as if you were making pesto (see p 66). Scrape down the ingredients from the side of the bowl if necessary. Pour in the rest of the oil in a thin stream with the machine running, as if you were making mayonnaise. As the authors say, 'the finished sauce *should look* like coarse, green mayonnaise'. Season to taste and serve in a bowl.

Salsa verde with preserved lemon

Excellent with barbecued fish, chicken and char-grilled vegetables. It is important to use bread with a good texture and flavour.

SERVES 4–6

1 bunch of parsley, leaves only
4 large sprigs of mint, leaves only
1 slice of decent bread, preferably 2–3 days old, crust removed and torn into rough pieces (about 45g/1$\frac{1}{2}$oz final weight)
1 clove garlic, chopped
$\frac{1}{2}$ preserved lemon (see p 21), rinsed, flesh and pith removed, and finely chopped
1 mild green chilli, seeded and finely sliced
1 tablespoon capers
100–150ml/3$\frac{1}{2}$–5fl oz fruity olive oil
lemon juice to taste

Put everything except the oil and lemon juice in a food processor. Pour the oil through the feed tube and process to a thick sauce. Stir in lemon juice to taste, and season with salt if necessary.

4

Vegetables

Vegetables play a central part in any modern diet. In many respects they have more potential for the cook than either meat or fish. They provide colour, different textures and a wide range of flavours in any meal. It is, indeed, the sheer diversity of vegetables that makes them so interesting both to cook and to eat.

The general rule that the fresher the vegetable the more simply it should be cooked holds true. Most are equally delicious raw. Contrary to the impression given in some vegetable cookery books, you do not need to do complicated or time-consuming things to vegetables to make them taste good. Vegetables are natural partners for each other. Simple vegetable medleys – grilled vegetable platters, vegetables and pasta, stir-fries, homely stews, Mediterranean braises, fragrant pilafs – never fail to please, and can be put together almost without having to think. Just about any combination of red, yellow and green vegetable looks spectacular and is instantly appetising.

BUYING VEGETABLES

Buying vegetables is very much a matter of experience. Really fresh vegetables – shiny bright and bursting with health – speak for themselves and will stay in good condition longer. It is worth remembering that the most expensive are not necessarily the best. Vegetables in their natural season, for example, are cheaper and better than their out-of-season counterparts. Similarly, cheap ripe tomatoes for soups and sauces or cheap ripe red peppers for grilling or roasting are better value than unripe expensive ones.

■ Inspect and feel before you buy (this is where self-service vegetable counters score). The feel of a vegetable tells you much about its quality. Firmness is the key. A fresh vegetable is a firm one and will stay in good condition longer.

■ Keep in mind that vegetables are not inert but living and breathing. Though most will keep for up to a week, it is better to buy them in small quantities, choosing what looks liveliest on the day.

■ Vegetables grown in their natural season always taste better than those that are forced. Seasonal vegetables that are available only briefly are a joy, and always match the weather.

■ Vegetables that are naturally sweet, such as peppers and tomatoes, have the best flavour when they are fully ripe.

■ Baby vegetables might be attractive and convenient, but they are expensive and have next to no flavour.

■ Leafy vegetables should be bright and turgid, not limp.

■ Inspect the base of cut vegetables such as fennel, lettuce and asparagus: a brown base indicates it was cut a while ago. Asparagus stalks should be moist.

■ Brassicas – cabbages, Brussels sprouts, cauliflowers – deteriorate quickly, becoming stronger-flavoured. Only buy fresh specimens, avoiding yellowing cabbages and Brussels sprouts and dull cauliflowers.

■ Don't buy potatoes that have started to sprout, look soft and wizened or have green patches.

Organically grown vegetables

Organically grown vegetables are produced without the use of chemical fertilisers or pesticides, in soil as opposed to high-tech growing mediums and by methods that work in harmony with the natural eco-balance. Because they are grown naturally, they tend to contain less water and hence often have a more concentrated flavour. Science has now confirmed that they also have higher nutrient levels.

Organic vegetables are now more widely available. If you want to be sure they have been grown to organic standards, look for the words Soil Association on the box or label. Organic mushrooms, potatoes and lemons can be found in large supermarkets, cost very little extra and are of consistent quality. Organically grown carrots, onions and tomatoes are generally available, too. Organic produce can also be obtained through specialist schemes (p 282).

Pesticide residues: a personal note

It is an unpalatable fact of life that many vegetables are grown with the aid of more chemicals and pesticides than most of us would care to know about. The debate about the long-term effect this may have on the environment continues, as does that about whether or not pesticide residues are harmful or safe, and so on. What can we, as concerned consumers who wish to enjoy good, fresh, genuinely healthy, vegetables, do? Kick up a fuss. Lobby MPs, demand that supermarkets provide a list of what each vegetable has been grown with and do our best to support those growers, organic or otherwise, who are doing their best to produce food we can trust.

The other thing we can do is to squash the myth that we demand cosmetically perfect vegetables. Beauty is, after all, only skin deep: a bio-friendly carrot has to be a better buy any day.

Frozen vegetables

Although there are honourable exceptions, most frozen vegetables are not worth buying. The best are frozen peas and sweetcorn (spinach is good too, but this can now be bought fresh all year round). Frozen broad beans are bland in flavour but useful. The same applies to home-grown vegetables or those you have bought from a pick-your-own farm. Peas, broad beans, sweetcorn cobs and spinach freeze exceptionally well; no other vegetable is worth the bother.

STORING VEGETABLES

Storing vegetables is a matter of common sense. Except for leafy greens and salad stuff, you don't necessarily have to keep them in the fridge, though this will prolong their life. Once vegetables have been cut, however, they should be stored in the fridge and used as quickly as possible.

- Keep potatoes in the dark; this helps prevent them turning green and starting to sprout.
- Good-quality tomatoes, peppers and courgettes are better stored at room temperature than in the fridge. This is because excess cold damages their texture. Underripe tomatoes and peppers will continue to ripen and will be perfectly fine for up to two weeks at room temperature.
- Vegetables bought wrapped in clingfilm stay in better condition than vegetables in thin plastic bags; keep them wrapped in their clingfilm until you come to eat them, rather than unwrapping them and exposing them to the air. An exception to this is mushrooms (p 100).
- Root vegetables bought sealed in thin plastic bags start to sweat quickly and will go mouldy. Open up the top of the bag or punch holes in it, or keep the vegetables loose in the salad drawer.
- Don't store leafy vegetables or salad stuff loose in the fridge; put them in thick plastic freezer bags, tying the tops loosely, to help stop them wilting. Store in the salad drawer of the fridge.

Preparing and Cooking Vegetables

Washing

It is a good idea to wash vegetables bought loose either under the tap or in a bowl of water to remove any dust, and to flush out any insects, etc. from home-grown leafy vegetables such as broccoli, cauliflower and so on. Pay particular attention to spinach and spring greens, which can be very dirty. Do not let them sit very long in the water as this can damage the tissues. A stiff vegetable brush makes short work of dirty root vegetables.

Prepacked vegetables have generally been cleaned; give them a brief wash and pick them over to check there are no yellowing leaves etc.

Peeling

Whether or not to peel vegetables is a matter for you – do what seems appropriate for the dish or what makes you happier. You may lose a few nutrients if you peel them, but not enough to feel guilty about.

The only occasions you really need to peel a vegetable are when the skin is so tough that it does not make good eating – celeriac, for example – or when, as with potatoes, the skin has a pronounced flavour of its own, which may detract from the dish. Contrary to popular opinion, most of the flavour does not reside in the skins. Except where the skin forms a thick protective coat, which helps prevent the vegetable becoming too watery when you cook it, peeling does not affect the flavour.

The skin becomes tougher as the vegetable gets older. Peeling certain vegetables can have the effect of tenderising them and shortening the cooking times needed. Some cases in point are the thick stems of broccoli florets, asparagus spears and the fleshy stems of Swiss chard. The only other reason for peeling vegetables is cosmetic. The skins of root vegetables, for example,

look grubby when cooked, while tomato skins curl up in a sauce (and then get stuck in your teeth).

- To tell if the skin of asparagus, French beans, broccoli or sugar snap peas is tender, press your thumbnail into the surface; if it goes in easily, the skin is tender.
- Mushrooms can be peeled, wiped with a damp cloth or washed; it doesn't matter which.
- The quickest way to peel shallots is to blanch them for a minute in boiling water. Drain them and slice off the bases, then the skins will slip off easily.
- The skins of garlic cloves keep the flavour inside the clove; so if you want a mild garlic flavour, in a pot roast, for example, leave the skin on.
- With starchy vegetables like potatoes and Jerusalem artichokes the skin helps to keep the vegetable together, which can be useful when cooking them.

Skinning tomatoes

Skinning tomatoes is tiresome and the reason for doing it is usually cosmetic. I think it is worth bothering only when you are making a cold or warm vinaigrette for salads and grilled fish and need a tiny dice of tomatoes, or when you need to blend raw tomato into an uncooked sauce. If you are making a cooked tomato sauce, you can fish the skins out once it is cooked.

A ripe tomato is far easier to skin than an unripe one; very ripe tomatoes can be peeled like an orange. If you need to skin them, the simplest way is to pour boiling water over the tomatoes, leave them for a few seconds, take them out using a fork and then hope the skins will come away easily. If you leave them longer in the hot water, the texture starts to suffer.

Cutting

The way vegetables are cut affects their appearance, taste and cooking qualities much more than you would imagine. Always take the shape and texture of vegetables into account when you cut them and bear in mind what the finished dish will be. Once cut, all vegetables begin to dry up and lose nutrients through oxidation by exposure to air. Though not a major factor, it is good practice, when you can, to cut them just before you need them.

■ Always cut vegetables to be eaten raw into bite-sized pieces, thin strips or thin wedges.

■ Finely grated raw carrot is much softer and sweeter to eat than coarsely grated carrot; the same holds for parsnip and beetroot.

■ To make vegetable 'pasta' or ribbons, use a potato peeler. Scatter celeriac, parsnip, carrot, kohlrabi or mooli ribbons over salads.

■ For salads or stir-fries, a julienne of root vegetables – long, thin, rectangular strips – looks nicer and tastes better than coarsely shredded root vegetables. Most food processors have a special julienne attachment, which can be brought separately.

■ A hash of chopped mixed vegetables – onion, celery, carrot, leek – is an excellent base for braised vegetable dishes, meat and fish stews and soups. The quickest and most effective way to prepare it is in the food processor: chop the vegetables roughly and process for 30–60 seconds.

COOKING

Vegetables are probably cooked with more care today than they have ever been. When serving them plain, the important thing is to choose whichever basic cooking method brings out the flavour most, cooking each vegetable to its proper state of doneness. The modern obsession with cooking all vegetables briefly should not be taken too far. Crunch is fine in some cases, but a perfectly cooked vegetable will always taste much better than a half-cooked one.

There is much confusing advice these days about how best to preserve the nutrients when you cook vegetables. There will inevitably be some loss of nutrients. Vitamin C, which is water soluble and largely destroyed by heat, is the major casualty. It is not the cooking method as such which is the most significant factor here, but the length of cooking time and how small you cut the vegetables. Once you take this into account, all the basic methods of cooking vegetables – steaming, blanching, stir-frying cooking vegetables in a covered pan with a small amount of water – are as healthy or unhealthy as each other.

■ The texture of a vegetable – hard, soft, leafy or crisp – tells you much about the way you should cook it.

■ The best way of telling when a vegetable is cooked is to taste a piece. Alternatively, you can insert the point of a sharp knife into the centre; it should penetrate quite easily with just a small amount of resistance.

■ Many recommended cooking times for vegetables are far too long. Apart from some tuberous and root vegetables, most are ready in 1–5 minutes. To ensure vegetables cook in the shortest time, cut or shred into pieces where appropriate.

■ To avoid sulphurous cabbage, cauliflower, spring greens and Brussels sprouts, cook them for no more than 5 minutes. After this time, the sulphur compounds start to break down and the vegetables will smell and taste like school dinners.

■ When serving green vegetables, leave them uncovered in the serving dish and they will stay bright green.

■ You don't need to plunge green vegetables such as French beans or broccoli into cold water to keep their bright colour. As long as they are cooked briefly, 1–2 minutes, the colour will not dull.

■ Vegetables should be served freshly cooked. Purées are one exception and reheat well.

Seasoning vegetables

Salt Most vegetables are high in natural salts and, contrary to accepted practice, need no extra added. Salt can detract from their natural sweetness and flavour. If you do salt them, do so after they have been cooked. Aubergines are the most notable exception to this.

Fried vegetables are a different matter. Here, salt cuts across the greasiness of the fat. The same is true for vegetables marinated in olive oil, or served with warm or cold vinaigrettes.

Sugar Sugar is a better seasoning than salt for many vegetables. This is particularly true for naturally sweet root vegetables such as carrots, beetroot and parsnip; for all members of the onion family; for tomatoes; for fresh peas past their best; for mangetout; and for stir-fry medleys. In all cases, it should be used as a seasoning, rather than by the spoonful. Add a sprinkling of sugar when cooking vegetables in their own juices with a little oil or butter; to help caramelise roast vegetables; or to bring out the flavour of root vegetable purées.

Butter Plain cooked vegetables are often ruined by the addition of too much butter. A fine-flavoured vegetable will be delicious on its own. Otherwise, dress them with a small pat of butter, or have the butter on the table so people can add their own.

Olive oil Olive oil is often used instead of butter to dress vegetables these days and suits most of them, including potatoes, beans, spinach, brassicas (cabbage, broccoli and cauliflower), and popular Mediterranean vegetables such as courgettes, aubergines, peppers, fennel and tomatoes. Carrots, celeriac, kohlrabi and parsnips, either grated or cut into batons and blanched briefly, are also good moistened with olive oil to serve as a salad.

Use a decent olive oil, drizzling a little over the vegetables just before serving. I find a mild buttery olive oil complements them best.

Easy Basic Ways to Cook Vegetables

The following are all excellent ways of cooking vegetables when you want to serve them on their own and appreciate their natural flavour. Apart from roasting, all are quick to do.

I have not included steaming, because it is more fiddly, is only useful for small quantities and I find it takes longer than any of the fast methods below. For general notes on steaming, see p 34.

When frying or roasting vegetables, a useful trick is to coat them with olive oil first rather than adding it to the pan. Put the vegetables into a bowl, pour over a little olive oil and toss, turning the vegetables to coat them evenly.

FRYING-PAN METHOD

This is also known as the 'conservative method' and is the basic method for plain vegetables. Arrange the vegetables in a single layer in a frying pan, cutting large ones into even, bite-sized pieces first. Pour in about 1.25cm/$\frac{1}{2}$ inch of water, cover and cook briskly until the vegetables are just tender, testing with the point of a knife or trying a piece to see. Remove the lid three-quarters of the way through cooking and start testing the vegetables then.

Good for Leafy vegetables, cauliflower florets, sliced broccoli, shredded cabbage, Brussels sprouts, mangetout, peas, French beans.

Cooking times These vary from 1–2 minutes for mangetout and shredded cabbage, to 2–5 minutes for French beans and Brussels sprouts.

STIR-FRY

For modern cooks this is the quick and easy method *par excellence* – adaptable, colourful and always appetising. You don't need a wok or necessarily to stick to Chinese flavourings. It is suitable for just about every vegetable except potatoes, aubergines and tomatoes.

Cut the vegetables into thin strips or thin slices as appropriate. Melt a little oil or butter and oil in a pan. Toss the prepared vegetables over a high heat for 1–2 minutes, with any additional flavourings. Add a few tablespoons of stock or water, sizzle up and serve. For more details, see Woks and Stir-fry Cookery, p 266.

STEAM STIR-FRY

This foolproof method for messy cooks (like me) who always manage to end up with half the stir-fry vegetables on the floor, or for anyone without a wok, was given to me by author and publisher Ann Dolamore. Melt a little olive oil in a heavy-based stock pot or other large pan with deep sides. Tip in your selection of vegetables and stir-fry over a high heat for 1–2 minutes. Clamp on the lid, turn the heat right down to the lowest it will go and leave for 2–3 minutes. The vegetables will emerge bright and juicy.

If you are using soft vegetables like bean sprouts, chopped tomatoes or thinly sliced mushrooms, add them just before you serve, stirring them in at the end.

If you want a Chinese flavour, fry chopped garlic and ginger for a few seconds before adding the vegetables, seasoning with a few shakes of soy sauce before serving.

THE GENTLE SAUTÉ

If you want your vegetables soft rather than crunchy, melt a little butter or olive oil in a pan, add the vegetables and cook gently for 3–4 minutes. Add a little stock or water – just enough to moisten – cover and continue to cook until the vegetables are soft. To ring the changes, add herbs – a big sprig of mint, tarragon or basil – or spices – cinnamon, cumin and coriander, or a few raisins or sultanas. A pinch of sugar brings out the sweetness of carrots, broad beans and hard fresh peas. This method is suitable for just about any hard or crunchy vegetable except potatoes. Cooking times are around 5–20 minutes.

BUTTER EMULSION

I picked this idea up from Raymond Blanc and it is a lovely way to cook peas, and other choice tender young summer vegetables such as baby turnips, French beans, broad beans, young asparagus spears, carrots, and strips of fennel and peppers. Melt a tiny knob of butter (about 10g/$\frac{1}{4}$oz) with a few tablespoons of water in a pan. Add the vegetables, cover and simmer for 5–10 minutes, until just soft. Arrange the vegetables in a dish, boil down the flavoured buttery juices and pour them over the vegetables.

A variation for carrots, summer turnips and baby onions is to put the prepared vegetables into a pan with enough water to cover, 1–2 teaspoons of sugar and a good knob of butter. Simmer gently, covered, until the vegetables are just soft. Remove the lid and boil down the juices until the vegetables become glazed and shiny.

GRILLING

This makes a splendid instant first course. See p 86 for the basic recipe.

BARBECUING AND CHAR-GRILLING

The fashionable way to cook vegetables. It is most suitable for aubergines, courgettes, fennel, peppers, mushrooms, red onion, tomatoes, corn on the cob, potatoes and blanched asparagus. For full details see pp 260 and 265.

ROASTING

If the oven is on, roasting vegetables is a splendid way to concentrate their flavour and gives them a rich, luxurious taste. You don't need bucketfuls of fat. Cut the vegetables into chunks, slice in half or leave whole as appropriate, paint with olive oil or dot with butter and arrange in a roasting dish. Roast them in a highish oven, 190–200°C/375–400°F/Gas Mark 5–6, for around 45 minutes or until they are soft and the edges are appetisingly charred. A sprinkling of sugar helps to caramelise the surfaces.

Good for Root vegetables, onions, tomatoes, peppers, aubergines, courgettes, squashes, baby sweetcorn.

Spiced roast wedgies

This instant way to jazz up roast vegetables is especially useful in winter, when a bit of aromatic punch is always welcome. Roughly pound a mixture of your favourite spices in a pestle and mortar, or use a mixture of ready-ground and pounded whole spices. Sprinkle over the vegetables and roast in the usual way.

BLANCHING AND BOILING

It has become *de rigueur* to decry any method of cooking vegetables that involves large amounts of water. This is misleading. The main reason why boiling vegetables is thought to be a bad idea is that in the past they were boiled for far too long. Blanching, however – cooking vegetables very briefly in a large pan of boiling water – is an excellent method of cooking spinach, all varieties of peas and beans, broccoli and cauliflower florets, and batons of celeriac and carrots. The golden rule is to blanch only small handfuls at a time. This ensures the water returns to the boil almost immediately and the vegetables cook through in 1–2 minutes, keeping their texture and bright colour.

Tradition also says that root vegetables should be put into cold water, whereas any vegetable grown above the soil should be put into boiling water. In practice, as long as you use small quantities of water, enough to cover the vegetables, and bring it up to the boil quickly, it doesn't matter whether you start the vegetables in cold or hot water.

Fresh Herbs

Fresh herbs are essential in modern cooking. Their great charm is the bright, fresh, aromatic quality they impart to food. Each has its own distinctive flavour, and can be used singly or in mixtures.

Having a supply of your own fresh herbs, even just a pot of chives or parsley, is better than relying on shop-bought herbs, which need to be used quickly. Most are easy to grow and will flourish in containers. Home-grown herbs will give you a constant supply and have more flavour than those bought in shops.

BUYING AND STORING HERBS

Supermarket herbs keep reasonably well in their cellophane boxes; otherwise wrap loose bunches of herbs tightly in clingfilm or place in a plastic freezer bag. Keep them in the salad drawer of the fridge and check them regularly, removing any yellowing or rotting leaves. Bunches of mint, parsley and coriander can be put in a jug of water. Keep them cool, change the water every two days and check regularly as before. Coriander, parsley, mint and oregano can also be chopped finely, left to dry on the work surface for a couple of hours, then stored in a bowl in the fridge for 1–2 weeks and used when required.

■ As a rule of thumb, the tougher the leaf (sage, rosemary, thyme) the longer the herb will keep. Most fresh herbs can be stored satisfactorily for a week or so. Fragile herbs (basil, dill, chervil) should be used quickly, within 2–3 days.

■ The young, tender leaves of any herb are more delicate in flavour and texture than mature leaves. Old leaves become stronger-flavoured and coarser in texture.

■ There is little difference in flavour between flat-leaf parsley and curled parsley; the difference is in their texture.

■ Herb vinegars are easy to make: stuff sprigs of herb into bottles of white wine vinegar and leave for a few days until the vinegar is well flavoured. Try tarragon, basil and mint.

■ Herb flowers have the same flavour as the herb, and make pretty additions to salads. Elderflowers and lavender make excellent flavoured vinegars.

■ The best way to make herb mayonnaise is to chop, then pound the herbs to a paste in a pestle and mortar. Stir into mayonnaise to taste. Basil, tarragon and sorrel mayonnaise are best.

ESSENTIAL CULINARY HERBS

These are the herbs that are most useful to have, or to cook with:

Spring herbs Chives, sorrel, mint, chervil.

Summer herbs Basil, dill, mint, French tarragon, parsley, oregano, sage, rosemary, thyme.

Autumn/winter herbs Rosemary, thyme, sage, parsley.

Fresh bay leaves are indispensable and are available throughout the year. If you have a garden, other herbs I would recommend are garlic chives, celery leaf and anise hyssop.

COOKING WITH FRESH HERBS

There is nothing complicated about herb cookery, nor are there any hard-and-fast rules about when to add herbs or how much to use.

The quickest way to chop fresh herbs is to snip them with kitchen scissors over a dish. If you need to chop them finely, use a large knife. A food processor will make short work of large quantities. Once herbs are cooked they become dull and stringy. If you are using sprigs of herbs in a dish, remove them before serving. To brighten the flavour, if it seems a good idea, add a little fresh chopped herb before serving.

Delicate herbs (for example, basil, chives, chervil, dill) On the whole these are not cooked but tend to be added last, to preserve their fresh taste, colour and texture.

Robust-flavoured herbs (for example, mint, tarragon, oregano, parsley, coriander, fennel) These can be either added at the end or incorporated during cooking.

Tough-leaved herbs (for example, rosemary, sage, thyme) Though there are exceptions, these are more often added to dishes early and used as flavouring agents, rather than being chopped and scattered over before serving.

Rosemary and parsley These are excellent chopped and frizzled briefly in olive oil to use in pasta sauces: for examples, see p 54.

Sorrel Sorrel is a special case. It can be used as a herb, salad leaf or vegetable and has a refreshing lemon acidity. It goes specially well with eggs, cream, fish, veal and tomatoes. Before using, it is a good idea to remove the tougher central midrib. To scatter raw over salads, roll up the leaves like a cigar, then shred finely.

It needs the briefest cooking – 2–3 minutes maximum – after which it wilts down to nothing and turns a dull khaki green.

TWO GOOD HERB PREPARATIONS

Basil and olive oil purée

This is the best way to store basil in the freezer, as a base for making pesto, etc. Made fresh, it can be used for a number of aromatic sauces and dips, or slipped under the skin of chicken breasts before baking. It is also heavenly stirred into hot plain rice, risottos, mash and summer vegetable soups.

Stuff 55g/2oz basil leaves, or more, into a food processor or blender. Process with enough fruity olive oil to make a stiff paste, about 5–6 tablespoons. Freeze in small amounts for up to 3 months.

For Basil and Olive Oil Purée sauces for fish, see p 185.

Fried sage leaves

This is the most delicious way to eat sage. You can either deep-fry the leaves – they take a minute or so – or use the following method.

Heat a couple of tablespoons of olive oil or butter in a non-stick pan. Throw in a big handful of sage leaves, stir around and cook for 2–3 minutes. The leaves change to a darker green and begin to frizzle and fry. They will absorb the fat – if they look too dry, add a little extra. Transfer to a shallow dish and put in a low to moderate oven to crisp. They take anything from 30 minutes–1 hour, and will keep in a low oven for a couple of hours or so.

Serve with chicken and calf's liver; pork, veal and rabbit; pasta; grilled red mullet; polenta; risotto; or scattered over green salads.

PARSLEY

If ever there was a herb that was due for a revival, it is parsley. It is the herb I would single out as having the most staying power and versatility. Almost wherever you go in the world there is parsley, and deservedly so.

Overshadowed of late by basil, parsley is unique among herbs in that its flavour marries well with just about everything. Unlike other herbs, too, parsley can be used in huge quantities, as a salad, in emerald-green frittatas, deep-fried as a vegetable garnish for fish, and to scatter over green salads – a good tip to know.

Parsley harmonises supremely well with other fresh herbs: for examples, see Parsley Pestos, p 68.

Parsley salads

The best way to make these is in the Middle Eastern style with bulgar, chopping large amounts of parsley finely by hand, mixing the greenery with diced tomato, a couple of tablespoons of bulgar and spring onions. Season to taste with ground cinnamon / allspice / finely chopped preserved lemon peel, olive oil and lemon juice. The salad should be virtually all parsley. For preparing bulgar for salads, see p 149.

A bowl of plain, finely chopped parsley is good on its own, to serve with fish or put on the table with other salads.

Deep-fried curly parsley

As delicious as deep-fried 'seaweed' and just as crisp, you can do this in a deep-fat fryer, a wok or a large saucepan. The parsley will shrink down to nothing, so make sure you prepare enough.

Wash and dry the parsley, and remove the stalks. You can make do with about 2.5cm/1 inch oil. Heat until frying temperature – to test, add a sprig of parsley, which should sizzle immediately; if the edges darken, the oil is too hot.

Throw in enough parsley to fill the pan in a single layer – don't overcrowd the pan. Fry for a few seconds only. It sizzles violently, shrinks and changes to dark shiny-green tufts. Remove with a slotted spoon and drain very well on kitchen paper. It becomes crisp on cooling. Season with salt.

MEDITERRANEAN BRAISE

This is a full-of-flavour, well-tempered dish that you can put together using any number of different vegetables and leave in a low oven for 1–2 hours until you're ready. What makes the dish is that, unlike a conventional braise, the vegetables are not covered; this allows the edges to char and concentrates the flavour. The vegetables are left whole, or in big rustic wedges, making it very easy and quick to assemble. An optional topping of fresh breadcrumbs adds a crisp contrast. Specific quantities are irrelevant, and are best judged by eye. As a rough guide, 675–900g/$1\frac{1}{2}$–2lb vegetables should serve 2–4.

Vegetables · A selection from:

■ Unpeeled shallots or small onions; whole fat unpeeled cloves of garlic; leeks; celery

Preparation Blanch shallots / onions / garlic for 2–3 minutes. Peel shallots/onions but leave garlic cloves unpeeled. Slice leeks thickly crossways. Peel away the stringy outside from celery and cut into 5cm/2 inch batons.

■ Aubergines, courgettes, peeled winter squash; peppers; tomatoes; whole mild chillies; sweetcorn; fennel

Preparation Cut aubergines and courgettes in half, or into thick slices or wedges. Cut squash and fennel into thick wedges. Leave chillies/small peppers/tomatoes whole; cut large peppers in half. Remove sweetcorn from cob; leave baby sweetcorn whole.

■ Potatoes; carrots; cauliflower florets; broccoli

Preparation Leave small potatoes whole; cut larger ones into thick slices. Cut carrots into long wedges. Blanch cauliflower florets and broccoli briefly, around 1 minute.

■ Broad beans (cooked or uncooked); peas; flat green beans; spinach/Swiss chard; chicory; cabbage

Preparation Cut flat beans into 5–8cm/2–3 inch lengths. Blanch spinach/Swiss chard for 1–2 minutes; drain then chop. Blanch chicory for 1 minute; leave whole or cut into half lengthways. Shred cabbage; par-cook briefly, around 1 minute.

■ Cooked dried beans such as chickpeas, haricot, borlotti or kidney beans

Flavourings · A selection from:

■ Basil, thyme, rosemary, parsley; bay leaf; lemon zest/slice orange peel; fennel/cumin/coriander seeds; dried chilli/toasted chilli flakes; olives; pine kernels

Preparation Leave basil leaves whole; chop other fresh herbs. Add olives 15 minutes before end of cooking. Add pine kernels with vegetables.

Moisten with

■ Tomato sauce / passata / *Sugocasa*

■ Chopped tomatoes

Top with

■ Dried breadcrumbs/dried breadcrumbs mixed with herbs/grated Parmesan or pecorino/finely chopped garlic, parsley and lemon zest.

■ Mozzarella

Preparation Add at end of cooking, then return to the oven until crisped/melted.

Method

1 Oil the base of an earthenware dish big enough to accommodate the vegetables comfortably in 1–2 layers – no need to be too fussy here, but avoid a jumble of several layers. Pile in the vegetables, together with any flavourings, and add chopped tomatoes or a little tomato sauce to moisten.

2 Drizzle with olive oil and bake in a lowish oven, 170°C/325°F/Gas Mark 3, for around 1½ hours, or until the vegetables are very soft.

3 If you want a breadcrumb topping, add it now. Ditto the olives, burying them in the vegetables. To brown the topping, either turn up the heat in the oven or pop the dish under a hot grill until the top is browned to your liking. If you are not using a topping and the vegetables need a little more browning, pop the dish under the grill if you want.

4 Serve from the same dish, with bread to mop up the juices. Pass extra olive oil round at the table. If you're not using a breadcrumb topping, scatter more fresh herbs over the top.

Cook's notes

- The vegetables should stew gently in their own juices and olive oil; adjust the oven temperature accordingly.

- The natural moisture from the vegetables should keep the dish from drying out, but keep an eye on it and add a little water if necessary.

- You don't need much in the way of tomato sauce or extra chopped tomatoes – just enough to moisten the base; use whatever seems right by eye.

- The vegetables will brown to a greater or lesser extent depending on the heat of your oven and whether it is gas or electric.

Grilled Vegetables

You can grill any number of vegetables using a normal domestic grill. It is quick and easy, with the added bonus of lovely brown bits on the surface of the vegetables. Arrange whatever vegetables you have on a large pizza tray or shallow baking tin. Grill as described below and serve as a first course with a warm vinaigrette, a jug of olive oil, a drizzle of cream or thick yoghurt, a dollop of pesto or a pat of savoury butter.

The following vegetables are all suitable:

General Asparagus; aubergines; chicory (radicchio and white chicons); courgettes; fennel; mangetout; mushrooms; peppers; tomatoes; spring onions; red onions.

Root Carrots; celeriac; parsnips.

Cooked Artichoke hearts; broccoli; cauliflowers; garlic cloves; Jerusalem artichokes; potatoes; shallots/baby onions.

Preparation

- Peel and slice hard root vegetables very thinly.
- Slice soft vegetables such as aubergines, tomatoes, mushrooms and cooked potatoes fairly thinly (about 7mm/$\frac{1}{4}$ inch thick).
- Slice long vegetables such as courgettes into thin slices lengthways and fat vegetables such as red onions and aubergines into thin slices crossways.
- Slice fennel from top to bottom to give a thin cross-sectional slice; slice chicory or radicchio from top to bottom, leaving leaves attached to the base.
- Slice peppers into quarters and remove seeds.
- Leave spring onions whole.
- Leave asparagus spears whole or slice lengthways into half, if necessary peeling away the tough outer stalk. You can also briefly blanch asparagus spears first, for 2–3 minutes.
- Boil shallots/small onions/garlic cloves in their skins first until just soft, then peel and grill whole.
- Slice florets of cooked cauliflower and sprigs of blanched broccoli into fairly thin strips.

Flavourings

Various spices, chopped herbs or pastes can be brushed on top to give extra interest. For example:

- caraway seeds for carrots, celery seeds for parsnips, cumin seeds for aubergines, fennel seeds/chopped thyme/rosemary for potatoes;
- sesame seeds lend a nutty flavour and go with all grilled vegetables;
- if you like chilli, use chilli powder, toasted chilli flakes or sliced fresh chilli;
- ready-made pastes – for example, harissa, Indian spice pastes.

Mix the seasonings/pastes/chopped herbs with a little olive oil and brush thinly on top of the vegetables.

1 Slice the vegetables. Arrange attractively in a single layer on a large flat oiled dish which will go under the grill, grouping together different vegetable to make a colourful display. To make it easy, choose a heatproof dish that you can take straight to the table. Paint the surface of the vegetables lightly with olive oil/flavoured oils. If you like, sprinkle a pinch of sugar over tomatoes and onions to bring out their flavour and caramelise the surface.

2 There is no need to pre-heat the grill. Just turn to the highest setting. Grill about 8cm/3 inches away from the heat source until the vegetables have softened and are patched with brown: 5–7 minutes, or a little longer, depending on how thick you cut the vegetable. If the outsides seem to be browning too quickly, reduce the heat.

Aubergines

Aubergines are enjoying a renaissance, but for all their new-found popularity, they are, in fact, a difficult vegetable to get to know. They are unpalatable raw and if you had to eat them plain I doubt if anyone would bother. However, they have two outstanding characteristics: their stunning looks and their ability to imbibe olive oil and generally soak up flavourings like a sponge. They have a unique woolly texture, which acts like an absorbent mat, and once cooked they are transformed into a creamy mass.

BUYING AND STORING AUBERGINES

■ Aubergines come in a range of colours, shapes and sizes: tiny green-pea ones used in Thai cookery, white and yellow egg-shaped ones, long, thin, lavender-striped ones and ones that are almost black. Their flavour varies, the best being mild and sweet. As a rough rule of thumb, the warmer the climate they were grown in, and the more naturally they have been grown, the better the aubergine.

■ Many of the familiar purple aubergines are grown in commercial greenhouses in Holland. These are very mild, with virtually no flavour; if you have ever wondered what all the fuss was about, or why your aubergine didn't have that elusive earthy flavour, this is probably why.

■ Choose firm aubergines with bright, glossy skins. Avoid dull or wrinkled aubergines. Big ones taste the same as small ones, so buy whatever is appropriate to the dish you want to cook. Keep in a cool place, not the fridge, and they will last in good condition for up to 2 weeks.

■ You can tell how mature an aubergine is by the colour of the pips inside: young aubergines have cream-coloured pips, older ones have dark-coloured pips.

SALTING AUBERGINES

The question everybody asks about aubergines is, 'Do you need to salt them?'

The bitterness in aubergines is due to the presence of compounds called saponins. The number of saponins alters with the variety of aubergine and its age. Young, immature aubergines have fewer than old, mature ones. Salting the aubergines first (known as 'degorging') draws out the bitter juices and this is why most recipes will tell you to salt them.

However, though traditional varieties may be bitter, modern commercial varieties available in all supermarkets and greengrocers are not, so they do *not* need salting.

But salting aubergines does have a useful function: it makes them soak up less oil. It also enhances their flavour and texture. For this reason, salting is a good idea, but it is optional. Be guided by the recipe, and by how much time you have.

How to salt aubergines

Salting aubergines is nothing like the fiddle it sounds. All you need to do is remember to start an hour or so ahead of the main preparation time. As a result of salting, the slices of aubergine become firmer and slightly compressed, rendering them less porous; this is why they soak up less oil when you then come to fry them.

Aubergine slices or cubes Sprinkle generously with salt and leave for 30 minutes–1 hour. Beads of juice form on the surface and a little brown liquid will collect in the dish. Rinse off the salt, squeeze gently and pat dry in kitchen paper or a clean tea-towel.

Whole aubergines Either make deep slits in the aubergine or peel away strips of skin so that the salt can penetrate the flesh. Soak in brine – a tablespoon of salt dissolved in enough water to cover the aubergines – for 30 minutes–1 hour. Rinse and pat dry as before.

COOKING AUBERGINES

- The two best simple ways of cooking aubergines are to grill or char-grill them and to bake them in their skins until very soft. They also make naturally creamy purées and dips, which can be whizzed up in a food processor in a matter of seconds and served with pitta bread.
- Aubergines are a good choice for summer and winter, and can be eaten hot or cold. Cold dishes should be served and eaten at room temperature.
- Aubergines need to be soft to be palatable; this is especially the case with baked aubergine dishes (see p 89). The cooked flesh is dense and retains its heat more than other vegetables. When cooking baked or stuffed aubergines, let the dish cool a little before serving.

. . . .

Frying aubergines

Aubergines need a certain amount of oil, which makes them taste better and develop a creamier texture. Use olive oil, which gives them a rich flavour; bland oils are not good for aubergines. The amount of oil you let an aubergine soak up is controllable:

To ensure aubergines do not become greasy when frying, make certain the pan and oil are hot before adding the slices or cubes. Use just enough oil to cover the base of the pan, adding extra only if needed.

If you want to fry aubergines with the minimum amount of oil, use a non-stick pan; if you want to grill them, brush the slices lightly with oil.

Basic grilled aubergines

This is the quick way to cook aubergines. They can be cooked plain but are better slathered with herbs and spices, etc. Aubergines look particularly impressive sliced lengthways into long, slim tongues and this is also the best way to slice smaller aubergines.

Slice the aubergines into 1cm/$\frac{3}{8}$ inch slices, brush generously with olive oil on both sides, season with salt, place on the grill rack or a flat baking tin/pizza tray, and put under a hot grill for about 5–7 minutes until the flesh is soft and the surface speckled brown.

Char-grilled aubergines

These can be done on the barbecue or a ridged cast iron grill. Slice and prepare as above. Slap the slices on to the hot grill or barbecue and leave undisturbed for a couple of minutes until well seared. Turn over and continue to cook for another 3–5 minutes, adjusting the heat if necessary (or move to a cooler part of the barbecue).

Eat with extra olive oil trickled over, or with pesto, salsa verdes, tomato sauces and salsas, etc.; marinate in olive oil, lemon juice and chopped fresh herbs and serve cold; or use as a base for aubergine platters (see opposite).

Char-grilled aubergines with chilli, thyme and oregano

Mix a little olive oil with a generous pinch of chilli flakes, salt, crushed thyme and chopped fresh oregano (or dried rigani if no fresh oregano is available). Dip the aubergine slices in the mixture, coating both sides, and leave until you want to grill them. Other flavoured mixtures can be made in the same way.

Aubergine platters

Slices of grilled or char-grilled aubergine are made for spreading things on top. They can be prepared ahead and serve cold (room temperature, not straight from the fridge) but are better warm: just reheat the slices in a frying pan until the aubergine base is nicely heated through. Good, easy toppings include:

- Pesto, thick salsa verde, tapenade and other olive pastes, and skordalia.
- Strips of roasted pepper flavoured with chopped garlic or slivers of preserved lemon, or topped with chopped olives, capers or snipped basil leaves.
- Thick yoghurt/crème fraîche topped with chopped dill/mint/basil/coriander and a pinch of chilli flakes.
- Horseradish cream topped with thin slices of smoked salmon, trout or eel.
- Toasted and crushed sesame seeds added to tahini.

Preparing aubergines

Aubergines are easy to prepare. Two tips:

- Aubergine skins are quite tough; they can be taken off, if you prefer. A good idea is to peel away strips of the skin, thus giving the slices a striped effect. Cooked aubergine skins can be used as edible wrap-arounds and make snazzy decorations: snip them into slivers or cut out fancy shapes and use on aubergine dips and such like.

- The flesh of aubergines darkens on exposure to air. There is nothing you can do about this, so don't worry. The flesh darkens once cooked anyway.

BAKED AUBERGINES

Aubergines can be baked and stuffed in any number of ways. They take longer to cook than you might think, so always allow plenty of time. Baked aubergines can be cooked in either a very hot, a hot or a moderately hot oven, depending on what is convenient. Corresponding approximate cooking times are:

Halved aubergines Around 20–40 minutes;
Whole aubergines Around 40 minutes–$1\frac{1}{4}$ hours (or longer if very large).

Allow a medium-sized aubergine per person, or a large aubergine for two.

········· **Tips** ·········

- Baked aubergine flesh should always be soft. To test, a skewer inserted into the centre should slide in easily; or gently squeeze the baked aubergine with your hands – the flesh should feel soft and yielding.
- The best way to bake an aubergine is to cook it in a very hot oven; the flesh becomes fluffy rather than soggy.
- If cutting the aubergine in half, oil the cut surface. If using whole aubergines, rub oil over the skins.

Quick baked aubergines

This is the quickest and most attractive way to bake aubergines to serve as a first course.

Slice the aubergines in half lengthways, slash the flesh with a knife to make a criss-cross pattern, oil lightly and bake in a very hot oven, 210°C/425°F/Gas Mark 7, for 20–30 minutes, until the flesh is soft. Dress with olive oil, pestos or salsas, and serve.

Moroccan tomato topping Mix 1 teaspoon of harissa paste with 2–3 tablespoons of olive oil and $\frac{1}{2}$ teaspoon of toasted and ground cumin seeds. Mix with 2 ripe, chopped tomatoes. Add lemon juice and seasoning to taste. Pile on top of the hot cooked aubergine and serve hot, or at room temperature.

Baked aubergine in the Sicilian style

This is the more conventional way to bake aubergines.

SERVES 2

1 large aubergine, cut in half

FOR THE STUFFING:

1 tablespoon chopped parsley
2 green olives, chopped
1 teaspoon toasted and ground cumin seeds
2 large anchovy fillets, chopped
2 tablespoons olive oil
good squeeze of lemon or Seville orange juice
Plus
about 300ml/$\frac{1}{2}$ pint tomato sauce/passata/ chopped tomatoes
30g/1oz fresh breadcrumbs
2 sprigs of mint

Slash the aubergine flesh in a criss-cross pattern. Mix the stuffing ingredients and spread the mixture evenly over the two halves, working it into the slashes. Place the aubergine in an ovenproof dish and sprinkle the breadcrumbs over the top. Pour in enough tomato sauce to come half-way up the aubergine. Tuck in a couple of sprigs of mint. Cover with foil and bake for 45 minutes in a moderately hot oven, around 190°C/375°F/Gas Mark 5, until the aubergine is soft. Remove the foil and flash briefly under a hot grill to brown the top. Serve from the same dish.

Variation Add grated Parmesan cheese, sprinkling it over the cooked aubergine just before you grill it.

Aubergine and tomato bake

A simple, tasty bake that you can flavour any way you want: fresh herbs in summer, warming spices in winter, or a judicious mixture of the two. I like mine laced with toasted chilli flakes.

SERVES 4

1 large aubergine, sliced and salted (see p 87)
about 600ml/1 pint tomato sauce, home-made or bought (for example, passata, *Sugocasa*)
1 tablespoon chopped herbs (for example, basil, parsley, oregano, mint, tarragon)
1 teaspoon spices (for example, toasted cumin and coriander seeds, cinnamon, allspice)
1 clove garlic, chopped
chilli, to taste
olive oil

Fry the aubergine slices in a little olive oil for about 5 minutes until flecked with brown, turning them once. Arrange in a wide, shallow ovenproof dish. Scatter over seasonings to taste, then pour in enough tomato sauce just to cover. Bake in a moderate oven, 180°C/350°F/Gas Mark 4, for about 45 minutes, or until the sauce is reduced and becomes thick. Allow to cool a little and serve from the dish.

You can also sprinkle the top with grated cheese: add after about 30 minutes and return to the oven to melt the cheese and complete the cooking.

Baking aubergines for purées and dips

Purées and dips provide countless possibilities and are easy to make. Rub the aubergine with olive oil, wrap in foil and bake in a moderately hot or hot oven until very soft – up to an hour or so, depending on the size of the aubergine: to tell if it is done, squeeze the parcel gently with your hands. Remove it from the oven when the aubergine yields to slight pressure. To double-check, a skewer inserted into the centre should slide in easily. Don't let the aubergine cook until it collapses or you'll end up with a much-shrunken aubergine and a lot of liquid. Cool.

The flesh can now be scraped out. It mashes easily with a fork or can be whizzed in a food processor to make a smooth purée. Flavour this, and you have a dip for spreading on bread or to serve with crudités, or a hot, smooth purée to serve as a vegetable accompaniment. A few suggestions to give the general idea:

With olive oil, lemon and coriander Mash the cooked aubergine flesh with a fork. Dry-fry 1 tablespoon of coriander seeds for 2–3 minutes to release their aroma. Pound them in a pestle and mortar, then stir into the aubergine, with olive oil, salt and lemon juice to taste. If you don't fancy the idea of crushed coriander seeds, use 1–2 teaspoons of ground coriander, adding to taste.

With garlic purée Mash or purée the cooked aubergine flesh, adding garlic purée (p 98) to taste. Beat in a little cream or olive oil and reheat, seasoning to taste. To make a cold dip, whizz the aubergine with half its weight of soft cheese and flavour with garlic purée.

Aubergine and butter bean purée

A beautiful purée, one of the best.

Allow equal quantities of cooked butter beans and cooked aubergine flesh – 110g/4oz of each will be enough for 4. Slip the skins off the butter beans, put the beans and aubergine in the food processor and blend to a soft paste with 3–4 tablespoons of olive oil. Season, adding extra olive oil and a squeeze of lemon juice to taste. Serve with crudités or bread.

To serve hot, omit the seasoning of lemon juice and heat through in a pan, loosened with a little creamy milk or cream.

Spiced aubergine dip with mint

Recipes for aubergines invariably contain garlic and lots of olive oil. Here is one that doesn't. The lemon and mint give it a fresh, summery flavour. You can bake the aubergine whenever it is convenient and keep it in the fridge for 2–3 days. Treat the quantities as a guide; like all dips, it invariably needs fine-tuning – that is, add a bit more of this or that until it tastes right to you.

1 large baked aubergine (see opposite)
Plus
leaves from 2 large sprigs of mint (about 15 leaves)
1 teaspoon lightly toasted cumin seeds, pounded with a good pinch of salt
2 tablespoons olive oil
juice of $\frac{1}{2}$ lemon, plus extra as necessary
salt to taste

Put everything in the food processor and process to a chunky purée. Taste, adding extra lemon juice and salt as necessary. The flecks of aubergine skin give the purée added texture (and flavour), but can be left out if you insist. In this case, slice the aubergine in half, scoop out the flesh and proceed as before.

The dip needs time to develop its flavours, tasting bland if you eat it straight away. Leave for a few hours, or preferably overnight in the fridge. Serve spread on dry-baked rounds of bread, with pitta or spread on grilled aubergine slices.

Chillies

Chillies, *Capsicum frutescens*, feature strongly in the food of many countries. They have become fashionable of late in the UK and are used extensively in modern cooking, but pose an ever-present problem: you never quite know how fiery they're going to be. This makes them confusing to buy and to cook with.

The reason for this is twofold. First, there are, in fact, countless varieties of chillies that differ enormously in size and degree of hotness, from extremely mild to mind-numbingly hot. Unless you know the variety or the label indicates whether it is mild or hot you have no way of knowing just by looking at the chilli. In addition, the amount of the compound responsible for chilli heat, capsaicin, differs not only with each variety but also with the growing season and how ripe each particular chilli is. This means that although each variety of chilli has a generally predictable level of hotness, individual chillies may be hotter or milder than expected.

The other sting in the tail is that each individual's tolerance of chilli heat is different, so that what seems pleasantly mild to one person may appear incendiary to another. The more you use and eat chilli, the more tolerant to chilli heat you become. This then levels off, so that each person reaches their own chilli plateau, finding the level of heat they like best. As long as you bear these points in mind when buying and cooking with chillies, you can cook with them successfully every time. A few more essential chilli facts:

- The hottest part of a chilli is the thin white membrane, which holds the seeds; this contains 90 per cent of the capsaicin. The seeds contain approximately the same amount as the flesh; although generally removed for cosmetic purposes, they are edible.
- How mild or hot a chilli is depends on its variety, not whether it is green or red. The smaller the chilli, usually the more fire it has. Dried chillies have a more concentrated flavour but the same amount of heat as a fresh chilli of that particular variety.
- Chillies are good for you, being a valuable source of vitamins A and C.
- Chillies are unique. Heat apart, they stimulate the tastebuds, promote a feeling of well-being and induce a tingling sensation inside the body. This is what makes them addictive.
- To relieve chilli heat, drink alcohol, milk or lassi. Water is cool to the mouth but will not dissipate the heat.

GREEN OR RED CHILLIES?

Recipes often stipulate green or red chillies. As long as the heat scale is approximately the same, it doesn't matter which you use, though red chillies undeniably look more attractive in a dish than green ones.

All chillies are green when they are unripe, gradually changing colour as they ripen. Their flavour and heat intensity also develop during ripening. This means that any variety of chilli will be milder in its green state. It does not mean, however, that all green chillies are mild. A green Habanero, for example, which is a hot variety, will be far hotter than the reddest Fresno, which is a mild one.

BUYING AND STORING CHILLIES

Fresh chillies

These are widely available. They may be green, yellow, orange or red in colour, and vary in size from tiny, pointed (hot) Thai chillies to long, tapering chillies, round, crinkly chillies and chillies large enough to be stuffed. Chilli heat is officially measured on a scale from 1–10. This gives a good indication of how hot the chilli will be and has been included in the descriptions.

- Supermarkets and greengrocers mainly sell unnamed chillies. Most are Fresno chillies, which have little or variable heat, are watery and flavourless. Named varieties of fresh chillies sold in supermarkets, like commercially grown sweet peppers, can also be disappointing, and do not necessarily reflect the character of that particular variety of chilli at its best.
- Ethnic shops sell a wider variety of chillies and are likelier to sell more typical and traditional varieties. They will probably be more knowledgeable and therefore able to advise you on how hot a particular chilli is.
- Buy fresh chillies in small quantities. They need no special storage conditions and will keep perfectly well in a bowl at room temperature. If left, fresh chillies dry out naturally in a month or so; green chillies often become riper, turning red and becoming hotter in the process.

Some of the best-known varieties you may find in the shops or will read about are as follows.

Anaheim Largish mild green chilli. A new American variety bred to be fleshier and large enough to be stuffed. Not as thick-walled as the Jalapeno but can be grilled or used whole for vegetable braises and meat stews. Heat scale 2–3.

Caribe Medium-sized, mild, sweetish-tasting, pale lime-green or pale yellow Mexican chilli. Good to use raw in salads, as a substitute for green peppers. Heat scale 2–3.

Dutch Bright-red, tapering, thick-fleshed, hottish, sweet chilli bred in Holland for export. Heat scale 6.

Fresno Smallish, typically squat and conical, this moderately hot green or red chilli is the variety most commonly available (see below), mainly imported from Kenya and the Gambia. They are usually a disappointment, with a thin, watery flavour and often no chilli heat. Heat scale 5–6, though often 2–3.

Habanero One of the hottest chillies in the world. Related to the Scotch bonnet and similar in appearance to a small, sweet pepper, it ranges in colour from green to orange and red. It has a very fruity flavour and fierce burning heat, but one that fades quickly. Heat scale 10.

Jalapeno A thick-walled, juicy green chilli, shaped like a bullet. Traditionally medium-hot when grown in Mexico, American hybrids are very mild. Sometimes they are mistakenly sold as Fresno chillies. To tell them apart, slice the chilli across. A Jalapeno will be round in cross-section and look like a cartwheel. Dried, smoked Jalapenos are known as Chipotle chillies. Heat scale 5.

Scotch bonnet Small, round, crinkly, fiercely hot yellow or red chilli popular in Jamaican cooking. Distinctive flavour and aroma Heat scale 9–10.

Thai Tiny, hot green or red 'bird's-eye' chillies sold in supermarkets as part of a packet containing fresh Thai herbs and seasonings, and in Chinese and Thai shops. Thai shops also sell mild varieties of Thai chillies. Heat scale 7–8.

Dried chillies

These are normally sold in the spice racks of supermarkets and in general delicatessens, usually with no indication of their variety, strength or age. Ethnic shops are likely to have a better choice. A wide range of authentic Mexican dried chillies, graded according to their heat, is slowly becoming more available and can be bought from selected Sainsbury's stores. They can also be obtained by mail order: see p 282.

■ The dried chillies used in southern Europe for tomato sauces, pizzas, seafood soups and stews, etc. are not hot Mexican or Indian chillies but sweetish, medium-hot *peperoncini* chillies. Remember this when making Mediterranean dishes.

■ Dried and toasted chilli flakes are very useful, and the most convenient way of using dried chillies in general cooking. I recommend them highly. They need no preparation and can be sprinkled on food, sauces, etc., and used for Mediterranean dishes.

■ All dried chillies will keep for years, though their flavours (if they have them) do diminish over time. Keep in a cool, preferably dark cupboard in an airtight jar.

PREPARING CHILLIES

Fresh chillies are prepared in exactly the same way as sweet peppers, with one very important proviso. They must be handled with care. Once cut, the capsaicin is released and can cause severe irritation to the skin and eyes. For this reason, ALWAYS wash your hands and knife immediately after chopping and seeding chillies, and take special care not to rub your eyes.

Whole, small dried chillies can be added direct to soups, sauces, etc. Large dried chillies can be chopped or roughly broken. For salsas they are usually rehydrated by soaking them in boiling water for 30 minutes first, then seeded and chopped in the usual way. They can also be puréed.

USING CHILLIES

Fresh chillies are easy to use. Slice, remove the seeds and either chop or slice very finely. As a flavouring – for example, for stir-fries – they are added first and fried briefly.

Large chillies can also be grilled or roasted like sweet peppers and then skinned. This is often done when making chilli salsas. It brings out their flavour and any sweetness they may have, though is fiddly to do and not worthwhile unless you have a thick-walled, fleshy chilli that has some flavour to it in the first place. Large chillies can also be stuffed.

Fresh fleshy chillies can be treated like peppers and added to pizzas, grilled vegetables, Mediterranean braised vegetables, etc. Slice in half and seed first. Large, mild or moderately hot dried Mexican chillies can be rehydrated and used in the same way.

CONTROLLING CHILLI HEAT

The secret of using and cooking with chillies is controlling chilli heat. There are several ways to do this.

Because of their unpredictability and because whoever created the recipe will have a different tolerance to chilli heat from you, use the amount of chilli specified in a recipe as a guideline only, adding more or less as you feel happy with. If in doubt, use less rather than more. A little chilli gives a pleasant background bite to a dish, whereas if you overdo it the dish will taste unpleasantly hot and may be overwhelmed completely.

Though it is fun to try different types of chillies it is also worth pointing out that all chefs I know tend to stick to one kind so they can be sure of how much to use. You can do this, too, if you like. Perhaps this is not the place to say so, but if you really do not like chillies at all yet want to try a recipe which contains them, for example, a Thai stir-fry, simply leave out the chilli.

Caribe salsa

This comes from chilli queen Dodie Miller, who imports fresh and dried chillies into the UK, packaging them in see-through bags with bright-yellow labels (p 282). She includes a recipe with every kind of chilli, of which this is one. If the oven isn't on, cheat and pop the chillies under the grill for around 5–7 minutes.

SERVES 4

2 fresh Caribe chillies, halved and seeded
4 ripe tomatoes
1 small onion (I use red onion), chopped
1 clove garlic
1 teaspoon ground cumin

Put the chillies on a baking sheet and roast in a hot oven, 200°C/400°F/Gas Mark 6, for around 15 minutes or until soft and beginning to brown. Meanwhile, halve the tomatoes and place skin-side up on a baking sheet under a hot grill for 2–3 minutes until the skins blacken (not too much).

Put everything into a food processor or blender and process to a chunky sauce. Scrape into a small pan and simmer for 5 minutes. Serve with grilled or barbecued meat or fish, or grilled vegetables.

Chilli Checklist

■ You can always substitute a mild for a hot chilli if you prefer. A mild chilli will give a bit of kick or bite to a dish. A hot chilli will make it spicy hot.

■ To find out how hot each chilli is, taste a small piece first, using this as a benchmark to adjust the quantity in the recipe accordingly.

■ Cutting the chilli releases its capsaicin and spreads chilli heat throughout the dish. If you use the chilli whole – for example, in soups and stews – this will contain its heat.

■ When using whole chillies, taste the dish half-way through and if the dish seems hot enough, remove the chilli. (This is called 'walking the chilli through the sauce', and is a good tip to know.)

■ Capsaicin is unaffected by cooking and cooking chillies does not dissipate their heat; a hot chilli will still be as hot whether it is raw or cooked, and be the same intensity at the end of cooking as at the beginning. If you have used too much, the only way to modify the heat is to add cream, yoghurt or coconut milk to the dish.

Garlic

Garlic has assumed a pre-eminence in modern British cooking that would have seemed impossible a few years ago. As with chillies, the key to garlic is to learn how to control it and how to use it to best effect. Whether or not you use it frequently, freshness is the other key. Think of it not as a store cupboard item that lasts indefinitely but as a vegetable like onions that should be bought regularly and every dish you make with garlic will taste immeasurably better.

Remember, too, that everybody's sensitivity to garlic is different and that some people find it much more digestible than others. Despite the status often given it in cookery books, it is not the ultimate seasoning and can always be left out if it is not for you.

. . . .

BUYING AND STORING GARLIC

The fresher the garlic the better it will be, with freshly harvested garlic (see right) being the best of all.

■ Good quality garlic has plump, smooth-skinned bulbs with firm cloves. Avoid wizened, stale-looking garlic or garlic that has started to sprout. Old garlic has discoloured cloves and an acrid rancid smell. Do not use.

■ Depending on where the garlic comes from (garlic is imported from Italy, Spain, Chile, Hungary, China, Thailand, California and Mexico), the bulbs may be small or large. As a rough rule of thumb, the smaller the bulb the stronger the garlic. Some shops also sell British garlic grown on the Isle of Wight, which is very good.

■ Garlic can be stored for about 6 months, though becomes progressively staler and more acrid. This is why it is important always to buy the freshest-looking bulb you can find and to use it quickly. It should not be kept in a steamy kitchen, which will hasten its deterioration and make it sprout. Keep it somewhere cool, dry and preferably dark.

Wet, green or fresh v. dried garlic

Contrary to accepted wisdom, garlic is *not* at its best when most potent but when it has just been harvested, that is, freshly dug out of the ground. The difference between this and the bulbs of garlic we are familiar with is that it has not been dried first. This is necessary in order to be able to store garlic for long periods, and increases its pungency dramatically, which is why all commercial garlic is dried as a matter of course.

■ The season for freshly harvested garlic is very short. It appears in the shops briefly in early summer, mainly imported from France, particularly from Provence. Snap it up when you can. It is easily recognised by its appearance and sweet smell: the bulbs are much larger and have a fat juicy neck, the skin is pure white or streaked with pink or purple and is supple, not dry and papery.

■ Fresh garlic perfumes the whole kitchen and is a joy to use. The cloves are plumper, juicier, crushing easily to a pulp, and are milder, sweeter and more digestible. It lasts no more than 2–3 weeks in this mild, heady state, before gradually drying out and becoming stronger in flavour. It will still, however, be much fresher than most of the dried garlic you will buy in the shops and can be stored in the same way.

Garlic shoots

Given time, all garlic will sprout, with a small green shoot appearing at the top of the clove. When this happens, the garlic is no longer fit to use. The green shoots, however, are a traditional springtime delicacy. Instead of throwing the garlic away, plant the sprouting cloves pointed-end up in the garden, or pop them into a pot of compost. The shoots grow like chives and have a lovely mild garlic flavour; they can be used like chives – snipped into omelettes, salads, stir-fries, etc.

Garlic shoots are now appearing in some shops to buy; they look like pencil-slim leeks and can be bought in spring and early summer.

PREPARING AND USING GARLIC

Garlic is power-packed and controlling its pungency depends both on how you prepare it and whether you use it raw, cook it briefly or cook it for a long time. Whichever way you use it, garlic breath is a fact of life.

■ Raw garlic is the most potent form and is more difficult to digest. If you are sensitive to garlic, a tiny amount of raw garlic will have the same effect as a large amount of cooked.

■ The action of chopping and crushing garlic breaks down the cells and releases the compounds responsible for the flavour. This means that the more you crush it or the finer you chop it, the greater the pungency and the more the flavour will be released and permeate the whole dish. If you want a less pungent garlic flavour, use it sliced. If you want a milder flavour still, use a whole clove, removing it when you want.

■ The simplest way to skin and crush garlic is to put the clove under a heavy knife and press down hard with the heel of your hand; the skin will then peel away easily.

■ Garlic burns easily and should be fried with care: move it about constantly and start frying it in cool rather than hot fat. The aroma is released almost immediately and it fries in a matter of a minute or so. Garlic becomes bitter when it is burnt.

■ The longer you cook garlic the more benign it becomes. Long, slow cooking breaks down its indigestible compounds and converts some of its starches to sugars, rendering it very mild and deliciously sweet, with fewer after-effects (see Ways to Cook and Serve Whole Garlic, p 99).

GARLIC AS A FLAVOURING

Garlic is most commonly used, like onions, as a flavouring in cooked and uncooked dishes. It is worth pointing out, however, that unless you like it, it does not necessarily improve a dish, but merely makes it garlicky.

If you want to add a hint of garlic flavour, without incorporating garlic, the following are good tips to know:

■ To flavour a salad, wipe a clove of garlic around the salad bowl or bury a piece of toasted bread rubbed with garlic in the centre.
■ To flavour a dressing, infuse a crushed clove of garlic for a few minutes and then remove.
■ To flavour a cooked dish, spear a clove of garlic on a fork and run it through the dish before serving. Or add a whole clove of garlic to the cooking water when cooking vegetables.
■ To flavour oil – for example in stir-fries – fry crushed garlic briefly, then remove.

Garlic lore

Chewing parsley does not take the smell of garlic away. It may make your mouth feel sweeter but offers no relief for your companions. People who have eaten garlic do not detect other people's garlic, whereas anyone who has not eaten it will smell it immediately.

BLANCHING GARLIC

This is the other way to temper the pungency of garlic and is the most useful garlic tip I know. The action of blanching drives off some of the volatile compounds and this makes it milder and more digestible. The golden rule, therefore, if you find garlic difficult to digest, or if it is too strong, or not as fresh as you would like, is to blanch it first. The same goes for whole heads of garlic which are to be roasted or barbecued.

Blanching is also the quickest way to skin a large amount of garlic. Put whole garlic cloves into a pan, cover with cold water, bring to the boil, cook for 2–3 minutes, then drain. To skin them, slice off the root end with a sharp knife. Squeeze gently and the clove will pop out of its skin.

Repeated blanching – another good trick – using fresh water each time, renders the cloves progressively milder. After 3–4 blanchings, very fresh cloves end up tasting sweet and only faintly 'garlicky'. Older garlic can be blanched 5–6 times.

Garlic purée

This is a revelation to anyone who has only ever experienced garlic as a pungent seasoning. It can be spread on dry-baked bread rounds to float in fish soups, added to mushroom and other vegetable purées and soups, and makes dreamy potato and garlic purées and mash. Let down with cream, it turns into a delicious sauce for rabbit, veal, chicken or lamb, and for vegetables like broad beans and carrots.

The method comes originally from Roger Vergé's *Cuisine of the Sun*, published many years ago.

Separate the cloves for 2–3 heads of new season's garlic. Blanch once and remove the skins as described above. Blanch another 3–4 times, using fresh water each time. The final time, simmer a little longer if necessary, until the

cloves are absolutely soft. Drain well, mash to a pulp and the purée is ready. Season to taste and use as described above. It will keep under a film of olive oil in the fridge for 3–4 days.

Frances Bissell's garlic sauce

This recipe, by the cookery columnist of *The Times*, is another way of making a simple, creamy garlic sauce. I blanch the cloves first, as a precaution.

Simmer blanched cloves of garlic (see above) from 2–3 heads of new season's garlic in about 300ml/$\frac{1}{2}$ pint of full-cream milk with a clove and bay leaf for about 15–20 minutes until soft. Blend to form a sauce, then sieve. 'The sauce can be thickened by stirring in some soft white breadcrumbs and beating in a little butter before seasoning.'

GARLIC AS A VEGETABLE

Garlic makes a delicious vegetable. It is important to use fresh, plump garlic (stale garlic will not make a delicious anything) and to cook it *slowly*. Whereas frying garlic releases its full potent aroma and flavour immediately, long, gentle cooking transforms it into nuggets of mild, sweet, meltingly tender flesh.

Whole cloves

Whole cloves of garlic are perfect to serve with any kind of roast meat, game or fish. The easiest way to cook them is in their skins, putting them into the pot roast or around the joint. To eat, simply squeeze the creamy pulp out of the skins. The skins protect the garlic flesh and also provide a barrier, so that however many cloves you use the garlic does not overpower the dish or the cooking juices, but imparts a delicate background flavour. For an example, see Pot Roast Pork, p 239.

Whole cloves may also be skinned and cooked separately. Allow anything from 6–12 cloves per person. Blanch them as above, drain, skin and arrange them in a small ovenproof dish with enough water to cover the base. Lubricate with a little olive oil or butter and cook in a low oven, 140°C/275°F/Gas Mark 1, for about an hour, adding a little extra water as necessary.

An excellent variation is to sprinkle the skinned cloves sparingly with sugar.

Barbecued garlic

Rub whole heads of garlic with olive oil and barbecue slowly, around 45 minutes, until soft, turning them frequently. Or you can blanch them first, which shortens the cooking time and makes them milder.

Roast garlic bulbs

For those who enjoy garlic and can take it neat, roast garlic is a feast. Depending on your garlic, choose either of the following methods. Use whole heads, with large cloves, allowing one head per person.

Very fresh mild garlic That is, freshly harvested 'wet' or 'green' garlic. Slice off the top of each bulb of garlic like a boiled egg. Arrange in a baking dish, drizzle over a little olive oil or dab butter on top, season with salt if liked, and roast in a hot oven, 200°C/400°F/Gas Mark 6, for about 45 minutes until the cloves are soft. To tell, squeeze the bulb gently: if the cloves pop up easily, the garlic is ready. Turn the heat down if the top looks as if it is browning too much.

New season's dried garlic That is, stronger-tasting garlic. Peel away most of the skin, leaving just a thin protective layer covering the cloves. Arrange in a baking dish. Drizzle with olive oil or dab with butter and add enough water to cover the base of the dish to a depth of 1.25cm/ $\frac{1}{2}$ inch. Bake in a moderate oven, 180°C/ 350°F/Gas Mark 4, for around 1–$1\frac{1}{4}$ hours depending on the size of the heads, or until the cloves are very soft. Baste frequently with the cooking juices, adding extra water as necessary. If you want a milder garlic feast, blanch the whole heads first.

Mushrooms

CULTIVATED MUSHROOMS

All fresh cultivated mushrooms have approximately the same flavour.

If you can, go for the chestnut-coloured Paris Brown, which has a slightly richer flavour than ordinary white mushrooms.

Conventionally grown mushrooms are heavily sprayed and sometimes bleached to make them whiter. Organically grown mushrooms are more widely available these days and are not much more expensive, so buy them when you can.

CULTIVATED WILD MUSHROOMS

These are generally overrated. They are more expensive and not as distinctive as is sometimes suggested. Oyster mushrooms are bland and have a slippery texture. Shiitake mushrooms have a slightly more meaty flavour and a rubbery texture, and are best suited to Chinese dishes.

WILD MUSHROOMS

Fresh wild mushrooms are becoming increasingly available. At the time of writing, two major supermarket chains have begun selling them in selected outlets. For anyone interested in collecting wild mushrooms, this offers a rare opportunity to see them and to begin to learn how to identify them.

Fresh wild mushrooms are much blander than their dried counterparts. Though their texture is usually different from that of cultivated mushrooms, their flavour is not and their taste is not all that distinctive. As a result, they are not worth paying a fortune for, though they are interesting to try. Truffles are the exception.

- Inspect thoroughly before you buy. Collected from the wild, very few mushrooms will be perfect or in tip-top condition. If they are badly bruised, slimy or very dirty, do not buy them. This also applies to those in the supermarket.
- Fresh wild mushrooms do not keep as long as fresh cultivated mushrooms and should be used as quickly as possible.

Mushroom Know-how

- All mushrooms, wild or cultivated, need to breathe. Never store mushrooms in a plastic bag. Remove the clingfilm from boxed mushrooms. Keep lose mushrooms in a brown paper bag or an open carton in the salad drawer of the fridge and they will last 4–5 days. Keep wild mushrooms on a plate lined with kitchen paper in the fridge.

- Water does not harm mushrooms. If the mushrooms are dirty, the best way to clean them is to rinse them very briefly, using a soft brush to remove dirt, then wipe dry with kitchen paper.

- There is no more flavour in the skins than in the flesh. If you want to peel mushrooms, go ahead.

- Mushrooms are good to add to stock.

COOKING WILD MUSHROOMS

Prepare and cook in the same way as cultivated mushrooms, washing them first with a soft brush. As a general guide:

All types Wild mushrooms make excellent pasta sauces, mushroom soups and risottos, and go well with grilled polenta.

Ceps (Porcini) Slice thickly and fry or char-grill with a drizzle of olive oil. Once soft, throw in finely chopped garlic and parsley, stir around and serve. Or char-grill as before and serve them as Franco Taruschio does at the Walnut Tree Inn in Abergavenny, on a bed of salad leaves with shavings of hard goat's cheese and toasted walnuts.

Chanterelles Fry gently in butter, add a little cream and serve. Or use to fill an omelette.

Morels Prized mushrooms that appear in spring. They need soaking first in water to remove any grit. They tolerate longer cooking times than other wild mushrooms, so they can be added to chicken casseroles, simmered in meat stocks, etc. They are usually fried in butter and cooked with cream.

Puffballs These have a soft texture, similar to marshmallows. Cut into thick slices and fry in olive oil, or butter and oil.

Mixed wild mushrooms Fry in olive oil or butter. Serve on baked bread rubbed with garlic and drizzled with olive oil, sprinkled with chopped chives, tarragon or parsley. Or mix with thick cream for a simple cream sauce and finish with herbs as before.

Truffles

Truffles are the most prized fungus in the world. There are two kinds, black and white. The white is the more prized, but as you are unlikely to come across them very often, this hardly matters.

They are round, knobbly, grow underground, and have a delicious, gritty, nutty texture and an intoxicating, addictive earthy perfume; if they do not have this aroma, they are not worth the large amount of money they command. Scrub very lightly to remove dirt if necessary, but do not peel – the skin has the most nuttiness.

Truffles are not cooked as such but are pared into gossamer-thin slices and served on pasta, fillet of beef, with shavings of Parmesan on a bed of salad leaves, or made into a truffle omelette. They are also used to flavour pâtés, and to slip under the skin of chicken before roasting for the perfume. Another idea is to chop them into tiny dark speckles, warm them through with the finest olive oil and serve as a pasta sauce. They freeze tolerably well and can be sliced finely with a very sharp knife while still frozen.

Truffle oil This is almost as expensive as the real thing and has some of its elusive flavour, though it is generally overrated. It is used primarily to dress pasta.

Peppers

Red peppers are sweet and delicious, with the same kind of universal appeal as frozen peas, and they are just about as useful. They have become the signature vegetable of the Nineties, which is no bad thing as they can be used in so many ways. Yellow and orange peppers are also sweet; green peppers are unripe peppers while brown ones are more unusual, insipid and generally tasteless.

Peppers are now available all year round. Regrettably, many of the ones on sale, particularly Dutch ones, have nothing like the intensity of flavour of those grown naturally in the Mediterranean sun. This is a fact of life. The best way round it is to roast the peppers (see opposite) first.

You can do almost anything you like with peppers. Because they cook so quickly and are so colourful, they have become a standard ingredient in stir-fries and salads. Because of their shape, they are wonderful stuffed and braised. They make vibrant soups, sauces and vegetable purées, are excellent with fish and are an essential ingredient in any Mediterranean vegetable medley.

- Red peppers are the best of the bunch.
- Red (and yellow and orange) peppers are high in vitamin C. The riper they are, the more they contain.

BUYING AND STORING PEPPERS

Peppers can be bought all year round, but are at their best late summer and autumn, the season when they naturally mature.

- All peppers are green when immature, changing colour as they ripen. This is why green peppers have a sharp, unripe flavour and are sometimes more difficult to digest.
- When buying red peppers, the deeper the colour the riper and sweeter the pepper will be, and the more flavour it will have. The same applies to yellow and orange peppers. Thick-walled peppers are juicier than thin-walled ones, though thin-walled ones often have more flavour.
- Peppers keep well, around 2 weeks or longer. Like tomatoes and aubergines, they should not be kept in the fridge. Leave them in a bowl, at room temperature, where they will continue to ripen.
- A ripe pepper will skin much more easily than an unripe one.

SKINNING, GRILLING AND ROASTING PEPPERS

These three basic operations are often confused with each other but they produce different results. Both grilling and roasting peppers can be used as a means of skinning them.

Skinning

As with tomatoes, peppers are skinned when it is felt that the skin would spoil the texture of a dish. If you just want to remove the skin but don't want to alter the texture or flavour of the peppers, use a potato peeler. Otherwise, you can either grill or roast them first. In each case, use whole peppers. For salads, thick, meaty peppers are preferable, to thin-walled, light ones.

Skinning

You do not need to put grilled or roasted peppers in a plastic bag to skin them. If they have been cooked properly, the skins will slip off easily of their own accord. If they haven't, the plastic bag will be of no help in loosening the skins.

Grilling

Grilling is essentially a method of skinning peppers and not a quick-fix substitute for roasting them. It blisters and chars the skin but the flesh remains firm, and, though it does enhance the natural flavour of the pepper, grilling will not bring out the full rich sweetness.

Place the pepper under a hot grill until the skin blisters, turning it around so that it blisters evenly. Unless the recipe specifically calls for it, don't let the skin blacken too much or the pepper will taste charred. Once the pepper is cool enough to handle, the skin can be peeled away easily.

You can also grill peppers over a naked gas flame, spearing them with a long-handled fork – though unless you do not own a grill why anyone should find this preferable defeats me.

Roasting

Roasting peppers is the method *par excellence* for cooking red peppers. It brings out their sweetness in a miraculous way and gives them a full, rich flavour and yielding soft flesh. Superb for instant salads, soups, sauces and pasta dishes, roasted red peppers have an entirely different character from either the crisp raw vegetable or the fried variety.

Orange and yellow peppers can be treated in the same way. It is not worth grilling or roasting green peppers (unless the recipe says so), since they have no inherent sweetness and therefore do not acquire the same kind of richness.

As a means of skinning peppers, roasting is less fiddly than grilling and produces an even result every time. To roast peppers for skinning, put them in a moderate or hot oven – it doesn't matter which, one is just quicker. Roast until the skins start to blister and the peppers start to feel soft: around 15–30 minutes, depending on the temperature. Do not leave them too long or the flesh will become very soft. Leave until cool enough to handle and skin; or leave unskinned in the fridge until required.

■ If roasting red peppers ahead of time, you will find they keep much better with the skins left on. Roast or grill them whole and cool. They will keep in the fridge for 4–5 days.

■ The juice from inside roasted red or yellow peppers is worth saving. Sweet and full of flavour, it can be added to whatever you are cooking with the peppers.

Baked or roast peppers as a vegetable

These are delicious either hot or cold and could not be simpler. It doesn't matter what temperature you cook them at. A hot oven will cook them quickly and brown them; a low oven will take longer but concentrate the flavour, giving the most luscious results.

Slice the peppers in half lengthways, taking out the seeds if you want. Small peppers can be left whole. Arrange in a shallow baking dish, drizzle with olive oil and a mean sprinkling of sugar and put in the oven. Leave for about 30–40 minutes in a hot oven, or up to $1\frac{1}{2}$ hours in a low oven. Serve with their juices and an extra dribble of olive oil.

Keeping roasted or grilled peppers under olive oil

Skinned roasted or grilled peppers are made even more luscious cut into thick slices and kept in the fridge in a small dish, covered with olive oil. Contrary to what you may read, because of the high moisture content of most commercial peppers they do not keep long, no more than a week. An extra bonus is that the olive oil takes on the flavour of the peppers. Use for instant salads, pasta sauces, etc.

Potatoes

Potatoes occupy a privileged position. They are our most important staple and can be cooked in more ways than any other vegetable. There are also more varieties of potato to choose from than ever before, with supermarkets offering a perplexing range of shapes, sizes and prices. Whichever you buy, the most important thing about potatoes is that they should have a decent flavour. This is not as easy as it sounds, for the flavour of a potato depends on both its variety and its inherent texture. More than is true for most vegetables, how a potato is grown, in what soil, in which part of the country, and the weather in any one season affect its flavour and quality. This is why buying locally or organically grown potatoes is good practice and why the same variety may be better at some times than others.

BUYING AND STORING POTATOES

Unless kept in perfect conditions, potatoes do not store well, sprouting quickly when it is too warm. For this reason, they are better bought in small quantities.

- You can judge how fresh, that is, how recently harvested, a new potato is by how easily it scrapes.
- Unless it is stated otherwise, main-crop potatoes bought after Christmas will probably have been sprayed with sprout suppressants. The alternative is to buy organically grown or new potatoes.
- Potatoes are a good source of vitamin C; this is highest in a freshly harvested potato and steadily decreases thereafter. The skins of potatoes are high in fibre. However, scrubbing them with water will not remove any chemical residues that may be present. If you want to eat the skins, it is better to use organically grown potatoes.
- Potatoes should always be kept in the dark in a cool place; brown paper bags are best. If you buy them in a plastic bag, make sure to tear the bag so that the potatoes do not sweat.

Greening in potatoes

Exposure to light causes potatoes to go green. Though the green colouring itself – chlorophyll – is harmless, the green parts also contain high levels of poisonous alkaloids and should never be eaten. Make sure all the green parts of the potato are cut away; the rest will then be safe.

Potato sprouts also contain high levels of these poisonous alkaloids and should never be eaten; again, make sure the area around the sprouts is cut away. Otherwise, a sprouted potato is safe to eat, though it becomes gradually softer and deteriorates in flavour.

'FLOURY' V. 'WAXY'

For cooking purposes, potatoes are divided into two broad groups, 'floury' and 'waxy'. The two have very different textures and this explains why certain recipes call for certain types of potato.

- A floury potato breaks up easily once cooked, has a lighter, more open texture and is generally recommended as the best kind of potato to use for mash, baking, chips and roast potatoes, where its fluffy texture is best appreciated. Typical floury varieties include Golden Wonder, Record and Kerrs Pink.

■ A waxy variety does not break up when cooked, has a creamy texture and is generally recommended for boiling, sautéing, salads and any dish where the potatoes need to remain intact after being sliced thinly and then baked, such as a hotpot or gratin. Waxy potatoes become gluey when over-processed, so are not recommended for potato purées. Typical waxy varieties include Ratte, Pink Fir Apple and Charlotte.

Both floury and waxy potatoes are good to eat and can be equally satisfying. Even though each is best for particular dishes as outlined above, there are no hard-and-fast rules. If a waxy potato is all you've got and you want to bake it, you can do so. You will just get a different-textured baked potato. Similarly, the majority of potato varieties are neither especially floury nor especially waxy. This means that most can be boiled, roasted, baked, chipped, etc.

POTATO VARIETIES

The following list of selected varieties currently available has been drawn up by potato expert, buyer and author Alan Wilson, with the kind permission of Waitrose.

Good general varieties*	Floury varieties	Waxy varieties	Waxy salad varieties**
Desiree	Ailsa	Ausonia	Belle de Fontenay
Estima	Fianna	Charlotte	BF 15
King Edward (Red King Edward if you see it)	Golden Wonder Kerrs Pink	Diana Nicola	Pink Fir Apple Ratte
Maris Piper	Pentland Dell	Spunta	Roseval
Saxon	Record		
Wilja			

*These include both floury and waxy potatoes, which can be used as all-purpose varieties and will suit most dishes.

**These are small oval or elongated varieties that are ideal for salads. All can be used wherever waxy potatoes are needed.

New potatoes Traditionally these are early varieties that are planted early in the year, grow fast, mature quickly and are harvested early summer, from mid-June to the end of July. They are eaten fresh and do not store well.

Modern 'new' potatoes are now grown all year, imported from various countries. Many are main-crop varieties, such as King Edwards, picked early when immature. This is why 'new' potatoes are often a disappointment.

Main-crop potatoes Main-crop potatoes are varieties that take longer to mature, grow larger and store well. They are harvested in autumn for use from autumn until the following spring.

Salad potatoes Salad potatoes are varieties with a pronounced waxy texture, which makes them particularly suitable for salads. They may be an early or main-crop variety.

Baby potatoes These are very expensive and are usually too immature to have any real flavour.

COOKING POTATOES

Everyone knows how to cook potatoes. A few miscellaneous tips:

■ Although raw potato has a hard texture, unlike other root vegetables this disintegrates once cooked. For this reason whole potatoes are put into cold rather than boiling water, so the whole potato can warm up at the same rate and will therefore cook evenly. This is important for floury potatoes but less critical for waxy ones, which do not disintegrate as quickly. If you are boiling potatoes to be mashed or puréed, it doesn't matter whether you put them into cold water or pour boiling water over them.

■ A sure-fire way of getting flavour into potatoes is to scrub them, wrap them in foil or greaseproof paper with dabs of butter and a big sprig of mint or tarragon, and bake them *en papillote* in the oven. You will need small potatoes of an even size. Allow around 45 minutes in a hot oven, 200°C/400°F/Gas Mark 6, and an hour or longer in a moderate oven, 180°C/350°F/Gas Mark 4.

■ A baked potato must be cooked in the oven (a microwave will merely give you a steamed potato with a wet skin). A large potato will take $1–1\frac{1}{2}$ hours to bake in a hot oven. Prick the potato in a couple of places with a fork to save any danger of it exploding or bursting apart. To shorten the cooking time, push a skewer through the centre of the potato. If you are short of time, cut the potato in half lengthways and paint the cut surface with olive oil. This will reduce the cooking time by up to 50 per cent.

■ A potato boiled in its skin will keep better in the fridge (3–4 days) than one which has been peeled and boiled. Leftover potatoes are very useful: see p 261.

MASH

Mash is ambrosial stuff. Olive oil mash made with decent olive oil is as good, if not better, than traditional buttered mash, specially with new-wave Mediterranean dishes. Whereas traditional mash is plain, modern mash is ritzy and comes flavoured. Whizz it up in a food processor and mash becomes purée. Enrich that purée further with cream or olive oil and it becomes a voluptuous sauce.

Perfect traditional mash is smooth, light and fluffy but requires some dedication, whisking and what-not. But less than perfect home-made mash is just as tasty. Just avoid watery or gluey mash and it will be fine. Remember, also, to cut the potatoes into even-sized pieces so that they all cook equally.

The character of your mash will depend on the quality of your potatoes, and whether they are floury or waxy. Similarly, mash can be stiff or soft, mashed roughly or whipped until it is light, depending on how you like it. The difference between mash and potato purée is one of texture and richness. A potato purée is more runny, and should be as smooth and unctuous as a thick cream sauce.

Mash know-how

■ A potato masher is the best and fastest implement to make mash.

■ Don't boil the potatoes in lots of water. If the basic potato mash is too watery, dry it off first in the pan before adding milk/butter, etc.

■ Any potato can be turned into mash. Floury varieties produce a fluffier mash (and a more watery one if the potato isn't up to much). Waxy potatoes produce a denser, richer mash, but are inclined to go gluey much more quickly.

■ The better the flavour of the potato the better flavour the mash will have.

■ Mash reheats well, but it does not freeze.

■ Use leftover mash for fishcakes, potato pancakes, potato rissoles and bubble and squeak.

Basic 10-minute mash

Peel the potatoes, cut into 7mm/$\frac{1}{4}$ inch slices and put in a pan, large enough to accommodate them in 1–3 layers. Pour over boiling water from the kettle barely to cover, put on the lid, bring to the boil and cook steadily until the potatoes are soft when pierced with a knife. This will take around 6–8 minutes from when the water comes back to the boil. Drain off the cooking liquid, leaving a little to moisten the potatoes in the pan. Mash with a potato masher, then beat in extra cooking liquid/milk/butter/olive oil to taste. Season and serve.

It's customary to add milk and butter or – these days – olive oil to mash, but if you have potatoes of character, basic mash made with just potatoes and the cooking water can be excellent too. If you should strike lucky and find yourself with a quality mash, full of potato flavour, try serving it with butter or olive oil on the table, rather than beating it in.

Tarted-up mash

Pile the mash into a shallow heatproof serving dish and rake the top with a fork, brush with a little olive oil and slap under a hot grill for 3–5 minutes to crisp the surface. Or sprinkle the top with finely grated Parmesan or a savoury herb and breadcrumb mixture.

Basic olive oil mash

Mashed potato flavoured with olive oil can be as addictive as the traditional buttery version (ditto olive oil with baked potatoes). The flavour of the olive oil comes through more than you would think, so it's worth using a good one.

Mash potatoes in the usual way, but instead of butter add 2–3 tablespoons of a fruity olive oil per 450–570g/1–1$\frac{1}{4}$lb mash. Serve as it is or pile into a dish, fork over the top, brush with olive oil and brown in the oven or under the grill. Especially good served with fried eggs, baked cod, grilled pork chops and kidneys and liver.

Leek and fennel mash

A good mash for fish. The leeks can be cooked in advance.

SERVES 2–4

675g/1$\frac{1}{2}$lb potatoes, peeled and sliced
225g/8oz prepared leeks, chopped (allow 2 large leeks, or about 450g/1lb leeks)
1 teaspoon fennel seeds
3–4 tablespoons olive oil

Start by cooking the leeks and fennel seeds gently in a little olive oil for 15–20 minutes until soft and limpid; keep the pan covered and don't let them colour. Meanwhile, cook the potatoes in a covered pan with just enough water to cover until soft. Drain off any excess liquid and mash with a potato masher. Purée the leeks with 2 tablespoons of your best fruity olive oil, then beat into the mash until smooth. Taste, season, adding a little extra olive oil if needed, and serve.

If you can't be bothered to purée the leeks, beat them into the mash as they are – less elegant but a good mash nevertheless. The mash can also be browned in the usual way under the grill.

Shaun Hill's basil and olive oil mash

This is my favourite olive oil mash, both fragrant and ambrosial, from Shaun Hill's *Quick and Easy Vegetable Cookery*. Let down with extra creamy milk or cream, it becomes a sublime sauce to serve with fillet of beef, calf's liver, veal escalopes or halibut. To get the full heady effect, make sure you add the basil/olive oil mixture at the last moment. The combination of grated nutmeg and basil, incidentally, is a winner: pinch the idea for other things made with basil – for example, Ricotta and Basil Sauce for pasta, p 52.

SERVES 2–4

450g/1lb floury main-crop potatoes, peeled and sliced
120ml/4fl oz double cream (or you can use single or whipping cream if you prefer)
1 large bunch of fresh basil (about 30g/1oz) or 2 supermarket packets
4 tablespoons olive oil
freshly grated nutmeg

Boil the potatoes as for Basic 10-minute Mash and drain well. Leave the potatoes in the pan and mash lightly but firmly until smooth – don't overwork them. Liquidise the basil and oil in a blender, adding some of the cream if the quantity is too small for the blender to work.

Stir the cream into the mashed potato over a low heat. Add the basil/oil mixture, season with nutmeg, salt, and pepper, if liked, beat hard for a few seconds to fluff up the potato and serve immediately.

Indian mash

Mash can be made spicy in any number of ways. This is Madhur Jaffrey's way, taken from her book *Quick and Easy Indian Cookery*. The surprise is the lemon juice, which makes this mash.

SERVES 4–6

1kg/2¼lb potatoes, peeled and sliced
1 green chilli, finely chopped
3 tablespoons finely chopped coriander
1 teaspoon garam masala
pinch of chilli powder
1½ tablespoons lemon juice
milk
butter

Make your mash in the usual way, beating in a little milk and butter to taste using a whisk to keep it smooth and light.

Mix in all the other ingredients and season to taste. Good with meat or fish, or with lightly fried liver or kidneys.

Note If you have no garam masala, a mixture of cardamom seeds (use the seeds from 2–3 pods), 1 teaspoon of cumin seeds and a couple of cloves ground together in a spice-grinder, plus a generous grating of nutmeg, makes a very fragrant mash.

Other good mashes

Potato, swede and rosemary mash A wondrous winter mash. Boil equal quantities of diced swede and potato. Mash with a potato-masher, adding a knob of butter and a little milk if you want. Frizzle 1 tablespoon of chopped rosemary in a little olive oil for a few seconds – it should sizzle and the aroma rise. Beat into the mash.
Saffron and caper mash For fish, liver and veal. Infuse half a packet of powdered saffron in 1 tablespoon of hot water for 30 minutes. Make the mash in the usual way, adding butter and milk/cream, or olive oil. Beat into the mash. Fold in lots (2–3 tablespoons) of rinsed small capers and serve.

ROAST POTATOES

Next to making mash, roasting potatoes in the oven in the traditional way is one of the best things you can do with them. A perfect roast potato – dry and crisp on the outside, soft and fluffy inside, with a flavour all of its own – is more difficult to achieve than you might think. Important things to remember:

■ Roast potatoes should never be greasy. If cooked properly, they do not soak up that much fat. Large potatoes soak up less fat than small ones. It doesn't really matter which type of potato you use: a floury potato produces a fluffy inside; a waxy potato produces a soft smooth inside.

■ The type of fat you use will determine the flavour of the potato. Beef or pork fat makes the best roast potatoes. Otherwise use olive oil, or a mixture of the two.

■ A perfect roast potato has a crunchy, uneven surface rather than a smooth skin. This is achieved by par-boiling the potatoes first, then roughing up the exterior.

■ Timing is critical – roast potatoes should not have to wait around and are best eaten straight from the oven. Decide what time you want to serve the dinner and then calculate the cooking time back from there.

The traditional way to roast potatoes is around the joint, but it's simpler and more convenient to roast them in a separate shallow dish, using some of the fat which comes out of the joint. This also avoids juices from the meat making the potatoes soggy. Par-boiling the potatoes first cuts down on the cooking time but more importantly enables you to get a nice crunchy exterior. The trick here is to drain the potatoes then shake them against the sides of the pan or score them roughly with a fork.

Roast potatoes were made for gravy. They are sublime with roast meat but don't seem to suit anything else particularly well.

Remember that a roast potato which has been deep-fried is not a roast potato. One which has been reheated, is greasy or has been left too long in the oven doesn't count either. Personally, I would not serve them with roast lamb, or cook them in lamb fat, which has a very strong flavour. An oval potato, about 225–285g/8–10oz weight unpeeled, sliced in half from top to bottom, makes, for me, the ideal-sized roast potato.

Cooking times will depend on the size of the potatoes and how hot the oven is. It doesn't matter if the oven is a little hotter or a shade cooler – just position the potatoes where the fat sizzles and the potatoes cook steadily. In hot ovens you need to watch that they don't brown too quickly or the bases will burn.

1 Peel the potatoes, cut in half lengthways, cover with water and boil for 4–5 minutes. Drain, saving the water to make the gravy. Either shake the potatoes against the side of the pan (put the lid on and shake vigorously) or rough up the surfaces with a fork.

2 Heat a thin layer of fat in a shallow oven-proof dish: where possible use the fat from the joint. Coat the potatoes by rolling them over in the hot fat. Arrange cut-side down in the dish and put in the oven. Roast in a moderately hot oven, around 190°C/375°F/ Gas Mark 5, for around 30 minutes, or almost done. They don't need basting or turning, though you can if you want.

3 Pour off any visible fat from the dish and continue to dry-roast the potatoes for another 15 minutes, or until they are cooked through and golden brown and crunchy on the outside.

4 Serve immediately, sprinkled with salt. If necessary, they can be kept waiting for a few minutes in the turned-off oven, but make sure you keep them hot.

RÖSTI

Rösti, or Swiss potato pancake, with its golden crisp crust and soft stringy centre, is very easy and virtually cooks itself. The potatoes are boiled in advance (the dish originated as a way of using up leftover potatoes), which is also handy. Ready-cooked röstis can be bought in supermarkets, though I wouldn't bother. Restaurants douse them in butter or fry them in lots of oil, which makes them greasy. Use a non-stick pan and this can be avoided.

Plain rösti is good with things like grilled sausages, liver and onions, and baked fish, and is often served on its own with a fried egg on top or with a tomato sauce. Add herbs, spices, pancetta or cooked bacon, etc. and you have fancy rösti. Mix with cooked dark green cabbage and you have new-wave bubble and squeak.

Classic rösti should be thick, about 3cm/a good 1 inch deep: 'a nice plump cushion', as friend and cookery writer Sue Style described it. Mine tend to be thinner, about 2cm/$\frac{3}{4}$ inch thick.

Rösti know-how

- Use firm waxy potatoes – for example, Charlotte, Ratte.
- The potatoes should be just cooked.
- The secret of a good rösti is to grate the potatoes when cold. This keeps the grated potato strands separate and avoids stodgy rösti.
- For the best crust, cook the rösti slowly, allowing round 15–20 minutes on the first side and 10–15 minutes on the second.
- Use a heavy-based pan.
- The rösti can be cooked slowly or more quickly, depending on how much time you have. If you want to cook it more quickly, cook over a moderate heat, allowing 10 minutes for the first side and around 5 minutes for the second.

Plain rösti

SERVES 2–4

| generous 570g/1$\frac{1}{4}$lb firm waxy potatoes |
| 15–30g/$\frac{1}{2}$–1oz unsalted or clarified butter |
| 1–2 tablespoons groundnut or light olive oil |

Boil the potatoes in their skins until just cooked. Drain, and leave to cool. These can be prepared in advance and left in the fridge overnight; in fact, the potatoes are easier to grate if they are chilled. Peel the potatoes, then grate into a bowl on the coarse holes of a hand grater; this takes only a couple of minutes but is a bit messy. Season.

Heat a heavy-based, preferably non-stick frying pan. For this amount of potato, a pan with a 19cm/7$\frac{1}{2}$ inch base is about right. Add half the butter and oil, swirl around, then add the grated potatoes, spreading them out lightly with a spatula or potato-masher to form a smooth thick cake about 2cm/$\frac{3}{4}$ inch thick. Turn down the heat and cook until the base is crisp and golden brown: lift an edge with a spatula to see.

Turn the rösti over to cook the other side. To do this, put a plate which just fits the rösti on top and flip the pan upside-down. The rösti is now on the plate, with the browned surface on top. Heat the rest of the oil and butter in the pan, slide the rösti back and cook until the underside is crisp. Serve immediately, cutting into wedges at the table.

This quantity serves 2 rösti addicts or 4 as a side dish; for 4–6 servings, allow 1kg/2$\frac{1}{4}$lb of potatoes and cook the rösti in a pan with a 23cm/9 inch base.

Short-cut rösti Once you have cooked the underside, slip the rösti under a hot grill, about 10cm/4 inches away from the heat source, and cook for about 5–7 minutes until the top is crisp and speckled with brown.

Mini-röstis These can be cooked more quickly. Form the rösti into small cakes and cook over a moderately hot heat for 3–5 minutes either side.

Fancy rösti

Fancy rösti is just as easy to make as plain, and you can match the flavourings to suit the rest of the meal. The added ingredients should be well mixed – the easiest way to do this is to use your hands. Using the same quantities of potato – 570g/1¼lb – and following the instructions opposite, here are a few suggestions:

Sweet onion and potato rösti Cook 225g/8oz finely sliced onion very slowly in a little butter or olive oil in a covered pan for 30–40 minutes until the onions are soft as butter. Shake the pan from time to time and sprinkle in a scrap of sugar towards the end to help the onions to caramelise. Mix into the cooked grated potatoes and cook the rösti in the usual way.

Thyme and sun-dried tomato rösti Add 1–2 tablespoons of chopped thyme and 2–3 chopped sun-dried or home-dried tomatoes kept under olive oil. If using plain sun-dried tomatoes, soften first in a little hot water.

Smoked pancetta rösti One of the best-flavoured röstis. You can use any kind of fatty smoked bacon, but pancetta or German smoked bacon is extra good. Allow 55–85g/2–3oz. Buy it in a piece, about 1cm/scant ½ inch thick, and dice into small strips. Fry briefly in a hot dry pan for 2–3 minutes until the fat begins to run. Mix into the grated cooked potatoes and cook the rösti in the usual way.

Cooked salmon and green peppercorn rösti A good way to use leftover salmon or salmon trimmings. Allow 110–170g/4–6oz cooked salmon and 1 heaped teaspoon of drained green peppercorns. Flake the salmon and crush the peppercorns in a pestle and mortar. Mix well into the grated potatoes, season to taste and cook the rösti in the usual way.

Spiced crab rösti A little crab goes a long way and is an excellent flavouring for rösti. Add more crab and you have crab cakes.

Allow 110–170g/4–6oz fresh crab meat. Mix with 1 finely chopped mild green chilli, 2 tablespoons of chopped chives or spring onion, ½–1 teaspoon of mild curry powder, salt to taste and, if possible, a finely crushed kaffir lime leaf (chop it finely if it's a fresh one). Alternatively, use the finely grated rind of a lime. Mix lightly with the grated cooked potato and make the rösti in the usual way.

JAZZED-UP BOILED POTATOES

Plain boiled potatoes can be jazzed up with more than a pat of savoury butter or pesto or new-wave pastes. It helps if the potatoes are small.

With anchovies and chives Melt a couple of anchovy fillets in a tiny pot with a little olive oil over a gentle heat. Pour over hot boiled potatoes, shaking the potatoes so they all become coated. Snip chives over the top and serve. Good with fish, grilled lamb and beef.

With toasted cumin, cayenne and tomato Toast 1 teaspoon of cumin seeds in a small pan, then pound with a pinch of salt. Heat 2–3 tablespoons of olive oil in a shallow heatproof dish. Add the cumin seeds, ½ teaspoon of cayenne pepper, a healthy squirt of tomato purée and 2–3 tablespoons of water. Mix together for a minute or so, then add cooked potatoes, toss to coat, scatter with chopped coriander, and serve hot or cold. Good with chicken and vegetables.

With crushed juniper berries and orange juice Roughly crush a tablespoon (or more) of juniper berries with a good pinch of salt. Fry in a little butter for 2–3 minutes until crusty. Add the potatoes, toss, squeeze over half an orange and serve. Good with game.

Pumpkins and Winter Squashes

Pumpkins and winter squashes are the winter equivalent of marrows. They store remarkably well (because their skins are so hard) and are one of the best winter vegetables for soups, bakes, pies and purées. They also belong to that exclusive group of vegetables that are equally good in savoury and sweet dishes, and come with their own container. With their bright stripes and wonderfully weird looks, why they have not caught on before is a mystery. Three important points:

■ Pumpkins have watery flesh, which disintegrates quickly once cooked, and a bland flavour; the larger the pumpkin, the more this is the case. Think of them as an inflated marrow with orange flesh.

■ Winter squashes, at least the best kinds, have deep-orange flesh which stays firm when cooked; as a rule, the harder the flesh, the better the squash. These are the ones to try. They have a dense, floury texture and a rich, sweetish flavour – soothing and rib-stickingly satisfying to eat. See list right.

■ Unlike any other vegetable I can think of, both pumpkins and winter squashes improve in flavour and texture with age – or rather, once they have been 'ripened' and are properly mature. The way to gauge ripeness is by the hardness of the skin: the harder it is, the riper the pumpkin or squash. Be prepared for this when you buy them from supermarkets: if you have read about how good, say, a butternut squash is and found it tastes just like a marrow, this is why.

There is more to pumpkins and winter squashes than Hallowe'en and pumpkin pie. A popular vegetable in most parts of the world: in Italy you'll find pumpkin gnocchi, ravioli and risotto; in Japan pumpkin tempura; in India fragrant spiced curries; in Jamaica 'meat-in-the-moon', a chilli-spiced Caribbean stew; in Southwest France they are cooked with peppers and sweetcorn and made into creamy gratins and soothing soups. They go with meat, cheese, nuts and pulses, are delicious stuffed with savoury rice mixtures, happily blend with every flavouring you care to think of from coconut to saffron, and make excellent desserts and jams.

Supermarkets, enterprising greengrocers and ethnic shops all sell a good selection of pumpkins and winter squashes. They are worth buying for their ornamental value alone. Buy the ones with the hardest skins which sound hollow when knocked. Kept at room temperature, they should store for 3–6 months.

SOME COMMON TYPES OF WINTER SQUASHES

Acorn Small ridged squash, usually green, with soft, smooth creamy flesh.

Butternut squash Pale-coloured, flask-shaped squash. Watery when first picked but develops in flavour and texture once stored.

Crown prince A large, handsome, grey-blue squash with deep orange flesh and a rich, sweet flavour. One of the best.

Gem squash Round, striped squash, often sold as small individual squashes. Pale fibrous flesh. Better once stored for a couple of months. for a couple of months.

Hubbard Pear-shaped, golden-orange squash with creamy but fibrous flesh that becomes more fibrous with storage.

Minchkin Miniature orange squash which looks like a clementine. Its other name is Jack-be-Little pumpkin. Dense orange flesh.

Onion squash A round, medium-sized, orange-coloured squash, with medium-soft orange flesh. Excellent when fully mature.

Turk's turban One of the most handsome squashes, medium-large, grey-blue, with deep-orange flesh and shaped like a turban. Excellent flavour and texture.

PREPARING AND COOKING PUMPKINS AND WINTER SQUASHES

Pumpkins and winter squashes are easy to prepare and cook, though there is considerable waste. As a rough guide, 450g/1lb squash will yield half that amount of usable flesh.

First, the skin. Soft-skinned squashes can be peeled with a vegetable peeler. If the skin is very hard, slice into wedges with a large, heavy knife and either slice the flesh away from the skin if this is easy or cook with the skin on, removing the flesh once it is cooked. The seeds and fibres can easily be scooped out with a spoon.

Hollowed-out shells also make stunning containers for soups, stews and bakes. The simplest way to retrieve them is to slice the squash in half and cook them first. Baby pumpkin shells can be dried out in the oven and used again.

Three simple ways to cook pumpkins and winter squashes are to steam them, to cook them with 1.25cm/$\frac{1}{2}$ inch of water in the bottom of a covered pan, and to toss cubes of flesh in a frying pan with butter or oil, adding spices if you like, or throwing in a handful of herbs for the last minute or so.

Unless using them in soups, pumpkins and squashes should be cooked in as little water as possible. Cook them just until a knife will go in easily. This depends entirely on the density of the flesh. Pumpkins and soft-fleshed varieties of winter squash are fibrous and cook down quickly. The smooth, denser-fleshed squashes cook more like sweet potatoes, take a little longer and do not readily break up. Diced into cubes or cut into wedges, allow 5–10 minutes depending on the size of the pieces and the density of the flesh.

EASY WAYS TO SERVE PUMPKINS AND WINTER SQUASHES

Plain cooked squash can be finished in various ways. Such as:

■ tossed in melted butter, with a sprinkling of coarse ground Sichuan peppercorns/black peppercorns/allspice/toasted chilli flakes;

■ tossed in melted butter with crumbled fried sage leaves (p 82);

■ dribbled with cream/crème fraîche/soured cream and scattered with chopped chives, tarragon, basil or parsley;

■ tossed in a mixture of the juice of $\frac{1}{2}$ lemon and 2 teaspoons of soy sauce, sweetened with a little runny honey to taste, and with toasted sesame seeds scattered over the top;

■ tossed in a mixture of finely chopped garlic, dried breadcrumbs and chopped parsley that has been fried first in a little butter or olive oil for 2–3 minutes.

Instant curried pumpkin or squash

Of all the various permutations of flavourings for pumpkins and squashes, mild curry or coconut cream are the outright winners. Choose Korma or Balti curry paste. The simplest way is to heat single or double cream in a pan, flavour with paste to taste and pour this mixture over hot cooked cubes of pumpkin or squash. Fleck with chopped coriander and serve.

You can do the same trick with yoghurt. Choose thick full-cream or Greek-style yoghurt. Melt a knob of butter (or ghee) in a small pan, add 2–3 generous tablespoons of yoghurt, bring to the boil, stirring, then add curry paste to taste. Let down with a spot of the pumpkin cooking liquid, add hot cooked cubes of pumpkin or squash, toss and serve with chopped coriander as before. If you want more of a sauce, use extra yoghurt, adjusting the quantities of paste, etc. accordingly.

Coconut cream and lime-flavoured pumpkin or squash

Melt a little coconut cream (about 15–30g/$\frac{1}{2}$–1oz) with a few tablespoons of the hot pumpkin cooking liquid to form a thin sauce. Stir in finely grated lime zest and lime juice to taste – it will take more than you think. Toss hot cooked cubes of pumpkin or squash in the mixture. Serve with a handful of toasted coconut flakes showered on top.

PURÉES

Dense-textured squashes make wonderful purées: cook the flesh with a little milk until soft, with a clove of garlic if you like, then mash with a potato-masher or purée in a blender.

The purée can be further enriched with a knob of butter or cream, or instantly enlivened with a dash of Tabasco, ground allspice, bottled House of Lee ginger 'n' shallot or Singaporean chilli sauce. For a fragrant spiced purée, add a little mild spice paste by the teaspoon, with cream to taste.

ROAST SQUASH

Dense-textured squashes can be roasted around the joint as you would carrots or parsnips; allow 30–45 minutes' cooking time. Alternatively, toss them in a little hot butter or oil and roast them separately, sprinkled with ground cinnamon or allspice if you like. To caramelise them, sprinkle sparingly with soft brown sugar.

BAKED PUMPKINS AND WINTER SQUASHES

Both are splendid baked – and can be cooked at any temperature which is convenient between 170°C/325°F/Gas Mark 3 and 200°C/400°F/Gas Mark 6.

Stand the squash in a shallow ovenproof dish with 2.5cm/1 inch of water, cutting large ones in half first. Allow 35 minutes–1 hour in a moderately hot oven, 190°C/375°F/Gas Mark 5. Shorten the cooking time for whole larger squashes, if they are a manageable size, by par-boiling them first: immerse them in boiling water for about 10 minutes and finish in the oven as before.

Small squashes are just right for one person: par-boil, slice off the top, scoop out the seeds, stuff and bake; or pour in a little cream, chopped herbs and a melting cheese such as mozzarella or Gruyère and bake until the filling is hot and the flesh is soft – 15–20 minutes should be enough.

Wedges of squash – squash wedgies – are the trouble-free way of baking them. Cut into thick wedges, paint with oil or dab with butter and bake until soft, around 30–45 minutes.

Orange peppercorn squash Not so much sweet and sour as sweet and peppery. Cut the squash into wedges and remove the skin. Place the wedges in an ovenproof dish and dab with butter. Thin down 2 tablespoons of marmalade with water to form a thin sauce. Add the juice of an orange and a lemon and pour over the squash. Scatter over 1–2 teaspoons of coarsely crushed peppercorns and bake until soft, topping up with extra water if the sauce dries up.

Tomatoes

Tomatoes have had a monumental influence on modern cooking and are one of the vegetables it is most handy to have, a chopped tomato improving a soup, a sauce or a braise, as well as just about any salad or sandwich you can think of. There are many such examples throughout this book. A really good tomato is truly delicious and a joy to eat. Ones that are not quite so good are better turned into sauces or chopped into salsas.

BUYING AND STORING TOMATOES

The most important thing for any tomato is that it should be ripe, which shop-bought tomatoes rarely are. Keep them at room temperature in a bowl for a week or more and they will improve. Tomatoes are tropical plants that originate from South America. This is why you should never keep them in the fridge; it dulls their flavour and damages their structure. This also goes for tomato salads and salsas, which should always be served at room temperature.

Choosing tomatoes

Matters have improved dramatically of late so there is a much wider choice of specific types and named varieties, which usually have more flavour than the tasteless ones we had become accustomed to. However, like potatoes, how good a tomato tastes depends as much on how it has been grown as on the variety or type of tomato it is. This means it is impossible to tell beforehand how good a tomato is likely to be, and a juicy beefsteak can be just as disappointing as an ordinary round tomato. Be mindful of this when buying speciality tomatoes, too, which can be twice as expensive. As a rule of thumb:

■ Tomatoes vary in flavour throughout the year depending on how and where they have been grown. Those grown in winter or in northern climates with large amounts of artificial light and heat will not develop the flavour of those maturing in summer or in hot countries with natural light and heat.

■ Organic tomatoes which have been grown more slowly and more naturally have a better flavour than commercial hot-house tomatoes.

Cherry tomatoes These are sweeter than other types of tomato. The best are superbly sweet, though they can be just as flavourless as round tomatoes. Use for scattering whole over salads.

Pear-drop tomatoes These are the latest salad tomatoes, yellow cherry tomatoes shaped like miniature pears. They are excellent, very sweet, and compare well to home-grown tomatoes in flavour.

Beefsteak tomatoes A juicy, full-flavoured, meaty tomato. The best are those grown in southern Europe. Dutch beefsteak tomatoes are usually tasteless. Use for bruschetta, Mediterranean salads with basil and olive oil, and barbecuing/grilling and stuffing.

Plum tomatoes These are grown outside in southern Europe and used specifically for drying and processing. They do not make good salad tomatoes and again are very variable, and may be as tasteless as standard commercial round tomatoes. Use for cooking in sauces and pizzas, for roasting and for making Home-dried Tomatoes (p 118).

Round tomatoes The standard commercial hot-house, general-purpose tomato which can be used for salads or cooking. They vary in quality from absolutely tasteless to very good. Named varieties, such as Sungold, are more expensive but do have a better flavour, as do varieties like Flavia and Manhattan, which have been left to ripen on the vine to develop their flavour. Use good ones for salads, salsas, fresh tomato coulis and soups; ordinary ones for sauces and general cooking.

Vine tomatoes These are another recent introduction and currently the most expensive type of tomato, though, in fact, the major difference between them and tomatoes like Flavia is presentation. Vine tomatoes are left to ripen on the vine and sold attached to their branches rather than being picked off. Those imported from Sicily and Spain are generally superb, the next best thing to home-grown tomatoes and worth paying extra for. Eat on their own.

PREPARING TOMATOES

Other than a brief wash, tomatoes need no preparation. The best knife to use for slicing tomatoes or removing the insides is a small serrated one with a pointed end. The only occasion you need to remove the core or seed tomatoes is when you want to stuff them. Otherwise, unless the recipe specifically tells you why, it is done for appearance's sake only. For Skinning Tomatoes, see p 76.

Passata

This is the Italian manufacturers' answer to instant tomato sauce. It is made from sieved tomatoes, and can be used on its own or as a base for whichever tomato sauce you're making. Despite the claims made for it, it is not as good as ripe, fresh tomatoes and the flavour varies more than you would think. The kind that comes in cardboard boxes can be pretty nasty, with a sickly, pasteurised flavour. The best comes in bottles; look for Italian brands and read the labels. *Sugocasa*, produced by Grand' Italia, is good and cheap.

Substituting tinned tomatoes or passata for fresh tomatoes

Although fresh is best, as long as you remember that a dish or sauce made with tinned tomatoes will taste different from one made with fresh tomatoes, which will be different again from one made with passata, it is perfectly possible to substitute tinned tomatoes or passata for most dishes which call for either fresh tomatoes or tomato sauce.

Unless it is heavily camouflaged with other ingredients, the basic taste of the dish will be that of whichever tomato base you are using. If you like tinned tomatoes, or are addicted to tomato passata, the dish will taste fine; if you don't, it may not.

Tomato purée

Tomato purée is a concentrated tomato paste. It has gone out of fashion recently, but is extremely useful. Rather than buying tins, go for tubes, which can be kept in the fridge once opened and will last for 1–2 months. A squirt or two can add depth to any tomato sauce which seems thin in flavour, braised meat and sweet-sour barbecue sauces. It can be added directly or mixed to a thin sauce with a little water first if this is more appropriate.

TOMATO SAUCES

You don't need a recipe for tomato sauce but you do need very ripe tomatoes. Frying tomatoes come cheap and are better than salad tomatoes. Check each one (taste a bit) before you use them, however, to ensure that they are not overripe and still taste good. Tomato sauces are just as easy to make in bulk and freeze very well.

■ If you have good fresh tomatoes, for the simplest and freshest-tasting sauce just chop them roughly and sweat gently with a little finely chopped onion in butter or olive oil for 5–10 minutes. The sauce will then be ready. For a smooth sauce – a tomato coulis – pass through a Mouli or a sieve.

■ If you have superb tomatoes, a glut of home-grown tomatoes from the garden or gardening friends, just chop them roughly and pile into a large pan with a chopped onion. Simmer for 20–25 minutes. Sieve, reduce down if necessary and the sauce is ready. This method will give you the purest-tasting tomato sauce.

■ To vary the flavour of either of the sauces above slightly, add some of the following: crushed garlic, chilli, bay leaf, basil, rosemary, parsley.

■ If your tomatoes are not so good, add some tomato purée and/or a little sugar; if you want to perk them up, add a few drops of Tabasco.

■ You can use tinned tomatoes, or a mixture of tinned and fresh tomatoes, for very good, albeit slightly different-tasting sauces. Make in the same way as the second sauce above, adding a squirt of tomato purée, and cook for 30–40 minutes. Buy good-quality canned tomatoes, without added anything.

Concentrated tomato sauce

This is a superbly rich, super-concentrated sauce. Its depth of flavour comes from the slow, gentle evaporation of the liquid, which cannot be hurried. To achieve this it needs to be made with a large quantity of tomatoes. It freezes perfectly and can be used as a pizza base, for pasta, lasagne and polenta, and by the spoonful to add extra richness to soups, sauces and braised/stuffed vegetable dishes.

MAKES ABOUT 900ml/1½ PINTS SAUCE

2.5kg/5lb tomatoes
1 large onion, sliced
1 large sprig of parsley, basil, celery leaf (or use whatever you have)
1 bay leaf
1 clove garlic (optional), peeled

Pile everything into a heavy casserole dish and bring gently to the boil. Either simmer over the lowest possible heat for up to 3 hours or leave to cook in a very low oven, 140°C/275°F/Gas Mark 1, until the mixture becomes very thick and concentrated. If cooking on top of the stove, give it an encouraging stir fairly frequently, especially towards the end, to check the sauce is not sticking or catching on the bottom of the pan. If cooking in the oven, you can leave it to cook itself, with just the occasional stir. Remove the bay leaf and garlic if used, and press the sauce through a Mouli (easiest) or metal sieve, sieving it thoroughly to extract as much of the sauce as possible. Pack into small tubs, label, freeze and use as required.

HOME-DRIED TOMATOES

I am not the world's greatest preserver of anything, but I make an exception for these. Anyone who has only managed to buy duff sun-dried tomatoes and has wondered what all the fuss is about will find these have a concentrated sweetness and a much fresher taste. They are also about the only genuine use I've ever found for a fan oven. You need a lot of ripe tomatoes; needless to say, the more flavour they have to begin with, the better the result. Home-grown tomatoes are ideal. Otherwise, make them in the summer when tomatoes are at their cheapest.

My method is based on the excellent one given in Delia Smith's *Summer Collection*. This quantity fills two oven shelves and involves about 10 minutes' work. If you want to get the hang of it first, do a trial batch with half quantities. The only drawback is that they taste so good that they are likely to disappear as fast as you make them.

2.6kg/6lb ripe but firm medium tomatoes, washed

1–2 level teaspoons salt

1 Cut the tomatoes in half: round ones horizontally, plum ones vertically. With a spoon, scoop out all the pulp, seeds and central pith into a bowl (use them to make tomato soup or sauce). Arrange the tomato cases, cut-sides up, side by side as you go, ready for the next step.

2 Sprinkle the tomato cases very lightly with salt – your fingers are better than a spoon. Put them, cut-sides down, close together but not touching, on wire cooling racks or oven shelves. Place a sheet of aluminium foil on the bottom of the oven to catch the drips: this may need weighing down with a couple of knives or something similar if you are using a fan oven.

3 Carefully place the racks in a very low oven, 60–80°C/150–175°F/Gas Mark 1/4–1/2, leaving space between them so that the air can circulate. If you have a fan oven, switch on the fan. Insert a skewer or knitting needle into the oven door as you close it, to stop it closing completely. This is important as it creates an airflow so that the tomatoes dry rather than cook.

4 Depending on your oven, the tomatoes will take anything from 8–12 hours. The oven should feel no more than comfortably warm throughout. If the tomatoes seem to be cooking, lower the temperature slightly or rearrange the shelves. Check the tomatoes from time to time. They will shrivel to half their size and are ready when almost all the moisture has evaporated yet they are still soft and pliable. The best idea is to try one or two to see. Don't let them get too papery or allow the edges to brown too much and remove any that are ready before the others. You will probably find that they have stuck to the racks slightly and need to be gently prised off.

5 Remove the tomatoes from the oven and leave to cool on the racks. You can use them straightaway or pack them into clean sterilised jars, fill to the top with olive oil and seal. They are delicious when freshly made but are even better in a month's time and will keep for 6 months.

Alternatively, freeze them on open trays, then pack into small boxes and keep in the freezer.

Alastair Little's home-dried tomatoes

These aren't really dried tomatoes at all, but are incredibly yummy. It's the sugar that makes them. Prepare the tomatoes as opposite but put them on baking trays that have been greased with olive oil. Sprinkle them with salt and sugar, allowing a mean tablespoon of caster sugar and about 4 tablespoons of olive oil per 16–20 large tomatoes. Drizzle a tiny amount of olive oil over the top, then put in a low oven, 150°C/ 300°F/Gas Mark 2, for 45–60 minutes, until the tomatoes have softened and collapsed, the oil has begun to 'fry' gently and the sugar has just started to caramelise. Remove from the oven and leave to cool.

Use fresh. You are supposed to be able to store them in sterilised jars under olive oil for 6 months, but as their moisture content is so high, I wouldn't recommend it. Better to keep them under oil in the fridge and use within 2 weeks. Great to eat on bread as a snack, to add to pizzas and pasta, to accompany grilled meat and fish, and to tuck into braises and stews at the end of cooking. They are also excellent served on their own, with Char-grilled Marinated Aubergines and Courgettes (p 265). Whatever you do, don't forget the delicious juices that remain on the baking trays. Mop up with bread or just use your fingers.

Variation: *Slow-roast tomatoes:* This produces the best baked tomato you will ever eat. Slice your tomatoes in half and place, cut-sides up, in a dish. Sprinkle with salt and sugar as left and drizzle with olive oil. Put in a low oven and forget about them for 2 hours until they have deepened in colour, are glistening and the cavities contain tiny amounts of clear tomato liquid. If the tomatoes do not look as I have described, leave them a little longer.

Serve as a first course on their own, or as a simple side dish for fish or grilled meat. They will keep in the fridge for 2–3 days. Serve at room temperature, as part of a Mediterranean medley, with Char-grilled Marinated Aubergines and Courgettes (p. 265).

5

Rice

Rice is one of the world's great staples and the ultimate convenience food. It needs no advance preparation, is even more versatile than pasta and can be cooked in innumerable satisfying ways. It is less understood than either pasta or potatoes, yet has more potential than either.

Rice cookery can bring a lifetime's pleasure, and it is worth pointing out that rice is far more than mere stodge. At an everyday level, there are many simple ways to enjoy it that are as easy to prepare as pasta. The key is to select the right kind of rice for the dish you are making, and to view it as rice-growing nations do – as a precious food that should be cherished, rather than something that can be boiled in a bag or goes on the side of the plate.

Types of Rice

The size, shape and colour of rice grains all help determine how it is cooked and therefore what dishes to use it for. It can be grouped into three main types: long grain, short grain and unrefined, or wholegrain, rice.

■ The essential difference between long and short grain rice lies in the starch make-up. Stickiness in rice is caused by waxy starch molecules called amylopectin. Long grain rice contains fewer of these than short grain rice, which makes it drier when cooked. The more amylopectin present, the stickier or creamier the rice, which is why some short grain rices are stickier than others.

■ The stickiness factor accounts for the different cooking properties of long and short grain varieties of rice. This is why it is important to choose the right kind of rice, and why you cannot use long grain rice to make a creamy risotto or short grain rice to make a pilaf.

■ All white rice is refined rice – that is, rice that has been milled to remove the outside bran layers and tiny embryo or germ. This makes the rice keep much longer.

LONG GRAIN

Long grain rice is used for savoury dishes, pilafs, stir-fries, salads and stuffings and served plain. The grains are long and slim, with some varieties longer and slimmer than others. Though there are exceptions, long grain varieties produce dry, fluffy rice when cooked. They generally absorb between one and two times their volume of liquid.

SHORT GRAIN

This is used for puddings and cakes, Italian risotto and Spanish paella. The grains are round and fat and may be short or medium in length. They stick together when cooked and dissolve into a creamy mass with long, slow cooking. Short grain rice absorbs more liquid than long grain rice, between 2 and 4 times its volume, depending on the variety. Glutinous rice and Japanese rice (see pp 121–122) are short grain rices used for savoury and sweet dishes.

UNREFINED OR WHOLEGRAIN

This is either long or short grain rice that has merely had its husk removed and been cleaned. This means it has a nutty taste and takes longer to cook. Commonly known as brown rice, this category also includes red rice, black glutinous rice and wild rice (see below).

Within these three broad groups there are about 2,500 different varieties worldwide, including medium grain rices which are usually cooked like long grain rice. The ones you are most likely to come across are:

Patna and Carolina

The generic names for long grain rice grown in Asia and America respectively. Both of these terms are now being dropped in favour of the more general description, long-grain rice. The packet should tell you where the rice was grown.

Basmati

The prince of long grain rice, grown in the foothills of the Himalayas in Northern India and Pakistan, this has a rich, fragrant flavour and long slender grains. Basmati is the best rice available and worth paying extra for. Again, there are different qualities of basmati rice. In India it is an expensive luxury. In the UK it is easily available, and I use it for all long grain rice cookery.

It is also available as brown basmati rice. This is lighter and less chewy than other forms of wholegrain rice and takes less time to cook.

Thai fragrant

Also known as jasmine rice, this is another top-quality long grain rice, similar to basmati. It is said to be highly fragrant, though this is somewhat exaggerated. The grains are slightly sticky and cohere naturally when cooked.

Arborio, Vialone Nano, Carnaroli

These are all kinds of Italian risotto rice. Though technically classified as medium grain, they behave like round grain rices when cooked. See Risotto, pp 135–40.

Wild

This dark, needle-like shiny grain is a distant relative of cultivated rice found in North America. Once only available in its wild form (and hence wildly expensive), it is now cultivated, and therefore becoming cheaper. Significantly higher in protein (14 per cent) than other forms of rice, it has a strong, dusky flavour and has recently become very fashionable. The best way to use it is as you would dried mushrooms, to give added depth, colour, texture and flavour to white rice.

The length of the grains varies, with top-quality wild rice having the longest grains. Wild rice may be bought mixed with brown or white rice. Cultivated wild rice is often scarified, which means that the outer skin has been scratched to faciliate the absorption of water and shorten the cooking time.

Red

This is the latest posh rice, a follow-on from wild rice. It is an unpolished variety grown in very small quantities in the Camargue region of France, and has a red outer skin. It tastes just like good-quality brown rice and is not to be confused with Chinese red rice, which is ordinary rice that has been dyed with a natural colouring.

Glutinous

This is sometimes referred to as 'sweet rice' or 'sticky rice' and is used in Southeast Asia for both savoury and dessert dishes. It can be bought from oriental shops. A round grain rice, it is quite unlike other varieties – more like chalky white pellets. Despite its name, it does not contain any gluten. 'Sticky' is slightly misleading, for it is not sticky in the way that pudding or risotto rice is. It is cooked in a special way: the grains are first soaked in water, then steamed. The grains remain separate but adhere together, as if joined by a very fine coating of glue, and can be pressed together easily. The usual way to eat glutinous rice is to roll it into small balls and pick it up with the fingers, and it makes a satisfying accompaniment to Thai or Chinese food.

Black glutinous

This unrefined black-skinned rice from Asia can be bought from Chinese supermarkets and deserves to be better known. A different kind of rice from white glutinous rice, the grains are longer and wide and flat rather than round. The flavour is more delicate and less nutty than brown rice. It is cooked in the same way as white glutinous rice (if cooking it in water, the water turns blue- black), and can be added to white rice in the same way as wild rice. It is also used for desserts.

Par-boiled

This is a particular type of processed rice. Whole rice grains are first soaked in water, steamed to par-cook them, dried, and finally milled to remove the outer skin – though why anyone should want to go to so much trouble to preserve

rice these days is not clear. It has a pale-gold, translucent appearance, a higher vitamin content than white rice, and takes longer to cook. The best known brand is Uncle Ben's rice. Follow the instructions on the packet.

Pre-cooked

Pre-cooked rice can be bought in various forms, all of which have led to a demise in the appreciation of the real thing. Rice takes so little time to cook, and can be flavoured so easily and deliciously, that there seems little point in wasting time or money on these.

Japanese

This is a naturally sticky short grain rice, used for making sushi. Both Japanese and American varieties are available and it can be bought from Chinese or specialist shops. It should be washed well, drained, then cooked by the absorption method (p 127).

American popcorn, jasmine, texmati, wahani, wild pecan

These are American varieties of rice. Though they are hard to obtain in the UK at present, they may well become more easily available in the future. American jasmine rice is the same variety as Southeast Asian jasmine rice; texmati rice is the American version of basmati.

BUYING AND STORING RICE

It is always worth paying extra for good-quality rice. If you look at it in terms of cost per serving, the difference is marginal for the benefits you get. Because it is so difficult to tell good rice from inferior-quality rice in a packet, it is better to buy a branded variety than cheaper own-labels.

■ Though most supermarkets and delicatessens sell a wide range of rice, ethnic shops specialising in their national type of rice are most likely to have the best brands and the best quality.

■ Buy rice from shops that appear to have a high turnover, and check the date stamp. When buying rice in packets, look for clean, unbroken grains that are free from dust.

■ Freshness is particularly important when buying unrefined wholegrain rice. This contains oils that go rancid in time so it does not keep as well as white rice.

■ Store all rice in a cool, dark, dry place. Stoppered glass jars are excellent storage vessels. Though I do not advocate it, white rice keeps for up to three years. Unrefined rice of whatever colour has a much shorter shelf life and should be used within six months.

Brown or white?

Both brown and white rice are good to eat, and have their own distinctive characteristics. Generally speaking, you can produce classier, more aromatic and more delicate dishes with white rice and earthier dishes with brown.

■ Brown rice is nutritionally superior to white, a complete food in itself. Rich in B vitamins, it has a nutty taste and tends to go better with strong flavours, particularly vegetables and vegetarian dishes. It is good with Chinese stir-fries.

■ White rice is blander yet more fragrant than brown. American long grain polished white rice is fortified with vitamins (a reason not to soak it, and to cook it in the minimum of water). It tends to go better with gentle, delicate flavourings and with meat and fish, is a must for risotto, and on the whole makes nicer stuffings than brown rice.

■ Both brown and white rice go well with cheese, and both make decent (albeit different) salads.

Storing cooked rice

Leftover cooked rice is excellent in salads, stuffings and vegetable tortas, the best rice to use for stir-fried rice or rice cakes, and will keep for 3–4 days in the fridge. The drier the rice, (that is, the less water you have used to cook it), the better it will keep.

However, giving advice on storing cooked rice is something that most cookery books are wary of, and for good reason. Cooked rice is susceptible to a bacteria called *Bascillus cereus*, which can cause severe stomach upsets. The organism cannot survive in temperatures below 4°C/39°F or above 60°C/140°F. For this reason, any leftover rice should be refrigerated as soon as it has cooled down, kept in the coldest part of the fridge and used as quickly as possible, preferably within 2–3 days. When reheating, make sure the rice is thoroughly hot.

How much rice should you serve?

Depending on how much liquid you add, rice will increase by two to three times its volume once cooked. People's capacity for it varies greatly. As a general guide:

■ If you are hungry, and the rice is served plain as the main accompaniment for everyday meals, allow about 85–110g/3–4oz per person. For light and moderate eaters, allow 55g/2oz per person.

■ At formal or more elaborate meals, and for larger numbers, allow 30–55g/1–2oz per person, always remembering that the more people are present or the grander the meal, the less carbohydrate you will need.

Cooking Long Grain Rice

It is always worth taking care over cooking rice. Perfectly cooked rice is a joy to eat, with a fragrant, nutty quality and a distinctive taste and texture. The grains should be soft but still slightly firm and distinct. Over-cooked or carelessly cooked rice is stodgy and unpleasant.

For much of the time, rice is cooked plain and eaten as an accompaniment, for which long grain is the usual choice. It is often said that for rice to be perfectly cooked each grain must be separate. This is not strictly true, for much depends on the character of the rice. Even basmati, for example, coheres together slightly, and the grains only become truly separate when served in a sauce or left to go cold, while Thai fragrant rice naturally sticks together.

Fluffiness is the other often quoted desirable characteristic. Again, much depends on the rice and personal preference. Soft cooked rice will be fluffier than rice cooked *al dente*, but will have a blander flavour. All rice, if left to relax for a few minutes in a warm place or on a warming tray, will become fluffier.

Once cooked, rice will keep perfectly well in a warm place for 30–45 minutes. Keep in a buttered covered dish on a warming tray or in the oven on its lowest setting.

Checklist

- Choose the right-sized pan for the amount of rice you are cooking – see opposite.
- The most common mistakes when cooking rice are to use too much water and/or to cook it for too long.
- You do not need to rinse long grain rice or to boil it in lots of water to prevent it sticking together. It only sticks when overcooked.
- Rice can be cooked very quickly. See Easy White Long Grain Rice, opposite.
- Wholegrain rice takes longer to cook because the skin acts as a barrier; again, there are short cuts. See Easy Brown Long Grain Rice, p 126.
- If you like rice to be nutty and full of flavour, cook it with less water. See pp 127–8.
- Printed instructions often say 'turn down to a very low simmer'. This is very difficult to do, except on gas hobs. On electric hobs, which take time to cool down, you will need to move the pan to another hob plate turned on to its lowest setting. Alternatively, see Easy White Long Grain Rice, opposite.
- Black pepper detracts from the flavour of plain cooked rice. Most recipes also advocate salting rice when you cook it, but this is not mandatory, especially for good-quality rice. As rice authority Sri Owen says, let its flavour speak for itself.

How soft should rice be?

All rice should be cooked through but exactly how soft is a matter of individual preference: nutty, firm, *al dente*, soft or very soft rice are all permissible. Furthermore, these varying degrees of softness are all controllable, depending on the amount of water and the cooking time.

Remember that rice for salads, pilafs and stuffings is better cooked *al dente* than very soft. Rice for frying should always be as dry as possible and should be cooked with the least amount of water.

Reheating rice

Rice reheats exceptionally well. The best way is to steam it in a fine-meshed sieve or colander over a pan of boiling water. Cover with a cloth, such as a clean tea towel or a J-cloth, to soak up evaporating moisture, put on the lid and steam for about 10–15 minutes until tiny holes appear between the grains and the rice is thoroughly hot.

EASY WHITE LONG GRAIN RICE

This cooking method may appear unorthodox but it works. It produces very nutty, *al dente* rice, a treat to eat and the way I like rice best, but you can produce much softer rice just as easily by adding extra water. It is vital to keep the rice covered and to let it stand for a few minutes to complete the cooking. For general notes on the absorption method, see p 127.

It is important to choose the right-sized pan for the amount of rice you are cooking.

- A small pan for 110g/4oz rice or less
- A medium pan for 225–340g/8–12oz rice
- A large pan for 450g/1lb rice or more

Any reasonably thick-bottomed pan will do, although heavy-based pans that retain the heat work best. Le Creuset dishes are excellent – the rice remains hot and can be served from the same dish. Soaking the rice in the cooking water beforehand for 15–30 minutes will help it absorb the water quickly.

1 Put the rice in a pan. For nutty rice, add water just to cover; for softer rice, add water

2 Cover the pan, bring to the boil and cook vigorously for 2–3 minutes, turning down the heat if the steam builds up too much inside the pan.

3 Remove from the heat and leave undisturbed for 5–10 minutes. During this time the rice absorbs all the moisture and continues to cook in its own steam.

4 Check the rice. It should be pitted with tiny steam holes and be ready to eat. It will keep perfectly in the pan in a warm place such as a warming tray, for 30 minutes or so. Fluff up lightly with a fork before serving.

········· **Tips** ·········

If the water has not been completely absorbed at the end of the resting time, put the pan back on a low heat for another 2–3 minutes, then leave to rest for another 5 minutes.

If the water has been absorbed but the grains are still hard in the centre at the end of the resting time, moisten with a little extra water, cover and cook for 1–2 minutes over a low heat, then rest for a further 5 minutes.

Do you need to wash and soak rice?

It is often said that washing rice prevents it sticking, but in fact if you overcook rice it will stick whether or not you have washed it. Washing removes some of the surface starch – the water becomes cloudy – and hence helps to produce a lighter, fluffier rice. This is why basmati rice is often washed, for example. I find it produces a slightly less flavoursome rice and I never wash long grain rice.

Occasionally, washing is included as part of a a specific dish. In this case, follow the recipe.

Rice does not need to be soaked either. However, soaking rice can be very useful and

can shorten the cooking time by up to 50 per cent. It will also make white rice whiter. Soaked rice can be used for all the basic cooking methods, and will absorb less water when you cook it by the absorption method.

The quick way to soak rice, picked up from rice expert Roz Denny, is to pour enough boiling water over the rice in a bowl to cover it by 2.5cm/1 inch, then cover the bowl and cool.

Alternatively, soak white rice in cold water for 30 minutes to 1 hour and wholegrain rices for 8–12 hours. If cooking by the absorption method, use the soaking water to cook the rice.

EASY BROWN LONG GRAIN RICE

Brown rice is just as easy to cook as white rice. The main problem is that recipes often advise you to cook it for far too long, so that the grains burst completely apart and become a soft, watery mush. In the process their unique chewy texture is destroyed and the flavour diluted.

There are two easy ways to cook brown rice. Both can be used for other types of wholegrain rice.

1. Absorption method

This is a variation of the cooking method for white rice. Again, the rice requires hardly any cooking (and therefore watching over). It produces soft grains and is as near to instant brown rice as you are likely to find. The initial cooking can be done well ahead, and the rice finished when you come to eat it.

1 Put the brown rice into a pan and add water to cover by 2.5cm/1 inch.
2 Cover the pan, bring to the boil and cook steadily for 5 minutes.
3 Remove the pan from the heat and let the rice cool in the liquid, still covered. The rice will now be almost cooked. It can be left until later if needed.
4 Drain off most of the remaining water. Cook over a gentle heat for another 5–10 minutes or until the water has been absorbed and the rice is soft but chewy.

2. Boil-steamed rice

This produces soft but entire grains with the skins intact, and is the best way to cook brown and other unrefined rices if you want their natural flavour. Instead of par-boiling the rice, you can soak it overnight instead, leaving it to soak until you are ready to cook it.

1 Par-boil the rice with water to cover by 2.5cm/1 inch for 5 minutes.
2 Drain and transfer to a steamer or fine-meshed sieve set over a pan of boiling water. The water should not touch the rice. Cover and steam the rice for 15–30 minutes, or until the grains are soft but chewy: how long depends on the type of rice and the length of soaking time if you have soaked it first.

Cooking wild rice

Wild rice is the exception. As I found out recently, its full smoky flavour develops only after 40–50 minutes' gentle simmering when the grains have burst. That said, if you do not like the mushy quality of burst wild rice grains, you can eat it when the grains are soft but still intact.

For general notes on wild rice, see p 121. Three good ways of cooking it are:

1 If cooking wild rice on its own, cook by the method for Easy Brown Long Grain Rice. Do not drain away the water when you come to finish the rice but simmer gently in a covered pan for 20–30 minutes or until the rice is soft and most of the grains have burst, adding a little extra water if necessary.

2 If you want to keep the grains intact, cook by the boil-steam method on p 128.

3 Mix it with white basmati rice, which is what I generally do, using 30–55g/1–2oz wild rice per 225g/8oz of white basmati rice. Follow method one above. When the wild rice is almost done, add the required amount of white rice to the pan, adding extra water if necessary to cover. Cover the pan, bring to the boil and cook for 2–3 minutes. Remove from the heat and allow the rice to rest for 5–10 minutes. It will keep perfectly for up to 30 minutes. Fluff up and serve.

Cooking Japanese sticky rice for sushi

Instructions are usually given on the packet. Wash the rice well and leave to drain for 30 minutes. Put the rice in a pan, add $1\frac{1}{2}$ times the amount of water to rice, cover and bring to the boil over a high heat. Simmer over a very low heat for about 10–15 minutes, or until the water has been absorbed and the rice is soft. This rice is naturally sticky.

OTHER COOKING METHODS

The problem with rice cookery is not that cooking rice is difficult but that there are almost as many confusing instructions on how to achieve perfect rice as there are types of rice. There is no magic formula; all methods work, but give slightly different results. To recap, the four basic methods are:

Boiling

This method involves stirring rice into a large volume of boiling water in an uncovered pan, then cooking it until soft. The water should be kept at a lively boil throughout so that the grains are kept moving. It is important to test the rice frequently towards the end of the cooking time so that it does not overcook. Taste a few grains or break them in half with your thumbnail to see if the rice is cooked through.

Depending on how firm or soft you like your rice, approximate cooking times are: Thai fragrant rice, 8–10 minutes; basmati rice, 9–12 minutes; American long grain rice, 11–14 minutes; brown basmati rice, 20–25 minutes; wholegrain rices, 30–40 minutes.

Comments Boiling rice has no special advantages and produces a steamy kitchen. It seems more suited to wholegrain rices, which have an outer protective layer. I find it dilutes any nuances of flavour in white rice and produces rice with a blander, more watery flavour.

Absorption method

This involves cooking the rice with a measured amount of water in a pan with a tight-fitting lid. The rice and water are brought to the boil, then simmered gently until the water has been absorbed and the rice is swollen. The rice is then left to rest for a few minutes, which completes the cooking.

The cooking times vary according to how much water you use and the type of rice, and may be anything from 2–3 minutes (see Easy White Long Grain Rice, p 125) to 15–20 minutes, and longer for wholegrain rices. The more water you add, the softer the rice becomes. By adjusting the amount of water, it is therefore possible to produce rice of varying degrees of softness.

- Using 1 part water to 1 part rice produces a firm, nutty rice with the most flavour, but which is *al dente* rather than soft. The water should just cover the rice; for 225g/8oz rice, you will need 300ml/$\frac{1}{2}$ pint of water.
- Using $1\frac{1}{4}$–$1\frac{1}{2}$ parts water to 1 part rice will produce a soft rice, with the grains fully swollen but mainly intact.
- Using 2 parts water to 1 part rice produces soft rice, with the grains burst apart.

Comments I find this is the easiest and most successful way of cooking rice, and there are many variations such as adding spices and replacing water with other liquids for a different flavour. Some cooks advocate simmering the rice in an uncovered pan, others in a covered pan. A heavy, thick-based pan is best and it is essential to let the rice rest. If the rice is soaked first, use the soaking liquid to cook the rice. Brown basmati rice takes around 25 minutes to cook, other wholegrain rices take about 35 minutes and need extra water. For further details, see Easy White Long Grain Rice and Easy Brown Long Grain Rice, on pp 125 and 126.

Steaming

This involves soaking the rice in water, then putting it into a covered steamer or fine-meshed sieve and steaming it over a pan of boiling water until soft. It is important that the steamer or sieve should not come in contact with the water.

Cooking times vary from 15–20 minutes to up to 40–45 minutes depending on the type of rice and how long it has been soaked for.

The best way to steam rice is to par-boil white rice for 2 minutes and brown/wholegrain rice for 5 minutes, drain and then steam it. This produces soft, fluffy white rice and softer wholegrain rice. Cooking times are 10 minutes for white rice and around 20–30 minutes for brown/wholegrain rices.

Comments This is an underrated cooking method, particularly for brown and other wholegrain rices. Because the grains do not come into contact with water they remain separate and undamaged and retain all their flavour.

Oven-cooking

This is a variation on the absorption method. The rice is first coated in a little melted butter or oil over a gentle heat, then cooked in a measured amount of water in a buttered, tight-fitting dish in a moderate oven, 180°C/350°F/Gas Mark 4, for 25–40 minutes, depending on the type of rice.

Comments Though many cooks swear by it, I find it has no particular advantages over the top-of-the-stove absorption method. Because the rice is coated with butter or oil it has a slightly richer, greasier taste. The grains at the edges and top of the dish tend to become crisp.

Rice cookers

Electric rice cookers are used in many Chinese, Asian and Japanese homes and restaurants. If you eat rice everyday or cook it in large quantities they are simple to operate, are suitable for all types of rice and produce perfect rice every time.

Easy Ways to Enhance Rice

Plain rice can be enhanced by stirring in a handful of chopped fresh herbs or a little savoury butter or pesto just before serving. You don't need much: about 30g/1oz savoury butter or 2 tablespoons of pesto is sufficient for 225g/8oz cooked rice. Stir it in very gently, being careful not to disturb the rice more than necessary. A few more ideas, collected over the years:

Basil rice

One of my favourites. Stir in Basil and Olive Oil Purée (p 82) to taste. Bliss.

Tarragon and lemon rice

Chop a good handful of tarragon leaves very finely, mix with 2–3 tablespoons of lemon olive oil, and add salt to taste. Stir into the rice and serve with fish, chicken or beef.

Orange liqueur rice

Melt a knob of butter and stir in a little finely grated orange zest and 1–2 tablespoons of Cointreau or, better, Grand Marnier. Mix into the rice and squeeze over a little juice from the orange. Serve with game.

Porcini rice

Put a small handful (about 10g/$\frac{1}{4}$oz) of dried porcini (cep) pieces into a small pan with 3–4 tablespoons of water. Bring to the boil, then cover and leave to cool. Take out the mushrooms, squeezing their liquid back into the pan. Chop the mushrooms very finely and mix with a lump of softened butter. Stir gently into the rice with the mushroom liquor, boiled down to 1 tablespoon.

Cinnamon and nutmeg rice

Break a 5cm/2 inch length of cinnamon stick into small pieces and cook with the rice. Dab with butter and fork up lightly. Just before serving, shower freshly grated nutmeg liberally over the surface of the rice.

READY-MADE SPICE PASTES

These are the best means I have found of flavouring rice (and other grains) instantly – for further details, see p 24. Any of the Indian spice pastes are well suited to rice. Stir 1–2 teaspoons, or to taste, into hot rice, mixing it in gently but thoroughly. If you prefer, the spice paste can be mixed with a little melted butter first, as for the Moroccan spiced paste below.

Moroccan spiced buttered rice

Melt a little butter in a small pan. Stir in enough harissa to make a shining orange-red sauce, then stir it into cooked rice.

This buttered spice paste is very versatile. Add it to cooked millet, couscous, hot chickpeas, courgettes, peas or spinach, or drizzle it over grilled aubergines or grilled or barbecued fish.

Thai chilli-basil rice

Stir Thai chilli and basil paste into hot rice to taste.

Reheated steamed rice

Reheated rice (p 124) can also be flavoured with buttered spice pastes, whole spices, etc. Stir the buttered paste into the rice or bury the spices as for Perfumed Rice (p 130), and steam until thoroughly hot.

Speckled saffron rice (p 130) can be made with reheated rice, too. Mix the two rices together and steam gently until thoroughly hot.

PERFUMED RICE

The cinnamon trick on p 129 is just one of literally dozens of ways that rice can be perfumed, either by burying whole spices in it when you cook it, by flavouring the cooking water or by using a cooking liquid other than water. Cook the rice as for Easy White Long Grain Rice (p 125). The following suggestions will perfume 225–340g/8–12oz uncooked rice.

Indian perfumed rice

There are countless possible combinations. The whole spices most commonly used are cinnamon, cardamom, cumin and cloves. An old favourite, adapted from a recipe in Madhur Jaffrey's *Indian Cookery*, is to add to the uncooked rice 1 scant teaspoon of ground turmeric, 3–4 cloves, 2.5cm/1 inch piece of cinnamon stick, 3 bay leaves and a pinch of salt. Cook in the usual way, then just before serving, dab the rice with butter or ghee. Fork in lightly and serve.

Coconut and lime perfumed rice

Pour 150ml/$\frac{1}{4}$ pint boiling water over 30–55g/1–2oz grated fresh coconut or creamed coconut. Add to the rice, together with a kaffir lime leaf broken into pieces. Add enough water just to cover the rice and cook in the usual way. You can also use canned coconut milk, diluted with water to taste. Serve curls of crisp, lightly toasted coconut flakes with the rice.

Variation Coconut and cinnamon perfumed rice – substitute a 5cm/2 inch piece of cinnamon stick for the kaffir lime leaf.

Simple saffron rice

Saffron is the classic flavouring for rice, used in India, Iran, Spain and Italy. For more information on saffron, see pp 25–7.

Infuse $\frac{1}{2}$–1 packet of powdered saffron in 1 tablespoon of hot water for 30 minutes. Add to the rice, basmati for preference, with a small glass (100ml/$3\frac{1}{2}$fl oz) dry white wine. Add enough water just to cover the rice and cook in the usual way as for Easy White Long Grain Rice, p 125.

Speckled saffron rice

A winner. You need 1–2 tablespoons of firm, dry cooked rice for this; leftover basmati is ideal.

Infuse a third of a packet of powdered saffron in 1 tablespoon of hot water for 30 minutes, or use 10–15 strands of saffron, toasting and crushing them first as described on p 26. Mix 1–2 tablespoons of dry cooked rice into the saffron liquor, adding enough to soak up all the liquid. Leave to 'set' the saffron for an hour, or until convenient; it will be fine for 24 hours or so in the fridge. Mix lightly into freshly cooked rice and serve. This is a good method to use for rice pilafs – see Carrot and Broad Bean Pilaf with Cardamom and Saffron, p 134.

Comment The attraction of this rice is that it is permeated throughout by the flavour of the saffron, yet it remains speckled with yellow. This is why you need to use very dry rice and to leave it to 'set'. If you stir hot rice into the saffron liquid and mix it directly into the rest of the rice, it will become coloured throughout.

Rice cakes

These can be made with leftover white, brown, red or wild rice or any other kind of long grain rice. A combination of different kinds is particularly nice. They are best thin, crisp and lacy, well spiced and freckled with fresh herbs. The easiest way to flavour them is to mix in ready-made Indian or other pastes, adding herbs, etc., as you see fit.

MAKES 8–10 SMALL CAKES

225g/8oz cooked long grain rice
1 tablespoon plain flour
beaten egg for mixing

Plus

2 teaspoons Indian spice paste such as garam masala, or ground garam masala to taste
2–3 tablespoons coarsely chopped coriander or parsley

or

2 tablespoons finely chopped spring onion
1 mild or hot fresh chilli, seeded and finely sliced
2 teaspoons finely grated fresh ginger
1 kaffir lime leaf, crumbled or finely snipped with scissors
a few drops of nam pla or Thai soy sauce, to taste

Put the rice into a bowl and mash roughly with a fork. Mix in the flour and all the flavourings, then add enough beaten egg just to moisten, without making them eggy. Heat a non-stick frying pan. When hot, drop spoonfuls of the mixture into the pan and press out into thin patties. Cook for 3–4 minutes over a steady heat until brown, crisp and set underneath. Turn over and cook for another 2–3 minutes. Serve as a snack or as part of a vegetarian meal.

Carrot rice cakes

Follow the previous recipe but use a mixture of grated carrot and cooked rice, allowing about twice as much rice as grated carrot.

Pilaf

A pilaf is not so much a dish as a style of cooking rice with other ingredients which is common throughout the Balkans (*plov*), Middle East (*pilaf*) and India (*pilau* or *pulao*). Richly fragrant, traditional Indian and Persian pilafs (*polow*), handed down through the generations, are a glory to eat and represent the high art of rice cookery. But pilafs are not necessarily grand or complicated dishes. At their simplest they are a way of enhancing rice with a few complementary ingredients. Like stir-fries, they are easy to assemble. You can either cook the rice with the other ingredients or cook the ingredients separately and combine them with the cooked rice. Although they are generally made with rice, they can be made from any grain. I learnt from Leslie Forbes' dazzling book, *Recipes from the Indian Spice Trail*, that the distinguishing feature of an Indian pilaf from other rice dishes is the greater proportion of rice to meat or vegetables. A useful rule of thumb for just about any pilaf.

■ A pilaf should be light, fluffy, fragrant and dry. The grains should be soft but distinct.

■ The vegetables, meat or fish should be cut into bite-size pieces, as for stir-fries.

■ Chicken and lamb are the most popular meats for pilaf. The meat can be used just as a flavouring, with a few strips of browned meat added to the pilaf at the end. Leftover roast meat is excellent for pilafs.

■ Pilafs often contain a sweet element in the form of dried fruit, and milky nuts such as almonds, pine kernels and cashew nuts. Almost any pilaf is enhanced by a tablespoon of juicy raisins, slivers of dried apricot and a handful of toasted almond flakes or lightly fried pine kernels.

■ Crisp browned onions or strips of fried carrot make a good addition to any pilaf.

■ Middle Eastern rice pilafs and pulaos from Southern India are often made fragrant with a few drops of rosewater or orange flower water, which can be added to the cooking liquid or sprinkled on top of the pilaf.

EVERYDAY PILAF

Pilafs are made in slightly different ways throughout the rice-eating world but they all follow roughly the same pattern. This simple method can be used for all rice and grain pilafs.

1 Soften a finely chopped onion in a little vegetable oil, butter or ghee.

2 Add the spices and cook for a minute until the aromas begin to develop.

3 Add the rice (or grain) and stir until coated with fat.

4 Add the required amount of liquid: this depends on whether you are using rice or another grain. For a good, nutty, firm-textured rice, use 300ml/$\frac{1}{2}$ pint per 225g/8oz rice. For softer rice, use $1\frac{1}{4}$–$1\frac{1}{2}$ times the amount of liquid to rice. For grains, see individual entries.

5 Bring to the boil, then cover the pot and simmer gently until the liquid has been absorbed and the rice or grain is tender but dry. This takes around 10–15 minutes for rice. For grains, see individual entries. Leave to rest for 5 minutes.

6 Add any extras – toasted nuts, dried fruit, crisp fried onion, fresh herbs, etc. Fluff up the pilaf to separate the grains. Turn out on to a hot platter, mounding the pilaf up in the centre, and serve.

Meat pilafs

To make a simple meat pilaf, cut the meat into strips and fry in a little oil or ghee or a mixture of butter and oil until browned on the outside and cooked through. Mix into the pilaf at the end along with a few other tasty ingredients such as fried pine kernels or toasted almond flakes, sultanas or chopped dried apricots, and strips of carrot fried separately until brown. Leftover roast chicken, pheasant or lamb is excellent cooked in this way.

Minced meat pilafs are also very good. Fry the meat (with or without spices) until browned and crisp and mix into the pilaf at the end. You can use raw or cooked meat for any pilaf made this way. For 225g/8oz rice, allow 55–120g/2–4oz meat.

Fish pilafs

A golden yellow or lightly spiced pilaf, using salmon, smoked haddock or fresh haddock or cod, and speckled with parsley, makes one of the best fireside suppers I know, and is easy to cook. Prawns also make excellent pilafs. Flavour the rice with whole or ground spices, with saffron or use a little mild spiced butter paste made with curry powder or mild curry pastes.

Poach the fish separately until barely cooked, then divide it into large creamy flakes and fold gently into the hot cooked pilaf just before serving. The poaching liquid can be used for cooking the rice. For cooked prawns, reheat them thoroughly in a little butter, then fold into the pilaf. For 225g/8oz rice, allow 120–170g/4–6oz prepared fish.

Vegetable pilafs

Don't swamp the pilaf with vegetables; aim for about a quarter to half vegetables to rice, or even less. Cut them into strips or small dice as appropriate. Either fry them gently with the onion until just soft, then continue to cook as for the Everyday Pilaf, or fry them separately, with or without spices. You can also moisten the vegetables with a little cream, either plain or flavoured with saffron, rosewater or orange flower water. Stir this into the vegetables once they are cooked. Fold into the cooked pilaf, fluff up and serve. See also grain pilafs, pp 154 and 155.

Dried fruit for pilafs

Apricots, dates, figs and raisins are the traditional and most popular kinds of dried fruit to add to pilafs. Tart fruits such as dried cranberries, blueberries and sour dried cherries, which can now be bought from most large supermarkets, are superb.

Unless the fruit is naturally soft – dates, semi-dried figs, etc. – it is better to soften it first. To do this, soak it in a little hot water for a few minutes. Raisins can be fried in a little butter for a minute or so to plump them, as can slices of dried apricot.

You will not need much dried fruit. A couple of tablespoons per 225g/8oz rice will give a pleasant sweetness without making the pilaf over-fruity. It is also better to cut large pieces of dried fruit – apricots, figs, dried pears – into strips, or to chop them roughly first.

Pilafs using leftover rice

So long as the grains are firm and not over-cooked, leftover rice makes excellent instant pilafs. Reheat the rice with a little butter in a steamer or in a buttered dish in the oven, fold in the other ingredients fried in the usual way, scatter with chopped herbs and serve. You can use white rice, or a mixture of white and other wholegrain rices.

■ Quarters of hard-boiled egg are an excellent accompaniment for any simple pilaf.

Carrot and broad bean pilaf with cardamom and saffron

This is based on the Iranian way of making a pilaf, whereby the rice is cooked first, then the other ingredients are mixed in. You can either serve it straight away or keep it over a steamer for 30–45 minutes, and it will still be perfect. The only major departure is that the rice is not cooked by the traditional pilaf method. It can also be made very successfully with leftover rice, or with a little cooked wholegrain rice (brown, red or wild rice) mixed in.

SERVES 2–4

225g/8oz basmati rice

225g/8oz carrots, cut into thin strips, 5–8cm/ 2–3 inches long

110g/4oz shelled fresh or frozen broad beans, cooked and skins removed

Plus

seeds from 4 cardamom pods

$\frac{1}{2}$ packet of powdered saffron, or 10–15 saffron strands, toasted and crumbled, infused in 1 tablespoon of boiling water for 30 minutes (see p 26)

2 spring onions, finely chopped (include green and white part)

30g/1oz pine kernels, lightly toasted

30g/1oz butter

1 teaspoon sugar

TO FINISH:

2 hard-boiled eggs, quartered

15g/$\frac{1}{2}$oz flaked almonds, lightly toasted

Melt a little of the butter in a non-stick pan, add the carrots, cover, and cook gently for 20–25 minutes until very soft, stirring occasionally. Add the sugar, turn up the heat slightly, and continue to cook, uncovered, stirring occasionally, for 5–10 minutes, until the carrots begin to go brown at the edges.

Meanwhile, cook the rice with the cardamom seeds as for Easy White Long Grain Rice on p 125. When the rice is done, take out 2–3 tablespoons, mix with the saffron and set aside.

If you want to eat the pilaf straight away, turn the rice into a hot serving dish and lightly mix in the carrots, broad beans, spring onions, pine kernels and saffron-coated rice grains. Melt the rest of the butter and drizzle it over the top. Arrange the quartered hard-boiled eggs around the edges of the pilaf, scatter with the toasted almonds and serve.

If you want to keep the pilaf, mix everything together as before, then transfer it to a large fine-meshed sieve set over a pan of simmering water. Cover loosely with muslin (or a clean J-cloth), put a lid on top and keep until required. Make sure the sieve doesn't touch the boiling water. When ready to serve, tip into the serving dish and garnish with the melted butter, eggs and almonds.

Variations You can use pistachios instead of pine kernels and fried onions instead of spring onions.

Simple red pepper or pea pilaf

This quick and colourful pilaf goes with just about anything. Flavour leftover rice with a spiced paste, either stirring it into the rice direct or mixing it first with a little melted butter. Good pastes to use are garam masala, balti, pasanda, or Thai chilli and basil paste. Add some diced red pepper and a few fresh bay leaves, then steam the rice until thoroughly hot. If using frozen peas, cook these for a minute or so in boiling water to cover and add last, mixing them into the hot fragrant rice.

Variation Shreds of fresh ginger, fried briefly in a little butter, or the seeds from 2–3 cardamom pods, can also be added to the rice when you steam it.

Risotto

Risotto is one of the simplest rice dishes there is, yet probably one of the most difficult to get right. The two critical things are judging how much liquid to add and when the rice is ready. The good news is that you can break almost all the rules and achieve the same unctuous result. One thing you cannot do is skimp on the ingredients: proper risotto rice, good quality butter or your best olive oil, and good home-made stock are essential. It is a wonderful dish, especially suited to vegetables and shellfish, and once you have mastered it you can make any number of variations.

For all its simplicity, there is no magic formula for making risotto. It is a dish you have to feel your way through. In this sense, it is a truly Italian dish, and you should approach it as an Italian would, with joy in your heart and a beady eye for detail. What I have tried to do here is unlock some of its secrets and to reveal its essential nature.

Consistency

The distinguishing feature of risotto, and what makes it so good to eat, is its consistency. Achieving the correct consistency is what is meant by judging a risotto. Though the consistency can vary, whichever kind of risotto you make it should always be creamy, with the rice soft but firm, each grain separate but clinging to each other and bathed in sauce. It should not be sticky or mushy or taste thin, but rich and satisfying.

The rice

It is important to use the right kind of rice for risotto.

■ Arborio, Vialone Nano and Carnaroli are the three varieties suitable for risotto. They are special for two reasons. Firstly, they plump up when cooked and can absorb a large amount of liquid without breaking up. Secondly, their starchy exterior dissolves into the liquid, giving body to the sauce. They contain the right amount of starchy substances to give the characteristic clinging consistency you need for risotto without making it too gummy.

■ Though aficionados often tend to favour one kind of risotto rice above another, they are all excellent. Arborio is the most widely available, has the largest grain and is good for all risottos. Carnaroli and Vialone Nano are more expensive and have smaller, stubbier grains. Carnaroli produces the creamiest risotto. Vialone Nano has small grains that remain more distinct. It produces a less creamy sauce than the other two and is often used for vegetable risottos and for soups. The words 'superfino' and 'fino', incidentally, refer to the length of the grains, not the quality grade of the rice; 'superfino' (Arborio and Carnaroli) is longer than 'fino' (Vialone Nano).

■ Each variety of risotto rice is capable of absorbing slightly different amounts of liquid, and needs a slightly different cooking time. Carnaroli rice absorbs more liquid than Arborio, and Vialone Nano less. In practice, this matters very little and does not significantly affect how much liquid you are likely to use. The difference in cooking times between Arborio rice, which has the longest grain, and Vialone Nano, which has the shortest, is only about 5 minutes.

The liquid

Most risottos call for a light meat or chicken stock but you can also use vegetable or fish stock where appropriate. All must be well flavoured and clean tasting. A few basic points:

- The stock may be added hot (the traditional method) or cold.
- Meat stock can be made from beef, veal or chicken, or a mixture of the three. Game stock is also very good, especially for mushroom risottos.
- Vegetable stock adds depth of flavour to vegetable risottos and can also be used for fish risottos if you have no fish stock. The soaking liquid from dried mushrooms and any vegetable cooking liquid can also be used, and added to the broth.
- If you have no home-made stock, use ready-made liquid stock, available in cartons from supermarkets.
- The other liquid used frequently in risotto is wine. This is added at the beginning.
- Water is not suitable as it produces a thin-tasting risotto, though it can be used to top up the stock if you run out. If you have no meat stock, use a simple vegetable stock.

How much stock?

Risottos require ample stock and, confusingly, different recipes call for different amounts. There are certain factors affecting how much is right for each risotto:

- It depends partly on the consistency you require. All risottos, while creamy, can be stiff to soupy, depending on individual preference and where in Italy the recipe originates. For example, traditional Piedmontese and Milanese risottos are dense, whereas traditional Venetian ones are slightly runny.
- The size of the pan, the quantity of risotto you are making and how well you regulate the heat source all affect the quantity of liquid you need. A bubbling risotto will absorb more liquid than one that gives the occasional blurp, or one

in which the rice is allowed to soak up the liquid off the heat.

As a general guide, risotto rice absorbs around three times its volume of liquid. Some recipes call for more, around four times the amount of liquid to rice, though personally I find this is too much.

To be on the safe side, allow three to four parts liquid to one part rice. A quick rule of thumb is to allow 900ml/$1\frac{1}{2}$ pints liquid for 225g/8oz rice, plus or minus up to 150ml/$\frac{1}{4}$ pint additional liquid.

In practice, each risotto cooks a little differently and the exact amount of stock required each time will vary. Don't feel you have to use all the stock. Alternatively, if you run out of stock and the risotto needs more liquid, use water.

Finally, if the finished risotto seems slightly sticky, loosen it with a few tablespoons of hot stock or water. Do this after the *mantecatura* (p 139).

Hot or cold stock?

Risotto cooks equally well using either hot or cold stock and the cooking time is not affected by more than 1–3 minutes. Because the stock is added in small amounts to the hot rice, it heats up quickly in the pan anyway. Using hot stock means that the cooking process is uninterrupted but makes no detectable difference to the quality of the risotto. Use whichever is convenient or whichever you prefer. Using hot stock is traditional, using cold is not.

The fat

Risotto is traditionally made with butter but many modern recipes use olive oil or a mixture of the two. Both make wonderful risottos.

- Use unsalted butter and a mild, buttery good quality olive oil. The fat is used to soften the onions and coat the grains of rice, with a little extra beaten into the risotto just before serving.

■ Bone marrow gives a delicious richness to a simple classic risotto. I use it whenever possible for plain or Milanese risotto or for mushroom risottos. Marrow bones, sawn into pieces, can be bought for a few pence from the butcher. You can either excavate the soft, opaque marrow with a sharp knife or put the bone in a low oven for 5–10 minutes, when the marrow will slip out easily in a piece. Add it to the risotto in small, thick lumps, placing it lightly on the surface seconds before serving so that it does not melt but just heats through. The marrow from a 10cm/4 inch length of marrow bone is sufficient for two servings.

■ Most recipes call for the onions and rice to be coated in 55g/2oz or so of fat (restaurants are likely to use more) for a risotto requiring 225–340g/8–12oz rice. You can use considerably less with equally good results. It is, however, important to add a little extra fat at the end.

Cooking

The general principles for risotto are as follows:

■ It must have an even, consistent heat and be cooked in a heavy-based pan, large enough to allow it to swell to at least three times its volume.

■ The initial softening of the onion and rice should be done gently. If wine is used, this is added before the stock and cooked until it has almost evaporated.

■ Then comes the stock, which is traditionally kept hot in a separate pan – although you can use cold stock. Once the stock has been added, the risotto should be cooked at a steady moderate heat – too low and the rice will become mushy; too high and it will burn at the bottom and not cook properly. The stock should be added gradually, about 150ml/$\frac{1}{4}$ pint at a time, and needs to be absorbed by the rice before the next batch is added. You may need slightly more or less than the amount stipulated.

■ Many of the best risottos are based on vegetables. These are generally softened first and cooked with the rice, so that the flavours become fused. They can also be cooked separately and added to the risotto towards the end of cooking.

■ Saffron is best added in two batches, a little at the beginning, the remainder at the end, so that its heady effect is still fresh.

■ Contrary to popular opinion, risotto needs frequent but not constant stirring: the important thing is that it shouldn't stick to the bottom of the pan.

Timing

Timing is critical. Risotto rice takes 15–18 minutes to cook and is judged perfectly cooked when *al dente*, i.e. tender but still firm to the bite. Once this point is reached you must stop cooking the risotto – if you cook it longer, the rice grains start to burst open and you end up with a plate of gluey stodge. For this reason, risotto needs to be served and eaten straight away. Left in the pan, it continues to cook and all your careful work is ruined.

■ Risottos are generally cooked straight through from start to finish, and need more or less constant attention. The alternative way of cooking risotto is to stop it half way through and finish it later. This works just as well as the traditional method and can often be more convenient.

■ Risotto continues to absorb liquid after it has cooked, so that a perfectly judged risotto, after standing for a few minutes, becomes more sticky and cohesive. This is the other reason why risotto should be served immediately it is ready.

■ An undercooked risotto can be rescued. An overcooked risotto is a disaster.

SIMPLE RISOTTO

The traditional method given here is how all risottos are made; the modern method stops the cooking half way through and has the advantage that you can get some of the preparation done in advance.

This quantity, and the recipes that follow, serves two as a main course or four as a first course. I have allowed 900ml/1½ pints of stock, though I find 750ml/1¼ pints is usually sufficient. You can use hot or cold stock.

225g/8oz risotto rice
about 750–900ml/1¼–1½ pints light but well-flavoured stock
1 glass (100ml/3½fl oz) dry white wine
1 small onion, finely chopped
15g/½oz unsalted butter or 1–2 tablespoons olive oil, or a mixture of the two
TO FINISH:
15–30g/½–1oz butter
1–2 tablespoons finely grated Parmesan or pecorino cheese, plus extra to serve

Traditional method

1 Melt the butter and/or olive oil in a heavy pan. Add the onion and cook gently until soft, about 5–7 minutes – it should not colour. If you are using hot stock heat it in a separate pan and keep hot over a gentle heat.
2 Add the rice and stir around until the grains are coated and glistening with the fat. You shouldn't need it, but if the rice seems dry, add a little more fat. Pour in the wine and cook steadily for 3–4 minutes, or until it has almost evaporated.
3 Add a quarter of the stock and cook fairly gently, stirring frequently, until it has been absorbed. Keep adding the stock, about 150ml/¼ pint at a time, waiting until the last lot of stock has been absorbed before adding the next. Stir to prevent the rice from sticking to the bottom of the pan. Cook until the

rice is *al dente*. This should take about 16 minutes for Vialone Nano rice, 18 minutes for Arborio or Carnaroli rice. Do not cook beyond this point.

4 The *mantecatura* (opposite): Remove the pan from the heat and stir in the extra butter and cheese. Stir the risotto vigorously for 30–60 seconds or until creamy. Check the seasoning and adjust the consistency if necessary. Serve immediately, handing round extra cheese and a jug of your best olive oil at the table. If you do not like olive oil, or have made the risotto using all butter, you can stir in a little extra butter when you season just before serving. If you omit the *mantecatura*, remove from the heat, add the extra butter and cheese as before, cover and leave to rest for 2–3 minutes. Check the seasoning and serve.

Modern method

This is the method I generally follow at home. It enables you to half cook the risotto in advance and then complete it when you are ready to eat. It tends to need slightly less stock. You can use either hot or cold stock.

1 Follow steps 1 and 2 of the traditional method.
2 Add a quarter of the stock and cook fairly gently, stirring frequently, until it has been absorbed. Now add stock just to cover, stir and bring back to the boil. Cover the pan and remove from the heat. The risotto can now be left for up to 4 hours.
3 To complete the cooking, first taste the rice: you will probably find it is almost cooked. Reheat it with another 150ml/¼ pint stock, stirring gently. Add more stock as needed, until the rice is just cooked.
4 Remove the pan from the heat and complete and serve as for the traditional method.

The final touch:
mantecatura

Though not essential, and though you will not find it in most risotto recipes you come across, this gives the finishing touch to risotto.

Remove the pan from the heat. Stir in a knob of butter (about 1–2 teaspoons per portion of risotto), plus a little finely grated Parmesan. Beat or stir the risotto vigorously (I use a balloon whisk) for 30–60 seconds until it becomes creamy. Check the seasoning, make any final adjustments to the consistency and serve immediately, handing round extra olive oil and grated Parmesan at the table if desired. A couple of important points:

- Finely grated Parmesan, 1–2 tablespoons per 225g/8oz rice, is usually included in the *mantecatura* to help bind the risotto. If Parmesan is not suitable you can use double cream or mascarpone.
- For the *mantecatura* to be successful the rice must be *al dente*; if it is overcooked, then it will not stand the vigorous beating and will break up. If this is the case it is better not to bother with the final beating.

Saffron risotto (risotto alla milanese)

Infuse 1 packet of powdered saffron or 20–30 toasted and pounded saffron strands in 1 tablespoon of boiling water for 30 minutes. Cook as opposite, adding half the saffron liquid when you begin to add the stock and stirring in the remainder about 5 minutes before the end of cooking.

This amount of saffron will give you a gloriously golden risotto, with a heady, potent saffron flavour, and is enough for up to 340g/12oz rice. Taste the risotto before you add the second batch of liquid, adding enough to give the flavour you like. For full notes on using saffron, see pp 25–7.

Saffron risotto with summer vegetables

Saffron risotto is a splendid partner for tender young summer vegetables. Make the risotto as above. Just before serving, stir in 110g/4oz freshly cooked skinned broad beans, cooked globe artichoke hearts cut into slices, or young asparagus tips cooked briefly in a little water until just soft.

Smoked salmon and basil purée risotto

Smoked salmon risotto is a new invention, worth trying if you have just a small amount of smoked salmon. For my taste, the salmon should be as mild as possible, since heat brings its salty nature to the fore.

Make the risotto as opposite. Just before serving, stir in 2–3 tablespoons of Basil and Olive Oil Purée (p 82) and 55–110g/2–4oz smoked salmon, cut into thick, short fingers. Serve immediately, with grated Parmesan if you like.

Red wine and mushroom risotto

A satisfying and rich-tasting risotto. For notes on bone marrow, see p 137. It can also be made without the bone marrow.

SERVES 4 AS A FIRST COURSE AND 2 AS A MAIN COURSE

225g/8oz risotto rice

about 600–750ml/1–1$\frac{1}{4}$ pints chicken stock

150–200ml/$\frac{1}{4}$–$\frac{1}{3}$ pint robust red wine

110g/4oz mushrooms, quartered or roughly chopped

15g/$\frac{1}{2}$oz dried mushrooms, preferably porcini (ceps), roughly broken

1 small onion, finely chopped

olive oil and butter for cooking

TO FINISH:

15–30g/$\frac{1}{2}$–1oz butter

1 tablespoon finely grated Parmesan cheese or 1–2 tablespoons double cream

bone marrow excavated from a 10cm/4 inch length of marrow bone, cut into 1.25cm/$\frac{1}{2}$ inch pieces

finely grated Parmesan or pecorino cheese to serve (optional)

Start by soaking the dried mushrooms: put them in a small dish, pour over a little boiling water to cover and leave for 5–10 minutes to swell.

To make the risotto, soften the onion gently in a little olive oil and knob of butter in a heavy pan. Add the rice and stir to coat the grains. Pour in the wine and cook steadily until it has almost evaporated. Add the fresh and dried mushrooms together with the soaking liquid and a quarter of the stock. Cook the risotto in the usual way (p 138), adding the extra stock if needed and finishing with the butter and Parmesan or cream. Season with salt if necessary, adding freshly ground black pepper for this risotto as well. Lightly stir in the pieces of bone marrow and serve immediately, before the bone marrow has time to melt completely. Hand round grated cheese if liked.

Squid, fennel and saffron risotto

SERVES 4 AS A FIRST COURSE AND 2 AS A MAIN COURSE

225g/8oz risotto rice

about 750ml/1$\frac{1}{4}$ pints light fish stock, or vegetable stock if fish stock is not available

1 wineglass (100ml/3$\frac{1}{2}$fl oz) dry vermouth or dry white wine

225g/8oz cleaned squid, sliced into 7mm × 2.5cm/$\frac{1}{4}$ × 1 inch strips

$\frac{1}{2}$ bulb of fennel, sliced down the middle then sliced across into fine strips

1 packet powdered saffron or 20–30 toasted and pounded saffron strands, infused in 1 tablespoon hot water for 30 minutes (see p 26)

1 shallot or $\frac{1}{2}$ small onion, finely chopped

olive oil and/or butter for cooking, plus best olive oil for serving

finely chopped fennel fronds, taken from the bulb, or use chopped fennel herb

Start with the squid. Pat dry on kitchen paper. Tip into a bowl, season with salt, then add 2 tablespoons of olive oil and stir around so that the squid gets coated with the oil – it's easiest to do this with your hands. Set aside.

Cook the fennel and onion in a little butter or olive oil as usual for 5 minutes, until softened. Add the rice, stir around until the grains glisten, adding a little extra fat if needed. Add the vermouth or wine and cook until evaporated. Pour in a quarter of the stock and half the saffron liquid. Cook the risotto in the usual way (p 138), adding the rest of the saffron liquid to taste 5 minutes before the end of cooking.

Just before serving, fry the squid over a high heat for 1–2 minutes until just cooked. Mix into the risotto along with any juices, scatter chopped fennel fronds on top and serve immediately, handing round a jug of fine olive oil separately.

6

Polenta

Once the poor man's staple in northern Alpine regions, polenta is now very chic. Made from ground cornmeal, it has a fairly bland, starchy flavour. It is cheap, convenient, colourful and easy to cook. It is also remarkably versatile. You can boil it, bake it, grill it, deep-fry it, make it solid enough to cut into slabs, or cook it long and slow until it melts to a creamy, custard-like consistency. It can also be flavoured and used to make deliciously gritty cakes and biscuits.

Depending on how much liquid is added when you cook it, polenta can vary in consistency from stiff to soft and can be used in a number of ways to accompany a wide range of dishes. Stiff polenta, for example, comes into its own char-grilled until crisp and then doused with olive oil, while very soft, sweet polenta is baked in the oven and makes comforting nursery puddings. Most of the time it is served plain or grilled, with melted butter or olive oil. It is excellent with grilled meat or sausages, bacon, sticky meat and game stews, Mediterranean vegetables, tomato sauces and mushrooms, or any kind of Italian cheese. As a comfort food *polenta dolce* – hot plain polenta, eaten straight from the spoon, dipped first into cold milk, and then into sugar – takes some beating.

Like all comfort foods, polenta is supremely satisfying to eat. Aficionados like me love it but it must be said there are others who do not take to it at all. It *is* bland, especially when cooked with plain water, and can be stodgy, more like wallpaper paste if you're not careful – though once you have tried it grilled on the barbecue you may well be hooked for life.

BUYING AND STORING POLENTA

It is important to buy the right kind of polenta:

■ Polenta should have bright yellow, gritty grains, and be labelled polenta or cornmeal. Only buy Italian brands; irrespective of what the shopkeeper may say, a label bearing only the words 'maizemeal' should be avoided. This may be better for bread or Caribbean dishes, but it does not make good polenta.

■ Instant polenta is twice as expensive but is very good. It has been partly cooked and needs only a further 5–10 minutes cooking. It has the same flavour as ordinary polenta.

■ Polenta should be stored in a cool, dark place. Instant polenta and ordinary packet polenta will keep for at least 6 months. It is also possible to buy stoneground polenta, which has much more flavour but is expensive and needs to be used more quickly.

COOKING POLENTA

Polenta is easy to cook. The essential points to bear in mind are:

■ You can make the polenta any way you like, be it stiff or soft, bland or creamy, plain or flavoured.

■ Whether polenta is stiff or soft, and how long it takes to cook, depends largely on the amount of liquid you add to it. The more liquid you add, the longer it takes for it to be absorbed and the softer the result.

Traditional v. easy method

The traditional way to cook polenta is to pour it in a thin stream into a measured amount of boiling salted water and stir vigorously and continuously for about 30–40 minutes, or until the polenta has absorbed all the water and comes away from the side of the pan. These are the instructions given on packets and in most recipes; instant polenta is cooked in the same way but takes only 5–10 minutes.

A much easier way, however, is to put the polenta into the pan with *cold* water. This is far less frenetic and there is no danger of lumps forming. The polenta and water are brought to the boil and cooked until the polenta is soft, stirring as necessary. If you cover the pan and simmer polenta over a very low heat, it needs hardly any stirring. Cooking times vary with the amount of water added and how much polenta you are cooking. Both ordinary and instant polenta can be cooked this way. For details see Easy Boiled Polenta on p 144.

Which liquid?

Polenta is usually cooked in plain water. A mixture of one-third to one-half milk and water produces a creamier polenta with more flavour. It is particularly recommended for soft polenta, which can seem very watery. Just milk can be used for polenta eaten as dessert.

Polenta can also be cooked in a light chicken stock, although this will alter the flavour.

········ **Tips** ········

■ When cooking polenta, add salt to taste rather than recommended amounts, which can make it too salty. As a general guide, allow $\frac{1}{2}$–1 teaspoon per 110g/4oz uncooked polenta. It can also be left out entirely if you prefer.

■ All polenta firms up on cooling – the less liquid used, the stiffer the set. It does not stick after you have turned it out, so there is no need to oil the serving dish.

■ Polenta is best served warm rather than piping hot; allow to cool a little before serving.

■ A crust often forms on the bottom of the pan. To remove, soak in cold water for a few hours, then clean. If the crust is very stubborn, soak overnight.

Deluxe boiled polenta

Plain polenta can be enriched with butter or cream or a mixture of the two. For 110g/4oz uncooked polenta, allow around 30g/1oz butter and 4–6 tablespoons of double cream. Beat either or both into hot polenta just before serving.

Storing cooked polenta

How long polenta keeps depends on its water content. Stiff polenta keeps for 4–5 days in the fridge, soft polenta 2–3 days. Polenta does not freeze.

Flavoured polenta

Boiled polenta can be flavoured in various ways. Beat the ingredients – just enough to flavour well – into the polenta as soon as it is cooked. Leave to cool, then slice and grill in the usual way. Quantities are best judged by eye and taste, though you won't need much. Dry ingredients such as chopped herbs, grated hard cheeses and toasted chilli flakes are easy to add. When adding cooked vegetables, make sure they are neither too moist nor too oily, as this loosens the polenta, making it more difficult to grill. Here are some suggestions for good flavourings to use with approximately 110g/4oz uncooked polenta:

- 2–3 teaspoons finely chopped rosemary with or without 1 finely sliced red chilli; 2–3 tablespoons chopped basil; 1–2 teaspoons toasted chilli flakes
- 30–55g/1–2oz finely grated Parmesan cheese
- 15g/½oz chopped black olives (about 6 large ones)
- 110g/4oz finely sliced and softened leeks; 2 tablespoons chopped garlic shoots (p 97); 110g/4oz chopped red pepper
- 55–110g/2–4oz fried onions; 30g/1oz crisp fried shreds of bacon; 55–110g/2–4oz finely chopped cooked green cabbage; 55g/2oz chopped cooked mushrooms; 10g/¼oz soaked, chopped and cooked dried mushrooms
- Mixtures such as leek and bacon, leek and mushrooms, cheese and olives and cheese and chopped herbs also work well.

Char-grilled/barbecued polenta

Irresistible. Probably the best way to eat polenta and the way most restaurants serve it. It is easiest with stiff polenta, though any kind of cooked or leftover cold polenta is suitable, as long as it is firm. Stiff polenta remains firm, while softer polenta will have a crisp shell and soft inside. Though you can cook it for less time, the secret is to char-grill/barbecue it slowly, up to 20 minutes or so, turning it once. This produces a golden, crisp crust. If you do not have a ridged cast-iron grill use a heavy non-stick frying pan.

Make a stiff polenta, using 1 part polenta to 4–5 parts water, following the method for Easy Boiled Polenta on p 144. Transfer it to a shallow dish to set in a layer about 2cm/¾ inch deep, smooth the top and refrigerate until needed.

Cut into thick squares or triangles, or stamp out shapes with a cutter, setting them on kitchen paper to absorb excess moisture. Place directly on a hot ridged cast-iron grill or the barbecue. Cook over a gentle heat and do not attempt to turn for 4–5 minutes, or until it forms a crust, when it will move easily (it will stick if you try and turn it before). Turn and cook the other side until crisp and golden. Serve with your best olive oil or a little melted butter poured over the top.

You can also grill polenta. Brush each slice on both sides with olive oil, arrange in a shallow heatproof dish and put under a hot grill for 7–10 minutes until the surface is crisp and browned.

Polenta crostoni

Squares of polenta are known as crostoni; grilled or fried they can be served as a hot snack. Top with a dollop of melting cheese such as mozzarella, Gorgonzola or dolcelatte, some spicy sausage, or a slice of tomato and a sprinkling of oregano, and you have an even tastier snack.

EASY BOILED POLENTA

The chart opposite gives the best proportions of water or other liquid to use when cooking traditional polenta. Use the comments and cooking times as a guide. Remember that cooking times are never precise, that the smaller the amount of polenta you cook, the quicker the liquid will be absorbed, and that polenta may be cooked for 10–15 minutes longer than the time stipulated and will come to no harm.

The chart and cooking method can be used for instant polenta. Because it is precooked it absorbs liquid much faster, so be careful to mix well with the cold liquid and not to heat it up too quickly as it may form lumps if you do so. Irrespective of how much liquid you add, it takes approximately the same time to cook, around 5–15 minutes, depending on whether you are making stiff or soft polenta. If cooking it in the oven, allow about half the recommended cooking times.

Allow 55g/2oz polenta per person. In all cases, cook until the grains are soft and the polenta firm enough to come away from the sides of the pan.

1 Put the polenta in a pan large enough for it to swell (for small quantities a small pan is okay), then pour in the required amount of liquid. Salt to taste, stir, cover and bring to the boil.

2 Stir again and turn the heat down to very low. Keeping the pan covered, simmer very gently, stirring occasionally, until the liquid has been absorbed and the grains are soft. If the polenta seems too thick, add a little more liquid and beat well until amalgamated; if too sloppy, remove the lid and cook for slightly longer.

3 Check the seasoning, give a final stir, and serve hot, plain or with melted butter or olive oil, or if appropriate cool until set and grill or barbecue as described on p 143.

Baked polenta

This is the modern alternative to cooking polenta on top of the stove, which I first came across in Claudia Roden's book, *The Food of Italy,* and is the easiest way to cook soft polenta. You can bake polenta in a moderate to hot oven, at any temperature from 180°C/350°F/Gas Mark 4 to 200°C/400°F/Gas Mark 6, depending on whichever is convenient.

Bring the polenta to the boil as above, and cook for 1–2 minutes until it begins to thicken. Pour into a greased shallow dish in a layer about 2–2.5cm/¾–1 inch deep and with about 2.5cm/1 inch headspace. Brush with melted butter or olive oil and bake in the oven until done to your liking – around 30–45 minutes in a hot oven, 200°C/400°F/Gas Mark 6, or 1–2 hours in a moderate oven, 180°C/350°F/Gas Mark 4, for very soft polenta.

Amount of liquid	Type of polenta when cooked	Cooking notes	Cooking time
1 part polenta/ 4 parts liquid	Thick, solid polenta, often recommended on packets and found frequently in recipes	Quickly forms a stiff mass that sticks readily to a spoon and needs beating rather than stirring. The liquid is absorbed almost immediately. Sets solid even when hot. Best for frying, grilling, barbecuing or cutting into shapes	Around 15 minutes; or 30–40 minutes in the oven
1 part polenta/ 5 parts liquid	Firm, good, all-purpose polenta that can be used for grilling or serving as an accompaniment	Midway between a stiff and soft polenta, easier to stir, but becomes firm quickly	Around 15–20 minutes; or 40–50 minutes in the oven
1 part polenta/ 6 parts liquid	Pale yellow polenta. Thick, creamy mass, blander flavour, soft and spreads easily but not runny. Sets to a soft firmness. Good for serving with stews or as an accompaniment	Easy to stir, developing the texture of thick custard. Not suitable for grilling or barbecuing as it is inclined to stick to the pan. Better flavour if cooked in part milk and part water. Good for desserts baked in the oven	Around 20–40 minutes; or 45 minutes–1 hour in the oven
1 part polenta/ 8 parts liquid	Pale, bland, spreading polenta with a custard-like consistency when set. Good for desserts. Unsuitable for grilling or barbecuing or serving as an accompaniment	Thin at first, gradually becoming thicker – it may take up to 1 hour before it is sufficiently firm to come away from the sides of the pan. Best made with just milk or milk and water and cooked in the oven	Up to 1 hour; or 1–2 hours in the oven

Char-grilled polenta with mixed mushrooms

Char-grilled polenta with mushrooms makes an easy meal and is a classic combination. Fresh wild mushrooms are particularly good; otherwise go for a mixture of cultivated mushrooms and a few soaked dried mushrooms. A ridged grillomat gives the best results but a heavy non-stick frying pan will do.

SERVES 2

110–170g/4–6oz mixed wild or cultivated mushrooms, cut into thick slices or quarters if small

about 1 tablespoon chopped parsley

1 fat clove garlic, peeled

7–10g/$\frac{1}{4}$oz dried mushrooms, or chopped pieces of dried porcini (ceps), soaked (optional)

olive oil

shavings of Parmesan or hard goat's cheese to serve

Chop the parsley with the garlic. Char-grill the polenta as described on p 143 and set it aside to keep warm. Throw the fresh mushrooms on to the grillomat or into the pan, drizzle with a little olive oil and cook over a high heat for 3–4 minutes until they are just softened and the juices have begun to ooze out, turning them with a spatula so that all sides become streaked with brown. If using soaked dried mushrooms, add those now and heat through. Add the parsley and garlic, stir to coat the mushrooms and pile immediately on top of the polenta. Serve with shavings of cheese and extra olive oil, seasoning at the table.

For a creamed version, after adding the parsley and garlic, pour in cream to taste, plus any soaking liquid from the dried mushrooms. Bubble up and pile on the polenta as before. This is better made in a frying pan rather than a ridged cast-iron grill, which is not suitable for sauces.

American polenta pudding with fresh pears

SERVES 4

110g/4oz instant polenta

750ml/1$\frac{1}{4}$ pints milk

2 large ripe pears, peeled and cored

2 large eggs, lightly beaten

55g/2oz white or light Demerara sugar plus 1 tablespoon

$\frac{1}{2}$ teaspoon almond essence, preferably bitter almond essence

Put the polenta and milk in a pan and bring to the boil. Add the 55g/2oz sugar and cook for 5 minutes or until soft, stirring often. Cool until lukewarm, then beat in the eggs and almond essence.

Dice one of the pears and fold it into the mixture. Pour into a medium-sized pudding dish in a layer about 2.5cm/1 inch deep. Slice the other pear thinly and arrange on top. Sprinkle with the remaining sugar and bake in a moderate oven, 180°C/350°F/Gas Mark 4, for 50–60 minutes: it will rise slightly and be firm to the touch. Flash under the grill to caramelise the pear slightly. Serve lukewarm. If you have it, hand round pear liqueur (Poire William) to pour over each serving.

Variations Fresh peaches or apricots can be used instead of pears; crushed amaretti biscuits or grated lemon zest can also be added, beating them in with the almond essence and eggs.

7

Good Grains

There are other grains to turn to besides rice or polenta. None has the ubiquitous appeal of rice or the fashionable status of Italian polenta. No matter what cookery writers say, this puts them firmly in the minority league. If you like bland, earthy flavours, you will enjoy using other grains regularly; otherwise they are pleasant for a change. All are as easy as rice to cook. The best – bulgar and couscous – are ideal convenience foods and can be bought from supermarkets; other grains are available from health-food shops and delicatessens. This chapter deals with couscous, bulgar, millet, buckwheat and quinoa. I have not included whole grains such as wheat, rye and barley, which you will probably use even less.

GRAIN COOKERY

Like dried beans and pulses, grains are cooked simply – usually either plain or as a pilaf. They can also be used in salads and as stuffings. As with pulses, salt brings out their flavour. Meat is not a strong feature of grain cookery, except with couscous, and neither is fish. Vegetables and nuts are. But the prize goes to dried fruit; any kind will do, with dried apricots raising grains to star status.

The natural, earthy flavours and textures that make grains comforting to eat also mean that you can cook them successfully with a wide range of foods and flavourings. In fact, you can treat them almost like a stir-fry, cooking them with whatever is to hand. So although grains are less familiar than potatoes, in many ways they are more convenient and easier to use, and offer more scope. They also marry well with pulses and any kind of tomato sauce.

If you are feeling lazy, it is also worth remembering that cooked grains can be instantly jazzed up by stirring in a spoonful of spice paste, butter paste or your favourite pesto. For ideas, see Easy Ways to Enhance Rice, pp 129–30.

BUYING AND STORING GRAINS

It is impossible to tell in the shop whether or not grains are good quality. For this reason, buy from shops with a high turnover and pay a little extra for reliable brands.

Grains do not last for ever. They have a shorter shelf life than white rice or packet noodles and should be used quickly. This applies to all grains, whether or not pre-cooked. Any grain that smells stale or faintly rancid should be thrown out. Light and heat affect keeping quality, so store all grains in a cool, dark place.

SOAKING AND COOKING GRAINS

None of the grains dealt with in this chapter needs soaking before cooking except couscous, which is moistened with water and left to swell for a little while before being heated through. Because bulgar and couscous are pre-cooked they can be rehydrated and used in salads without further cooking.

Two important points that apply when cooking all grains are:

■ Like dried pulses, grains cook by absorbing water and are done when they are soft, which takes about 20–25 minutes. It is the texture that counts. Overcooked grains become soggy, stick together, and are bland, uninteresting and leaden to eat. Cooked properly, they are light and fluffy, each grain separate, and have a pleasant nuttiness.

■ The key to achieving a light and fluffy texture is simply the amount of water you add. Often, as with rice, recipes call for too much liquid. If you have tried grains before and been unimpressed with the mush that is sitting on your plate, try cooking them with less liquid and you may be pleasantly surprised.

Grains could not be simpler to cook. The basic method is set out on p 153 and can be used for all the grains in this chapter except couscous, which is rehydrated and then reheated.

How much liquid to add?

Different grains absorb different amounts of liquid. Furthermore, you can adjust the amount according to how soft or nutty you like it. The more you add, the more the grain will swell and the blander the taste, until eventually it will become saturated. To illustrate this, try soaking a small amount of couscous in half, the same, and one and half times its weight or volume of water. The first bowl will be very nutty, the last much softer, while the middle one will probably be perfect.

Different cookery writers also tend to recommend different quantities of liquid, which can be confusing. Gauging how much liquid to add as a proportion of the grain is a much easier system to remember, and works every time. For the best proportion to use with each grain, see under individual entries.

Grains are usually cooked in water. For a richer flavour, you can use vegetable stock or half stock and half water. In lieu of anything else, a tablespoon of soy sauce added to the water gives a little extra depth of flavour.

Storing cooked grains

Plain cooked grains keep for 4–5 days in the fridge and reheat well, either wrapped in greased foil in the oven or put in a fine sieve set over a pan of boiling water and steamed until hot. They do not freeze well.

How much should you serve?

Grains double in bulk once cooked. As a guide, allow 55g/2oz (uncooked weight) per person for a main course accompaniment or pilaf. Otherwise, follow the same general guidelines as for How Much Rice Should You Serve? (p 123).

Tips for success

■ The key to achieving perfectly cooked, light and fluffy grains is the amount of liquid you add. This can be varied according to how soft or nutty you want the grain.

■ When calculating how much liquid to use, proportions are far easier to remember than specific amounts, and work every time.

■ Grains are easy to cook. They do not need as much liquid or take as long to cook as is often suggested, and are ready in 20–25 minutes.

Bulgar

This is most often sold in health-food shops as cracked wheat but is also known, for example, as bulgar in Bulgaria, bulgur in Turkey, burghul in Lebanon and pourgouri in Greece. Best known in the form of the Lebanese salad, tabbouleh, bulgar is a staple throughout the Middle East, especially Turkey, where it is combined with minced meat to make patties called *kibbeh*.

Bulgar is made by boiling wheat grains until they crack – hence the name cracked wheat – which are then dried and ground between rollers. It looks like pale brown granules, has a warm nutty smell and can be used equally successfully for salads, stuffings and pilafs. It is available either fine (salads), medium (stuffings) or coarse (pilafs) – though supermarkets and most other shops only sell the coarse grain bulgar.

Bulgar goes especially well with minced lamb and with vegetables such as carrots, peas, celery, courgettes, peppers, pumpkins and aubergines. It is less successful with fish. Warm spices, fragrant fresh herbs, dried fruit, walnuts, pine kernels and sharp citrus dressings suit it best. The other thing to try is pomegranate. Pomegranate juice is used instead of lemon juice in a traditional form of tabbouleh, and you can add pomegranate seeds to bulgar for a lovely autumn salad.

COOKING BULGAR

Bulgar is the easiest grain in the world to deal with. Because it is pre-cooked it only needs rehydrating, which takes about 5–10 minutes if you follow the basic method on p 153. A proportion of 1:1, that is, equal quantities of liquid and grain, produces perfect results. Simmer gently until the liquid has been absorbed, fork up lightly and serve.

Bulgar pilafs are cooked in the same way as millet pilafs (p 151). Because bulgar cooks so quickly, make sure the vegetables are softened first. The other simple way to produce a bulgar pilaf is to cook the other ingredients separately and fold them into the cooked bulgar.

Preparing bulgar and couscous for salads

The usual way to prepare bulgar and couscous for salads is to leave them to soften in ample water for 20–30 minutes, drain and squeeze out the excess moisture with your hands. This produces a 'wet' mix and messy fingers. If you are organised enough to think ahead, a simpler and better way, which produces soft but dry grains, is as follows.

Put the bulgar or couscous into a bowl, sprinkle over an equal quantity of water (or up to half as much again if you prefer a slightly softer grain) and leave to soften – about 30 minutes for couscous and 45–60 minutes for bulgar. Or leave until you want to make the salad. Using a fork, lightly break up the grains and make the salad in the usual way. The moisture from the salad ingredients and dressing will soften the grain further, giving you a perfect salad, neither wet nor dry.

If you want to soften bulgar quickly, pour boiling water over it and leave for 20–30 minutes.

Make the salads at least 1 hour before you eat them, to allow the flavours to mingle.

Couscous

Couscous is a great grain, the national grain of Morocco and North Africa, popular in Sicily and Brazil, and currently the most fashionable grain in California. It is made from grains of hard durum wheat semolina, which is dampened, then rolled in fine flour which accounts for its globular appearance. The flavour is similar to semolina, though more distinctive. Of all the alternative grains to rice, this is the one with the most scope, having a natural affinity with just about anything. Chickpeas and couscous are inseparable bedfellows, and it is excellent with lamb, spicy sausages, and Moroccan spices such as cinnamon, saffron, turmeric and the spice paste, harissa (p 24).

Unlike traditional couscous, which is made by hand and needs repeated moistening and lengthy steaming, modern couscous is pre-cooked and needs merely moistening and reheating. This means you can ignore instructions in cookery books that tell you to prepare it in the traditional way.

COOKING COUSCOUS

Perfect couscous is as soft and fluffy as newly fallen snow, and is well worth taking a little trouble over. The procedure, which never fails, comprises two simple operations:

■ Put the couscous into a bowl, sprinkle over the required amount of water (see right) and set aside for 10–15 minutes until the water has been absorbed. Using your fingers, gently separate the grains – about 2–3 minutes' pleasant work. The couscous can now be left until you need it. Just before reheating, you may need to break the grains up again.
■ The moistened couscous can be reheated either in the oven or in a steamer set over a pan of simmering water or whichever stew you are making to serve with it.

The steam method

You can use any fine-meshed sieve as a makeshift steamer. Pile the swollen couscous loosely into the sieve and set over a pan of boiling water. The grains become mushy if they are in contact with the water, so make sure the sieve or steamer is well clear of it. Steam, uncovered, until the couscous is thoroughly hot and has little holes between the grains. Depending on the quantity you are making, this will take 15–30 minutes. Check that the pan of water does not dry out, adding extra water as necessary. Halfway through cooking mix the couscous lightly, bringing the bottom half to the surface, to ensure that all the couscous is heated. If you prefer, place a clean J-cloth or piece of muslin lightly on top to keep the heat in.

When the couscous is done, transfer it to a hot serving dish, mixing it lightly to break up any lumps.

The oven method

Put the moistened couscous into an oiled or buttered serving dish, cover very tightly with oiled or buttered aluminium foil and reheat in a hot oven, 200°C/400°F/Gas Mark 6, for about 10–15 minutes or in a moderate oven, 180°C/350°F/Gas Mark 4, for 15–25 minutes. Fork up lightly and serve.

Leftover couscous can be reheated successfully by either method.

Proportions of liquid

Once you decide how soft or nutty you like your couscous, you can adjust the amount of liquid accordingly. You will need about $\frac{1}{2}$–1 part water to 1 part couscous. Any more liquid and it starts becoming very soft. Traditionally couscous is served with a wet stew, so the grain should be dry and nutty.

A few other points about couscous

- Cooking couscous over a stew does not flavour the grain but is a handy way of reheating it. Burying spices in the couscous, on the other hand, will flavour and perfume it and is an excellent idea. Try a broken cinnamon stick, crumbled bay leaves, dried orange peel or whole cloves.
- Stirring oil or a little melted butter into the couscous before reheating it adds flavour and helps to keep the grains separate, although it is not necessary for this purpose.

- It does not matter when you season the couscous. You can add salt either when you moisten it or when you reheat it. If the stew or sauce is already highly seasoned, it is quite nice to have unseasoned couscous.
- The way to achieve feather-light couscous is to use less water and to separate the grains after you have moistened them.
- Couscous can be substituted for bulgar in salads (p 149).

Millet

The problem with this sweet, nutty grain is that it is fed to birds. Which is a shame, because unless you think up a different name you are unlikely to persuade people to give it much of a chance. It is a popular staple in India and Africa, has a crunchy texture and makes a good accompaniment for a vegetable stew. Millet on its own is fine, but enhanced with one or two flavouring ingredients it is much better. Any kind of tomato sauce goes well with it. It makes excellent pilafs and can also be cooked with milk, sweetened and eaten as a dessert. Butter suits it better than olive oil.

COOKING MILLET

Millet absorbs more liquid than most grains. As a general guide, use twice the amount of liquid to grain, adding more if you want a slightly softer texture. The grains should not be cooked until they burst completely and lose all their nutty crunch; they are best when they are soft but just beginning to burst. This should take about 25 minutes and the millet can be kept hot without spoiling for up to half an hour. Cook as for the basic method on p 153.

Like couscous, millet is a versatile grain and can be flavoured with a wide range of herbs and spices. Spicy mixtures with chilli or chilli paste suit it particularly well, as do warming spices such as cinnamon, allspice, nutmeg, mace, turmeric, cumin and fennel seeds. Smoked bacon and spicy sausages are reliable partners. For herbs, try parsley, coriander, chervil, dill, rosemary and thyme. It is also good enriched with savoury butters such as Moroccan spice paste (see p 129) or pesto, stirred into the cooked millet by the spoonful. For the basic idea, see Tomato and Thyme Millet on p 155.

Millet pilafs

Millet goes well with a wide range of vegetables, with frozen peas coming out on top. Choose from red or yellow peppers, courgettes, mushrooms, aubergines, fennel, celery, carrots, sweetcorn, broccoli, cauliflower, blanched spinach, shredded dark green cabbage and mangetout. Make the pilaf in the usual way (p 132). Vegetables that are best cooked briefly such as courgettes, broccoli, cauliflower and mangetout should be cooked separately and folded in at the end; others can be cooked with the millet. Add the frozen peas last, cook until heated through and serve.

Buckwheat

This is a popular staple in Russia and Eastern Europe and has an unmistakable smoky, almost chocolate flavour. It comprises triangular-shaped seeds that are toasted (see right) and used to make kasha (buckwheat porridge) and pilafs. The other place buckwheat crops up is in Northern Italy, where it is ground and added to polenta. It is very much a northern, that is, cold weather grain, good with root vegetables, such as carrots, beetroot, celeriac and parsnips, and with cabbage and mushrooms. It also goes well with soured cream, spices such as caraway and nutmeg, and dairy produce, rather than anything remotely Mediterranean. Buckwheat flour is made from ground buckwheat seeds and used for blinis, Japanese noodles (soba), pasta, crêpes and pancakes. Because it has no gluten it is a difficult flour to use neat and it is usually combined with white flour.

BUYING BUCKWHEAT: PLAIN V. ROASTED

Buckwheat seeds can be bought from health-food shops and delicatessens and are available plain (pale green-beige seeds) or ready roasted (pale chestnut-brown seeds). Ready-roasted buckwheat seeds sound a good idea until you come to cook and eat them. Freshly toasted buckwheat (see right) has a better, fresher and sweeter flavour. Most importantly, ready-roasted buckwheat cooks to an unpleasant mush, about which there is little that can be done.

The quality of buckwheat varies. Inspect the packet as best you can and try to avoid ones with a lot of broken grains.

COOKING BUCKWHEAT

Buckwheat takes only about 10 minutes to cook and is nicest when the grains are soft but still nutty. You can cook it to a soft porridge but I wouldn't recommend it. Use about one and a half to double the quantity of liquid to weight of grain. Unlike other grains, buckwheat disintegrates completely once it has burst.

Buckwheat seeds need to be toasted before being cooked. This brings out their nutty flavour, takes off their very slight bitter edge and also shortens the cooking time. I find them deliciously crunchy and will happily eat them on their own. Despite what the packet may say, ready-roasted buckwheat seeds do not need re-toasting. The method is simple:

Pour the seeds into a hot heavy-based frying pan and dry-fry for 4–5 minutes over a moderate heat, stirring them around until they have become light brown and pleasantly crunchy.

To cook, add water, milk or stock, cover, and simmer for 5–10 minutes until the liquid has been absorbed. Remove the pan from the heat and leave for a further 5 minutes or so to complete the cooking. Plain buckwheat is generally served with butter or soured cream.

Comments The problem with cooking buckwheat is that any broken seeds cook to a soft mush in about 5 minutes, while the whole seeds remain crunchy. Ready-roasted buckwheat is awful in this respect, the broken seeds turning to cotton wool almost immediately. The best way round this is to simmer ready-roasted buckwheat in an uncovered pan until the liquid has been absorbed. Cover and let rest, then serve.

Buckwheat pilafs

Follow the basic recipe on p 132, mixing in cooked vegetables once the buckwheat is ready. Buckwheat can be substituted for quinoa in Caraway, Lentil and Mushroom Quinoa Pilaf (p 155).

Quinoa

This tiny, protein-packed pale brown grain is the most recent to hit the high street, although it has been grown and eaten in the Andes since ancient times. It becomes soft and globular when cooked. Plain quinoa is bland and does not exactly shout at you with promise. However, butter cheers it up enormously, and it is also pleasant mixed with cooked brown lentils or served with game. It goes with the same kind of flavourings as buckwheat, and can be used for pilafs, salads and stuffings.

COOKING QUINOA

Despite its diminutive size, quinoa can absorb a large amount of liquid. As a general guide three parts liquid to one part grain is about right, and it takes 10–15 minutes to cook. Cook by the basic method below.

BASIC COOKING METHOD
FOR GRAINS

This is the basic method for cooking all grains except couscous. Although bulgar needs only to be rehydrated, it is excellent cooked in this way, too. Use a heavy-based pan that will retain the heat and allow the grains to finish cooking in their own steam.

1 Melt a little butter or oil in the pan, add the grain and stir for 2–3 minutes until it smells pleasantly nutty. If you want, soften a little finely chopped onion in the fat first before you add the grain.

2 Add the required amount of liquid, stir, and bring to the boil.

3 Cover and simmer over a low heat until the liquid has been absorbed. This will take anything from 5–20 minutes depending on the grain. Remove the pan from the heat and leave undisturbed for 5–10 minutes. The grain will continue to cook in its own steam.

4 Season, fork through lightly and serve. Prepared like this, grains will keep for up to half an hour in a warm place.

Variation

This basic method can be varied by adding herbs and spices for extra flavour, or by cooking diced vegetables with the grain – see individual entries and recipes for ideas. Spices, garlic and chilli should be added with the grain, while fresh herbs should be stirred in just before serving.

Finally, if you like your grains buttery, distribute a few shavings of butter over the top and stir lightly into the cooked grains just before serving.

Pilaf of couscous (or rice) with curry butter, pistachios and sultanas

An idea from *Grain Gastronomy* by Janet Fletcher, this produces as fragrant a pilaf as you could wish for – which is to say it smells and tastes comfortingly like your favourite curry house.

SERVES 2

| 110g/4oz couscous or cooked basmati rice |
| 1 generous tablespoon plump sultanas |
| ½ red onion, finely sliced |
| 1 generous teaspoon curry powder of your choice |

Plus

| 15g/½oz butter or ghee |
| 2 tablespoons shelled roasted pistachio nuts, coarsely chopped |

Prepare and steam the couscous in the usual way. If using rice, reheat it in a steamer covered loosely with a clean J-cloth. After 5 minutes, add the sultanas to heat through and plump up. Meanwhile, melt the butter or ghee in a small pan and gently soften the onion for 5–7 minutes. Turn the heat up slightly and let the onion brown a little. Remove the pan from the heat, stir in the curry powder and leave for a minute or so to cook in the heat of the pan.

Mix the cooked onion into the couscous or rice; to make sure you get all the curry flavour, tip a little of the grain into the pan the onion was cooked in, stirring it around to collect all the bits, then mix it back in with the rest. Mix in the pistachios, pile into a hot dish, and serve.

If your storecupboard contains curry paste instead of curry powder, simply stir 1–2 teaspoons into the cooked grain.

Variations Substitute garam masala or harissa (p 24) for curry powder. Add 1–2 tablespoons of cooked frozen peas and/or 1 tablespoon of finely chopped coriander, stirring it in last.

Spicy bulgar or couscous salad with melon and cucumber

SERVES 4

| 110/4oz bulgar or couscous, soaked in 125ml/4fl oz water |
| 1 teaspoon garam masala paste |
| 1 tablespoon plain yoghurt |

Plus

| ½ small ripe melon, cut into small dice |
| ½ cucumber, peeled and cut into tiny dice |
| 3–4 spring onions, thinly sliced |
| 1 tablespoon raisins |
| 2 tablespoons finely chopped parsley |
| 1 tablespoon finely chopped mint |
| 1 tablespoon finely chopped coriander |
| juice of 1 lime or lemon |

Put the soaked bulgar or couscous in a roomy bowl. Stir the garam masala into the yoghurt and mix lightly with the grain. Add all the rest of the ingredients and mix in lightly. Taste, adding extra herbs if necessary, season if required, and let the salad stand for an hour before serving. Serve in a frill of plain crisp lettuce leaves.

Variations If you have no melon, you can substitute mango, peaches or apricots, or even tomato. If you want a nuttier salad, add 1 tablespoon of very finely chopped walnuts.

Creamed couscous

This adds a new dimension to couscous, and became a lifesaver for a time while I was writing this book. The recipe is also based on one in *Grain Gastronomy* by Janet Fletcher. It is as softly comforting as rice pudding but only takes 5 minutes to make. Strictly feel-good food, for private pleasure. I eat mine out of the pan.

SERVES 1

| 55g/2oz couscous |
| 300ml/½ pint creamy milk and water mixed; use approximately two-thirds milk and one-third water |

Toast the couscous lightly for 2–3 minutes in a dry pan set over a moderate heat. Pour on the milk and water, stir, and simmer gently for about 5 minutes, stirring frequently, until the mixture is thick and creamy. Beat it a little to lighten it slightly. Serve hot, with a spoonful of your best strawberry, raspberry, damson or apricot jam, or sprinkled with brown sugar. You can pour cream over it, too, or maple syrup, if that is your tipple.

Tomato and thyme millet

This is a simple way of enhancing millet and can be served on its own or with meat, fish or vegetables.

SERVES 2–4

110g/4oz millet
300ml/$\frac{1}{2}$ pint water or light stock
2 tablespoons tomato purée
1 dessertspoon thyme leaves
butter or olive oil

Sauté the millet in a little butter or oil in a heavy pan over a moderate heat for 1–2 minutes until it begins to smell pleasantly nutty. Add the liquid, tomato purée and thyme, stir and bring to the boil. Cover and simmer gently until the liquid has been absorbed, about 15 minutes. Turn off the heat and leave undisturbed for another 10 minutes. The millet will continue to cook and soften in its own steam. It is ready when the grains are beginning to burst and are soft but still a little crunchy. Season to taste, fluff up lightly and serve. You can enrich it, if you want, with flakes of butter dotted over the surface and then gently mixed in, though try the plain version first.

If you prefer a softer result, add an extra 4–5 tablespoons of liquid and cook for another 5 minutes, or until the liquid has been absorbed.

Variation Moroccan spicy tomato and thyme millet: Stir in 1 teaspoon of harissa sauce, adding it with the tomato purée and thyme.

Caraway quinoa

SERVES 2 AS AN ACCOMPANIMENT

55g/2oz quinoa
150ml/$\frac{1}{4}$ pint water or light stock
1 generous teaspoon caraway seeds
butter

In a small heavy pan, fry the quinoa and caraway seeds in a little butter over a moderate heat for 1–2 minutes, until the grains smell pleasantly nutty. Add the liquid and bring to the boil, then cover the pan and simmer gently for about 10 minutes, until the liquid has been absorbed. Remove from the heat and leave for 5 minutes. Check the seasoning, stir in a little extra butter if wanted, and serve.

Caraway, lentil and mushroom quinoa pilaf

SERVES 2

110g/4oz quinoa
300ml/$\frac{1}{2}$ pint water or light stock
1 tablespoon caraway seeds
a few pieces of dried mushroom, or 55g/2oz fresh mushrooms, sliced

Plus

110g/4oz cooked small brown lentils or Puy lentils
2 tablespoons sultanas (optional)
2 hard-boiled eggs, quartered
butter

Follow the recipe above, adding the dried mushroom, if using, with the liquid. Meanwhile, gently heat the cooked lentils. Fold them into the quinoa with the sultanas, if using. If using fresh mushrooms, put the lid back on the pan of quinoa while you quickly fry them in a separate pan, tossing them in a little butter over a high heat for 3–4 minutes until just cooked. Check the seasoning of the quinoa, pile into a warm dish, arrange the quarters of egg around the outside and serve.

8

Pulses

Dried pulses are good, cheap, versatile and becoming more popular by the minute. They are very nourishing, and all the various types share three fundamental characteristics: a satisfying creamy texture, earthy 'peasant' tastes, and a wonderful ability to absorb flavours.

As the Greeks say, olive oil brings beans to life. Herein lies the first clue to the secret of cooking with dried pulses. By and large, tried and traditional ways of cooking them are best. Haricot beans may be very nice with paw-paw but are much better with tomatoes and parsley, and heaven cooked with lamb or pork. Similarly, split pulses – dhal – are glorious with Indian spices, and so on. Nut cutlets and mock pâtés are generally the kiss of death. To appreciate this unique group of foods at their best, take my advice and head straight for the cooking of the countries where they are a staple.

BUYING AND STORING DRIED PULSES

Pulses are the dried edible seeds of various legumes (peas and beans). Contrary to popular opinion, they do not keep indefinitely; they are best bought in small quantities and used sooner rather than later. Store in a cool, dry place.

■ Avoid packets that contain a lot of broken beans or ones with a tired, shrivelled appearance. The older they are, the longer they take to cook.
■ Good dried beans look plump and have a soft sheen to their skins. Recently dried beans, that is, the current year's crop, are always better than old ones. Recently harvested dried beans, fresh from the pods, are a revelation: tender and creamy, they have the satisfying texture of dried beans combined with a fresh, green bean flavour; they need no soaking and will cook in under half an hour.
■ Most varieties of dried pulses can be bought in supermarkets and health-food shops. The freshest and best, however, tend to be found in Italian, Spanish, Greek, Indian, Chinese and

other specialist shops, who each sell their own nation's favourite bean.
■ You used to have to pick over dried pulses meticulously for stray pieces of grit or small stones. Quality control has improved enormously and this is rarely necessary nowadays.

Canned beans and lentils

These are certainly convenient and some people swear by them, though I still feel home-cooked are better. The best brand is Suma, which has no added salt or sugar and is canned in spring water. Whichever brand you buy, rinse the beans thoroughly in fresh water to get rid of their canning liquid before use.

COOKING DRIED PULSES

Dried pulses are simple to cook. You need to soak them first until they have doubled in bulk, then simply drain, cover with fresh water and simmer until soft. Aromatics – onions, garlic, herbs or spices – are sometimes added to the cooking water, but more often than not these will be added afterwards, or the pulses simmered further in a sauce.

■ Soaking them first rehydrates them, shortens the cooking time and makes them cook evenly. The longer they soak, the softer they become and the quicker they cook – see Soaking Chick-peas, p 161. Dried beans can be soaked for 1–2 days. If soaked longer, they begin to sprout and then ferment. The quick-soak method (see below) reduces the soaking time by half. Lentils are the exception. They do not require soaking and take less time to cook.

■ For cooking purposes, dried pulses can be divided into two broad types; those that take ages to cook and those that do not. Most dried beans need about 4–8 hours' soaking and take 1–2 hours to cook. The timing depends on the type of bean and how long it has been kept in store.

■ It has become customary to advise boiling all dried beans vigorously for 10 minutes when you start to cook them. This is unnecessary except for red kidney beans, which *must* be boiled for 10 minutes to destroy toxins.

■ Dried pulses need seasoning with salt, which brings out their flavour in a miraculous way; without it they can be decidedly bland. This should be added once they have been cooked.

■ Dried beans cook perfectly well on top of the stove, but the slower you cook them, the better the result; and they are best of all, becoming unctuously creamy, when baked in the oven in an enclosed pot with pork rind or olive oil. Oven-cooked dried beans tend to break up less.

■ For the best flavour and texture, dried beans should be cooked in less rather than more water.

Add enough to cover them and stop them drying out but not enough to swamp them (if you use a lot of water, more proteins and carbohydrates will leach out of the beans).

■ How soft the pulses should be depends on how you intend to use them. Almost all over-cooked pulses disintegrate quickly to a mush. This is fine for purées and soups but not for salads or anything else.

■ Whole lentils and split pulses (dhal) cook much more quickly than beans, requiring only 15–30 minutes. They do not need soaking beforehand, though if you soak whole lentils first you will reduce the cooking time to a few minutes.

■ Because they take a long time to cook, it is always worth cooking more dried beans than you need. They are fine re-cooked, make good additions to soups, salads and the mid-week stew, and freeze perfectly.

■ When making salads, add the dressing while the beans or lentils are hot, to absorb all the flavours.

Quick-soak method

Put the dried beans in a saucepan with plenty of cold water. Bring to the boil, boil for 2–3 minutes, then remove from the heat. Cover and leave to soak for about an hour or until the beans have doubled in bulk and are fully re-hydrated. Rinse, cover with fresh water and cook as usual.

Cooking liquids

Water is the usual cooking liquid for pulses. Vegetable and chicken stock add flavour, though this is not necessary for most dishes. An exception to this is whole lentils, which are delicious cooked in game stock or with wine. Otherwise, if you want to add extra flavour but don't want to make stock, use half (or less) of a decent stock cube, preferably the unsalted variety. Another trick is to add a few bacon rinds to the cooking water.

Beans and fat

Beans and fat have a remarkable affinity. Olive oil and pork fat feature in traditional bean cookery more strongly than butter or cream. You can use vegetable oils (as they do in Latin America and India), but it seems a bit of a waste – both for your waistline and the beans.

As a rough rule of thumb:

- White beans go best with pork fat; just about everything except mung beans and aduki beans goes with bacon fat; all beans and chickpeas are excellent with olive oil.
- Lentils go well with butter and cream; butter beans and sweet-tasting pulses such as split peas and broad beans also suit cream; purées will take either, depending on your preference.

Salting beans and adding tomatoes

It is often said that you should never add salt when cooking beans as it toughens their skins, nor cook them with acidic ingredients such as tomatoes and onions. These both turn out to be red herrings.

- Adding salt to beans does not seem to make any difference to the skins. However, you can gauge the amount of seasoning needed much better if you add it once the beans have been cooked.
- Beans cooked with tomatoes and other acidic ingredients such as lemon juice are likely to take longer to cook (anything up to an hour or so), but will soften eventually just the same. It makes no difference to the cooking time of thin-skinned pulses (lentils are often cooked with onions and tomatoes), and adding the odd tomato to your beans won't hurt, either.

Storing cooked pulses

Plainly cooked pulses, that is, pulses cooked in plain water with aromatics but no onion, will keep for 5–6 days in the fridge. Drain them well and store in a plastic box. Use any pulses cooked with onion in 2–3 days, since cooked onion sours quickly and will make the pulses taste sour, too. Any surplus can be frozen for 3–6 months.

Which bean for which dish?

Though there is a certain sameness to all dried beans it is not true that one type can always be substituted for another with equal success. Some are sweeter, some more starchy and some, like chickpeas, have a distinctive flavour of their own. As a general rule, unless you feel the flavours will work it is better to stick to the type of bean in the recipe, or another which you know to be similar in flavour.

Dried pulses and flatulence

All dried pulses can cause flatulence, but not to the same degree. Haricot beans apparently cause the most, and lentils the least. I say 'apparently' because it also depends on each person's digestive system, so don't blame it all on the beans.

How to make dried pulses less windy

The compounds that cause flatulence leach away into the soaking liquid, so to make beans more digestible, throw away the soaking liquid and cook them in fresh water. To get rid of more of the offending compounds, change the water 2–3 times and/or par-boil the soaked beans for 5 minutes, then drain, add fresh water and cook until tender.

Checklist

- Dried beans and peas need soaking before they are cooked. This significantly reduces the cooking time and improves their digestibility. If you can, soak them overnight; they can be cooked when convenient any time the following day. Or use the quick-soak method on p 157. Make sure that all the beans have rehydrated, otherwise the outsides may begin to disintegrate before the insides of the beans are soft.

- Soaked beans are ready to cook once they are plump and fully swollen. They should have smooth skins and be approximately doubled in bulk. If the skins show wrinkled patches, leave to soak for a little longer.

- It is impossible to tell exactly how long dried beans will take to cook and recommended cooking times are only a guide. So cook them before you need them whenever possible.

- Always throw away the soaking liquid and cook dried beans in fresh water. Use enough water to cover them by 2.5–5cm/1–2 inches and stop them drying out, but not enough to swamp them.

- Dried beans should be cooked gently. They also have a tendency to cook unevenly, with some beans being soft before others. This is another reason to cook them gently.

- Red kidney beans should be boiled fast for 10 minutes to destroy toxins.

- With the exception of chickpeas, dried beans disintegrate to a mush if overcooked. Once they are soft, do not cook further unless you want to purée them.

- 110g/4oz dried beans will swell to twice their volume and yield 225g/8oz cooked beans.

- Once cooked, lentils disintegrate quickly; when cooking whole lentils, watch them carefully.

- All dried pulses are concentrated protein and carbohydrate. This means they fill you up.

. . . .

A Quick Guide to Pulses

There is an enormous range of dried pulses to choose from. Below is a brief list of those you will find readily available. Not surprisingly, the most familiar tend to be the best. Approximate cooking times are given; these are for soaked dried beans and peas and are from the moment the cooking liquid comes to the boil. Remember that old beans may take up to twice as long to cook.

HARICOT, NAVY OR KIDNEY BEANS

This is the largest group of dried beans. All belong to the same botanical species, *Phaseolus vulgaris*, and are the seeds of different varieties of French beans. The name 'kidney bean' comes from their shape. All take about an hour to cook.

Haricot

The bean of baked bean fame, smallest of the white-skinned beans and one of the most popular. Haricot beans have a mild flavour and are not too starchy. Soissons haricot beans from France are particularly prized. The classic bean for cassoulet, they go supremely well with garlic, tomatoes, parsley, bacon, pork and lamb. Excellent for soups, salads and as an accompaniment to lamb and pork.
Approximate cooking time: 1–1½ hours.

Cannellini

This medium-sized white bean has the same flavour as haricot beans, and the two are fairly interchangeable.
Approximate cooking time: 1 hour.

Flageolet

These pale green beans are noted for their creaminess and delicacy. They are not, as is often thought, the semi-dried version of white haricot beans but a distinct variety which keeps its green colour. Twice as expensive as haricot beans, good flageolet beans do not take as long to cook although old/cheaper brands do. Excellent with lamb or ham, and lovely in salads.

Approximate cooking time: 1 hour.

Borlotti/rose cocoa

This pretty pink, speckled large bean from Italy has a slightly sweeter flavour and softer texture than the haricot bean but can be used in the same way. In Italy borlotti is a favourite for soups (it purées to beige-pink) and risottos.

Approximate cooking time: 1 hour.

Pinto

Similar in appearance to borlotti beans but smaller, these are popular in Latin America. They are good in Crusted Beans (p 165) and Latin American bean soups, and have a slightly more refined flavour and creamier texture than red kidney beans.

Approximate cooking time: 1 hour.

Red kidney

Red kidney beans, with their meaty, savoury flavour and starchy texture, are very popular. They keep their colour and shape well, making them one of the best choices for bean salads. Used in chilli con carne, Mexican bean soups, Crusted Beans (p 165) and Jamaican rice and peas.

Approximate cooking time: 1 hour.

Black kidney

The same size, shape and flavour as red kidney beans, these are popular in Latin America, especially Mexico and Brazil, and the Caribbean. They are used to make Brazil's national dish, *feijoada*. They turn an attractive deep russet brown when cooked.

Approximate cooking time: 1 hour.

White kidney

These are the same size, shape and flavour as red kidney beans.

OTHER BEANS

Butter beans

These large, mild, starchy beans from South America disintegrate rapidly once cooked. They have a distinctive taste, not dissimilar to potatoes, and thick skins, which slip off easily when they are cooked. Good with leeks, in soups, and with mustard vinaigrette. Though often recommended, they are not really a good substitute for other white beans. Lima beans, which originate from Peru, are a smaller version of butter beans.

Approximate cooking time: $\frac{1}{2}$–1 hour.

Black-eyed peas

Small and cream coloured with a black 'eye', these play a major role in African and Creole cooking and are popular in the Caribbean and India. They are also found in Catalan cookery and in Spain and Portugal. They have a creamy texture and, as the name suggests, a faint pea flavour. Black-eyed peas take less time to cook than most beans, making them a useful addition to soups. They are also good in mixed bean salads.

Approximate cooking time: 30 minutes.

Dried peas

These need no introduction. Modern nutritionists advise against cooking them with bicarbonate of soda – the traditional method – as it leaches out nutrients. They make excellent soups.

Approximate cooking time: 1 hour.

Split peas

These come in two colours, yellow and green. The yellow kind, which is used to make pease pudding, has a sweeter flavour. Both are best cooked with ham stock.

Approximate cooking time: 45 minutes.

Chickpeas

A wonderful bean with a distinctive nutty flavour. They are popular throughout the bean world but can take for ever to cook and are much nicer skinned. Chickpeas keep their shape and do not readily disintegrate, making them the ideal choice for casseroles, pilafs and couscous. They are also excellent in salads and with pasta, brilliant with lamb and heavenly with aïoli. In India and Italy chickpeas are ground into flour and used to make pancakes and patties.

Approximate cooking time: 2–3 hours or even longer – though this can be considerably reduced by lengthy soaking.

Skinning cooked chickpeas Submerge the cooked chickpeas in a large bowl of water. Gather up handfuls of them and gently rub them between your fingers – the skins should slip off easily. Drop the chickpeas back in the water. They will sink and the skins will float. Pour off the water and the skins. If any remain behind, fill the bowl with water and pour it off again.

Soaking chickpeas

Chickpeas are better for a very long soak – 2 days. They soften more quickly and thus need a shorter cooking time. It also sweetens their flavour very slightly. Leave them to soak in a cool place or in the fridge.

Broad beans

Dried broad beans have a floury texture and strong, earthy flavour, but an unappetisingly drab brown appearance and tough skins. They need long soaking and cooking. Popular in Greece and the Middle East, they are most often used to make purées.

Approximate cooking time: $1\frac{1}{2}$–2 hours.

Ful Medames

Used to make the dish of the same name, these are a small, round variety of broad bean, popular in Egypt. Available from Lebanese and Greek shops.

Approximate cooking time: 45 minutes.

Mung beans

These small, green 'bean sprout' beans have a mild, sweetish flavour and are popular in India, both whole and split (moong dal). Good with rice.

Approximate cooking time: 30 minutes (whole bean).

Aduki beans

Aduki are small, dark red, starchy beans popular in the Orient and in macrobiotic cooking. They are primarily served with rice or made into small sweet cakes.

Approximate cooking time: 45 minutes.

Soy beans

'The world's most important bean – and God's worst joke.' They have the highest protein content and are the hardest bean, requiring a long soak and long cooking (3–4 hours). Their flavour is bland and slightly sickly, which is why they are usually cooked in a spicy tomato or other robust spiced sauce, or disguised in pâtés or smooth veggy patties.

LENTILS

There are two types of lentils – whole and split ones. All are earthy without being aggressively so, and are easy to digest. They cook quickly compared to other dried pulses and disintegrate fairly readily. Soaked lentils cook in a matter of minutes. Split lentils cook down to a soft mush and make wonderful purées and dhals.

Lentils, particularly split lentils, can be dusty so rinse them well before use.

Continental lentils

These are the large, flat green-brown lentils popular throughout the Mediterranean and Middle East. They have a delicious earthy flavour and keep their shape fairly well once cooked. They make the best accompaniment for any kind of feathered game, and are delicious cooked in game stock or made unctuous with butter and cream.
Approximate cooking time: unsoaked, 30 minutes; soaked, 10–15 minutes.

Small brown and red-brown lentils

Smaller than continental lentils, these are the same variety as red split lentils but are whole.
Approximate cooking time: unsoaked, 20–25 minutes; soaked, 5–7 minutes.

Red split lentils

The common red split lentil cooks quickly to a soft, pale orange mush. It has a sweet taste, and a handful will thicken and pleasantly flavour any kind of chunky mixed vegetable soup.

Cooked red split lentils can be beaten to a purée, enriched with butter or laced with spice paste (p 129), and served with chopped coriander.
Approximate cooking time: 10–15 minutes.

Puy lentils

Dubbed the posh lentil, this is the superior French variety, and has its own *appellation controllée*. More expensive and much smaller than the continental lentil, they are a striking slate green-grey colour and have a gentle, suave flavour. Save them for game, fish and salads.

Puy lentils cook very quickly and become overcooked, turning to a disappointing mush, in a matter of minutes. Aim for the firm side of nutty, draining them as soon as they are ready. For this reason, there is no point soaking them beforehand.
Approximate cooking time: 15–20 minutes.

Indian dhal

Several kinds of split pulses are used to make dhal, and preparation and cooking methods vary according to the recipe. Split pulses can be bought from Indian shops. Remember that all dhals (and split peas) firm up on cooling.

Some of the common ones are:
masoor dhal – common red split lentil
arhar dhal – yellow split lentil
urad dhal – ivory-white split seed of the black gram bean
moong dhal – split mung beans
channa dhal – split chickpeas

Bean Cuisine

Dried pulses are used extensively throughout the Mediterranean and the Middle East and also feature strongly in Creole and Caribbean cooking. In Latin America and India they are a way of life. Each nation has its favourite pulses and favourite ways of using them: bean and pasta soups in Italy; cassoulet in Southwest France; falafel and hummus in the Middle East; *frijoles refritos* (refried beans) and chilli con carne in Latin America; Boston baked beans in North America; and fragrant dhals and lacy crisp pancakes in India.

Wherever you find dried pulses you will come across them used in soups and salads, in creamy dips and velvet purées, made fragrant with garlic, fresh herbs or spices, and added to meat to eke it out. You will find them, too, combined with pasta and grains, rice and couscous. In Europe they form the backbone of traditional frugal peasant stews of onion, potatoes and cabbage, made savoury with a piece of pork, bacon or spicy sausage, and are inevitably cooked with garlic, parsley, sage and tomatoes. They are rarely enriched with butter or cream but with olive oil, lard, bacon fat or, in Southwest France, goose fat. In the Middle East they are spiced with cumin, laced with lemon juice, sprinkled with mint and eaten with yoghurt. In Latin America they are made hot with chillies, pepped up with cumin and eaten with hard cheeses, tortillas, corn and pumpkin. In the Caribbean, meanwhile, you will find them cooked in coconut milk and seasoned with lime juice.

Pulses are one of the glories of Indian cooking and ways of cooking and eating them are legion. Here, they are cooked in ghee (which adds its own distinctive flavour to dhal) or vegetable oil, and perfumed with spiced butters – *tardka*.

Spices that aid the digestion, such as ginger, asafoetida and turmeric, are commonly included in whichever heavenly mix of spices the recipe calls for, and Indian flat breads and yoghurt are popular accompaniments.

Elsewhere, dried beans and pulses feature less. China prefers soy beans in other forms, mung beans sprouted and black beans salted. The tiny red aduki bean is found in Japan, cooked in a dish called red rice and made into small, sweet cakes. The English contributions to the great pulse dishes of the world are pease pudding and mushy peas – not a lot, but all we've got.

Although pulses are natural partners for meat, you won't find many dishes combining them with fish, although this is changing fast. Current restaurant favourites are butter beans and lentils with cod and skate. Try them. Other exciting trends include new-wave purées and sauces blending warm, spicy flavourings such as cinnamon with sharp, fragrant tastes such as lemon grass.

Pulses go supremely well with vegetables. Any root vegetable is a winner, while spinach and other dark greens are especially good, forming as comforting and earthy a twosome as you are likely to find. Finally, a few leftover cooked beans, or a can of beans, can be added to any Mediterranean braise (p 84) and will go very nicely.

Beans cooked in a pot

There are many variations on the theme of beans ticking away by themselves in a low oven, but this version of the Greek dish fasoulia, taken from Colin Spencer's *Vegetable Pleasures*, is as good as they come. You can either soak them overnight or use the quick method of soaking (p 157).

SERVES 4

225g/8oz haricot, cannellini or large white kidney beans or chickpeas, soaked until doubled in bulk and then drained

4–5 tablespoons olive oil

2 cloves garlic, crushed or chopped

1 small sprig of rosemary

$\frac{1}{2}$ teaspoon oregano

1 bay leaf

2 tablespoons tomato purée

juice of $\frac{1}{2}$ lemon

TO FINISH:

$\frac{1}{2}$ large white or red onion, thinly sliced

Put the beans, olive oil, garlic and herbs in an earthenware crock or ovenproof dish. Place over a gentle heat and let everything sizzle for about 5 minutes. Pour in enough water to cover the beans by 2.5cm/1 inch, then add the tomato purée and lemon juice. Cover with a lid and cook in a very low oven, around 140°C/275°F Gas Mark 1, until tender. This will take anything from 4–6 hours. Check after 1 hour that the liquid is barely simmering, and adjust the temperature if necessary.

Inspect the pot after 4 hours. The beans should be soft and gooey but still reasonably intact, and bathed in a delicious sauce. Once cooked, stir in the onion and season to taste. Cover and leave off the heat for 4–5 minutes for the onion to soften. The beans are usually served cold with bread as a salad but I also like them hot. Fasoulia will keep for a day or so in the fridge; if you want to keep it a little longer, don't add the onion until you serve the beans.

Beans with sage and tomato

Beans in tomato sauce – the home-made kind – cannot be bettered. Here is a classic Italian way. Quantities are not important; use the ones given as a guideline, adjusting to the flavour you like. Serve with a good fruity Italian olive oil to pour over the beans.

A popular dish in Tuscany. It is supreme made with freshly harvested semi-dried beans from your garden, which need no soaking and will cook in around 15 minutes.

SERVES 4

450g/1lb cooked beans (allow 225g/8oz dried uncooked beans)

about 300ml/$\frac{1}{2}$ pint plain tomato sauce, passata or sieved, canned tomatoes, or use 2–3 tablespoons tomato purée diluted in about 300ml/$\frac{1}{2}$ pint water

1–2 large cloves garlic, crushed

4–6 sage leaves

olive oil

Heat a little olive oil in a shallow pan and add the sage and garlic. When the aroma arises, add the cooked beans, stir around for a couple of minutes, then add the tomato sauce. You need enough sauce to cover the beans. Cook gently for about 15 minutes, until the flavours are well blended, topping up with water if necessary. Check the seasoning and serve with good olive oil poured over the top.

Variation Substitute 2 large sprigs of basil for the sage leaves. Remove the basil before serving.

Creamed butter beans and mustard

Butter beans have a special affinity with mustard. For a simple accompaniment to grilled or baked white fish, mix 1–2 teaspoons of Dijon mustard with 2–3 tablespoons of cream, or to taste. Stir into hot, seasoned butter beans, sprinkle with a little chopped parsley and serve.

Emerald beans (Beans with dark green cabbage)

Left to my own devices, this is the kind of food I like most of all. It is best made with beans that have been cooked slowly with lamb or pork. As a general guide, aim for one-third to one-half cooked beans to cooked cabbage, remembering that the greens shrink by half once cooked. The exact proportions are not that important, though the kind of cabbage is; it needs to be spring cabbage, kale or Swiss chard. My all-time favourite is a combination of chickpeas and Swiss chard spiked with toasted chilli flakes. Again, use a decent fruity olive oil for serving.

SERVES 1–2

| 225–285g/8–10oz greens, coarsely chopped |
| 110g/4oz cooked flageolet, haricot, cannellini or pinto beans, or chickpeas |
| 1 sprig of rosemary/1 clove garlic, crushed/toasted chilli flakes (optional) |
| olive oil |

Cook the greens in boiling water to cover for 2–3 minutes until just soft. Drain and squeeze out the excess moisture. Heat a little olive oil in a pan, add the greens, cooked beans and any aromatics and cook gently for 5–10 minutes. Season with salt if necessary and serve in a shallow dish with extra olive oil poured over. Good with roast quail, rabbit, pasta or on its own with bread.

Crusted beans

This is my version of refried beans, which I find addictively tasty. Use any member of the haricot bean family or chickpeas – it is worth cooking extra just to make this.

Soak and cook the beans and divide them in half. Mash one half with a fork (you can do this in the pan). Heat a non-stick frying pan and fry the mashed beans in a little olive oil over a fairly brisk heat for about 5–7 minutes, until they become dry and crumbly. Keep stirring and, as

soon as they begin to brown slightly, drizzle over 2–3 tablespoons of olive oil, tip in the rest of the beans and season generously with toasted chilli flakes, cayenne, paprika or chilli powder, plus a good shake of cumin seeds, if you like them. Stir everything together for another couple of minutes, until the beans become encrusted with the crispy mixture. Season with salt and eat as a snack, with bread and a tomato salad, or straight from the pan. For my money, one of the best ways to tart up leftover beans yet.

Fragrant pea purée

This recipe is based on one from Jane Grigson, published in the *Observer* many years ago. Serve with grilled fish or lamb, or with Indian flat breads as part of a spiced vegetarian meal.

SERVES 4–6

| 225g/8oz green split peas |
| 1 medium onion, peeled and stuck with 1 clove |
| 1 large potato, peeled and quartered |
| 1 clove garlic, peeled |
| 1 dessertspoon coriander seeds |
| butter/ghee/cream to serve |

Put everything into a medium pan and add enough water to come 5cm/2 inches above the peas. Bring to the boil and skim off any scum. Reduce the heat and simmer gently, covered, for about 45 minutes or until the peas are soft and you have a thick mixture. Pour off any excess liquid and reserve. Remove the clove and push everything else through a mouli, which is best, or whizz (very briefly) in a food processor, adding some of the reserved liquid if the purée is too thick. Season with salt. Reheat, adding a lump of butter – or ghee if you are serving it Indian style – and/or a little cream to taste if you like.

Variation You can cook red split lentils or other dhals in the same way.

Lentils cooked in wine

Wine can have a remarkably cheering effect on lentils. The simplest way to achieve this is to add a spoonful or two to the hot lentils just before serving. Both a robust red wine and a rich sweetish white wine go well. You can also add a glass of wine to the cooking liquid; red wines darken the lentils, giving them a deep red hue.

Mulled lentils

A winter warmer. Seville oranges come into the shops in January and are around for a few weeks only. They have an intense sharp flavour that is lacking in sweet oranges and can be used in many ways. Freeze a few, and hoard any skins.

SERVES 2–4

| 110/4oz whole lentils, soaked for 4 hours or longer and then drained |
| 150ml/$\frac{1}{4}$ pint robust red wine, plus an extra hefty splash |
| 1 small onion or shallot, finely sliced |
| 2 whole star anise |
| peel from $\frac{1}{2}$ Seville orange, cut into segments |
| butter |

Start by softening the onion or shallot in a little butter in a smallish pan over a moderate heat, about 4–5 minutes. Add the lentils, wine, star anise and orange peel. Bring to the boil and bubble for a minute or so, then add enough water to cover the lentils. Cover and cook for 15–20 minutes, or until soft. Season with salt. Just before serving, add an extra splash of wine and enrich with a little butter if liked.

Stuffed mushroom caps

Another useful idea which makes the most of Puy lentils, or for when you have any lentils leftover from the previous recipe. Depending on the size of the mushroom, allow 1–2 tablespoons of prepared stuffing.

Soak 2–3 large pieces of dried porcini (cep) mushrooms in wine, sherry, stock or water for a few minutes until soft. Squeeze, reserving the liquid, and chop. Add the porcini and their soaking liquid to the cooked lentils. Remove the stalks from large, washed open-capped mushrooms. Chop finely and mix with the lentils. Spread the mixture in a thick layer on the underside of the mushrooms. Arrange the mushrooms in a shallow ovenproof dish and moisten with a little extra wine or stock; if you don't have these, use water and a dash of soy sauce. Dot with butter and bake in a moderately hot oven, 190°C/375°F/Gas Mark 5, for around 30 minutes, until the mushrooms are cooked. Pour the dark juices over the mushrooms and serve as a first course with salad leaves.

COOKED BEAN SALADS

The nutty quality and inherent softness of cooked beans make them admirable for salads, either on their own or with pasta. A few tips:

■ Don't have the beans so soft that they fall apart, and mix the other ingredients in lightly.

■ Dress the salad while the beans are warm and serve at room temperature.

■ You don't need to stick with just one type of bean; all dried beans harmonise well with each other, and colourful mixed bean salads make a change from the ubiquitous red kidney bean or white bean salads – as indeed does adding a few cooked fresh green beans.

■ Quarters of hard-boiled egg laid around the edge of the dish are an excellent addition to any bean salad.

■ Finally, as cookery writer Glynn Christian points out, if any bean salad fails to excite, add wine vinegar by the teaspoon, which does indeed have a wondrous effect.

Here are a few suggestions for flavouring simple, everyday bean salads.

Haricot, borlotti, cannellini, pinto and flageolet beans Onions, spring onions, garlic, chopped tomatoes or tomato sauce, parsley, basil, sage, lemon zest, spicy salami, sausages, pancetta, pesto, anchovies, canned tuna and olives.

Butter beans As above, plus orange, apple, celery, mustard, bacon and leeks.

Whole lentils As for haricot beans, plus frozen peas, raw carrot and celery, ham, game, smoked meat, tarragon, chives and chervil.

Red beans Onion, garlic, chilli, tomato sauce, parsley, coriander, sweetcorn, coconut flakes, raisins, lime zest and juice, avocado, ripe fruit such as pineapple, bananas and peaches.

Chickpeas Onion, garlic, chilli, courgettes, tomato paste, harissa, cumin, mint, parsley and coriander.

Bean salads are not *haute cuisine*. Judge the proportions of the other ingredients by eye and by taste. As a rough guide, allow 110g/4oz cooked beans per person, less if you have provided a lot of other salads as well. A couple of spoonfuls of an interesting bean salad (see below) set in a fringe of mixed salad leaves or spooned into a hollowed-out tomato makes a simple first course and won't overload anyone's digestion. A few more ideas, based on familiar themes:

Bean and walnut oil salad

This is based on an idea tucked away in Glynn Christian's good book, the *Delicatessen Food Handbook*. Mix some finely sliced red onion with warm cooked pinto, flageolet or cannellini beans. Season with salt and dress with walnut oil and a splash of good wine vinegar. Add chopped garlic if you like.

Lentil, celeriac and lemon olive oil salad

A nice salad for autumn and winter. Use whole cooked lentils, Puy lentils for preference, and an equal amount or more of celeriac. Dress the lentils with equal proportions of sherry vinegar and lemon olive oil. Stir in some finely chopped tarragon or lemon thyme and a little finely chopped preserved lemon (p 21), if you have it. Cut the celeriac into thin dice no bigger than your fingernail and blanch for 1–2 minutes until just soft. Drain, moisten with extra lemon olive oil and mix into the lentils. Finish with thin strips of sun-dried tomato, snipped over the top with scissors.

Lentil and lemon salad

This pursues the lemon flavour one step further, making a refreshing, tangy salad. Dress the lentils as on p 167, with lemon olive oil, sherry vinegar and finely chopped preserved lemon if you have it. Add chopped capers and peeled segments of fresh lemon, sliced across to give tiny triangles of flesh.

The combination of lentils with lemon olive oil and sherry vinegar is particularly good and can be used for other salads too. Lentils, celeriac and walnut oil are another obvious trio; dress with balsamic vinegar rather than sherry vinegar.

Kidney beans with avocado and chilli

Mix kidney beans with diced ripe avocado, keeping the dice small. Add finely sliced spring onion and as much finely chopped fresh chilli as you like. Season with salt, then dress with olive oil and enough lemon or lime juice to make it feel like summer.

Bean and chicory salads

Sliced chicory adds crunch in a way that lettuce never can. Use either white chicory or radicchio, and shred coarsely. Mix lightly with cooked beans, add segments of orange and a few stoned olives, then dress with olive or walnut oil and a splash of balsamic wine vinegar. Good for all members of the haricot bean family.

Greek bean salad

Another one for the haricot bean family. Mix cooked beans with feta cheese cut into tiny dice. Moisten with olive oil and finish with finely shredded rocket or watercress and slivers of stoned black olives.

Sweet-sour aduki bean, radish and ginger salad

Having bought a token packet of aduki beans and cooked them with rice, you may be wondering what to do with the rest. Here is one idea. Allow an equal quantity of cooked beans and radish. Pickled radish is best if you can find some, but fresh, crunchy mooli will do.

SERVES 2–4

110–170g/4–6oz cooked aduki beans
110–170g/4–6oz pickled radish or peeled mooli, cut into small, thin dice
$\frac{1}{2}$ red onion, finely sliced and separated into individual half-moon slivers
1 small knob of preserved ginger, cut into tiny dice
1–2 teaspoons peeled and finely grated fresh ginger
tamari sauce to taste

Lightly mix all the ingredients together, adding fresh ginger and tamari sauce to taste and sprinkling the tamari sauce over the salad last. If you have no tamari sauce, use Japanese teriyaki sauce.

Green salads with beans

A few leftover cooked beans or whole lentils can be added to green salads to great effect. Lentils in particular lend an earthy warmth to the salad without making it noticeably beany.

If you are using whole lentils, just scatter them over the salad. Dress other beans with a vinaigrette of your choice and place a dollop in the centre of the salad, or turn them into Crusted Beans (p 165) and scatter over the top of the salad.

9

Fish

In many respects, fish is the perfect food: healthy, easy to digest, low in calories, high in protein, quick to cook and good to eat. With the exception of the herring family, mackerel and mussels, though, it is rarely cheap nowadays. A prime cut, or a choice fish, can cost as much, sometimes more, than fillet of beef. For this reason, take extra care when buying it, and try not to be too ambitious when you cook it. The importance of freshness cannot be overstated: bad experiences of eating fish all come from eating it when it is stale.

Where fish is concerned, most people fall into one of two categories; those who eat fish regularly and will try anything and those for whom fish is still largely untried territory and who are more cautious in their approach. Two fish I would single out as made for modern cooks and suitable for both groups are skate and squid – see pp 180–1 and 182–4.

As for fish cookery, it has never been brighter or more eclectic than it is today. Modern fish cookery is quick and easy, with the emphasis on letting the flavour of the fish come through, and it employs Mediterranean and Asian flavourings, spices and fresh herbs with panache. I cooks fish in olive oil instead of butter, uses lime juice as well as lemon, and has replaced cream sauces with pestos and zesty salsas.

BUYING FISH

Freshness is paramount with fish, which means that it is vital to learn how to choose it well. It differs from choosing meat in two major respects. Firstly, all fish, apart from farmed ones such as trout and salmon, are wild food. As a result, supplies are erratic and the quality varies throughout the year – fish are least good to eat when they have just spawned, for example, and best when they have fattened themselves up in readiness to spawn. Where a fish has lived and what it feeds on – hence where it is caught – also affects its eating quality.

Secondly, truly fresh fish that has been caught, landed and sold within 24 hours is a rarity. Most fresh fish is considerably older than this by the time it reaches the shops, and its quality depends largely on how it has been treated in transit *from the moment it was caught*. This, rather than 'freshness' per se, is the critical factor. Good-quality fish will have been handled carefully and kept chilled at all times, and thus will stay in good condition longer. Ideally, the less it travels after being caught, the better. This is not something anyone except an expert can recognise easily by looking at fish, so whom you buy fish from is almost as important as the fish itself.

Fish is not something most of us buy every day, so never be afraid to ask your fishmonger for advice.

Always bear in mind that you can do a lot more with less than ideal meat than you can with second-rate fish. If in any doubt, leave it and buy fish another day.

What to look for

■ Fresh fish is slippery to the touch, has lustrous, shiny bright eyes, red gills, an opaque 'mother-of-pearl' sheen to the flesh and a sweet, fresh, sea-breeze smell.

■ Really fresh fish speaks to you, almost asking to be bought. It stands out above the rest, shines with quality and is always easy to recognise. Dull, flabby-looking fish, or ones that smell fishy, are past their best and will be dull to eat.

Why fish is delicate and deteriorates quickly

There are only two things to know about fish: it is either fresh or it isn't, and it should never be overcooked, because the flesh is delicate and dries out easily. This is basically due to the composition of the fibres that make up the flesh. Whereas meat fibres are long, resilient and come in bundles, fish fibres are short and separated by long, thin sheets of fragile connective tissue that dissolve into gelatin with very little cooking. This is also why fish dries out and becomes stringy in the freezer much more quickly than meat does. In other words, you can't treat fish in the same way as meat and expect to get the same results.

Because fish are cold-blooded and live in a cold environment, they deteriorate quickly once caught, unless they are kept on ice at all times. They also contain polyunsaturated fats, which oxidise and go rancid easily on exposure to air.

STORING FISH

Fish should be consumed as soon as possible. However, as long as it is stored properly, high-quality fresh fish, including fillets, keep perfectly well for 24 hours in the fridge. As a general guide:

■ Once home, take the fish out of its bag and pat dry with kitchen paper, then put it on a plate, cover with clingfilm and place in the coldest part of the fridge immediately.

■ If you have bought a whole fish and want to keep it for 24 hours, gut and clean it now, if the fishmonger has not already done so, rather than before you come to cook it.

■ The modern way to keep fish in tiptop condition is to have it vacuum packed when you buy it. Check whether your fishmonger can do this for you. Vacuum-packed fish keeps perfectly in the fridge for 2–3 days and emerges as fresh as when you bought it.

FREEZING FISH

Avoid freezing fish when you can. Though most of us do freeze it, it does not have the resilience of meat and, no matter what experts say, does not keep well in a domestic freezer. The exception to this is vacuum-packed fish, which freezes very successfully.

■ Fish for the freezer must be well wrapped. Exclude as much air/moisture as possible.

■ The quality of fish deteriorates quickly in the freezer, so use it as soon as possible, preferably within a month. Vacuum-packed frozen fish will keep in good condition for 3 months in the freezer.

■ After 1–3 months, oily fish, including salmon and halibut, develop off flavours. Use within a month of freezing if possible.

■ Freezing damages the texture of fish. To minimise this, thaw it slowly, overnight if possible, in the refrigerator. Dry thoroughly with kitchen paper before cooking.

Where to Buy

Fishmongers' are still the best place to buy fish. A fishmonger will fillet a fish for you, give you advice and supply ice if necessary. A knowledgeable fishmonger will also have a good network of suppliers, deal with fishermen direct and be selective in his choice of fish. Another excellent place to buy fish is from a friendly local fisherman when you are on holiday – this could be a rare opportunity to enjoy really fresh fish.

Many large supermarkets have wet fish counters and sell a wide range of fish, including exotic species flown in direct from New Zealand, the Caribbean and elsewhere. Though the quality is good, it rarely matches the best you can buy from a fishmonger, and you need to be extra choosy. Though things are improving, most supermarkets do not offer the know-how of fishmongers. Check whether they will clean fish for you, as some do not.

Fish vans offer a valuable service for those who have neither a fishmonger nor a large supermarket nearby; again you need to be choosy.

········· Checklist ·········

■ Buy what looks best on the day, get it home as soon as possible and decide how to cook it later. You don't need to dress up good fish with a number of ingredients, so this is never a problem. For the best choice, shop early in the day and collect the fish just before you go home.

■ You do not need to worry if you can't find a specific fish. Fish is very adaptable and most recipes are suitable for several different types.

■ It is much harder to judge how fresh fillets of fish are, so buy whole fish whenever possible and have them filleted on the spot. Similarly, if you can, have steaks cut from a large fish while you wait.

■ No matter how fresh it may look, some of the fish that appears on the fishmonger's slab has previously been deep frozen at sea. Although all fish treated this way should be clearly labelled by law, it is always worth checking that fish has not been previously frozen if you want to keep it until the following day or freeze it.

■ When buying whole fish, halve the total weight to calculate how much there will be to eat. As a general guide, allow 170–225g/6–8oz prepared weight of fish per person.

■ Whole fish often contain roe and will therefore appear to have more flesh than is actually the case. The roe are usually left in but, if you prefer the fishmonger will take them out so they can be cooked separately. If you do not want the roe, ask the fishmonger to select another fish for you.

■ Fish is messy stuff to gut and clean. Often, it will have been gutted beforehand but if not, ask your fishmonger to do this for you. A fishmonger will also remove the head, scale the fish if necessary, gut and clean squid and open up crabs, etc.

The ideal fish

The ideal fish would have firm, sweet, delicate-tasting flesh, large flakes and as few bones as possible. Though very few have all these attributes, it provides a useful role model for assessing the array of fish on the counter. A quick checklist of questions to ask yourself – or the fishmonger if the fish is new to you – is:

■ How soft and friable or firm and meaty is the flesh?
■ How bony is the fish?
■ How dry or oily is it?
■ Does it have a delicate flavour, best suited to savoury butters, pestos and cream sauces, or a strong or distinctive flavour, which can take spices and robust sauces?

PREPARING FISH

There's not much to preparing fish, except cleaning and (sometimes) filleting it. As long as you have a sharp, flexible fish knife, both are easy. Even easier, of course, is to ask the fishmonger to do it for you.

Modern recipes rarely call on you to do any fancy preparation work, other perhaps than slashing the fish so that it grills evenly or cutting it into thin slices or cubes. Whether or not to leave the heads on whole fish is purely cosmetic and a matter for personal preference. If the fish doesn't quite fit the dish you are cooking it in, trim off the fins and tail with a pair of scissors. Two things that do make a difference are:

■ Make sure you clean all the blood out of the cavities of the fish. This has a bitter taste and taints the flesh next to it and the cooking juices. Scrape out with a knife or rub with a little coarse salt, then wash the fish briefly.
■ Crisp grilled fish skin is wonderfully good to eat but must be free of scales. A cheap Japanese fish scaler which you run along the back of the fish does the job quickly. Do this in the sink – the scales fly everywhere if you don't.

Do you need to wash fish?

Generally speaking, the less fish comes into contact with water, the better. If you prefer to wash it to remove slime, etc., do so as briefly as possible when you get the fish home and then pat dry with kitchen paper. Store in the fridge until needed.

Essential fish equipment

Dealing with fish is much easier if you have a few essential tools. They are:

■ Sharp fish filleting knife, about 18cm/7 inch long, with a flexible blade
■ Cheap fish scaler
■ Kitchen scissors for cutting off fins and the undersides of prawn shells, etc.
■ Pair of tweezers for removing fine bones
■ Pair of fish baskets, for barbecuing
■ At least one crab pick
■ Wooden hammer or claw crackers for dealing with crab and lobster claws

Fish smells

Though it may come as a surprise to anyone who enjoys cooking fish regularly, the smell can be offputting. Apart from opening the window, there is no way to avoid this. Oily fish, such as mackerel, herrings and sardines, are the worst offenders by a long margin. Otherwise, grilled and fried fish smell more than steamed or baked ones, for obvious reasons.

To minimise the cooking smells, soak the pan in water immediately you have finished cooking, and line the grill pan with foil, which you can dump into the dustbin with similar speed.

Liquids to use for cooking fish

The range of cooking liquids for fish is not large.

- The best liquid for poaching smoked fish is a mixture of milk and water; use this also when poaching white fish between two plates.
- Except for poached whole salmon, fish is rarely cooked in plain water.
- The three main liquids suitable for moistening baked or braised fish or making fish sauces are white wine, vermouth and cider. Red wine can be used for specific dishes and makes very good butter emulsion sauces for fish such as salmon and red mullet: be warned, the sauce will be a murky red.
- Most recipes use only a few tablespoons of wine. Rather than open a bottle specially, use whichever wine you are drinking with the dish.
- If a recipe calls for a little white wine and you have none at hand, dry vermouth makes an excellent substitute.
- Light chicken stock can be used instead of fish stock or wine to moisten baked fish, or when a few tablespoons of liquid are required to make a sauce.
- When making sauces, soups and stews you will achieve a better result if you use fish stock as a base. If you don't have any fish stock, make a simple vegetable stock (p 41), or flavour the cooking water with a little chopped onion, celery and carrot, plus a bay leaf and parsley stalks if you have them. For details on sauces for fish see p 185–6.

Serving fish

Unlike meat, fish does not wait around happily and should be served as soon as it is ready. Remember it will continue to cook a little after it has been removed from the heat. For this reason, don't leave it in a turned-off oven but take it out as soon as it looks ready.

Fish is best served hot. It cools more quickly than meat – another reason to serve it as soon as possible.

Serving whole fish Cooking fish whole and serving it from the same dish is the perfect way to enjoy it when cooking for one or two. The best way to tackle flat fish is:

Run the knife down the centre of the backbone and ease the flesh from either side of the skeleton. Lift out each half with a fish slice. Lift the backbone and gently pull it away from the fish to expose the underside. Lift out each half with a fish slice as before.

What to serve with fish

Starch Potatoes are the classic filler to serve with fish. Plain, mash or a creamy purée are best. Rice is quicker, easier and nine times out of ten suits fish just as well as potatoes. It also matches modern sauces better.

Of the other possibilities, pasta is tricky, unless the fish is part of a pasta dish, such as a seafood pasta salad or squid with pasta. Couscous is excellent, makes a pleasant change from rice and is a must for tomato-based Mediterranean-style fish stews. Proper chewy bread is also good with these.

Vegetables The two outstanding vegetables to serve with fish are peas and spinach.

Salad Green salads are excellent with any kind of fish. Tomato salad runs a close second for bream, red mullet, sea bass, John Dory and 'queer-gear' fish flown in from the Southern hemispheres.

BASIC METHODS OF COOKING FISH

Anyone can cook fish well. The two easiest methods for everyday use are grilling and frying. Frying also doubles up as a means of braising fish. Barbecued fish is incomparably good. These three methods are suitable for most fish and provide ample scope and variety.

Of the other regular methods of cooking fish, roasting and baking are simplicity itself, and make it easy to judge when the fish is cooked. Wrapping fish in foil or greaseproof paper is trickier to judge but produces fragrant results.

With the exception of a few classic examples, poached fish is rarely used in modern recipes. Poaching is not as simple to do well as it sounds. Steaming is the other gentle way of cooking fish, and also the 'purest'.

Finally, stir-frying is perfect for prawns, squid, scallops and rounds of monkfish but is not particularly suited to anything else.

Grilling

A starred way of cooking whole flat, oval or torpedo-shaped fish, and also suitable for thick steaks. For easy cleaning, cover the grill rack with foil or cook the fish in a heatproof shallow dish and serve from the same dish. For examples, see recipes on pp 187–9.

- Grill fish in their skins to protect the flesh and keep it moist. Paint the skins and fish steaks lightly with olive oil.
- Put the grill on its highest setting and place the fish so that the top is 10cm/4 inches below the heat source. This distance allows it to cook evenly – any closer and the skin tends to burn or the fish cooks too quickly on the outside; with oily fish, the oil spits and causes smoke.
- Score whole fish before grilling. This means it cooks slightly more quickly and it is easier to tell when it is ready. Criss-cross flat fish to make a diamond pattern on the surface; slash

other fish with diagonal slits down each side. Small flat fish such as Dover sole do not need scoring first.
- Grilling oily fish such as sardines, herrings and mackerel is a smelly business.

Barbecuing

The best way to cook fish – see pp 258–60.

Char-grilling

See p 264.

Pan-frying

This is an excellent way to cook fish and does not have to involve using large amounts of fat. Think of it more as grilling on top of the stove in a frying pan. You sear the fish on both sides, then cook it gently until done. Perfect for fish steaks and thick fish fillets. For examples, see Cod in a Polenta Crust on p 193.

- Use a heavy non-stick pan.
- Seal the fish in a hot pan over a moderate-high heat; thereafter cook over a gentle heat.
- Once sealed, if you cover the pan and turn off the heat the fish will virtually cook itself.
- Soak the pan in water immediately you have finished cooking.

Roasting

Roasting is a troublefree way to turn any fish into a feast. Less frenetic than grilling, it is suitable for whole fish and for large thick pieces of meaty fish such as monkfish, tuna and swordfish. See Roast Monkfish on a Vegetable Base with Garlic, Saffron and Chilli on p 192.

- Roast the fish in a single piece where possible.
- For an instant accompaniment, roast fish on a bed of vegetables.

Cooking in a parcel

This is an excellent way to bake fish. The fish effectively steams inside the package, its juices mingling with the added flavourings to produce a fragrant sauce. It is also very clean – no fishy pans to deal with later.

Cooking in a parcel is suitable for whole fish of any size, fillets and fish steaks. (See Sea Bass under Wraps on p 195.) The parcel should be opened at the table.

You can use greaseproof, silicon paper or aluminium foil to wrap the fish in. Foil is easier and does not soak up any juices. Greaseproof and silicon paper are see-through and look more impressive at the table (the parcel balloons up in the oven).

The only drawback to cooking in a parcel is that you cannot see the fish, which makes it more difficult to judge exactly when it is ready. Here, you need to trust the cooking times in the recipe – or use aluminium foil (which means you can peek inside 5 minutes before the end of the cooking time and easily reseal it) and miss out on the presentation. See p 194 for more tips.

Steaming

Steamed fish has many enthusiasts. If you like fish to have a 'pure' flavour and do not find steaming fiddly (I do), it may be the perfect method for you. If you like gutsy, full-flavoured fish and crispy skin, don't worry about what you are not missing.

Steaming is only suitable for very fresh fish, and is best suited to delicate fish and fillets. Moistening fish fillets with milk or milk and water and steaming them between two plates is old-fashioned, but still one of the best ways to cook friable white fish. Otherwise, Chinese flavourings – spring onions, ginger, soy, star anise – go best with steamed fish. If you want to add sea flavour, lay the fish on a bed of seaweed or samphire (p 205). The method is always the same: lay the fish on a deep plate and set it on a makeshift stand or in a steamer in a pan containing a little simmering water. Cover and steam gently until just done.

■ You don't need a purpose-built steamer. A collapsible perforated one that expands to fit any size of pan is suitable for small whole fish. For large fish, a fish kettle is excellent.
■ There is no point in flavouring the water: it does not permeate the fish.
■ Never put too much water in the bottom of the pan: the water should not touch the steamer. It should not boil vigorously but should be kept at a constant simmer instead.
■ Cooking times depend on the thickness, not the weight of the fish, and the texture of the flesh. Friable fish such as plaice steam more quickly than dense-textured fish such as halibut.
■ Check the water levels in the pan and top up with extra boiling water from the kettle as necessary.

Poaching

Apart from poached salmon, poached smoked haddock, cod and jugged kippers, this is a rather outdated method of cooking fish. It has little to offer modern cooks and requires fine judgement if the fish is not to be a watery disappointment. Fish are usually poached in a court bouillon, which is water flavoured with vegetables, lemon juice or a little vinegar and the fish bones. My feeling is that it is best suited to fish that are to be eaten cold, such as salmon and trout. It is also the classic way to cook skate wings, but grilled or baked skate wings are better.

To call it 'poaching' is a misnomer, for the liquid should never boil but barely shimmer. If poaching smoked haddock or cod, place it in a pan, cover with a mixture of milk and water and bring gently up to the boil, then remove the dish from the heat and leave to stand, covered, until the fish is cooked.

Cooking Fish

It doesn't matter whether you grill, bake, fry, roast, poach or steam fish, the crucial thing is learning to recognise when it is done. Do that and every dish will be a success, for whereas undercooked and overcooked fish are both equally unpleasant, a perfectly cooked fish will send everyone into raptures.

Fish should be *à point*, or just cooked, and should fall apart easily when pressed gently with a fork. The flakes should be moist and succulent, the flesh soft, and warm rather than hot, while the colour should have changed, usually from opaque to white, but still retain its mother-of-pearl sheen.

■ Undercooked fish is raw in the centre; overcooked fish is dry and hard.

TIMING

Fish cooks very quickly, and at lower temperatures than most meat. In practice, all this means is that you need to watch it closely and be diligent. Depending on the cooking method, the difference between an undercooked, perfectly cooked and overcooked fish is about 5–10 minutes (maximum) for steaks and whole fish, less for thin fillets.

The texture and thickness of the fish both affect the cooking time:

■ The softer the flesh, the more quickly it will cook. Plaice and whiting are examples of soft-fleshed fish, while monkfish and tuna are examples of firm, meaty fish.

■ Thin fillets cook proportionally much more quickly than thick steaks.

It is also worth remembering that if you are unfamiliar with cooking fish, by far the easiest way is to cook it on the bone, protected by its own skin. For details, see recipes on pp 187–9.

Finally, as one expert pointed out, cooking fish is largely a question of what you can get away with – in this case how little you can cook it without it being unpalatably underdone. This varies depending on the type of fish. Oily fish are decidedly unpleasant if undercooked; semi-oily fish such as sea bass or red mullet need to be cooked *à point* rather than underdone; salmon is best when slightly underdone; and white fish can take slightly more cooking without spoiling.

What happens when fish is cooked

Various changes take place when fish is cooked, all of which are visible proof that it is ready. To quote from Alan Davidson's *Seafood Cookery*: 'The first is that the protein in the flesh coagulates, resulting in the white, curdy appearance which is a characteristic of cooked fish. This coagulation liberates a substantial proportion of the water present in the flesh, together with flavouring substances in it. Secondly, the thin membranes which hold the flakes of fish together are broken down so that the flakes separate easily. Thirdly, chemical changes take place; and it is these which produce the odours and flavours which we associate with cooked fish.'

Butter or olive oil?

Until recently, it was virtually unheard of to cook fish in anything except butter. In fact, olive oil suits many fish, including white fish, just as well, if not better. Grilled and barbecued fish are obvious examples. At home, too, a jug of olive oil often replaces the traditional knob of butter put on top of fish before serving. Lemon olive oil is particularly suited to good-quality white fish and sea bass.

There are exceptions, of course. Four that come to mind are salmon, salmon trout, trout and Dover sole.

How to tell when fish is done

There are several ways, and the best for domestic cooks, which should be used in conjunction with each other, are:

■ Insert the tip of a pointed knife or a skewer into the thickest part of the flesh, or by the backbone if the fish is whole. If the flesh parts easily, it is ready.

■ Look for creamy white beads of curd on the surface in the spaces between the flakes of fish. When these appear, the fish is ready (see below).

Fish juices

In general, the aim with fish cookery is to keep the juices inside the fish. This results in moist flesh that is good to eat and has lost none of its flavour components. The juices noticeably start to come out of the fish only when it has cooked, which makes it one of the most reliable ways of telling whether it is done. Contrary to the impression often given, it also means that you never have to worry about losing the juices – for example by scoring the fish – *before* the fish is cooked, because they do not exist. As a rough rule of thumb:

■ Fish that is cooked *à point* has creamy curds and no juices.

■ Fish that is fully cooked but still moist and very good to eat has creamy curds and a small amount of juice.

■ Overcooked fish looks obviously cooked and has a pool of juices; the more juice, the harder and drier the fish will be.

Baking fish

There is no need to preheat the oven for whole fish, steaks or large pieces. In fact I find the fish cooks more evenly if I do not preheat the oven first. Allow 5–10 minutes (maximum) extra cooking time, depending on how quickly your oven heats up and how thick the fish is.

Average cooking times

To be precise about cooking times for fish is to enter dangerous waters. What really counts is its appearance. Nevertheless, it can be a help to have some guidelines, especially if you are trying a particular fish or cooking method for the first time. Remember that the shape, texture and thickness of the fish will all determine how long it takes to cook. For details of cooking methods, see p 174–5.

Grilled Thick fish steaks, 5–7 minutes (no need to turn); whole round fish, 5–7 minutes first side, 3–5 minutes second side; whole flat fish 7–10 minutes (no need to turn).

Poached Thin fish fillets, 3–5 minutes; thick fish steaks, 5–7 minutes. See also poached salmon, p 194.

Fried Thin rounds, escalopes of fish, 1–3 minutes; thick fish steaks, 5–7 minutes. See also char-grilled fish, p 264.

Steamed Thin fillets, 1–3 minutes; thicker fillets of fish, 3–5 minutes; steaks, 7–10 minutes; small whole fish, 10–15 minutes; medium whole fish, 15–30 minutes.

Roast Medium fillets/steaks of fish and small–medium whole fish, 10–15 minutes in a hot oven; large sections of whole fish and large whole fish, 15–25 minutes.

Baked Fish is generally braised or baked in a moderate to moderately hot oven. Small–medium fish, thick fish fillets, fish steaks, 10–20 minutes; large fish, 20–30 minutes.

Baked in foil or paper Thin steaks, fillets and small fish, 10–15 minutes in a moderately hot oven; thick steaks, thick fillets and medium fish, 20–25 minutes in a moderately hot oven.

Which Fish for Which Dish?

Classifying fish according to type, whether it be round or flat, dry or oily, can be a great help when you come to cook it or when, as is often the case these days, you are faced with a strange-looking fish flown in from the other side of the world.

Fish from the same family or a closely related one tend to share the same culinary features. This means they can be prepared in the same ways and substituted for one another easily. Here is a brief guide to the main groups.

FLAT WHITE FISH

Flounder – dab – plaice – witch sole – lemon sole – Greenland halibut – halibut – megrim – brill – turbot – Dover sole.

This is the easiest group to remember. All are white fish, simple to fillet, quick to cook and easy to eat. The differences between them are their size, the relative softness of the flesh and the perceived eating quality, all of which are reflected in the price. The sweeter and more refined the flavour and the firmer the flesh, the more desirable the fish. Not surprisingly, then, Dover sole, turbot and halibut are the most expensive fish in this group.

Dab, flounder and plaice have the softest flesh, which breaks into small flakes when cooked, while megrim, witch and lemon sole are slightly firmer; Dover sole (a separate but related species) is accredited with the finest flavour and is the firmest of all. Though traditionally often sold and cooked as fillets, the best way to cook these fish is to grill or bake them whole.

Halibut and turbot are huge, firm-fleshed fish with an excellent flavour. Both are usually sold as steaks and fillets, and are expensive. Turbot is rich in gelatin, which keeps it succulent, whereas halibut is dry and needs careful cooking. They are best poached, fried, baked or braised. Cream sauces suit them admirably. Brill and Greenland halibut are smaller and therefore more manageable (and cheaper). Whole ones can be grilled or baked. Megrim and brill are related to turbot. Halibut is a separate species.

ROUND WHITE FISH (THE COD FAMILY)

Whiting – cod – haddock – hake.

These are the most popular white fish. Whiting has the softest flesh, while cod and haddock are characterised by large, firm, juicy flakes. Hake has denser flesh but is softer. The flesh should look milky white, with a soft sheen when fresh. Fish in this group are best poached, fried, baked or braised. Whiting is good steamed. Cod and haddock are particularly suited to pilafs, chowders, fish pies and fishcakes.

It is worth pointing out also that cod is a versatile fish, equally suited to spices and robust sauces as it is to cheese sauce, and absolutely delicious served with aïoli.

John Dory

This is not a white fish, nor does it belong to the flat fish family, but it has a similar shape. It looks like a weird tropical fish, with a huge head and the famous thumbprint marking on its side that has led to its common name, St Peter's fish. Because of its large head and gut there is considerable wastage, but the flesh is firm and has an excellent flavour. It is usually cooked in fillets. Like many fish found in the Mediterranean, it pairs admirably with aïoli.

OILY FISH

The herring family

Whitebait – sprats – herrings – sardines –
pilchards – anchovies.

Slim, silvery and rich in valuable omega-3 and
omega-6 fatty acids, the only problem with the
fish in this group is their pervading smell when
grilled or fried – the best cooking methods.
They also contain more than their fair share
of bones.

Whitebait are the baby fry of several fish,
while a sprat is a young herring. Sardines are
best for barbecuing. Fresh pilchards, which are
adult sardines, are rarely available, and anchovies
tend to be preserved rather than eaten fresh
(though this is not the case in Turkey and Latin
America). For a note on anchovies see p 22.

All have soft flesh and, when fresh, a plump
shiny brightness matched with a delicate flavour
that is not in the least bit fishy. The secret of
cooking them is speed and heat – have the grill
or frying pan hot and cook them briskly until
the skin is crisp; if frying, use a non-stick pan –
they will need no extra fat. A squeeze of lemon
counteracts their oiliness.

Mustard is the best flavouring for sprats and
herrings. For sardines, read Mediterranean –
barbecue, stuff or bake in the Sicilian manner
or serve with pasta (see p 57). Herrings are
remarkably good value and can be baked, soused
or salted and eaten raw – no smells here.

Mackerel

A powerful swimmer and thus more muscular
than herring, mackerel is still one of the cheapest
fish. It has a high oil content, soft flesh and
spoils easily. Though not everybody likes mackerel – the flavour can be strong sometimes – an
absolutely fresh mackerel is as much a delicacy
as herring can be. It is best grilled and served
with gooseberry sauce, soused, baked in wine
or cider or rubbed with Indian spice pastes. It
belongs to the same family as tuna.

Salmon and sea trout

These magnificent fish are very strong and have
powerful muscles – which means large, succulent
flakes of firm flesh – and enough oil to stop them
being dry. They almost fit the description of the
ideal fish on p 171, and are one of the few categories that taste good hot or cold. They are excellent grilled, barbecued, poached, fried or baked,
and for fishcakes, kedgeree and pilafs.

There is little to choose between salmon and
salmon trout, though the latter has paler flesh
and a more delicate flavour. Farmed salmon has
become as common as cod once was. Like
farmed trout, the quality varies so much that
it has become debased. The quality of farmed
salmon is difficult to judge just by looking at
the fish, though it is immediately apparent once
you come to eat it, cheap, inferior farmed
salmon having a flavour reminiscent of chemical
pink blotting paper. The best advice is to pay
extra for good-quality farmed salmon.
Premium-quality Scottish farmed salmon, available in most major supermarkets, is sold under
the Tartan Quality Mark (TQM). Salmon trout
is also farmed, though nothing like as extensively
as salmon.

Even slightly overcooked, the flesh loses its
soft succulence and becomes dry. Perfect salmon
or salmon trout are slightly under-cooked, the
flesh still a shade rosy.

Salmon is also a surprisingly good substitute
for most firm-fleshed fish – cod, tuna, etc. Like
cod, it marries well with spices, and can also be
flavoured with ginger, spring onions and soy.

Wild salmon has become an expensive luxury.
A prime wild salmon is undoubtedly a finer
fish than farmed salmon, with an unsurpassed
richness of flavour. Because it is a wild food,
however, the quality varies. Be especially wary
of bruised or flabby-looking fish. The best time
to buy is when it is at its most plentiful, generally
July to August. The same remarks apply to
salmon trout, which is usually cheaper and
therefore better value than wild salmon.

DENSE-FLESHED 'MEATY' FISH

Tuna – bonito – swordfish.

This group contains powerful fast swimmers – hence their flesh is close grained, the texture is as dense as meat, and the flavour is meatier than most other fish, too. They are invariably sold as steaks – tuna looks like fillet steak – and are best treated in the same way: grilled, barbecued or pan-fried. Good tuna can be roasted. All should be bought fresh – frozen tuna and swordfish are invariably a disappointment. They are inclined to dryness and benefit from being marinated in olive oil and lemon juice before you cook them.

Tuna and bonito are related species. Tuna can be enormous; when buying it, avoid any steaks with dark, bloody patches, as this taints the flavour. Bluefin tuna is found in the Mediterranean and is the type most commonly on sale, while yellowfin tuna is found in the Tropics and the Pacific. Skipjack tuna (also known as oceanic bonito) is not a true tuna but is a related species and is cooked in the same way.

Monkfish

Monkfish does not really belong to this group, but because you only eat the tail, which is dense and muscular, and it has no small bones, it is treated in similar ways. It is best roasted in slices or a thick piece (see p 192), or the individual muscles can be cut away from the central bone, sliced into medallions and briefly fried. The thin membrane on the outside of the flesh is tough and should be removed first. The sweet-tasting flesh can take robust flavourings such as garlic or bacon, and strong herbs such as thyme and rosemary. Excellent either cooked in the Mediterranean style with olive oil, tomatoes, red peppers and saffron, or in the European style with butter, mushrooms, cream and herbs. See Roast Monkfish on a Vegetable Base with Garlic, Saffron and Chilli on p 192.

NON-BONY FISH

Skate – thornback ray – shark – dogfish.

The important thing about rays and skate is that they have no true bones – a positive bonus – and are gelatinous in nature. They deserve to be better known. Unique among fish is their whiff of ammonia. Only the wings are eaten, and they can be poached, grilled or baked.

Skate

Skate has many advantages. Despite its bony appearance, the flesh on a skate wing – the part you buy for eating – has no bones, comes away easily in long ribbons when cooked and has a soft creamy texture. Other than a brief wash, it needs no preparation.

Buying and storing skate

Skate wings should look thick and glossy, with a rose-pink tinge to the flesh. A large wing has proportionally more flesh and is better value than two small ones: a skate wing weighing 570–675g/$1\frac{1}{4}$–$1\frac{1}{2}$lb will feed two handsomely.

Skate keeps better than most fish. There is some debate as to when it is best. To quote Rick Stein, whom I reckon has seen and cooked more skate than anyone: 'Skate is tough and tasteless when totally fresh; it needs to be refrigerated for two to three days, after which it will be quite tender. For three days it will then be in perfect condition; after that it will start to smell faintly and then distinctly of ammonia. A faint smell is acceptable; a strong smell is not.'

A fresh, sweet-smelling skate wing will therefore keep in satisfactory condition for 1–2 days in a domestic fridge. Do not buy skate that already smells of ammonia.

Sometimes you can buy skate knobs, small round nuggets of flesh taken from the cheek bones, which are a delicacy.

Cooking skate

The traditional way to cook skate is to dust it with flour, fry it in a little butter and then serve with extra butter, browned first in the rinsed-out pan, and capers.

However, I usually grill or bake skate wings (see Grilled Skate with Tomatoes, Celery and Capers, p 188, and Fish on a Platter with Roasted Vegetables, p 191) and serve them with extra olive oil, which suits skate flesh admirably. Because skate is wedge shaped, it will always cook a little unevenly. Check that the thickest part of the flesh is cooked to your liking.

Skate wings can also be cut into fingers, floured and fried, then served with green salad leaves as a first course. Skate knobs should be fried in a little butter or olive oil, moistened with cream, or served with a warm vinaigrette, as for grilled skate. Leftover skate is excellent in salads.

Shark

Shark is normally sold in steaks, and is best treated like tuna. Like skate and ray, it has no true bones but a cartilaginous skeleton that comes away easily when cooked and develops an ammoniacal smell. A dry, meaty fish, its flavour is often likened to veal.

Dogfish

Also known as huss or rock salmon, this is similar to shark, with the same kind of eel-shaped torso and cartilaginous skeleton, but softer flesh and a milder flavour. It is nicer than you might think; best fried.

MISCELLANEOUS MEDITERRANEAN AND EXOTIC FISH

Sea bream/porgies – red mullet – sea bass – gurnard – groupers – grey mullet – snappers – parrot fish – red fish – tilapia – African pompano.

These are just some of the members of this huge group of fish. It contains several of the most prized and expensive fish, such as red mullet and sea bass, as well as the cheapest, such as gurnards. Though diverse, multi-coloured and belonging to different species, from a cooking point of view they share similar characteristics: round, oval or torpedo-shaped, with thick skins and firm, distinctive-flavoured flesh. Some are bony and many have tough, scaly skins – check when you buy. All are admirable barbecued or grilled whole, make good stews and can be cooked with robust flavourings – Mediterranean, Middle Eastern, Chinese, Pan-Asian or Caribbean. They are less suited to traditional white fish dishes, such as cheese and cream sauces, pies or fishcakes.

Red mullet and sea bass deserve a special mention. These are very fine fish, with firm but delicately flavoured flesh, and are in a class of their own.

Squid

Squid is the fish equivalent of chicken, and is just as lean. Ideal for modern cooks, it offers first-class value and is one of the easiest fish to cook. Furthermore it has no bones.

Don't be put off by its strange, monster-from-the deep appearance. Its sweet shellfish flavour is truly excellent stir-fried, char-grilled or barbecued, invaluable added to Mediterranean fish soups and stews, and brilliant with pasta. It complements mussels and prawns and can be cooked either in the Southeast Asian manner, with coconut, ginger, lime, chilli, lemon grass or coriander, or with Mediterranean flavourings such as olive oil, garlic, saffron, bacon, peas, red peppers, parsley, etc. Squid and rice are natural partners.

BUYING AND STORING SQUID

Fresh squid is available all year round: it should look slithery and be pearly white. Squid freezes much better than most fish, and frozen squid is generally good quality.

■ The smaller the squid, the tenderer it will be. For general purposes, small-medium squid (up to about 25cm/10 inches long) are the best. Very large squid have tougher flesh.

■ If it has not already been gutted and cleaned, this should be done as soon as you buy it. It will then keep for 1–2 days on a plate covered in clingfilm in the fridge. Alternatively (and a better idea), freeze the squid in handy portions. It thaws quickly and can be sliced from frozen with a sharp knife.

PREPARING SQUID

Though your fishmonger should be happy to do this for you, squid is easier to prepare than it looks (see diagram below).

■ The fishmonger will remove the head and soft parts but the squid should still be cleaned: rinse the tubes out thoroughly with water, making sure they are clean inside, then pat dry with kitchen paper and store in the fridge.

■ The ink sac, which contains a concentrated black ink, is prized for use in risottos or for colouring pasta. It is difficult to find and in any case has usually been removed or already burst by the time the squid gets to the fish counter.

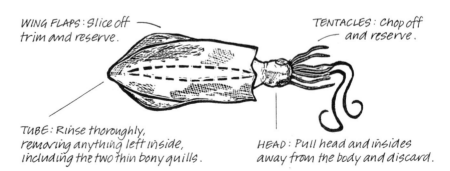

WING FLAPS: Slice off trim and reserve.

TENTACLES: Chop off and reserve.

TUBE: Rinse thoroughly, removing anything left inside, including the two thin bony quills.

HEAD: Pull head and insides away from the body and discard.

Which parts can you use?

There is no waste on squid: tentacles, body and wing flaps can all be used and all taste the same.

Tubes This is the prime part of the squid. Cut into rounds for deep-frying and seafood salads, thin, bite-sized strips for stir-fries, pasta, risotto and soups, or leave whole for stuffing.

When grilling or barbecuing squid, cut the tubes into large squares and score one side with a criss-cross pattern.

Tentacles The best way to use these is to slice them into dainty pieces and serve as hors d'oeuvres – see A Nice Way of Serving Squid Tentacles and Squid with Anchovies, right. If stuffing squid, include the tentacles.

Wing flaps Trim rigorously and use in the same way as the tentacles, or add to soups.

Baby squid The tubes are nice served whole. They can be grilled, stir-fried or barbecued. They are also good stuffed with a cooked filling such as a rice or pasta mixture, painted with olive oil and grilled for 5 minutes, turning once, until the stuffing is hot and the squid cooked.

COOKING SQUID

Squid has a naturally chewy texture. The secret of cooking it is to do so as briefly as possible, just until the flesh has turned opaque. In this way it remains tender, and only takes 1–2 minutes for sliced squid. Overcooked squid is just plain rubbery.

Bear in mind that the resilient texture of squid is more enjoyable eaten in small mouthfuls. When using squid in a pasta dish, risotto or fish salad, be sure to cut it in thin, bite-sized strips or rounds.

A nice way of serving squid tentacles

Wash and pat dry the tentacles, then chop them into bite-sized slices and put in a small bowl. Marinate for a minimum of 1 hour and up to 24 hours in a mixture of olive oil and slivers of fresh red (hot) chilli or toasted chilli flakes.

Heat a small shallow heatproof dish, then tip in the squid mixture and fry, stirring constantly, over a high heat, for about a minute, just until the squid changes colour. Remove from the heat and add a crushed clove of garlic. Stir this around so that it permeates the mixture, then leave to cool. Season liberally with Thai soy sauce or nam pla (p 277) to taste. Finish with a dusting of finely chopped coriander or basil. Serve at room temperature and eat with tooth-picks, with drinks or as part of a *mezze*. One of the best ideas in the book.

Strips of squid can be cooked in the same way and served with salad leaves as a first course.

Squid with anchovies

This idea comes from *New Food* by Jill Dupleix. Use chopped tentacles, strips or rings. For 110–170g/4–6oz squid, heat a finely chopped large clove of garlic with a couple of anchovy fillets in a small heatproof dish over a gentle heat. Stir around to melt the anchovies, then turn up the heat, add the squid and fry for about a minute, until the squid turns opaque. Scatter with a little finely chopped parsley and serve. For a squid antipasto, serve this with a portion of the two following dishes. Serves 2–4.

Squid with pesto

Stir-fry strips or rings of squid in a little olive oil. Season with salt, pile on to a plate and serve with a pesto of your choice (pp 65–9).

Easy deep-fried squid with polenta crust

Use the tubes for this. For notes on deep-frying, see p 33.

Wash the squid, shake off excess water (do not dry the fish) and slice into rings. Put a small amount of polenta on a plate and dip each ring into it, making sure it is well coated – this only takes a couple of seconds and you can do 3–4 rings at the same time. On a large plate sprinkled with extra polenta, spread the rings out so that they do not touch each other. They can be prepared up to this stage a couple of hours beforehand and left in the fridge until you want to cook them.

Take a small heavy saucepan and pour in about 1.25cm/$\frac{1}{2}$ inch of oil – use half peanut oil and half olive oil. Heat until very hot but not smoking: the way to tell is to dip the end of one squid ring into the oil – if it sizzles violently, the oil is hot enough. Keeping the heat high, slip in 3–4 squid rings, or however many you can fit in the pan in a single layer without crowding them. Cook for 30 seconds, turn the rings over with a fork, and cook for a few seconds longer. Remove immediately and put on a plate lined with 2–3 sheets of kitchen paper to soak up excess oil. Keep warm while you fry the rest. Sprinkle with salt and serve immediately.

Variation Mix chilli powder into the polenta. You can also use fine matzo meal as a coating.

Squid with pasta, peas, fennel and sun-dried tomatoes

During the course of writing this book I have come to the conclusion that squid is *the* fish to serve with pasta. You don't need much, it cooks in a flash, is resilient enough to match the firm bite of pasta, and harmonises well with vegetables you are likely to have around, such as peas, peppers, aubergines and mushrooms. This is just one example, and it can be adapted to whatever you have in the larder. Use pasta shapes such as conchiglie (shells), fusilli (spirals) or orecchiette (little ears).

SERVES 2

225g/8oz dried pasta shapes
110–170g/4–6oz prepared squid, cut into small bite-sized pieces
110g/4oz peas, fresh or frozen
1 small onion, preferably a mild red one, or 1 leek, finely sliced
2 tablespoons finely chopped fennel bulb
2–3 sun-dried tomatoes in oil, preferably home-dried ones (see p 118), finely sliced
1 teaspoon fennel seeds
2–3 tablespoons olive oil

Put the squid, fennel, sun-dried tomatoes and fennel seeds in a small dish with 1–2 tablespoons of olive oil. Stir to coat and set aside. Soften the onion or leek in the rest of the olive oil for about 5 minutes in a non-stick pan.

Meanwhile, put the pasta on to boil and cook the peas in a little boiling water.

Turn up the heat under the onion or leek, add the squid and fennel mixture and toss for 1–2 minutes, until the squid is cooked. Drain the pasta and put it into a hot serving dish. Add the peas and squid mixture to the cooked pasta, and season to taste. Toss thoroughly and serve immediately, handing round a good-quality olive oil.

SAUCES FOR FISH

Sauces for fish do not need to be complicated, delicate or rich. A few suggestions:

Tomato salsas

These are perfect with grilled, fried or barbecued fish, and suit everything from salmon and sole to oily fish such as mackerel – see p 71.

Tomato sauces

Tomato sauces are as useful with fish as they are with pasta, particularly grilled, fried or barbecued fish.

Aïoli

This is wonderful with cod and hake, prawns and crustaceans, but no good for oily fish and a waste with Dover sole. Stir it into flavoursome fish juices and you have a simple bourride. Stick to plain mayonnaise, or mayonnaise laced with a few drops of Pernod, for crab and lobster.

Pestos

Brilliant with all fish. See pp 65–9.

Mustard

Ready-made mustard complements oily and white fish extremely well. Mild, sweet ones are best.

The most common way to use it with oily fish is to spread the mustard over the fillets before grilling. Another trick, gleaned from Elizabeth David's book *An Omelette and a Glass of Wine*, is to flavour a simple tomato sauce with 2–4 teaspoons of mild mustard. This is good served with cod.

Simple sorrel sauce

For salmon, salmon trout and quality white fish. Melt a knob of butter in a pan and cook a good handful of sorrel leaves for 2–3 minutes until wilted. Pour in thick cream to taste, bring to the boil and pour the sauce around the fish.

Mustard and cream sauce

This is useful for any white fish that has been baked in the oven or braised with cider. Taste the cooking juices from the fish, boiling them down if necessary until well flavoured. Stir in 1 tablespoon of mild mustard and add cream to taste. Bring to the boil, check the seasoning, adding a squeeze of lemon juice if necessary, and pour over or around the fish. See also Laverbread Sauces, p 205.

Basil and olive oil purée sauces

Basil and Olive Oil Purée (p 82) can be used to make simple sauces for fish. Three ideas:

- Add chopped capers and preserved lemon (p 21) to taste to make a chunky sauce-cum-dip. Serve as a relish for grilled fish.
- Add mashed anchovy fillets plus enough thick cream to make a thick sauce. Serve with white fish or salmon.
- Add toasted chilli flakes and blend in an equal quantity of butter to make a fairly stiff paste. Serve with grilled prawns, squid and steamed mussels.

Skordalia

Nut sauces go surprisingly well with fish. This one is the Greek equivalent of aïoli, made with ground almonds instead of egg yolks. Useful for all grilled and baked fish, and for vegetables. This is the way I make it.

SERVES 2

55g/2oz ground almonds
1 small slice good white bread, crusts removed (about 15g/½oz)
4 juicy cloves garlic, peeled
4–6 tablespoons olive oil
a few drops of lemon juice or wine vinegar

Soak the bread in water to cover for a few minutes until swollen, then squeeze out all the moisture and transfer to a blender. Meanwhile, blanch the garlic for 2–3 minutes in boiling water. Drain and add to the blender with the almonds and olive oil. Blend to a thick paste, then add about 4–6 tablespoons of hot water, until the sauce has a dropping consistency. Season with a few drops of lemon juice or vinegar, add salt if necessary and serve.

Walnut and horseradish sauce

This is a cheat's version of a sauce made famous by Escoffier. Serve with poached salmon or trout. Blend 55g/2oz finely ground walnuts with 2 tablespoons of horseradish cream and up to 150ml/¼ pint thick cream, crème fraîche or Greek yoghurt to taste, making sure the yoghurt is well drained first. Stir in 1–2 teaspoons of sugar and lemon juice, both to taste. Serves 3–4.

Spanish hazelnut and pepper sauce

The classic name for this is romesco sauce, for which many recipes exist. This version is based on one in Jane Grigson's *Fish Cookery*. It is a splendid sauce for all grilled and baked fish. The correct variety of dried pepper to use is the Spanish romesco pepper, a sweet medium-hot one, but you will probably have to improvise as suggested below.

SERVES 2–3

12 hazelnuts
1 large ripe tomato
1 large juicy clove garlic, the fresher the better
1 medium-hot dried chilli, seeded, or ½ teaspoon Spanish or Hungarian paprika plus ½–1 teaspoon toasted chilli flakes
90–125ml/3–4fl oz olive oil
1 tablespoon sherry vinegar, or to taste

Bake the hazelnuts, tomato and garlic in a moderate oven, 180°C/350°F/Gas Mark 4, for about 15–20 minutes; after 10 minutes, add the whole dried chilli, if using, to crisp up. Transfer to a blender; if using paprika and chilli flakes, add these now. Blend with enough oil to make a smooth thick sauce, then stir in sherry vinegar to taste and check the seasoning. Serve in a small bowl for people to help themselves.

SIMPLE WAYS WITH GRILLED WHOLE FISH

Grilling whole fish in a shallow dish with a few extra flavourings is one of the easiest and most successful ways to cook it. Apart from in summer, when fish can be barbecued, this, and the baked version on p 191, Fish on a Platter, is the way I cook most fish at home.

The method given here takes no more than 5 minutes to prepare and is suited to a range of whole fish. It is particularly good with whole white flat fish, such as plaice, lemon sole, etc., skate wings, and Mediterranean or exotic fish, such as bream, snapper, tilapia or parrot fish. You could also try it with something as common as trout or mackerel.

1 Choose a shallow heatproof dish from which you can serve at the table. If you have nothing else, a pizza tray is fine. Brush the dish with olive oil.

2 Score the fish with a sharp knife. This gives it an attractive appearance, helps it cook more quickly and makes it easier to tell when it is cooked. For flat fish, score the upper surface in a criss-cross pattern; for torpedo- or oval-shaped fish, make diagonal slits on both sides.

3 Lubricate the fish with olive oil – this prevents it drying out.

4 Cook under a hot grill, turned to the highest setting, arranging the dish so that the top surface of the fish lies 10cm/4 inches under the heat source. There is no need to heat the grill beforehand.

5 There is no need to turn the fish over to cook both sides – the heat from the dish cooks the underside. If you are cooking fish that is easy to turn, or if you want the skin on both sides crisp, you can turn it half way through cooking if you prefer.

6 Serve with rice, mash, or hunks of bread.

GRILLED FISH WITH AROMATICS

This involves rubbing spices, spice pastes or highly aromatic flavourings into the fish.

Grilled fish with lemon grass and olive oil

This is uncommonly good – and superb with sea bass. Leek and Fennel Mash (see p 107) makes a good accompaniment.

SERVES 2

1 whole fish, cleaned, descaled if necessary, head removed if preferred. Allow around 570–675g/$1\frac{1}{4}$–$1\frac{1}{2}$lb fish
2 sticks of lemon grass – use the inner, tender basal portion only (p 277)
2–3 tablespoons fruity olive oil, preferably lemon olive oil
$\frac{1}{4}$ teaspoon salt
extra olive oil and lemon wedges to serve

1 Slash the sides of the fish and lay it in an oiled heatproof shallow dish. Bruise the lemon grass with the heel of a knife, chop finely and mix with the oil and salt. Pour this over the fish, working bits of lemon grass into the slashes. Leave to marinate for at least 1 hour, or for several hours, covered, in the fridge if convenient.

2 Baste with the marinade, sprinkle with an extra pinch of salt and cook under a hot grill until the skin is crisped and browned and the flesh just cooked. This will take about 5–8 minutes depending on the size and shape of the fish.

3 Serve immediately from the same dish, spooning the juices over. Hand round a jug of best olive oil and wedges of lemon if you like.

Grilled lemon sole with garlic, oregano and crushed coriander seeds

SERVES 2

| 1 large fish, approximately 570g/1¼lb |
| 1 tablespoon coriander seeds |
| 1 tablespoon chopped oregano |
| 1–2 cloves garlic, chopped |
| 2–3 tablespoons olive oil |
| ¼ teaspoon salt |

Cut the fins and tail off the fish, remove the head if you prefer, and slash the upper surface (the white one) in a criss-cross pattern. Lay the fish in an oiled shallow heatproof dish into which it will fit snugly. Crush the coriander seeds in a pestle and mortar, stir in the rest of the ingredients, and mix into the slashed surface of the fish. Leave in the fridge for up to 8 hours, or until required. Grill for about 5–8 minutes, until the skin browns and the flesh has turned white at the bone. Serve with extra olive oil at the table.

Grilled fish with spice paste

This is the cheat's way to spice fish. Mix 1–2 teaspoons of your favourite spice paste with 1–2 tablespoons of olive oil. Mild curry pastes or garam masala work well. Smear the fish with the mixture, rubbing it well into the slashes, drizzle over extra olive oil, and grill as before.

GRILLED FISH WITH HOT SALSA

Here, the fish is surrounded with a piquant mixture of chopped tomatoes, or other soft or easily cooked vegetables such as red pepper or thin slices of red onion. The 'salsa' cooks in the same time as the fish, and is served as a sauce or accompanying vegetable.

The following two suggestions can be used for any grilled white fish, fish steaks including salmon, and for whole grilled fish such as red mullet and bream.

Grilled skate with tomatoes, celery and capers

SERVES 2

| 1 large skate wing, about 570–675g/1¼–1½lb |
| 450g/1lb ripe tomatoes, cut into quarters |
| 1 small celery stick, finely chopped |
| 2 heaped teaspoons capers |
| pinch of sugar |
| fruity olive oil |
| handful of celery leaves, chopped |

Wash the skate wing briefly, pat dry with kitchen paper and put it thick-side up in the centre of a large flat oiled tin – a pizza tray or something similar is ideal. Surround with the tomatoes, then scatter the celery and capers over the tomatoes and sprinkle with a few grains of sugar. Drizzle olive oil over everything. Grill for about 7–10 minutes, until the skin is beginning to brown and bubble and the flesh from the thickest part of the wing parts easily.

Scatter the tomatoes with the celery leaves, season the skate with salt and serve immediately, with extra olive oil and saffron rice (p 130).

Grilled fish with charred red pepper, onion, parsley and coriander salsa

SERVES 2

1 large fish, approximately 570g/1¼lb

FOR THE SALSA:

1 large ripe red pepper, seeded

1 small onion, preferably a mild red one, finely sliced

1 generous tablespoon chopped parsley

1 generous tablespoon chopped coriander

3–5 tablespoons fruity olive oil

juice of ½ lemon

Cut the pepper into thin strips, then fine dice. Blanch the sliced onion, unless you are using a red one or prefer it strong or crunchy: put it in a small pan, cover with cold water, bring to the boil and cook for 1 minute. Drain. Mix the salsa ingredients together to form a thick sauce, adding a little olive oil and lemon juice to taste. This can be prepared in advance.

Arrange the fish in a shallow, oiled heat-proof dish roomy enough for the salsa to be scattered around the fish. Drizzle with the remaining olive oil and grill until half cooked, about 3–5 minutes depending on size and thickness, then spoon the salsa around. It should only cook for about 5 minutes and chars easily, so you need to watch it quite closely, turning it over if the exposed edges are charring too much. Cook until the fish is done and serve immediately.

GRILLED FISH WITH WARM VINAIGRETTE

This idea comes, again, from Rick Stein's Seafood Restaurant in Padstow, and is a winner. Grill the fish as above, then pour over a warm olive oil vinaigrette, flavoured with chopped herbs, olives, capers, etc., and serve immediately. The vinaigrette can be made from whatever ingredients you have to hand and mingles with the fish juices to form a sauce. Suitable for all the vinaigrette white fish – whole, steaks or fillets – and can also be used with baked fish (see p 191).

Suggested flavourings

- Finely chopped chives, garlic shoots, spring onion, garlic.
- Chopped olives, capers, anchovies, saffron, crushed green peppercorns, fennel seeds.
- Finely chopped parsley, coriander, fennel, dill, mint, chervil, tarragon, basil, celery leaves.
- Finely diced fresh ripe tomato, finely chopped fennel bulb.
- Fruity extra virgin olive oil, lemon olive oil.
- Lemon, lime or Seville orange juice, balsamic vinegar, lemon or lime zest.
- Salt and pepper.

Making the vinaigrette All you need to do is put your chosen ingredients in a small pan and heat gently. The idea is merely to enhance the olive oil with a little extra flavouring. As a rough guide, for 2 servings allow 4–6 tablespoons of olive oil, 2–3 teaspoons of wine vinegar or citrus juice and 1–2 dessertspoons of other flavouring ingredients. A few tips:

- Use a good-quality, fruity olive oil.
- Stick to 2–4 additional flavourings and use just enough to provide interest without in any way overwhelming the olive oil.
- Taste as you go along, until the vinaigrette has the balance of flavours you like.
- Have hot plates ready for serving the fish.

Simple bourride

Stir aïoli into concentrated fish poaching juices or a simple stew and you have bourride, one of the most glorious fish dishes you can make. The best white fish to use are cod and hake. For fish stews, choose any combination of sweet, firm-textured fish fillets, mussels, clams and shellfish such as large prawns and langoustines. The only thing to remember is never to add the aïoli to boiling liquid or over a direct heat or it will curdle. Stir it in off the heat and all will be fine. If you have no fish stock, make a simple vegetable stock by simmering water, finely chopped onion, carrot and celery, a chopped tomato and bay leaves for 15 minutes, then strain.

SERVES 4

4 thick cod steaks
approx 300ml/$\frac{1}{2}$ pint fish stock or simple vegetable stock
up to 150ml/$\frac{1}{4}$ pint aïoli (p 262), plus extra for serving
dry baked bread rounds for serving

Arrange the fish steaks in a shallow ovenproof dish into which they will just fit snugly. Pour in enough stock to come half way up the sides of the fish, cover loosely with aluminium foil and poach in a moderate oven, 180°C/350°F/Gas Mark 4, for 15–20 minutes or until just done – the flesh should look opaque and there will be beads of white curd beginning to appear on the surface. Do not overcook.

Strain off the cooking liquor into a wide pan and keep the fish warm in the dish while you finish the sauce. Boil down the liquor to about 150ml/$\frac{1}{4}$ pint, or until well flavoured and concentrated: this is important – the aim is to produce a richly flavoured sauce not a watery one. Take the pan off the heat and add the aïoli, a spoonful at a time, stirring it in until it dissolves; add until the sauce is creamy and the balance of flavours seems right. At this point, if the sauce has cooled too much, you can reheat it *very* gently, shaking the pan constantly just until the sauce is hot. Pour the sauce over the fish, mixing it in with any extra juices in the bottom of the dish, and tuck in the baked croutes. Serve immediately, on hot plates, with plain boiled potatoes that have been dried off in the oven for a few minutes first. Hand round extra aïoli at the table.

Brill with fennel or celery and mustard sauce

Brill is a relative of the turbot and tastes almost as good, with a sweet, fine flavour and creamy, slightly firm flesh. Think of it as cheap turbot rather than expensive plaice and you may be encouraged to buy it more often.

SERVES 2

1 whole brill, about 570g/1$\frac{1}{4}$lb, cleaned
150ml/$\frac{1}{4}$ pint white wine, cider or a mixture of dry vermouth and water
2 tablespoons finely chopped fennel bulb (use the stalks) or celery
1 tablespoon mild mustard, or to taste
a little cream or thick Greek-style yoghurt

Cut the tail off the brill, trim the fins with kitchen scissors, and lay it in a shallow oval ovenproof dish. Pour over the liquid and scatter the chopped fennel or celery on top. Bake in a moderate oven, 180°C/350°F/Gas Mark 4, for about 25 minutes, or until the fish is done and the juices are bubbling.

Strain the juices and vegetables into a wide pan. Bring to the boil and reduce slightly, then stir in mustard to taste. Finish with a little cream or thick yoghurt to taste. If you use yoghurt, move the pan away from the heat and don't let the sauce boil again. Season if necessary, pour the sauce over the fish and serve with saffron rice (p 130). If you do not like eating the fish skin, serve the sauce separately.

FISH ON A PLATTER
WITH ROASTED VEGETABLES

Suitable for whole fish or steaks, this is a crafty way to bake fish and turn it into a visual feast. The fish is placed on a dish and surrounded by piles of vegetables, then put in the oven to cook.

Because of their shape, skate wings are ideal. The best potatoes to use are salad potatoes, that is, creamy, waxy ones that do not break up. Leftover boiled potatoes are fine. The vegetables should be sliced fairly finely so that they cook in time.

SERVES 2

1 large skate wing, about 570–675g/1¼–1½lb
225–340g/8–12oz potatoes, cooked, peeled and sliced
1 large leek, shredded
1 large celery stick, shredded
55g/2oz hazelnuts, roasted or toasted
1–2 tablespoons chopped chives (optional)
olive oil

1 Rub the fish with olive oil on both sides and arrange in the centre of the tray.

2 Moisten the potatoes with olive oil and pile them in separate mounds around the fish.

3 Rub the skins off the hazelnuts as best you can – no need to be fussy – then crush or chop them coarsely and put into a bowl with the leek and celery. Moisten with 2 tablespoons of olive oil, then add salt to taste and some chopped chives if you have them. Mix well and distribute in 3–4 piles around the fish between the potatoes.

4 Bake in a moderately hot oven, 190°C/375°F/Gas Mark 5, for 20–25 minutes, or until the fish is done and the vegetables are beginning to brown.

Serve from the platter, letting people help themselves. Mayonnaise goes nicely with this dish.

Cod on a platter with sweetcorn, green peppers, chilli and potatoes

SERVES 2

2 large cod steaks
225–340g/8–12oz potatoes, cooked, peeled and sliced
110–170g/4–6oz cooked sweetcorn, either fresh from the cob or frozen/canned kernels
1 green pepper, seeded and sliced
1 fresh green chilli, seeded and chopped, or 1 teaspoon toasted chilli flakes
olive oil

Make in the same way as above. Bake as before, allowing 15–20 minutes or until creamy curds appear on top of the fish. Serve with mayonnaise.

Cod on a platter with shredded cabbage, bacon and potatoes

SERVES 2

2 large cod steaks
225–340g/8–12oz potatoes, cooked, peeled and sliced
110g/4oz green or white cabbage, finely shredded
55g/2oz thick bacon such as pancetta, diced
1 small onion, finely sliced
olive oil

Fry the diced bacon in its own fat in a small pan for 2–3 minutes until beginning to brown, then follow the recipe above.

ROAST MONKFISH ON A VEGETABLE BASE WITH GARLIC, SAFFRON AND CHILLI

This is a two-in-one dish, requiring no more than 5–10 minutes' work. Setting the fish on a bed of previously cooked vegetables gives you an instant accompaniment to serve with it. The fish is bathed in olive oil and aromatics, and the vegetables soak up the flavours from the fish. All you need is some rice and you have a complete meal. You can adapt the recipe to other thick, meaty chunks of fish and other flavour combinations. For some strange reason, the garlic does not show itself strongly, nor does it seem to have the usual lingering effect.

SERVES 2

450g/1lb monkfish, cut in a thick even piece, preferably from the centre

FOR THE MARINADE:

1 large clove garlic, finely chopped

$\frac{1}{2}$–1 mild or strong red chilli, seeded and finely shredded

$\frac{1}{2}$ packet of powdered saffron infused in 1 tablespoon Pernod, vermouth or white wine for 30 minutes

3 tablespoons olive oil

$\frac{1}{4}$ teaspoon salt, or to taste

FOR THE VEGETABLE BASE:

2 large leeks, fairly thickly sliced

1 red pepper, seeded and cut into strips

olive oil

1 Cut away the outside membrane of the monkfish (a sharp filleting knife is best for this).

2 Mix all the marinade ingredients together in a shallow bowl. Turn the monkfish in this, coating both sides. Leave for at least 1 hour or place in the fridge for up to 8 hours, turning the fish occasionally.

3 Meanwhile, simmer the leeks in a few tablespoons of water in a covered pan for about 15 minutes until soft. Set aside, in their liquid.

4 To assemble the dish, spread the leeks and their cooking juices over the base of a medium-sized shallow ovenproof dish – a Le Creuset oval gratin dish is ideal. Place the fish on top, spooning over the marinade. Make sure you add it all, and use your fingers to scrape out the dregs if necessary, drizzling them directly over the fish. Scatter the red pepper around the sides, and drizzle a little extra olive oil over the vegetables.

5 Put the dish into a cold oven, set to 400°F/200°C/Gas Mark 6, and cook for 20–25 minutes. When beads of white curd start to show on the surface of the fish, check it by inserting the point of a knife into the thickest part of the flesh by the bone. Alternatively, roast it in a preheated hot oven for 15–20 minutes.

To serve, cut away the 2 fillets of fish from either side of the bone and slice crossways into thick penny pieces, with a dollop of leek and pepper braise to the side.

Variations Add 1 tablespoon chopped fennel bulb to the marinade mixture. For a serious garlic dish, simmer whole unpeeled cloves of garlic in water until soft, around 15–20 minutes, and mix into the leek mixture. When the dish is cooked, squeeze the flesh from the garlic skins to spread over the fish at the table.

Roast monkfish with tomatoes and fennel

Fennel and monkfish are perfect partners; don't omit the fennel seeds, which add their own distinctive anise flavouring. If you have none, use chopped tarragon to taste instead.

SERVES 2

monkfish and marinade ingredients as opposite

FOR THE VEGETABLE BASE:

340–450g/12–16oz ripe tomatoes, cut into wedges

1 bulb of fennel, thinly sliced

1 small onion, thinly sliced

1 teaspoon fennel seeds

olive oil

Gently fry the fennel, onion and fennel seeds in a little olive oil for 5–10 minutes until soft. Mix with the tomatoes. Cook the dish as above, spreading the fennel and tomato mixture over the base of the ovenproof dish.

Coated fish

The idea of using couscous or similar grains like breadcrumbs to form a crispy coating that also protects the fish has been around for some time. As well as salmon, it is suitable for cod, haddock, hake and halibut and for dry, meaty fish such as tuna and swordfish. You can also vary the flavour of the couscous with herbs, pesto, spices, Tabasco, etc.

Cod in a polenta crust with spicy tomato sauce and fresh coriander

A straightforward recipe, using cod steaks and uncooked polenta, which forms a golden, extra-crisp crust.

Pour 7mm/$\frac{1}{4}$ inch polenta straight from the bag into a shallow bowl and season it. Remove the skin from the fish steaks and dip them first in beaten egg and then into the polenta. Pat on firmly on both sides and leave in the fridge until required. To cook, heat a little olive oil or a mixture of olive oil and butter in a heavy non-stick pan. Use a spatula to slide in the fish steaks. Depending on their thickness, cook over a moderate heat for 5–7 minutes on each side, until nicely crusted, adding a little extra oil or butter if necessary. The fish should cook steadily and the crust become browned a little – adjust the heat accordingly.

Serve with a simple tomato sauce (p 117) laced with slivers of chopped fresh red chilli or Tabasco or Jamaican hot pepper sauce to taste. Hand round a separate bowl of chopped fresh coriander to sprinkle on the fish and sauce.

POACHED SALMON

There is no finer dish in the world than a per-fectly poached silky-smooth salmon (or salmon trout), served with home-made mayonnaise, new potatoes and green salad. The salmon is best freshly cooked and should always be served slightly tepid or at room temperature, never chilled. Use a tail piece, a whole salmon trout or a small salmon. You can fiddle about and put lemon zest, tarragon, peppercorns, etc. into the cavity or cooking water if you like, but I think plain is best. It is important not to overcook the fish. It tastes best when moist and slightly underdone, still showing a rosy tint.

Clean the fish, making sure you remove any blood along the spine. Lay it on a sheet of aluminium foil, season generously with salt inside and out, then wrap tightly, crimping the edges of the foil well.

Lay the fish in a pan into which it will fit snugly, cover it completely with water and set over a moderate heat. Bring to just below boiling point – that is, when the water begins to shimmer; do not heat it to a rolling boil, as this may overcook the fish. Give it a minute or so, then take out the fish and leave to cool on a plate. By the time it has cooled, the fish will be perfectly cooked.

Open the foil and pour off any liquid (save this for making stock or soup). Either serve on a clean white plate in its silvery skin or remove the skin first. Garnish with greenery.

Comments

▪ A fish kettle is only necessary for large salmon; for tail pieces or small fish improvise with a large pan or casserole dish.

▪ Salting the fish overnight beforehand improves the flavour, and is useful to know if you need to keep the fish anyway. Sprinkle it with salt on both sides and leave on a plate covered with clingfilm. The next day, rinse briefly, wrap in foil and cook as above.

▪ Most recipes for poaching salmon by this method suggest leaving it to cool in the water. I find this unnecessary for salmon tails and fish smaller than, say, 1.8–2kg/4–5lb, for they cook more than I like – but you can do so if you prefer.

BAKING FISH IN A PARCEL

This is both clean, convenient and impressive, specially so for individual servings. First, a few general tips.

▪ It is better to make the wrapping too large and roomy than too small, when you will be unable to seal the edges easily.

▪ Always butter or oil the foil or paper, other-wise the fish will stick. If using oil, it is simpler to coat the outside of the fish than coat the paper.

▪ Include a little butter or oil and liquid – wine, citrus juice or chopped tomatoes – in the parcel to baste the fish and keep it moist.

▪ Crimp the edges of the parcel very tightly to prevent the juices oozing out. If using grease-proof paper, to make an effective seal use two sheets rather than one.

▪ For a quick and easy way to seal greaseproof paper packages, a tip from cookery writer Sybil Kapoor is to fasten the edges together with a stapler or paper clips.

▪ The fish continues to cook in its parcel and should be served straight away.

SEA BASS UNDER WRAPS

This recipe illustrates how to cook fish in a parcel. You can use the method for any whole fish, varying the aromatics and other ingredients to suit. For general remarks, see p 174 and opposite.

Sea bass is the king of fish, and one of the most expensive. Similar in appearance to salmon, with a shiny silvery coat and slim body, it has firm but soft-textured flesh and a delicate, sweet flavour. Only buy it when it looks absolutely fresh. The remarkable thing about it is that it will take both Eastern and Mediterranean flavours equally success-fully – in this recipe I have opted for Eastern influences, with shiitake mushrooms, ginger and soy sauce. Its success depends on using a sweet wine and judging the amount of soy sauce properly: the soaking liquor shouldn't taste heavily of soy but rather be nicely sea-soned with it. Thai soy sauce (p 277) is the best to use with fish. The mixture can also be used for oriental-style steamed fish.

SERVES 2

| 1 large sea bass, 675g/1½lb, cleaned |

FOR THE STUFFING:

| 4 dried shiitake mushrooms |
| 5–6 tablespoons sweet white wine |
| 3–4 spring onions, chopped |
| 1 tablespoon chopped chives |
| 1 tablespoon finely diced cucumber |
| 1.25cm/½ inch piece of peeled fresh ginger, cut into julienne strips |
| 1 clove garlic, sliced |

Plus

| 1–2 tablespoons light soy sauce, preferably Thai soy sauce or Japanese teriyaki |
| olive oil |

1 Soak the shiitake mushrooms in the wine for 10 minutes, then remove them, reserving the wine, and cut into strips. Mix the mush-rooms with the spring onions, chives, cucumber, ginger and garlic to make the stuffing.

2 Place a large sheet of aluminium foil or a double thickness of greaseproof paper in a shallow dish big enough to hold the fish or on a baking sheet. Rub the cleaned fish with olive oil and lay it in the centre of the foil or paper. Drizzle over a little extra olive oil.

3 Put some of the stuffing mixture in the cavity of the fish and scatter the rest over the top. Fold the paper around the fish, leaving a gap in the centre. Aluminium foil will crimp easily and hold its shape. If using greaseproof paper, fold the ends over the fish, draw up the sides and secure with paper clips, leaving a slit along the centre.

4 Flavour the wine with soy sauce to taste, pour over the fish and stuffing, then seal the paper or foil tightly.

5 Bake in a moderately hot oven, 190°C/375°F/Gas Mark 5, for about 25 minutes; open up the parcel and sneak a look after 20 minutes to check how it is doing and then reseal. Serve with plain rice and green salad – don't forget to recover all the delicious juices at the bottom of the parcel, spooning them over the fish.

To serve the fish, ease out the flesh by insert-ing a knife along the length of the backbone. The fillet will slide away easily. Turn the fish over and repeat.

Fishcakes

Fishcakes can be made from several different types of fish. They can also be varied by the addition of herbs and spices at the whim of the cook, though don't feel you have to use these. A traditional fishcake is one of those tried and tested combinations that is difficult to better. It is also fair to point out that, though easy enough to make, fishcakes take longer to prepare from scratch than most of the recipes in this book.

■ Fishcakes should be made from freshly cooked floury potatoes (p 104); waxy potatoes are not suitable. If you have no floury potatoes, use a general-purpose variety.

■ Fishcakes can be made from white fish, smoked fish, salmon, crab and canned fish such as tuna and sardines.

■ The fish should be lightly cooked. Poach smoked fish and white fish gently with milk to cover.

■ You need at least the same amount of fish as mashed potato.

■ Leftover fish is suitable.

■ You do not need to coat fishcakes in egg and breadcrumbs. They can be dusted with flour or rolled in uncooked polenta or matzo meal instead.

■ They can be any size you like but should be about 1.25–2.5cm/½–1 inch thick.

■ Fishcakes should be cooked briskly in hot oil, otherwise they become greasy. Shallow- or deep-fry them in a non-stick pan. Drain on kitchen paper before serving.

■ Serve with mayonnaise or plain or spicy tomato sauce.

Seasonings

On the whole, the more delicate the fish the more delicate the seasoning should be. That said, do not be frightened to try robust spices with plain or smoked cod or haddock.

Fishcakes are best with one or two extra flavourings; chopped capers and grated lemon zest for tuna fishcakes, for example; chopped parsley or dill and crushed green peppercorns for salmon; toasted cumin seeds and turmeric for haddock. It is wise to make up a tiny amount and taste first before adding the flavourings to the entire batch.

Reliable flavourings are:

Herbs Parsley, dill, coriander, chives, chopped spring onion.

Oriental flavourings Lemon grass, fresh chilli, crumbled kaffir lime leaf.

General seasonings Mustard, anchovy, tomato purée, capers, crushed peppercorns, finely grated Parmesan cheese, finely grated lemon or lime zest.

Spices Mild spice pastes, harissa, cumin, coriander, turmeric, powdered saffron.

■ Fishcakes made with smoked fish need no salt. For plain fish, add 1 teaspoon of anchovy essence. If you have no anchovy essence, mash 2 anchovy fillets to a pulp and add to the potato mixture. If you do not like anchovy or have none, season with salt to taste.

■ Smoked fish is best poached to remove some of the salt. Plain white fish can also be poached, while other fish, such as salmon, can be baked with dabs of butter, grilled, or cooked in a non-stick frying pan with a little butter.

■ Fishcakes soak up a fair amount of oil. If you prefer, you can reduce the amount.

Basic fishcakes

MAKES 6 LARGE OR ABOUT 12 SMALL FISHCAKES

generous 340–400g/12–14oz lightly smoked
haddock or cod

scant 450g/1lb floury potatoes, peeled and cut
into thick slices (this should give 285–340g/10–
12oz peeled weight)

about 300ml/$\frac{1}{2}$ pint milk, or milk and water
mixed for cooking the fish

1 egg, beaten

30g/1oz butter

2 tablespoons finely chopped parsley

flour, uncooked polenta, matzo meal, or 1
beaten egg, and dried breadcrumbs, for coating

vegetable oil, clarified butter (see p 39), or a
mixture of olive oil and vegetable oil for frying.

Put the fish flesh-side down in a pan and add
milk or milk and water mixed to cover. Set
over a low heat, bring to simmering point, then
remove from the heat. The fish should be
cooked; if not, cover and leave it in the hot
poaching liquid for a little longer. Drain, skin
and flake the fish, removing any bones.

Meanwhile, boil the potatoes until soft in
water or extra milk and water to cover. Drain
thoroughly and mash lightly with a potato
masher.

Mix the fish with the mashed potatoes, egg,
butter and parsley. Season with freshly ground
pepper. Flour your hands, divide the mixture
into equal portions and shape into flat, round
cakes. If coating with polenta, matzo meal or
egg and breadcrumbs (see right), do this now; if
dusting with flour, do this just before you cook
them.

Heat about 7mm/$\frac{1}{4}$ inch oil, clarified butter,
or oil and butter in a non-stick pan over a high
heat. Using a palette knife, transfer the fishcakes
to the pan and cook briskly for about 3–4
minutes on each side until brown and crisp.
Drain on kitchen paper and serve immediately.

Coating fishcakes

This is simple, but messy, and needs to be
done methodically.

In order of messiness:

Egg and breadcrumbs

You need two large shallow soup bowls,
arranged side by side, a palette knife and a
large plate to put the prepared fishcakes on.

Put a beaten egg in one soup bowl and a
deep layer of fine dried breadcrumbs in the
other. The trick is to try not to touch the
fishcakes with your hands, since this makes it
progressively messier and more difficult.

Using a fork, fish slice or palette knife, dip
the fishcake into the beaten egg, making sure
the top surface is coated with egg as well. Lift
out, draining off the excess egg, then transfer
to the bowl of breadcrumbs. Using a clean
palette knife – not the same one you used to
dip the fishcake into the egg – cover the
fishcake with breadcrumbs, pressing them on
firmly. Lift out and put on to a plate. Other
foods can be coated in the same way.

Polenta

This is simpler. Put a layer of uncooked
polenta in a shallow soup bowl or on a plate.
Using a palette knife, coat each fishcake with
a thin layer of polenta as above and transfer
to a clean plate. Use matzo meal in the same
way.

Flour

Put some flour on a plate. Just before you
want to cook the fishcakes, lightly flour your
hands and dip each fishcake into the flour,
patting off all the excess. Put on a clean plate
while you do the rest, then cook.

Other coatings

Fishcakes can also be coated with ground nuts
or sesame seeds. Brush with beaten egg first,
then press the coating into the fishcakes using
a palette knife.

Shellfish: a Brief Guide to Crustaceans and Molluscs

Crustaceans – prawns, langoustines (Dublin Bay prawns), lobster and crab – are truly delicious when fresh but not worth eating otherwise. Molluscs – mussels, clams, etc. – are generally cheap and easy to prepare. Their sweet juices taste of the sea and should always be used.

All crustaceans and molluscs, in fact, contain sugars and are naturally sweet-flavoured. All, too, are concentrated protein, with very little waste.

I do not have many blind spots but eating raw oysters is one. This section does not, therefore, include any notes on oysters.

BUYING AND STORING SHELLFISH

■ The quality of crustaceans and molluscs varies throughout the year. When buying crab or lobster, feel the weight: it should feel heavy for its size. Light specimens will contain little flesh and will not be of decent quality. If already cooked, ask the fishmonger to open up the crab or lobster and check this for you.

■ Mussels are cultivated under stringent controls and undergo purification before being sold, so they are perfectly safe to eat at any time of year.

■ Scallops should be pearly white and glistening with natural moisture; if possible, buy them in their shells. Off-white, grey or drab-looking scallops should be avoided. Large scallops make much better eating than queenie scallops. Though expensive, there is no waste and they can be sliced across into two or three pieces.

■ The best way to keep live crustaceans and molluscs is to put them in a sealed container, covered with a damp cloth or kitchen paper, and store them in the bottom of the fridge. They will keep for 1–2 days.

■ Lobster and crab are best to eat when they're allowed to cool after cooking and served at room temperature. Chilling dulls their flavour. The same is true for freshly cooked langoustines and prawns. Once cooked, lobster and crab keep for 1–2 days in the fridge; bring to room temperature before serving.

■ Most lobsters and crabs are bought ready boiled. Live lobster and crab are easy to cook but it is not a particularly pleasant task. Ask your fishmonger to cook them for you and, if possible, ask him not to chill them.

■ The dead man's fingers (feathery gills) of lobster and crab are easy to spot and even easier to remove. They are not poisonous, but are not for eating either.

■ Where possible, buy crustaceans in their shells. Use the shells to make stock and to add to soups (p 43).

Buying frozen shellfish

Frozen prawns are a fact of life and vary tremendously in quality. One exception is the large, uncooked frozen Asian tiger prawns, which I find consistently good. Otherwise buy the best you can afford. Shell-on prawns are better value, and the shells make excellent stock (see p 43).

Most frozen crab is truly awful. Though I am reliably informed that good-quality frozen scallops are available, many are left in water until bloated to twice their size before being frozen. Who'd be a scallop?

COOKING SHELLFISH

Crustaceans and molluscs bought from a reputable fishmonger and which smell and look good enough to eat are perfectly safe. Shellfish are scavengers and indiscriminate feeders so, as a matter of common sense, always remove the dark threads (intestines) from crustaceans and scallops before cooking and check that the mouth parts and stomach have been removed from crab and lobster. The shells of langoustines, crab and lobster are often dirty. Scrub these first if you intend using them for soups or stock.

All shellfish need only the briefest cooking over high heat: overcooking produces tough, rubbery flesh. Cooking times can be as little as 30–60 seconds for mussels and sliced scallops, and 1–2 minutes for raw prawns. Shellfish are cooked when they change colour, molluscs when the shells have opened.

Langoustines and prawns

Langoustines look like mini lobsters, have long front claws and are also known as Dublin Bay prawns. Freshly cooked, allowed to cool to room temperature, and served with mayonnaise they make a summer feast. To cook them, put them in a large pan of boiling salted water, bring back to the boil and cook steadily for 2–3 minutes. Drain and allow to cool. Remove the heads and take off the outside shells. Check, discarding any dark threads that run down the back of the flesh before eating. To get at the claw meat, use a crab pick or skewer. Save the shells for soup.

A favourite way to cook large raw prawns is to fry them for 4–5 minutes in a shallow heatproof dish with olive oil that has been flavoured with chopped garlic and a dried hot chilli. Eat from the dish with good bread to mop up the juices. They are also excellent barbecued for 4–6 minutes until the shells are crisp and served with aïoli.

Scallops

Scallops are all meat. To prepare, remove the membrane around the girth and the small piece of tough muscle (this is the bit that attaches the scallop to its shell). Slit open the coral with the point of a sharp knife and remove the dark vein. Scallops are unadulterated enjoyment, and the more simply you cook them the better.

Queenie scallops are not young or small scallops but a separate species. They are not as fine flavoured as large ones and are generally tougher. The best way to cook them is in the traditional style, gratinéed with garlic, cheese and breadcrumbs.

Though bought frozen scallops are not generally to be recommended, fresh scallops can be frozen at home more successfully than most fish. They lose their elusive sea-fresh sweetness but the texture remains firm and succulent.

Mussels and clams

For anyone who likes them, mussels represent outstanding value. Even if you are not keen, they are worth buying for their juices and the sweet sea flavour they give to fish soups and stews.

Mussels should be clamped tight when you buy them – too many open ones are a sign that they are not as fresh as they should be. The two best ways of cooking them are to steam them in a pan with a few extra flavourings, or to steam them open briefly, then spread them with a savoury butter / pesto / breadcrumb filling / ground nut paste and flash under a hot grill until the filling is browned.

To prepare mussels, see Spicy Thai-style Mussels on p 200. Clams are less familiar but are prepared and cooked in the same way. They are also served in chowders and fish stews and in Portugal are cooked with pork in casseroles.

Crab

Lobster has all the kudos, though crab if anything is the greater delicacy. You can also do more with crab – make soup, fishcakes, potted pastes – than you can with lobster.

Large crabs are better value than small ones since they contain proportionally more meat. A male crab has more white meat; he is the one with larger claws and a smaller tail flap on the underside of the belly. A freshly cooked crab you prepare for yourself is infinitely better than one bought ready-prepared. Crabs are best in May/June and September, when they will be full of juicy meat. In summer they have other things on their minds and in winter they hibernate. A crab yields about a quarter to a third of its weight in edible meat and a large crab, about 1.5kg/3$\frac{1}{4}$lb will feed 2 handsomely for tea.

Lobster

Imported Canadian Atlantic lobsters from Nova Scotia, available in good fishmongers and large supermarkets, are of excellent quality and make lobster an affordable luxury. They are generally available cooked and ready to eat. The problem here, as with any cooked lobster you buy, is that lobster flesh toughens so easily that unless it has been cooked with consummate care the meat is often a rubbery disappointment. For this reason, too, cooked dishes containing lobster, such as risottos, etc., are never particularly successful. Use the shells and roe to make shellfish bisque (p 43).

You can expect a quarter of the lobster's weight to be edible meat. A 450g/1lb lobster will serve one (though if you like lobster you will probably manage one twice this size).

SPICY THAI-STYLE MUSSELS

Mussels are cheap, cheerful and, once scrubbed, take just 2 minutes to cook. Throw them in a pan with a few flavouring ingredients and you've got yourself a first course to be proud of. This recipe gives the basic cooking method and you can use it to devise infinite ways of flavouring mussels. It's a good idea to serve crusty bread and to provide a bowl of water for your fingers.

As a general guide, 450g/1lb mussels will serve 2 as a first course.

450g/1lb mussels
3–4 spring onions, finely sliced
4–5 tablespoons dry white wine, fish stock or water
1 teaspoon Thai curry paste (mild or hot, as you prefer)
30g/1oz creamed coconut, diluted in 2 tablespoons boiling water
juice of 1 lemon
shredded basil leaves

1 Rinse the mussels in cold water. Scrub them and pull off the hairy beard poking out of the shell. Throw away any that do not close when you tap them. Store in the fridge until needed.

2 Pile the mussels into a wok or large frying pan, together with the spring onions and the liquid. (If you have no wine or fish stock, you could add a mean splash of nam pla or Thai soy sauce to the water.)

3 Cover the pan tightly and place over a high heat. Bring to the boil and cook for 2 minutes. In the meantime, mix the curry paste into the creamed coconut.

4 Lift off the lid: all the mussels should have opened. Discard any that remain firmly shut. Mix the flavoured coconut paste into the juices, adding lemon juice to taste (you will need a fair bit).

5 Divide the mussels between 2 hot soup plates, spooning the juices over them, scatter with basil and serve.

Mussels with tomatoes, saffron and cream

A hedonistic favourite. Cook the mussels as before, with 3–4 chopped ripe tomatoes, a little finely chopped onion or leek, chopped parsley and 4–5 tablespoons dry white wine or water mixed with $\frac{1}{2}$ packet of powdered saffron. Stir in single cream to taste and sprinkle with parsley.

Prawns with marmalade, lime and ginger

Raw tiger prawns have beautiful gossamer-blue shells and are available in most large supermarkets that have a decent fish counter. Despite the fact that they are frozen, they still taste good, with sweet and tender flesh. And they are good value: they come without heads, so you are only paying for the flesh. This recipe, meanwhile, is nothing like as startling as it sounds.

About 14 meaty prawns weighing 170g/6oz will feed 2 generously as a starter.

SERVES 2 AS A FIRST COURSE

12–14 large raw tiger prawns (about 170g/6oz), defrosted

1 dessertspoon clear marmalade, minus peel

1 teaspoon finely grated fresh ginger

juice of $\frac{1}{2}$ lime, or to taste

Wash the prawns briefly and pat dry. Snip off the legs and remove most of the shell – this comes away easily – leaving just a little shell on the tail so you can pick up the prawns and eat them with your fingers if you want. Remove any dark threads along the back of the prawns.

Mix together the marmalade and ginger and add lime juice to taste: it should be pleasantly sharp. Arrange the prawns in a shallow oven-proof dish and pour the sauce over. Either grill for 5–6 minutes or bake in a moderately hot oven, 190°C/375°F/Gas Mark 5, for 8–10 minutes or until the prawns are just opaque and the shell turns pink. Serve from the same dish, with a plain salad of bitter leaves.

Chicory and scallop salad with an orange jus

A simple festive starter with a sweet sauce. The orange sauce is Pierre Koffmann's, from his book, *La Tante Claire*.

SERVES 4

2 heads of white or red chicory

10 large scallops

about $\frac{1}{2}$ oz/15g butter

FOR THE ORANGE JUS:

150ml ($\frac{1}{4}$ pint) freshly squeezed strained orange juice (bottled is fine)

150ml ($\frac{1}{4}$ pint) double cream

2 tablespoons Grand Marnier

1 teaspoon finely chopped shallot

small nut of butter (7g/$\frac{1}{4}$ oz)

Put 4 plates to warm in the oven. Separate the chicory. Prepare the scallops by removing the membrane around the outside of each one, taking with it the tough piece of muscle on one side and the coral on the other, to leave you with a shining clean piece of scallop. Slice in half, pat dry and set aside. Using a sharp knife, tease out any black veins from the coral and set aside also.

Make the sauce: in a very small pan over a gentle heat, cook the shallot in the butter for about 5 minutes, until softened. Add the orange juice, cream and Grand Marnier and simmer gently for 5–7 minutes until just thick enough to coat the back of a spoon.

Heat up a non-stick or heavy frying pan. Arrange the salad leaves on the hot plates. Melt the butter in the frying pan and quickly brown the scallops and corals, giving them no more than 30 seconds on each side. Pile the scallops in the centre of the plates and drizzle the sauce over. Serve immediately.

Smoked Salmon

Smoked salmon has become *the* affordable luxury of modern times – the perfect ready-to-eat food which happens to be good for you, too. It is worth getting to know well.

BUYING SMOKED SALMON

The quality and flavour of smoked salmon varies considerably, and generally you get what you pay for. Wild smoked salmon is a more individual product but is not necessarily better: it all depends on the quality of the salmon and the skill of the smoker. Cheap smoked salmon should always be avoided.

- Smoked salmon should be plump and moist, not oily or flabby. It should be neither over salty nor over smoked. The best is moist and yielding, rich yet delicate, with a silky-smooth, melt-in-the-mouth texture and a natural fish flavour enhanced with an overlay of smoke.
- Colour is no indication of quality; usually the brighter it is, the more colouring it contains and the more inferior the quality.
- One of the best ways to buy smoked salmon is by mail order from specialist suppliers. The quality is guaranteed and the price generally compares favourably with retail shops and supermarkets.
- Smoked salmon varies enormously, from mild, buttery and subtly smoked to something approaching kippers. Check with the suppliers which kind they sell. Supermarkets tend to sell a middle-of-the road salmon.
- Though ready-sliced is convenient, a side of salmon is much better value and keeps far longer.

Storing smoked salmon

Smoked salmon should be kept chilled; store it, well wrapped, in the fridge.

Pre-cut sliced smoked salmon This deteriorates rapidly and should be eaten as soon as possible. To store, wrap tightly in greaseproof paper, then in clingfilm and use within 2–3 days.

Sides of salmon Once cut, these keep well for 7–10 days. Wrap tightly, folding over the skin first to make a parcel, then wrap completely in clingfilm.

Freezing smoked salmon

Smoked salmon freezes well for up to a month but deteriorates thereafter. Vacuum-packed salmon freezes perfectly for 2–3 months.

Slicing smoked salmon

There is nothing difficult about slicing smoked salmon, which is as soft as butter. Keep it chilled in the fridge and slice it just before you serve it. With your fingers, feel for the pin bones that run down the side and remove them with tweezers. Use a sharp fish filleting knife or a carving knife to cut wafer-thin slices at a shallow angle towards the tail. Take off what you need, rewrapping the remainder.

To make smoked salmon milder

- Most of the smoked flavour is on the outer surface of the salmon. If you find your smoked salmon too smoky, shave this off and you will find the flesh underneath much milder.

Serving smoked salmon

Serve smoked salmon slightly chilled; warmth makes it oily and sweaty. If you are serving smoked salmon on its own it should be cut in wafer-thin slices; if you use it in cooking, for example with pasta (p 52) it is better sliced more thickly.

The best way to serve smoked salmon The best way is the traditional way; on its own, in thin slices, as a first course with a few bitter salad leaves and the traditional sprig of watercress. A few refinements:

- Thinly sliced dark rye or pumpernickel bread is the best bread to accompany smoked salmon. Spread it with unsalted butter or leave un-buttered.
- Stronger/saltier smoked salmon benefits from a squeeze of lemon or (better) lime; milder, subtly smoked salmon is better without.
- For a first-class dressing, drizzle your best olive oil or good-quality lemon olive oil over the smoked salmon.
- Simple, sharp-tasting relishes go well with smoked salmon. Try a few plump capers, cucumber pickles or blanched julienne shreds of ginger moistened with sweet rice wine (mirin). Serve in tiny quantities on the side of the plate.

USES FOR SMOKED SALMON

There is much you can do with smoked salmon in the way of salads and tit-bits. Smoked salmon quiches and soups have their fans, though I am not one of them. With one or two honourable exceptions, heat brings out the worst in smoked salmon. If you are using it in cooked dishes, add it at the last moment. It mashes easily to a paste, so there is no need to use the food processor unless making large quantities. Generally, stronger-flavoured smoked salmon works best with other ingredients. Trimmings from mild smoked salmon can be disappointingly bland when mixed with cream cheese, etc. Use them as a luxury garnish for green salads instead.

Smoked salmon trimmings

Smoked salmon trimmings add instant luxury to canapés and salads, are easy to use, and stretch a long, long way. Whizz with soft cheese to make an instant pâté. Toss with buckwheat noodles and seasonings to make a pasta salad, or mix with scrambled eggs or baked potatoes.

Smoked salmon butter

Mash smoked salmon with an equal quantity of unsalted butter, or to taste, then season with lemon juice. Serve on toast, with soft-boiled eggs, asparagus or broccoli, or with hot boiled potatoes.

Smoked salmon parcels

Bite-sized parcels of smoked salmon can be stuffed with cottage cheese or other soft cheese flavoured with grated cucumber (salt lightly and squeeze out the juice first), chopped basil, dill, chives, tarragon, capers, gherkins or horseradish. Or wrap the salmon around teaspoons of rice salad dressed with lemon vinaigrette, or mashed or chopped avocado seasoned with lemon or lime juice, or a little finely chopped spring onion and fresh tomato.

Scrambled eggs and smoked salmon

A glorious mixture. The scrambled eggs must be barely set and remain very creamy, while the smoked salmon should be added at the last moment. Cut the salmon in small neat strips, about 7mm/$\frac{1}{4}$ inch wide and 2.5–4cm/1–1$\frac{1}{2}$ inches long. Make the scrambled eggs in the usual way and scatter the salmon over them. Pile on to fingers of toast, or place in a dish and tuck triangles of toast around; for canapés, use the scrambled eggs to fill hot cooked miniature pastry cases or squares of dry toast cut into fancy shapes.

Baked potatoes stuffed with smoked salmon

Make a slit in each baked potato, add a dollop of cream cheese/soured cream/fromage frais/thick Greek yoghurt, and top with diced salmon trimmings plus, if you like, chopped chives, dill or basil. For canapés, boil baby new potatoes, stuff them in the same way and eat with your fingers.

Smoked salmon and warm potato salad

Any combination of hot potato and cold salmon works brilliantly. Choose waxy salad potatoes with a good creamy texture, like Ratte or Belle de Fontenay. Arrange hot sliced potato over some salad leaves. Drizzle with your best olive oil and scatter smoked salmon trimmings over the top. Fried caraway seeds, a few capers, chopped chives or dill can also be added.

Fresh dates and smoked salmon

Stone the dates, stuff with a tiny blob of cream cheese and top with smoked salmon.

Smoked salmon tartare

This makes an elegant first course and is adapted from a recipe in Shaun Hill's *Gidleigh Park Cook Book*.

PER PERSON

55–85g/2–3oz smoked salmon
finely grated lime zest and juice to taste
about 1 teaspoon thick Greek-style yoghurt, sheep's milk for preference
a little chopped dill or mint (optional)
thinly sliced cucumber to serve

Slice the salmon into neat strips, about 7mm/$\frac{1}{4}$ inch wide, then cut them across into the smallest possible dice, being careful not to squash them. Mix lightly in a bowl with grated lime zest and juice to taste (it will take more than you think). Bind with a little plain Greek yoghurt; you can also add a hint of chopped dill or mint. Mound on individual plates and set in a garland of thinly sliced cucumber.

Variation Another way to serve this is to pack it lightly into individual ramekins and turn it out by placing each ramekin upside down on the centre of a large plate. Surround with a few endive and white chicory leaves, dressed with good olive oil. Scatter over a few capers if you like them, and a few toasted and crushed hazelnuts if you have some.

See also Pasta with Smoked Salmon, Crème Fraîche and Nutmeg, p 52.

Seaweed, Samphire and Laver

Seaweed has become sort of fashionable. It is full of vitamins and minerals, and particularly high in iron, which pleases nutritionists. However, its taste is generally strong, so it is not the kind of thing you tuck into every day. Its main attraction is its salty sea taste, which makes it good to serve with fish.

Dried seaweed

Dried seaweed can be bought in packets and needs to be rehydrated in water for 5 minutes before boiling. Most commonly associated with Japanese cookery, its use elsewhere is very limited, strictly for seaweed fans! Try placing fish on a bed of seaweed when steaming it, or adding a small piece of seaweed to fish stocks.

There are several kinds of dried seaweed available, such as kombu and dulse. Nori, which comes in thin sheets, is the most pleasant to eat. Toasted under the grill for a few seconds until crisp, it can be scattered over salads. Wakame is another mild-flavoured seaweed.

Laver

Laver, a common seaweed, is bought ready prepared, cooked to a dark green purée. A traditional Welsh speciality, it is commonly served with lamb, or mixed with oatmeal to make laverbread and fried in bacon fat for breakfast. Snap it up if you see it. It is fairly strong tasting and has a glutinous seaweed texture, which I find is too overpowering eaten on its own but which makes an excellent instant sauce for grilled or baked fish. You need very little. Add a spoonful to the cooking juices, season with orange juice or enrich with butter or cream, and the sauce is ready. It freezes well.

Samphire

Rock samphire is not a true seaweed but a small plant, found growing on rocky seashores along the South and West coast, particularly in Wales and East Anglia. Once a curiosity, it can now be bought from many good fishmongers in early summer. It looks like thin sea-green strands of succulent cacti, and has a delicious mild flavour with a pronounced salty tang. It needs to be bought fresh: look for bright green samphire and avoid any that is going slimy. Contrary to popular opinion it does not need cooking and is best eaten raw. Simply wash it, drain it and pick it over thoroughly, removing any slimy threads. Damp dry with kitchen paper, and keep it in a sealed box in the fridge. Use within 24 hours.

Serve samphire as an accompaniment to any fish or shellfish, or eat it on its own or scattered over salads. It can be steamed briefly for 30–60 seconds, and served with butter.

Samphire vinegar is one of the best vinegars you can make; pack samphire into good-quality wine vinegar and leave for 1–2 weeks before use. The samphire can be eaten as a pickled relish.

10

Meat and Chicken

Over recent years meat – especially red meat – has assumed less importance in the modern diet. We are eating fewer meat meals and even though meat may still be the traditional focal point of a meal, it is just as likely to play a secondary role – in stir-fries, for example, or in pasta sauces, and to bulk out vegetable dishes.

In recent times, too, the trend in meat cookery has been for dishes that are perceived as being quick and easy, using lean, ready-portioned meat. I feel that the time has come to redress the balance and return to 'proper' meat cookery, which is much simpler than most people imagine.

Where meat is concerned, I have come to realise that being 'choosy' is the crux of the matter. Everyone who cares about what they eat cares about how it is produced, and this is especially true with meat. There is no pleasure – or flavour – to be had from second-rate meat, or from meat produced in highly intensive ways. For this reason I have covered buying meat in some depth.

People also say we have lost the skills to cook meat, but I do not think this is true. Meat cookery is no more complicated than other forms of cooking. What has happened is that the quality of our meat has deteriorated. Recipes tend to ignore this fact and presume that you can get a tender, moist and delicious result irrespective of the meat you buy. This is not so. Add to this the modern trend of selling 'roasting', 'frying' or 'stewing' meat, with no indication as to which part of the animal it comes from, and it is all too easy to end up with a disappointing dish through no fault of your own. The answer is to take responsibility for your own meat. Meat remains incredibly good value. Whatever sort you choose, and whichever personal strategy for buying meat you settle on, apart from quality the important factors for success are choosing the right cut for the right dish and not being misled into believing that the leaner the meat, the better it will be. In reality the best meat is meat with the correct amount of fat.

Mike Richards, a traditional butcher with a lifetime's experience, has pointed out that many people, worried that they know nothing about meat, are too embarrassed to seek advice, or even to come into the shop, preferring to opt for the convenience and anonymity of supermarkets. A fair point. All I can say is, if this is you, please don't be. Every good butcher I have ever known has been delighted to offer assistance. Give yours a try next time and see.

TYPES OF MEAT

The manner in which animals are reared – animal husbandry – has a profound effect on their eating quality. Much publicity has been given to the unsavoury aspects of modern animal husbandry, but happily there are various alternatives available giving the consumer a much wider choice. These break down as follows:

'Real meat'

This is a term coined in the Eighties to describe meat that has come from animals raised in non-intensive ways. It includes three main groups: organically reared meat, conservation-grade meat and meat produced by the Real Meat Company. In all three, methods of husbandry, feed and medication are strictly controlled. The animals are raised outdoors and given natural feeds with no growth promoters or routine antibiotics. The result is high-quality meat with a fuller flavour. It may or may not be hung for longer than conventionally reared meat. Naturally, it costs more (up to 30 per cent), but is worth every penny.

Real meat can be bought from certain butchers, from shops selling organic produce and direct from the producers. The Real Meat Company has various shops throughout the UK. It also operates an overnight mail-order delivery service, Real Meat Express (p 282), which is worth taking advantage of.

In the UK a limited supply of 'real meat' is available in some supermarkets. Safeway sells organic beef, pork and chicken in many of its outlets. Sainsbury's sells organic beef and lamb in a few stores. Conservation-grade meat is sold in ASDA. See also UK Suppliers, p 282.

Traditional v. modern breeds

There are fundamental differences between traditional and modern breeds of animals raised for meat. The most important are that modern breeds concentrate on leanness and, because of the way they are reared, reach commercial weights far more quickly than traditional breeds. This means that while they are more tender, they do not attain the maturity of flavour that traditional breeds, which reach maturity more slowly, do. Modern breeds not only have less fat but that fat is not distributed evenly throughout the animal. Beef cattle, for example, are 18 months old before marbling fat is laid down. Traditional breeds are raised by small suppliers. For this reason, they tend to be reared by non-intensive feeds and are likely to have been raised on grass.

These differences are reflected in the eating quality of the meat. Meat from traditional breeds has a richer flavour – which you may or may not like – and is fattier. It is more succulent and has a closer grain and a coarser, 'meatier' texture. It feels firmer and tighter when raw, and generally is less sweet, soft, pappy or milky than modern breeds. If you value real meat flavour, you will like traditional breeds; if you prefer blander meat, you are likely to prefer modern breeds.

The best traditional breeds include Aberdeen Angus, Devon Red, Hereford, Galloways and Longhorn cattle; Tamworth and Gloucester Old Spot pigs; and Shetland and Scottish Black Face sheep. All chickens are modern breeds.

Unless stated otherwise, meat bought in supermarkets and from most butchers will be from modern breeds. (Angus beef, incidentally, is a modern cross-breed and not pure Aberdeen Angus.) In rural areas, where butchers sell locally raised meat, it may sometimes be from traditional breeds.

Free range

This is a term used for chickens and other poultry. Regrettably, the common perception that a free-range chicken has led a contented life pecking around the farmyard is false. Unless reared by a small producer and unless stated explicitly otherwise, all free-range chickens have been reared in highly intensive conditions. The only real difference between free-range and battery-reared chickens is that free-range ones are not kept in cages and are allowed access to the outside. This is why there is often very little difference in flavour between a free-range and other types of intensively reared chickens. The best chicken? Snap up an organic or 'real meat' chicken when you can.

Supermarket labels

'Traditional', 'Naturally reared', 'Farmhouse', 'Heritage', 'Nature's choice', 'Outdoor reared', 'Tenderlean', etc. are terms used by UK supermarkets to describe their premium-priced meat, produced to their own specifications of animal husbandry and welfare. The terms do *not* mean that the animals have been raised using organic or 'old-fashioned' methods of husbandry. However, they are often applied to meat that has been aged (usually in vacuum packaging) longer than other non-premium meat for sale in the store.

BUYING MEAT

Buying meat ought to be simple but it isn't. This is because you need to be more selective than with other major groups of food. The best way I have found is to buy meat in a piecemeal fashion. This may mean, for example, snapping up an authentic free-range chicken when you find a supplier and doing without chicken at other times; or buying certain kinds of meat in bulk and freezing it; or eating meat less in order to eat better meat more and so on.

Many people presume that the quality of meat depends solely on how it is produced, but this is not so. Aftercare – what happens to the meat once it has left the producer, how it is killed, butchered, hung and stored – is also vitally important.

Although it is easy enough to give basic guidelines on buying meat (see below), it is actually very difficult to tell the cooking and eating quality of meat simply by looking at it. High-quality meat depends on many inter-related factors. When buying meat, you are depending on the expertise of your supplier – which explains why choice of supplier is crucial.

Butchers

The secret to buying good meat is to find a butcher you can trust and then build a relationship with the shop and its staff. I appreciate that this takes time, but it is the best way I know of buying meat.

A good butcher will buy only good-quality meat, handle and condition it properly, hang it to your requirements, cut it exactly how you want it, and be happy to give advice on various cuts and how to cook them.

Not all butchers, however, are good. Butchers who care about their meat care about their customers and are enthusiastic. If you are unused to buying meat from a butcher, go first when the shop is quiet. Have a good look outside first and take your time. Then discuss what you'd like. If necessary, to save embarrassment, have a think while the butcher serves the next customer or come back later. Even after twenty years of buying meat from butchers, this is the strategy I follow every time and it has never failed me yet.

Q Guild butchers This is an association of independent butchers who operate their own high quality standards of hygiene, buying, butchery, hanging and sales service. They may or not sell 'real meat'. For their address, see p 282.

Hanging meat

All meat needs to be hung. This tenderises it, softening the muscle tissues, and develops the flavour, which becomes deeper and richer. During the process, the carcass may lose up to 10 per cent of its moisture (and therefore profit). Though matters are improving, the problem with the majority of modern meat is that it is not hung for nearly long enough. This applies to pork and chicken as well as to beef and lamb. All would be significantly improved if aged for the correct time. This is where your butcher comes in. Joints of meat hang as well as whole carcasses:* as long as the meat is hung at the correct temperature, with air circulating around, it is perfectly safe.

Though butchers hang meat in the traditional way, it is perhaps worth pointing out that to prevent moisture loss, most meat is now aged in vacuum-packaging, rather than hung on the hoof. The carcass is boned, cut into large sections, vacuum-packed and left in controlled temperatures to age.

Note also that although hanging improves all meat, it won't, as one leading butcher has remarked, make bad meat good. It will, however, make good meat superb.

Beef

Beef should be hung for a minimum of 10 days and preferably 2 weeks or longer. Between 2–3 weeks it develops its optimum rich, beefy flavour. It can be hung for longer, but the flavour generally does not improve any further, becoming slightly gamy. These times are based on my own experience for sirloin of beef, but correspond to accepted practice. The best butchers will hang sides of beef for 2–3 weeks or longer. Only prime cuts of beef are aged. See Beef, p 211.

Veal

Veal is generally sold fresh. It should be hung for up to 1 week and may be hung longer.

Lamb

Lamb should be hung for a minimum of 1 week. Anything up to 2 weeks is fine. Beyond this lamb does not improve and develops a mutton-like richness.

Pork

Pork is generally eaten fresh and is not usually hung for more than 2–3 days. However, it should be hung for 1 week. Hanging it for 7–10 days will improve the eating quality and help develop a proper pork flavour. Only prime cuts are aged.

Chicken

The old-fashioned practice of hanging whole chickens improves the flavour dramatically. A good butcher should be able to buy whole chickens and do this for you. They should be hung for a minimum of 1 week and anything from 1–2 weeks is fine.

Note You *cannot* hang an oven-ready chicken. They can be plucked but otherwise must be left whole and uneviscerated (as with game).

* The processes responsible for the tenderising and maturing of meat operate at microscopic levels, so size is not critical.

Supermarkets

Supermarkets take their meat seriously and offer a wide range of pre-prepared meat, of a quality consistent with their own standards. Marks and Spencer have a reputation for the highest standards. The larger the supermarket, the greater the choice will be and the higher the probability of the store having a fresh-meat counter where you can buy meat cut to order. The expertise varies. My impression is that meat bought from a supermarket is blander in flavour than that bought from a decent butcher. You tend to get what you pay for. As a general rule, pay extra and choose premium meats. Cooking instructions are often provided with the meat, though I find they cater for those who prefer well-cooked meat.

Buying direct from the producer

Many small producers offer delivery services or will sell their meat through mail order. As with butchers or supermarkets, you need to be choosy; though the meat itself is of the highest pedigree, farmers and small producers are not butchers: ask and check that the meat has been handled and conditioned properly, otherwise you may find the eating quality a disappointment. For two excellent supppliers of organic meat, see p 282.

STORING MEAT

Unlike fish, meat will store perfectly well for a few days in the fridge. Large pieces can be kept longer than small or thin pieces. A joint of meat can be kept for 4–5 days, or even a little longer. Minced meat and offal should be used as quickly as possible. All meat should be kept in the coldest part of the fridge. A few storage pointers:

- Unwrap meat as soon as you get home. Wipe dry and keep on a plate, covered with fresh clingfilm or aluminium foil.
- Check regularly and wipe off any blood which has collected on the plate with kitchen paper.
- The best way to store chops, steaks, small fillets such as tenderloin and escalopes is to seal both sides with olive oil, then cover loosely with clingfilm. This will protect the meat surfaces from oxidation and spoilage. Store pork and veal for up to 2–3 days, lamb and beef for up to 4–5 days. If you do not seal them first, use within 2–3 days. The exception is joints or pieces of chicken, which should be used within 1–2 days, or frozen instead.
- Raw meat contains bacteria. If they are allowed to come into contact with cooked meat, they may contaminate it, and unless the cooked meat is recooked to destroy the bacteria, this

Checklist

- Meat should look fresh, reasonably dry and recently cut, and smell sweetly of meat. Avoid dull, stale- or sweaty-looking meat or meat lying in pools of liquid. Fat should look firm, not oily or waxy.
- Ask how long the meat has been hung for.
- If in doubt, seek advice. Wherever possible, ask for the meat to be cut on the spot exactly to your requirements.
- Unless in special circumstances – for example, buying meat from a small producer – don't buy frozen meat. You cannot judge the quality.
- When buying roasting joints, order well in advance and get your butcher to hang the meat for you.
- Never buy cheap mince.
- When buying meat in bulk from a farm shop, etc., check to see if it can be vacuum-packed. If it can, it will keep better and freeze much more successfully.

can lead to food poisoning. For this reason, *never* let raw meat come into contact with cooked meat and *never* let meat blood drip on to other food in the fridge.

- When buying poultry, remove any bag of giblets, etc. from the cavity immediately and clean out the insides with kitchen paper.
- *Always* wash your hands before and after handling meat. Wash knives, chopping boards, etc. immediately. This is to prevent any possible bacterial contamination of other foods you may go on to prepare immediately after handling meat.

Freezing meat

Meat freezes better than any other category of food. It should be wrapped in heavy-duty freezer bags (or better, vacuum-packed first) and frozen as quickly as possible, using the fast-freezer. Beef and lamb will keep satisfactorily for up to 12 months. Pork, veal and poultry should be used within 6 months.

WHICH MEAT?

The important factors that contribute to the quality of meat are the breed of animal and how it was reared (expert butchers will tell you that what the animal has been fed on is more significant than the breed, grass being best); how long it has been hung for; and how lean or fatty the meat is. All are interrelated. An intensively reared animal that is sold fresh and is very lean is mere protein. It will have very little flavour and, frankly, is not worth eating. An animal that has been raised carefully, has been properly hung and has a correct covering and marbling of fat will exceed expectations and taste glorious. It is as simple as that.

Various cuts of meat are discussed elsewhere: see Roast Meat, pp 225–6; Slow Meat Cookery p 233; and Barbecuing and Char-grilling, pp 255–6. Here, I have confined myself to a few general remarks.

Beef

Beef is the richest-tasting meat. Because of its size, there is also more variation in the tenderness of different cuts than in other meats. Though not generally appreciated, only the prime cuts will be aged by hanging (either using the traditional method or by sealing in vacuum-packaging). Braising and stewing cuts are removed from the animal 2 days after slaughter and sold fresh.

The prime – that is, tender – cuts start halfway down the back through to the top part of the back leg. In order, these are wing rib, sirloin, fillet, rump, silverside, topside and thick flank, also known as top rump.

Braising and stewing cuts come from the rest of the animal. These are brisket and shin (front leg), neck, chuck and blade (shoulder), middle rib and fore rib (on the back, next to the shoulder; the wing rib joins the end of the fore-rib), thin flank or skirt (underbelly) and leg (back leg).

The best beef is that which has been fed on grass and is 2 years old. Most modern beef is killed at around 12–16 months; 18 months is reckoned to be the dividing line between beef which has and has not developed its proper flavour. A bright-red colour is not an indication of quality. Fresh beef will remain bright red for hours; aged beef will be burgundy instead and will dull quickly on cutting.

Though much depends on the age of the animal, the less tender cuts of beef need more cooking than other types of meat.

Veal

Though not traditionally a popular meat in the UK, humanely reared veal, being naturally tender and succulent, has much to commend it. It has a mild and sweet but positive flavour. It is also rich in natural gelatin, which once cooked yields delicious sauces. Being small, the joints are of a more manageable size than beef. All cuts are good.

The whiter the veal, the more you will not wish to hear about how it has been produced. Humanely reared English veal is stocked by most major supermarkets and will be a deep pink. The best veal is organically raised, though this is not generally available. It is usually sold at 3–4 months old.

Lamb

Lamb offers the best all-round value and is less intensively raised than either beef, pork or chicken. The flavour varies depending on the breed, where it was raised and its age. Hill or mountain lamb generally has the richest flavour. Lowland (and much supermarket) lamb is, I find, milder in flavour.

All lamb is tender and the whole animal is aged. The sweetest-flavoured joints – shoulder, neck chops, breast – have the highest fat content. Providing you have a freezer, half a lamb is excellent value, providing a good range of roasting and braising joints, and is not too much to cope with. A good time to buy half a lamb is during the summer. Spring lamb is highly prized but I find it overrated, with little flavour.

The younger the lamb, the paler the colour of the meat. Most lamb is sold between 4–9 months old; spring lamb is 3–4 months old. A lamb that is older than 9 months is called a hogget. Hardly any lamb is sold at more than 12 months old.

Lamb is a rich meat – which is to say that you can eat less lamb than other meats.

Pork

Pork is the cheapest meat and has suffered most as a consequence. Along with chicken, it has been subjected to the most intensive farming methods, with the result that the majority of modern pork is very lean, with a bland, sickly flavour and a dry, uninteresting texture. Real pork is much better; organic pork from a recognised old-fashioned breed the best.

There are more misconceptions about pork than about other meats. Contrary to popular opinion, all cuts are relatively tender and nearly all can be grilled or roasted. Like lamb, the most flavoursome cuts have the most fat, but remember that this is relative. Pork is no longer a fatty meat; indeed most cuts are leaner than chicken (one of the prime reasons why today's pork has become so tasteless).

Most pork is around $3\frac{1}{2}$ months old. Real and organically raised pork will be a month or so older. It is generally sold fresh. If hung at all, like beef, only the prime cuts of pork will be aged: the loin, chump and back leg. Belly and shoulder pork (blade and spare ribs) will not be aged. Pork should always look fresh and glistening.

Salt brings out and improves the flavour of pork more than it does other meats. Rubbing coarse salt over a joint of pork 8–24 hours before cooking, then rinsing it off thoroughly, or submerging the pork in brine (30g/1oz salt per 600ml/1 pint of water) is a good tip to know if you fear your pork might lack flavour. Pork rind and pig's trotters are invaluable as additions to stews and daubes, and to cook with dried beans.

The traditional view, which every cookbook tends to restate, that pork needs to be well cooked, is, in fact, no longer relevant. In earlier times pork was well cooked to safeguard against the possibility that it may have been infected with a small tapeworm (*Taenia soleum*). There is no chance of this occurring in modern pork and no case has been reported for decades. A different kind of worm infestation (trichonella) sometimes occurs in foreign pork: again, British pork has a clean bill of health. Trichonella is also killed at a temperature of 58°C/130°F, far below that which most pork is cooked to.

The usual recommended cooking temperatures for pork, around 75°C/170°F, are unnecessarily high. Lean, tender joints of pork in particular become dry and tough when well cooked: try cooking them less so that they remain a little pink and they will stay tender.

Chicken

Chicken is by far the most popular meat sold in the UK. Ironically, it is more difficult to buy a decent chicken than any other kind of meat. As, I explained on p 208 a free-range label is no guarantee of either caring farming or flavour. Like pork, most modern chicken is bland and lean to a fault. The two simple ways to improve such a chicken are to cook it with the skin on (where the fat will baste the meat and add some flavour) and to poach it in chicken stock, which will also add flavour.

Jointing a chicken is very easy (see diagram). Chicken joints should be eaten as soon as possible; whole chickens can be kept for 2–3 days in a cold fridge. The carcass can be made into stock (pp 40–1).

The modern chicken is very young and tender. Most birds are killed at 7–8 weeks old. Proper free-range chickens will be killed at around 10 weeks old. If you want to buy a real free-range chicken but have no local supplier or butcher, the Landais chickens from France, available at Tesco, are your next best bet.

Breast meat takes about half as long as leg meat to cook and quickly becomes dry when overcooked. For this reason, when making chicken casseroles, etc. with joints of chicken, it is a good idea to remove the breast meat when it is done, returning it to the dish to reheat once the legs are ready. This also explains why roasting a chicken is always a compromise.

Maize-fed chickens These are not superior chickens, nor do they have a better flavour. Unless specifically stated otherwise, they are intensively reared birds with a yellow colour due to the presence of corn in their feed.

Poussins These are baby chickens around 4 weeks old. They are intensively reared.

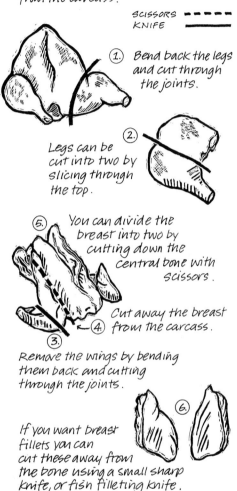

Use a sharp heavy knife to cut through the leg joints; these can also be bent back and the joint will break naturally.
Use stout serrated kitchen scissors, or poultry scissors to cut away the breast from the carcass.

SCISSORS ▬ ▬ ▬ ▬
KNIFE ━━━━

1. Bend back the legs and cut through the joints.

2.

Legs can be cut into two by slicing through the top.

5. You can divide the breast into two by cutting down the central bone with scissors.

Cut away the breast from the carcass.

3. 4.

Remove the wings by bending them back and cutting through the joints.

6.

If you want breast fillets you can cut these away from the bone using a small sharp knife, or fish filleting knife.

Cooking Meat

If you have taken the trouble to buy good meat, then it is wise to cook it extremely simply, in ways that bring out the best of its flavour. The methods that do this supremely well are frying, barbecuing/char-grilling and roasting for tender meat; pot roasts/braises for medium-tough meat; and slow casseroles/daubes for very tough meat. All require minimum effort and preparation by the cook, yet give superb results.

The aim in meat cookery is to produce meat that is tender, succulent and full of flavour. This means hanging on to the tenderness and getting rid of the toughness. As with cooking fish, controlling the heat is the key. Fat, or lack of it, is the other significant factor. Otherwise, the general rules are very few.

Tenderness v. toughness

Meat is either tender or tough. *How* tender or *how* tough determines the ways it may be cooked and depends on three interrelated factors: the amount of collagen in the connective tissue, how young (tender) or old (tough) the animal was when it was killed and how long the meat has been hung for.

Collagen This is a protein found throughout all meat that helps to hold muscles together and to give them their strength and structure. Generally referred to as connective tissue, it can take many forms and ranges from the thin, silvery skin which surrounds certain muscles, to the grainy structure of certain cuts, such as silverside, and muscle tendons and gristle.

The more collagen or connective tissue present, the naturally tougher the meat. Collagen dissolves during cooking to form gelatine.

This is why tough cuts of meat produce the richest dishes. Young animals contain 'soft' collagen, which breaks down easily. The older the animal, the tougher the collagen becomes and the longer it takes to break down.

In practice, tender cuts of meat, which contain the least collagen, can be cooked rapidly. Tough cuts of meat, which contain more collagen, need prolonged cooking to dissolve it.

Any cut of meat can be made more tender by stripping away the connective tissue. This is why trimming meat is important if you are cooking it by fast or relatively fast methods.

Muscle activity The more a muscle has to work, the tougher it becomes. Tough cuts of meat therefore come from those parts of the animal, such as the neck (which has to hold the head), shoulder or front legs, which bear the brunt of the work. The back and rump of the animal do the least work and so contain the tenderest meat. Note that each muscle, too, has its own degree of tenderness. This is one of the main reasons why joints of meat, which often contain a collection of muscles, do not cook evenly; and why the 'eye' of a chop is considerably more tender than the tail.

Hanging meat As discussed on p 209, hanging meat breaks down some of the proteins in the muscle fibres, making them softer and more tender. The longer the meat has been hung, the more tender it will be.

The aim, obviously, is to get meat that is tender, succulent and full of flavour. Here, a cook is faced with several choices.

How to tell when meat is cooked: the tender trap

Meat goes through various stages when you cook it. Tender meat will remain tender until it is well cooked, when it becomes dry. If you add moisture and cook it longer, it will become more tender again. Finally, it will disintegrate. Tough meat requires prolonged cooking first with moisture before it becomes tender. It, too, will eventually disintegrate, though this will take longer. Put simply:

tender meat – tender – tough – tender – rags;

tough meat – tough – tender – rags.

Judging when meat is tender is therefore a question of stopping the cooking at the right time. The best way to tell this is by sight and feel for tender meat and by taste for tough meat.

Lean, tender meat This is cooked when it is pink throughout. The flesh is softly firm and juicy. Note that rare cooked meat is not as tender as pink meat. The flesh is softer but somehow slightly more 'slimy' or resilient. Overcooked tender meat is dry. The flesh is firm, more like cardboard. See also How to Tell When Meat is Done, p 257.

Tough meat Because tenderness varies from one piece of meat to another, the only way to tell when a tough piece of meat is cooked is to cut off a piece and taste it. Tough meat is naturally chewy; how chewy you like your meat is a matter of preference. A tough piece of meat is cooked when the meat feels tender to the taste but is still firm. It will be parting away from the bone and can either be cut into pieces easily with a knife (medium-tough meat) or will break easily into pieces with a fork (very tough meat).

Both tender and tough meat, if cooked too long, will turn literally to 'rags'. The meat fibres separate into strands, or dissolve into a mush, and the texture becomes soft and pappy.

Cooking temperatures

This is one of the most confusing areas of meat cookery. The theory that meat needs to be cooked at a particular temperature for a particular amount of time, or that there is one correct temperature for roasting, etc., is not true. Apart from the two extremes listed below, meat is far better tempered than most people imagine and can be cooked successfully in a wide range of temperatures. Furthermore, because each piece of meat will vary in tenderness, it is impossible to give exact cooking times. For more information on cooking temperatures see also Calculating the Cooking Time, pp 221–2, and Meat Thermometers, p 224.

- The only meat you can accurately predict cooking times for is small, lean, uniformly tender cuts such as tenderloin or fillet. The meat needs to be of the same thickness and from the same muscle.

- All cuts of meat, tender or tough, can be cooked at very low–moderate temperatures.

- Only tender cuts of meat can be cooked at high temperatures.

- Tough and very tough cuts of meat must be cooked at low temperatures.

- Timing is never critical for meat cooked at very low temperatures and it can be kept for a considerable time without spoiling.

How to get tender meat

There are three ways to get tender meat: by choosing a tender cut, by long, gentle cooking and by methods of cutting the meat.

The cut Tender cuts of meat are generally the leanest cuts. They should be cooked briefly and will be at their optimum tenderness and juiciness when pink. Cooked too much, they become dry and firmer and, because of this, will seem tougher to eat.

Note also that tender cuts of meat can either be cooked rapidly over a high heat or be poached very gently, and give the same succulent results.

Medium-tender cuts of meat are better cooked more gently with a little added moisture.

Long, gentle cooking Any medium-tough or tough cut of meat will become tender if given enough time. Because you need to cook the meat for a long time, it will need extra liquid to stop it drying out. If you want to use a small amount of liquid, the meat will need to be cooked in a sealed pot. If you use a large amount of liquid, the meat can be cooked uncovered.

Tough cuts can be divided into two broad groups:

- Medium-tough cuts – these are any cuts described as 'braising' or 'casseroling' meat. They take around $1\frac{1}{2}$–$2\frac{1}{2}$ hours to cook.
- Very tough cuts – these are any cuts described as 'stewing meat'. They are best cooked as slowly as you can, for 3–4 hours or longer, but depending on the kind of meat can take around $2\frac{1}{2}$ hours.

Cutting The way you cut (and carve) meat affects its perceived tenderness and texture. A very thick steak, for example, will have a different feel from a very thin one. Pot-roasting/braising cuts, if trimmed of all connective tissue and cut into thin strips the correct way, against the grain, can be stir-fried briefly and will be tender.

How to get succulent meat

Two factors contribute towards succulence in meat: fat and moisture.

Fat You can either choose meat with the correct amount of fat or add fat. This latter can take the form of cooking chicken in its skin or adding extra fat when roasting or braising, which will baste the meat.

Moisture Meat is 75 per cent moisture. When it is cooked, the moisture is progressively expelled from the meat. This is why tender cuts of meat should not be overcooked: the longer you cook meat, the more moisture is lost. This is also why tough cuts of meat need to be 'wet' cooked, with added moisture.

To summarise:

- **tender meat** – do not overcook;
- **tough meat** – cook with added moisture.

Flavoursome meat

The simplest and yet at the same time most difficult thing to achieve is meat that is full of flavour. It has very little to do with the way you cook the meat and everything to do with the meat's quality.

- Buy good-quality meat that has been aged to develop its flavour.
- If you are unsure of the quality of the meat, choose naturally fattier or tougher cuts. These have more flavour than lean meat.
- Add fat. Ideally, this should be the same fat as the meat you are cooking – that is, beef fat if cooking beef – because this carries the essential flavour of the meat and will impart extra flavour to it. Otherwise use pork rind to cover the meat. Clarified butter is a good fat to use for choice tender cuts and imparts its own flavour; or use a mixture of butter and mild olive oil.

Meat fat

Sadly, meat fat has suffered an unwarranted bad press: the notion that meat fat is wholly bad for you is not true. There is far more saturated fat, for example, in convenience foods than there is in meat. Learn not to fear fat, but make it work for you, and the quality and flavour of every meat dish you make will instantly improve.

■ Less than half the fat in meat is saturated – lamb fat contains the most (52 per cent). The remaining fat is, like olive oil, predominantly mono-unsaturated, recognised as a healthy fat.

■ Marbling fat – the fat found within the lean tissues of the meat – has a higher proportion of poly-unsaturated fats than visible fat.

■ Fat is responsible for the flavour of a particular meat. It also has an appetising effect, being responsible for initiating the flow of gastric juices.

■ Without fat, meat is less tender and less succulent. In particular, 'marbling' fat provides internal basting. Only a small amount of fat is needed. Beef, for example, requires 3 per cent marbling fat to give it sufficient flavour and succulence.

The best way to deal with fat is to harness its flavour-enhancing and succulent qualities until it has done its job and then to remove it before serving. When cooking meat:

■ Cut off obvious excess fat from the joint and use a non-stick frying pan to seal meat.

■ Religiously skim off any fat from the surface of meat casseroles and sauces before serving: for how to do this see Mopping Up Fat, p 39.

■ Cut off the remaining visible fat when you eat the meat. An exception to this is the crispy fat on the outside of roast meat. Nothing is more delicious or makes a finer accompaniment to the meat itself.

Marinades

Another vexed subject. Recipes often advise you to marinate meat beforehand, believing that it will help to tenderise the meat. In fact, this is rarely the case.

■ Marinades – for example, wine and olive oil mixtures – alter the flavour of the meat but they do not 'tenderise' it. For the flavour of the wine to permeate the meat, it should be marinated for 8 hours or more.

■ Acid ingredients such as vinegar and citrus will tenderise meat but they have no effect on connective tissue. They do this by causing the protein in the meat to absorb water and swell, thus making it more tender. However, you need a fairly concentrated acid solution and the meat needs to be in contact with it for a reasonable length of time. Though the surface of the meat will be tenderised, the inside will not.

■ Certain plant enzymes can tenderise meat, breaking down both the muscles and the connective tissue. The best known is papain, found in fresh pineapple and papaya. Again, only the surfaces which come into contact with the enzyme are affected. The enzymes are really only effective when you cook the meat. Tinned pineapple does not have this effect, as the enzyme is destroyed during canning.

See also Barbecuing and Char-grilling, p 254.

Seaming

Seaming is the continental method of butchery: here the joints are cut so that they comprise the same muscle instead of several different muscles. This helps to ensure that the meat will cook evenly. You can do this yourself at home – when making lamb kebabs, for example, from leg of lamb – by separating each muscle out, trimming off the silvery skin and cutting it into cubes. Each piece of meat will then be uniformly tender.

Roast Meat

Roasting meat has a primitive simplicity. It takes 30 seconds to put a joint into the oven and 30 seconds to take it out. The knack, and it is the only knack, is learning to judge when the meat is cooked to your idea of perfection. This is achieved by a combination of basic science and common sense. The look and the smell of a joint of meat as it roasts, for example, will help to tell you when it is ready, and are as important as calculating so many minutes to the pound, meat thermometers or other such devices.

Obviously, to get a decent roast out of the oven, you need to have put a decent one in. Whatever the label may say, only tender prime cuts of meat are suitable for roasting. You then need to look at the joint, for its shape and thickness affect how long it will take to cook as much as its weight. Once the meat is out of the oven, it needs to relax. None of this is difficult, but it makes the difference between success and failure. In the end, roasting meat comes down to experience – keep your own notebook and you will become an expert in a very short time.

Roast meat is, without doubt, the crowning glory of meat cookery. Even with all the trimmings, it is a lot more straightforward to prepare than cookery writers often suggest and certainly more so than many modern meat recipes. And you don't have to cook for large numbers to enjoy the occasional roast joint.

If you are unused to roasting meat, start with the easiest, which is pork. Then, despite its awkward shape, a half leg of lamb is excellent value and another good choice, while my favourite joint for 2 is loin or best end of lamb. What I wouldn't do is go for a large or expensive joint, a second-grade joint of beef or anything that is more risky to roast, until you have gained a little experience and confidence.

. . . .

On or off the bone?

There is much debate about whether or not meat is better roasted on the bone; I find it is, and always roast classic joints on the bone. A few points to bear in mind:

- Boned and rolled joints give the appearance of being convenient but are not necessarily better value or easier to cook. This is because most of them comprise different muscles, some of which are less tender and therefore roast less well.
- There is *no* need to have joints on the bone chined to break the bone away from the meat when buying sirloin or rib of beef, or loin of lamb or pork. Chining cuts into the meat and this means it may not cook evenly. Much better is to leave the meat on the bone and then remove it once cooked, before carving.
- Bone-in joints support themselves, so you don't have to worry about tying the joint to prevent it falling apart when you carve.
- When cooking meat on the bone, arrange it bone-side down in the roasting dish, leaving the fat side uppermost. There is little practical difference in cooking times for most joints between meat cooked on the bone or boned joints. This is because bone is a very good conductor of heat. An exception to this, I find, is sirloin or rib of beef, where there is a large amount of bone. Joints on the bone that are appreciably thinner than their equivalent boned-and-rolled joints are also likely to cook a little more quickly.

Buying and choosing meat

Only the best cuts of meat should be roasted (see p 225). If you want the best flavour, the meat should be aged properly and have a good covering of fat.

■ Contrary to popular wisdom, small joints can be roasted just as successfully as large ones. However, larger joints make economic sense even when cooking for 2. Many, for example, can be divided up at home to provide 2–3 different cuts, which can be cooked separately. Roast meat is also excellent either cold or recooked.

PREPARING THE ROAST

The meat should be brought to room temperature to ensure it roasts evenly. Allow 1–2 hours for this.

■ Other than removing surplus fat, a roast joint needs no preparation, especially if cooked on the bone. Other ingredients – slivers of garlic pushed into the meat or stuffings – are purely optional.

■ Meat contains ample natural salt, so it is not necessary to salt it first. Whether or not you pepper it is up to you. The exceptions are pork and chicken because salt enhances their flavour.

Weighing

Weighing the joint is important to give you a rough guide to how long it will take to cook: see Calculating the Cooking Time, p 221.

······· Tips ·······

■ The shape and thickness of a joint will affect how long it takes to cook as much as its weight: a thick piece of meat will take longer than a slim piece. For a joint to reach the same degree of doneness throughout, the meat should be of even thickness. This is why awkward-shaped joints like leg of lamb will always cook unevenly, no matter what temperature the oven or which method of cooking you use.

■ Small joints of meat are relatively quicker to cook than large joints. In their turn, large joints hold their heat longer and continue cooking out of the oven longer.

■ Stuffed joints take longer to cook than unstuffed joints: Allow an extra 5–10 minutes per 450g/1lb.

■ If put in the roasting dish, potatoes and other vegetables get in the way. They soak up the juices that collect there and so are better roasted separately, using some of the meat fat from the pan.

■ Remember that meat continues to cook when it comes out of the oven. Depending on the size of the joint, the internal temperature will rise by up to 2–3°C/5–7°F, and the meat continue to cook at any internal temperature above 50°C/122°F. For this reason, if you prefer pink meat, it is always better to take the joint out of the oven 5–10 minutes sooner rather than later.

COOKING THE ROAST

It doesn't matter what temperature or combination of temperatures you roast meat at: see Which Cooking Temperature?, opposite.

········ **Checklist** ········

■ It is up to you whether you set the joint on a trivet. Doing so allows air to circulate around the joint and prevents its bottom part from coming into contact with the hot fat, but it will cook just as well without.

■ You can roast meat in any heatproof dish. Choose one that can be used on top of the stove, so that you can boil up the meat residues and make the gravy in it.

■ You do not need to sear meat first in a hot oven for it to roast successfully. Meat will become brown during the cooking process, even at moderate temperatures.

■ To roast all meat apart from lamb – which is naturally fatty – successfully, it is important to use a little fat. If the joint has a covering of fat, no extra will be needed. If the joint is very lean, cover it with a piece of beef suet (if beef) or pork rind or a layer of pork fat. This will not make the meat fatty, or make it taste fatty, but it will help prevent the joint becoming dry.

■ Though not necessary, basting the meat with the fat that collects in the roasting dish is a good idea. It adds flavour to the outside of the meat and creates a temporary barrier, preventing excess moisture loss and thereby helping the meat to remain succulent.

■ Do not cover the joint with foil, as this has the effect of steaming meat.

■ When cooking pork, remove the rind first and cook it separately if you want crisp crackling: see p 231.

Resting the joint

Letting the meat rest when it comes out of the oven is essential and evens out the temperature throughout the joint. The meat fibres become less taut. The joint thus becomes moister and seems more tender when you eat it. It also becomes easier to carve.

You do not need to let the meat rest for long or to let different meats or sizes of joints rest for any given time.

■ Lamb is best eaten hot, on hot plates, because its fat congeals quickly. A small loin of lamb needs only a brief rest, around 5 minutes.

■ Joints need only 10–15 minutes' resting time. Moderate-sized joints will remain warm for 30 minutes or so. Large joints can be left for up to an hour. Though it is often recommended, I find covering the joint loosely with aluminium foil is never necessary.

■ Let the joint rest in a warm place on a warm carving dish or meat board. The kitchen is usually warm enough, especially for meat that is to be eaten soon. Be careful not to leave it in too warm a place or this will cook the joint further. Leaving it in the turned-off oven is often suggested. Be careful as the residual heat may cook the joint further. Make sure the door is opened first, check that the inside feels no more than comfortably warm and leave the door ajar.

Resting grilled or fried meat, incidentally, in a warm place or very low oven has a similar effect, and is good practice also.

The A–Z of Roasting a Joint

This is the nitty-gritty bit. Roasting meat well revolves around temperature, timing and judgement and are as easy to grasp as ABC.

Which cooking temperature?

This is the most perplexing aspect of roasting meat. The truth is that meat can be roasted equally successfully at a range of temperatures and roasts perfectly well from either a hot or a cold start (p 14). Similarly, it doesn't matter if you roast at a high or a moderate heat, or a combination of the two. Comparative cooking charts are given on p 223. In brief:

■ Only the most tender prime cuts are suited to high-temperature roasting.

■ All roasting joints can be cooked at a combination of high heat to brown the outsides and moderate heat to complete the cooking.

■ All roasting joints can be roasted at a moderate heat throughout.

■ Less tender roasting cuts, or very large joints, should be roasted more slowly.

■ There is no advantage in cooking either pork or veal at high temperatures. Both are best roasted gently, 170–180°C/325°F–350°F/Gas Mark 3–4.

So, which temperature you choose is primarily a matter of personal preference and convenience. The most common variations are:

High-temperature roast Here the meat is cooked at very high temperatures, 210–230°C/425–475°F/Gas Mark 7–9, for the shortest time possible. My feeling is that there is little advantage in cooking meat above 210°C/425°F/Gas Mark 7.

This is suitable only for sirloin, rib and fillet of beef, and loin of lamb. It produces a good crust, rich caramelised surfaces and crisp fat, but also a thin layer of well-cooked meat next to the skin. Timing for high-temperature roasts is critical.

The fat spits more in high-temperature roasts and tends to burn. Be careful when you open the oven door or take out the roasting dish.

Combination-temperature roast This is the method most commonly used; it is suitable for all meat and poultry. The meat is started in a very hot oven, 210–230°C/425–475°F/Gas Mark 7–9, to sear and brown and enable the fat to start melting quickly. After 15 minutes, once the meat has started to brown, the temperature is reduced and cooking completed at the reduced temperature. Beef and lamb are reduced either to 200°C/400°F/Gas Mark 6 or 180°C/350°F/Gas Mark 4. Pork and veal are reduced to 180°C/350°F/Gas Mark 4.

Moderate-temperature roast Here the meat is cooked at 180°C/350°F/Gas Mark 4 throughout. The method is suitable for all meats and all joints, and is the one recommended by the Meat and Lifestock Commission, who find it produces less shrinkage and will also result in a well-browned joint.

Calculating the cooking time

Roasting times are generally given as x minutes per 450g/1lb of meat, plus (usually) x minutes over. By and large, these correspond reasonably well to actual cooking times. The calculations are based on set temperatures, so if you cook a joint at a lower temperature it will need more minutes per pound than if you cook if at a higher temperature. Watch out for this when reading recipes, as different authors give different versions.

The main exceptions are very small joints of meat, such as loin of lamb or fillet of beef. Here, the x minutes per 450g/1lb formula is irrelevant and what matter are the thickness of the eye of the meat and the overall depth of the joint. Irrespective of the weight, for example, depending on the thickness, in a hot oven a loin of lamb takes 20–30 minutes to cook and fillet of beef 25–35 minutes. I also find loin of pork takes around 50 minutes–1 hour to cook in a moderate oven.

Looking back through my roasting notes the times I use are as follows:

Roast beef 15 minutes per 450g/1lb, plus 10–15 minutes if necessary. This is for pink beef, either sirloin or rib, cooked on the bone in a hot oven, around 210°C/425°F/Gas Mark 7.

Roast veal and roast pork 25–30 minutes per 450g/1lb meat, plus 15–30 minutes if necessary. This is for cooked but not overcooked veal or pork, on or off the bone, cooked in a moderate oven, either 180°C/350°F/Gas Mark 4 or 170°C/325°F/Gas Mark 3 respectively.

Roast lamb 15 minutes per 450g/1lb, plus 10–15 minutes if necessary. This is for pink lamb, cooked on the bone in a hot oven, around 200°C/400°F/Gas Mark 6.

If you prefer medium-done beef or lamb, add approximately 5 minutes per 450g/1lb meat.

If you want to roast meat in a moderate oven, add an extra 5 minutes per 450g/1lb.

Doneness

Conventional wisdom says that roast meat can be served 'rare', 'medium' or 'well cooked', allowing the cook the choice. In fact, this is fair neither to the meat nor to the cook. If cooked beyond the pink stage, tender cuts of meat become progressively dry and less tender (p 215). For this reason, any prime roasting joint of beef or lamb cooked beyond medium will be disappointing. If you genuinely prefer well-done meat, it is better to choose pork or a pot-roasting joint. This is also why loin of lamb and fillet of beef are at their best very pink. See also Two Simple Remedies for Undercooked Meat, p 224.

How to tell when a joint is cooked

Whatever temperature you choose to roast your meat, the skill is in learning to recognise the various signs that tell you how the joint is cooking. The three important indicators are when the fat starts sizzling, the meat juices start coming out of the joint and the joint starts to smell like roast meat.

What happens is that cooking the meat tightens the fibres and coagulates or 'cooks' the proteins, causing moisture to be released. It takes time for this to seep to the surface. The fat, meanwhile, starts to come out of the joint. So, when it starts sizzling, you know the joint has begun to start cooking in earnest. When the juices start coming out of the meat and actively sizzling in the pan, this is a sign that the heat has penetrated to the centre of the joint. This is what you are looking for. If you want pink roast meat, you are almost there. To check how rare the meat is, prod the centre of the meat: the more it yields, the rarer the meat. From this point on, the more juices that come out of the meat, the more well cooked it will be.

The temperature of cooked meat

The way to judge when meat is cooked is to measure the internal temperature. As the following chart shows, this is surprisingly low. The temperatures vary slightly for different meats: see the roasting charts opposite. Always remember, too, that figures are not writ in stone and, irrespective of what the temperature chart says, one person's 'rare' may be the next person's 'medium'. What matters is how you like your meat and finding the temperature that corresponds to this. For example, I prefer an internal cooking temperature of 55°C/130°F for pink meat, 60–65°C/140–150°F for medium meat and 65–70°C/150–160°F for well-done meat.

ROASTING CHART • COMBINATION TEMPERATURE

Source: *The Real Meat Cookbook,* Francoes Bissell

	Starting temperature			Turn down after 15 minutes to			Cooking time: minutes per 450g/1lb		Temperature on meat thermometer	
	°C	°F	Gas Mark	°C	°F	Gas Mark			°C	°F
Beef	250	475	9	200	400	6	Rare	12	51	125
							Medium	16	60	140
							Well done	18–20	70	160
Pork	220	425	7	180	350	4		20–25	75	170
Lamb	250	475	9	200	400	6	Rare	12	51	125
							Medium	16	60	140
							Well done	18–20	70	160
Veal	220	425	7	180	350	4		18–20	75	170

ROASTING CHART • MODERATE TEMPERATURE

Source: British Meat

	°C	°F	Gas Mark	Cooking time: minutes per 450g/1lb		Temperature on meat thermometer	
						°C	°F
Beef	180	350	4–5	Rare	20 + 20	60	140
				Medium	25 + 25	70	160
				Well done	30 + 30	80	175
Pork	180	350	4–5	Medium	30 + 30	75–80	170–175
				Well done	35 + 35	80–85	175–185
Lamb	180	350	4–5	Medium	25 + 25	70–75	160–170
				Well done	30 + 30	75–80	170–175

The above charts, adapted with the author's permission, give two examples of approximate standard cooking times for roasting meat.

Meat thermometers

A meat thermometer measures the internal temperature of the meat and is often recommended as the foolproof answer to successful roasting. But thermometers are not as accurate as they appear to be, nor will using them teach you anything about how to cook a roast. For this reason, it is best simply to view them as an aid, to be used in conjunction with estimated cooking times and the outward signs outlined previously. If you do use one, remember:

■ The temperature readings on a meat thermometer tend to be between 5–10°C too high, which means that the meat will be more well done than it needs to be. While this does not matter very much for well-cooked meat, it is critical for rare and pink meat. Here, you need to take readings at a lower level. For temperature guidelines, see the roasting charts on p 223 and The Temperature of Cooked Meat on p 222.

■ For an accurate reading, the meat thermometer must be inserted into the thickest part of the joint. The reading applies to this part of the meat only. Thinner parts will be more well cooked.

■ To be sure the reading is accurate, you need to insert 5cm/2 inches or so of the thermometer spike into the meat; if you insert less, the reading will not reflect the true temperature of the meat. For this reason thermometers are not suitable for thin pieces of meat, such as steak, breast of chicken or loin of lamb.

Two simple remedies for undercooked meat

■ Meat often appears very pink or bloody while you are carving it or removing the bone. This is, in fact, a good rather than bad sign and does not necessarily mean that the meat is too rare. Once cut and served on hot plates, it quickly changes colour. The hotter the plate, the more the slice will cook. Conversely, to keep meat perfectly pink, serve on warm rather than hot plates.

■ Once you remove the joint from the oven for resting, it takes only 5–10 minutes for the juices to seep to the surface. If these are very red, it indicates the joint is very pink and likely to be rare in the centre. If you would rather have the meat a little more cooked, simply return it to the oven for another 5–15 minutes depending on the size of the joint.

Using a notebook

Keeping a small notebook specifically for roasting meat is invaluable. This is a practice I always follow. Every time you roast a joint, jot down the weight, shape of the joint, cooking temperature, cooking time and any pertinent remarks – how it cooked, how evenly done the meat was, how it tasted, etc. When you next come to roast that particular joint of meat, you will have your own record to refer back to, which will serve you better than any cookery book.

THE BEST ROASTING JOINTS

The following brief descriptions are of the best cuts for roasting. Beef cuts are sold on or off the bone, lamb is usually sold on the bone, while most pork and veal joints are usually sold off the bone.

Beef

The top-notch roasting joints are fillet, sirloin and wing rib. Because they are expensive, and are likely to be bought only occasionally, it is wise to wait and buy them from a first-class butcher. Topside, top rump and other roasting joints are less tender and/or naturally drier, so unless they are first class, they will not roast as well.

Beef fat is excellent for cooking roast potatoes in and the juices from the joint make very good gravy.

Fillet Fillet of beef, the most expensive cut, is exquisitely tender. Being very lean, it is not always the best flavoured, dries out quickly and needs careful timing. It is best cooked wrapped in pastry. Attached to the sirloin, it can be removed and cooked separately. If buying it separately, insist on a piece which is of even thickness throughout its length – fillet of beef tapers off at one end – otherwise one end will be grossly overcooked.

Sirloin The classic roasting joint. For the best all-round value, buy it on the bone. It is not worth buying less than about 2kg/4½lb in weight. This gives you 3 joints in one: a piece of fillet, the sirloin itself and a strip of flank (breast meat) which joins the top of the sirloin. From these, you can produce 3–4 first-class meals, thus spreading the cost of what is always an expensive joint. Make sure the joint is of even thickness, is from the sirloin proper and that the butcher cuts away most of the excess fat lying on the inside of the joint before weighing. It should not have a large piece of flank attached.

Wing rib This is a fairly fatty joint, with a sweeter, richer flavour than sirloin. It is slightly less expensive. Buy with the same care as sirloin and to the same specification. Remove the top flank and use for braising. It is not so good cold as sirloin of beef, but makes excellent hot eating.

If buying boned and rolled sirloin or rib of beef, check to see whether the flank has been included; this is much tougher than sirloin and is not suited to roasting. The best idea is to remove it, cook it separately and retie the joint.

Topside, top rump and other roasting joints These lean joints are slightly tougher and are inclined to become dry if overcooked. For this reason, they are better cooked at lower roasting temperatures and should be basted well with added fat. They vary in quality enormously. If at all possible, wait until you can buy them from a first-class butcher.

Pork

The best joints are leg and loin of pork, but almost all of them will roast successfully. Pork should be roasted at lower temperatures. It is better tempered than beef or lamb and is the easiest meat to roast successfully because cooking times are less critical, though roast pork will always be more succulent when still slightly pink. Cloves of garlic, sage leaves or sage and onion stuffing inserted into/spread on to the meat enhance roast pork.

Pork fat is the best for roasting potatoes in and pork juices make the richest gravy.

Loin of pork The remarks for loin of lamb also apply to loin of pork. A whole loin will feed 4 handsomely. Remove the crackling and cook this separately.

Leg of pork The remarks for leg of lamb also apply to leg of pork, except that you don't need to worry about overcooking. Because of its large size, it is advisable to tie the joint with string so it will keep its shape. To be sure of crisp crackling, remove it and cook separately.

Lamb

The joints that roast well are loin, best end and leg. All are excellent value. Shoulder of lamb is delicious but fatty, and is better braised and roasted as on p 243.

Lamb fat is strong-tasting and greasy. Do not use it for roasting potatoes or making gravy. Lamb should be served on very hot plates.

Loin of lamb This is the perfect joint for 2. A full loin consists of 6–7 chops and will feed 3, but you can ask for 4–5 chops only. Do *not* have it chined. For how to prepare and cook, see p 227.

Best end of lamb As good as the loin, but with a smaller 'eye' of meat and a sweeter-tasting flavour, it is slightly less expensive. Buy in a piece, as for loin. Do *not* have it chined. Cook as for loin of lamb, allowing approximately 5 minutes less.

Leg of lamb A whole leg of lamb is an awkward shape and contains different muscles. For this reason, it is impossible to cook it evenly to the same 'tenderness' throughout. It is generally divided into two. The top half (the fillet end) is a more convenient shape than the bulging calf end, though this contains the largest, most tender muscle. Slivers of garlic or small pieces of anchovy fillet can be inserted into the meat with the point of a knife.

Veal

Roasting joints of veal are very expensive, and include leg, loin, rump and silverside. All are very lean with no waste and will need extra fat to keep them moist. Like pork, most joints are suited to roasting or pot-roasting, and should be cooked in the same way, at moderate temperatures. Contrary to popular belief, veal does not need to be thoroughly cooked, and I find it is best undercooked so that it remains pink. Like pork, too, veal yields rich juices, which make excellent gravy.

ROAST SIRLOIN OR RIB OF BEEF/LOIN OR BEST END OF LAMB/PORK

These joints are all prepared and cooked in the same way, requiring minimal attention from the cook.

Sirloin of beef and loin of lamb

Cut off the flap of breast meat straight across the top of the joint, just above where the eye of the meat ends. This is a tough cut, not suitable for roasting: for suggestions on how to cook, see Simple Braises, p 240.

Turn the joint over so that the bones are facing you and remove the fillet (beef) or underfillet (lamb). Reserve for char-grilled fillet steaks, lamb kebabs or Chinese stir-fry. Remove any lumps of visible fat.

You now have a perfect roasting joint. Slash the skin in a criss-cross fashion with a sharp knife. If roasting beef, weigh the joint.

Lay the joint in a roasting tin along the length of the bone, with the fat uppermost.

Wing rib of beef This has no fillet attached. Remove the breast flap (use as before) and any visible lumps of fat. Score the skin.

Best end of lamb This has the bones attached to the chops and no underfillet. Remove any lumps of visible fat. Score the skin. There is no need to scrape the delicious meat from between the bones unless you want to.

Loin of pork This usually comes ready-trimmed of the breast flap. Remove the tenderloin and use either whole or for Chinese stir-fry. The kidney may also be attached; it can be removed and cooked separately or just left. Remove the rind, score it well and cook separately. Season the joint with salt.

Best end of pork This corresponds to best end of lamb – that is, it has bones attached to the chops and no tenderloin. It needs no preparation apart from seasoning with salt. If you want crackling, remove the rind, score it well and cook separately.

Cooking

1 Look at the thickness of the eye of meat and make a mental assessment of its comparative thickness: obviously, a fat loin will need more cooking than a thin one.

2 If using sirloin or rib of beef, calculate the approximate cooking time using the charts on p 223 or suggestions on p 222.

3 Now you can roast the joint. Baste sirloin or rib of beef and loin of pork 2–3 times during cooking; basting is not necessary for loin or best end of lamb as it cooks so quickly.

4 Once it is cooked, leave the meat to rest while you make the gravy, prepare the vegetables, etc.

Loin and best end of lamb It is better to undercook them rather than risk overcooking, which can happen easily with such small joints. Resting the joints and serving on hot plates will cook them a little more anyway.

Because they are such small joints and the meat is of even thickness running along one side, cooking times are the same whether cooking a short (say 4 chops) or a full length. As cooking times are short, the joints are best cooked in a preheated hot oven, 200–210°C/400–425°F/Gas Mark 6–7. At 200°C/400°F/Gas Mark 6, depending on the thickness of the eye of meat, a small loin and best end will take 20–25 minutes to cook; a thick loin will take 25–30 minutes maximum.

If the skin is not crisp enough, flash it under a hot grill for a couple of minutes before serving.

Loin and best end of pork Roast at 170–180°C/325–350°F/Gas Mark 3–4. Depending on how well cooked you like your pork, allow 45 minutes–1 hour for a short length and around $1\frac{1}{4}$ hours for a full one.

ROAST CHICKEN

Although chicken is delicious when cooked well, it is not the easiest meat to roast. It needs more attention than most roasts because the breast and leg meat are very different, making it impossible to cook both perfectly in the same time. The legs take around 50 per cent longer than the breast, which, being very lean and tender, quickly becomes dry when overcooked. If you manage to keep the breast moist, then the legs, which are fattier and slightly tougher, may not have been roasted enough to reach peak crispness.

For this reason roasting chicken is something of a juggling act. Basically, because it is necessary to cook all parts of the bird thoroughly, if you want to eat the whole chicken you will need to protect the breast in some way. And because the breast meat is so dry, it will need additional lubrication in some form. Butter is the best choice. It enhances the flavour of the chicken and produces delicious juices. This is the secret of succulent roast chicken.

As with pork, seasoning improves the taste.

Remember, if you are cooking for only 2, you can always remove the legs, reserving or freezing them for another dish, and roast the breast meat on the bone on its own.

Trussing a chicken

Chickens are bought trussed, that is, tied with string so that the legs are held in shape next to the body. It keeps its shape when cooked and looks more attractive at the table, but it does not affect the cooking process: the chicken will roast equally well trussed or not. I prefer roasting chickens untrussed because the legs seem to cook slightly better. To untruss the bird, cut and remove the string.

Irrespective of whether or not the chicken is trussed, always roast it in a tin or dish into which it fits reasonably snugly, rather than one which is too large. This will also help an untrussed chicken to keep its shape.

Protecting the breast

There are several ways you can do this:

- Cover the chicken breast with slices of streaky bacon. These add flavour and can be served as an accompaniment. Remove for the last 20 minutes or so for the skin to become crisp and brown.
- Cover the breast with a thick layer of pork fat or rind. This acts as a blanket and both protects the breast and bastes it. Remove for the last 20 minutes or so for the skin to become crisp and brown.
- Cover the breast with its own fat, taken from the cavity.
- Put a protective layer of cream cheese mixed with garlic, herbs, etc. under the breast skin, or spread plain or flavoured butter under the skin.
- Spread butter on the breast, cover (the breast, not the legs) loosely with aluminium foil, removing it for the last 20 minutes or so for the skin to become crisp and brown.

Roasting times

Chicken roasts well at any temperature from 180°C/350°F/Gas Mark 4 to 200°C/400°F/Gas Mark 6. The higher the temperature, the faster the chicken will brown (don't forget to protect the breast) and cook.

As a guide, allow 20 minutes per 450g/1lb, plus 20 minutes or so. In practice, at a temperature of around 190°C/375°F/Gas Mark 5, a small chicken takes around 45 minutes–1 hour to roast, a medium-sized chicken around 1–1¼ hours and a large chicken around 1½ hours.

To tell if the chicken is cooked, pierce the thighs with a cake skewer. The juices should run clear.

Turning the chicken

Although unnecessary, many people like to roast chicken this way because it ensures the bird browns evenly on all sides. It does not protect the breast as such but does give maximum exposure to the legs, thus helping them to cook properly. Start with the chicken on its side. After 20 minutes, turn it over to the other side. After another 20 minutes, sit the chicken on its back and complete the cooking.

Basting a chicken

It is a good idea to baste the bird a couple of times, starting half-way through the cooking; this will help keep it moist and add flavour.

Resting a chicken

This is as important for chicken as it is for other roast meat. Leave for 15 minutes; it will remain hot for 30 minutes or so.

Gravy

The juices from a chicken are rarely sufficient and you will need to add extra chicken stock to make a well-flavoured gravy. Once the chicken is cooked, tip any juices from the cavity into the roasting pan; juices from the chicken, once it has rested, should also be added to the gravy.

Though often recommended, the giblets do not make a particularly pleasant-tasting liquid with which to prepare the gravy. Wash them first, add to the stockpot and use proper chicken stock instead, which can be made from the carcass or bought ready-made in cartons.

Variations There are countless ways to vary plain roast chicken. The three common methods are rubbing the skin with spices or spice pastes; slipping a stuffing/flavoured butter/pesto/slivers of garlic under the skin; or rubbing the chicken with lemon/lime/or orange and pouring the juice over it. Porcini Butter or Moroccan Spiced Butter (p 129) are both excellent.

Stuffing the cavity with herbs – rosemary, tarragon, lemon thyme and bay leaves – does not flavour the chicken meat but will flavour the juices that come out of the cavity, which can be used to make the gravy. Breadcrumb stuffings are often suggested though I find they remain soggy and are not particularly successful.

For a spectacularly golden bird, rub the skin with a strong saffron infusion (see p 26). The flavour of saffron will come through to the juices in the pan and can be made into a simple cream sauce, with the addition of cream and extra saffron if needed.

Roasts: A Miscellany

Meat juices

You will often be advised to use the meat juices to make your gravy. This is fine, except that as one of the main aims in roasting meat is to keep the juices inside, thereby helping to make it succulent, unless the meat is well cooked, as in pork or veal, there should be very few juices in the pan. In this case, you will need to supplement the gravy with extra meat stock or added flavouring.

The same applies to advice to deglaze the meat residues and juices with, say, wine to make a thin gravy. This will work satisfactorily only if you have a reasonable quantity of residue and juices to start with.

An alternative way of using roasting juices

When you have only a small amount of roasting juices and don't want to make gravy with it, you can try tossing cooked spinach in the residues of the roasting pan.

First, mop up almost all the fat from the roasting tin, then mix 1 teaspoon of potato flour with the roasting juices. Add cooked spinach and reheat over a gentle heat, turning the spinach. Its moisture will dissolve the dark meat residues in the roasting dish, while the potato flour will bind any excess moisture from the cooked spinach. The spinach should not be wet but glisten nicely and will become deliciously impregnated with the meat juices. I allow 170–225g/6–8oz cooked spinach for 2, but you can use whatever quantity you like. Lightly cooked, shredded dark green cabbage also works well.

Gravy

Personally I am not a fan of using wine to make gravy, and for me the old-fashioned way remains the best. Beef and pork make the best gravy; I find redcurrant jelly or mint sauce a better accompaniment for lamb. A few tips:

- A chopped onion added to the roasting dish will help flavour the gravy.
- Always use a little of the meat fat to make the gravy; this improves the flavour.
- The cooking water from the vegetables will also add a little flavour.
- In the absence of stock or sufficient meat juices, an excellent instant flavouring for gravy is soy sauce. About 1–2 tablespoons is usually sufficient. Add it a little at a time to taste.
- Be careful if using stockcubes instead of home-made stock, as these can be overpowering. Use them at half-strength. A better choice if you have no home-made stock is stock from a carton.
- You don't need to make a specific quantity of gravy. If the gravy is too thick, add a little liquid; if is too thin, boil it down a little longer.
- If your gravy is lumpy, pour it through a sieve.
- Add any juices which come out from the meat while it is relaxing to the gravy.

As a rough guide, use 1 scant tablespoon of plain flour per 300ml/½ pint liquid for 2 people. For a very lightly thickened gravy, use half the quantity of flour.

Pour off most of the fat from the roasting tin, then sprinkle in the flour, stirring it around over a moderate heat so that it soaks up the fat and meat residues. Cook until light–medium brown.

Add your liquid, which can be water, stock and water, or vegetable cooking water. Stir vigorously and bring to the boil.

Reduce the heat and simmer for 10–15 minutes, until the gravy is well flavoured and the desired thickness. If the flavour is still too thin, add 1–2 tablespoons of soy sauce to taste.

Unthickened gravy If you prefer an unthickened gravy, omit the flour. Pour off most of the fat, add the liquid as before and simmer, scraping up the residues from the bottom of the pan with a wooden spoon, until the gravy is well flavoured, as before. If you want to you can deglaze the meat residues with a glass of dry white wine first, but make sure you boil most of it off before adding extra liquid.

Crackling

One of the pleasures of roast pork is the crackling. Everyone seems to have their own pet theory or 'secret' recipe, but there is really no mystery. All you need do is to cook the crackling for long enough and it will become crisp. A few tips:

■ The tougher the skin of the breed of pork, the chewier the outside of the crackling will be; there is nothing you can do about this.

■ Ideally the rind should include 1cm/generous $\frac{1}{3}$ inch of fat; if there is too little fat, the crackling will be all rind and no 'crackle'.

■ It is important to score the rind thoroughly using a small, very sharp knife. This allows the fat to come out of the crackling at a steady rate.

■ Unless you are cooking large joints of meat for a long time, the crackling will not usually be crisp enough if left on the joint. Therefore, to ensure crisp crackling, remove the rind and its layer of fat from the joint and cook it separately. If the joint is very lean, place the rind on top of it, removing it three-quarters of the way through the cooking time. Place the crackling in a separate tray and place in the hottest part of the oven.

■ If the crackling is still soft by the time the pork is cooked, remove the meat, turn up the heat to around 200°C/400°F/Gas Mark 6 and continue to cook the crackling until crisp. This can take anything from 15–30 minutes, or a little longer.

Yorkshire pudding

■ Yorkshire pudding should be cooked in a hot oven and the batter should be thin, not thick. Use a little of the fat from the meat to cook the Yorkshire pudding. This will give it a good flavour. The fat should be hot.

■ Do not attempt to cook the Yorkshire pudding under the meat. Cook it separately.

■ A purpose-made Yorkshire pudding tin, which has 4 wide, shallow depressions for making single-portion Yorkshire puddings is the best tin to use and saves having to cut up the pudding. Otherwise, use a thin baking tin, which will conduct the heat very quickly.

■ The best way to serve Yorkshire pudding is in the traditional northern way, with gravy, as a first course, before the beef.

■ Yorkshire puddings reheat very successfully.

The following method, sufficient for 2, will fill one Yorkshire pudding tin with 4 depressions. For 4 people, double the quantities and make in a large roasting tin or use 2 Yorkshire pudding tins.

1 Put about 55g/2oz plain flour and a good pinch of salt into a small bowl. Make a well in the centre.

2 Add 1 egg to the well, beating it lightly with a fork, then draw in the flour, adding enough water, or milk and water mixed, to form a thin batter, no thicker than thin custard – you will need around 150ml/$\frac{1}{4}$ pint. Leave to stand for at least 30 minutes.

3 Spoon 1 teaspoon of meat fat taken from the roasting dish into each depression of a Yorkshire pudding tin. Heat the tin on top of the stove for 30 seconds or so until the base and fat are hot. Whisk the batter briefly, then divide between the 4 depressions. The batter should start to set immediately.

4 Transfer the Yorkshire puddings to the oven on the hottest shelf. Cook for around 20–25 minutes, or until crisp; the centres should not be soggy. Serve immediately with gravy.

Slow Meat Cookery

Slow meat cookery – pot-roasting, braising, casseroling and stewing – is the easiest and most gratifying of cooking methods. It requires few ingredient and minimal preparation. Timing is never critical: most dishes can be cooked in advance (which often improves them) and reheated without spoiling. Slow cooking also gets the very best out of cheaper cuts of meat which, though tougher, often have more flavour than many prime cuts. They emerge as soft as butter and produce their own wonderfully dense-flavoured sauces. Once you have tried a few, the method becomes second nature and a recipe unnecessary.

It is commonly supposed that only large joints of meat are worth cooking this way, but I do not find this to be the case. I regularly cook as little as 450g/1lb meat, though because the dishes keep and freeze so well, cooking enough for 2 meals is never a problem. A small amount left over makes an excellent ragù to serve with pasta: chop the meat, reheat in its sauce and it is ready.

Slow meat dishes usually need only some kind of starch to mop up the juices. Unless included in the dish, vegetables are best served as a separate course and make excellent starters. The other thing to serve first is a simple salad. You only ever need fruit to finish; this refreshes the palette and rounds off the meal splendidly.

Cooking in the oven v. on top of the stove

The methods described here can all be cooked in the oven or on top of the stove. In all cases, I find the oven is preferable, for the following reasons:

■ It is much easier to control the heat in the oven than on top of the stove; this is particularly important for tough cuts of meat which need very gentle cooking over a prolonged time. An oven also produces all-round gentle heat, which enables the meat to be cooked evenly.

■ The gentle cooking in the oven allows the flavours to develop and merge together evenly, and produces a better, clearer sauce. The fat remains separate, rather than combining with the liquid, and can be skimmed off easily.

■ When cooking a casserole or stew in the oven, you can remove the lid to brown the surface of the meat and to enable the liquid to reduce without boiling it.

If you prefer to cook on top of the stove:

■ Choose a deep, wide, heavy-based pan which will accommodate meat and vegetables in a single layer. If cooking a pot-roast, make sure the meat fits in the pan snugly.

■ Check the heat regularly, using the lid to give extra control if necessary. If cooking in a sealed pan, use a heat diffuser.

■ The meat should cook as gently as possible. For this reason, never let the liquid boil. Boiling will also produce cloudy, greasy sauces.

TYPES OF SLOW MEAT COOKERY

A wide variety of cuts can be used, the most common of which are listed below. Any cut of meat cooked gently will produce excellent results; only the more tender cuts can be used for pot-roasting.

The average cooking times given below are for small–medium-sized joints, up to around 2kg/4½lb weight. Joints of chicken take around 30–50 minutes.

Pot-roasting

The name is a misnomer, for it does not involve roasting. It is used for meat that is tender enough to be roasted but not quite as tender as classic roasting joints, and for poultry. In effect, a half-way house between roasting and braising, the meat is cooked in a sealed dish at a moderate heat, often on a bed of vegetables and with a little liquid; to create a roasted effect, the meat is traditionally browned first.

The recommended oven temperature is around 180°C/350°F/Gas Mark 4 for chicken, pork and veal and 170°C/325°F/Gas Mark 3 for beef and lamb. Average cooking times are from 1–2½ hours, depending on the kind of meat and size of joint.

Suitable for Topside, top rump, silverside, brisket and forerib of beef; boned shoulder, breast and topside of veal; leg and shoulder of lamb; all boned joints of pork, for example leg, shoulder, belly, blade; chicken.

Braising

This is the general term used to describe slow meat cookery: all terms mentioned here are ways of braising meat. Virtually synonymous with pot-roasting, it is used specifically for moderately tough cuts of meat, which are either sliced or cooked in a single piece, in a sealed dish in the oven, with enough liquid to come a third of the way up the meat. The meat may or may not be browned first.

The recommended oven temperature is around 170°C/325°F/Gas Mark 3. Average cooking times vary from 1½–2½ hours depending on the kind of meat and size of joint.

Suitable for Braising steak – chuck, blade, thick rib, 'frying steak' and pot-roasting joints of beef as above; pot-roasting joints of veal; shoulder, chump chops and breast of lamb; all cuts of pork; joints of chicken.

Casseroling

This is a term used for cubed pieces of meat cooked in a sealed dish with added vegetables and a generous amount of liquid, which is often thickened. It may be cooked either in the oven or on top of the stove and is suitable for both moderately tender and moderately tough cuts.

The recommended oven temperature is around 170°C / 325°F / Gas Mark 3. Average cooking times are the same as for pot-roasting or braising, depending on the cut.

Suitable for Braising steak – chuck, blade and thick rib; shoulder of veal and pie veal; chump chops and 'cubed' lamb; shoulder, chump chops, spare rib chops and 'cubed' pork; joints of chicken.

Stewing

This is a term used for cooking tough and very tough cubes or pieces of meat in ample liquid. Stews are traditionally cooked on top of the stove but may be cooked in the oven also.

The recommended oven temperature is around 150°C/300°F/Gas Mark 2 to 170°C/ 325°F/Gas Mark 3, but these cuts of meat in particular benefit from being cooked at much lower temperatures. Average cooking times vary from 2–4 hours and can be longer, depending on the kind of meat and size of joint.

Suitable for 'Stewing' beef – shin, leg, neck, clod and skirt; shin (osso buco) and pie veal; neck of lamb.

Mastering the Braise

These are the main rules that apply to slow-cooked meat dishes:

- Choose the right cuts.
- Buy and cook the meat in a large piece wherever possible. It cooks better and is more satisfying to eat. Slice into thick pieces just before serving.
- A heavy, ovenproof casserole dish that holds its heat is the best type of dish to use. *Always* choose a dish in which the meat, etc. will just fit comfortably.
- When cooking beef, chicken or rindless pork, try and include a piece of pork rind. This adds succulence to the dish and gives the sauce extra depth. It is especially important for beef. For large joints or a substantial quantity of meat, a split pig's trotter has the same effect and will produce a rich jellied sauce.
- When cooking braises with a small amount of liquid, it is imperative to cook the meat in a totally sealed dish to prevent it drying up. Aluminium foil does not produce an air-tight seal. A sheet of greaseproof paper inserted between the dish and the lid is much better.
- Toughness varies from one piece of meat to the next. For this reason, cooking times may be anything from 2–4 hours, or even longer if cooking at very low temperatures.
- Testing the meat with a knife or fork is not enough. The only way to judge when it is done – that is, tender – is to slice off a small piece and eat it; if it is not done to your liking, cook a little longer.
- Leave the dish to cool in the turned-off oven. This seems to have a beneficial mellowing effect. If eating straight away, leave the dish to 'relax' in a warm place for 30 minutes or so.

- Daubes and braised meat dishes, which are essentially meat and sauce, are better for being made in advance and served 1–2 days later. Keep in the fridge, take off all the fat and reheat gently. They will keep for up to 6–7 days in the fridge and freeze perfectly. If freezing, however, do not include garlic.
- Lamb stews and any casseroles containing vegetables to be eaten with the dish are better not reheated but eaten fresh.
- Always remove any fat from the dish before serving. Do this before you thicken the sauce: see Mopping up Fat, p 39.

Sealing the meat

It is commonly believed that browning and searing the surface before you add liquid 'seals' in the flavour and 'keeps in the juices' when cooking braised meat. In fact, as American writer Harold McGee has shown – and as anyone who has observed the amount of liquid that comes out of meat knows – this is not the case. It neither keeps the flavour in nor stops the meat juices coming out. Sealing the meat caramelises the surface, which makes it appetising to look at and contributes extra flavour, but that is all. You can seal the meat or not as you wish and it will cook just as well and be just as successful. As a general guide:

- If you want to brown the surface of the meat – for example, when pot-roasting – to give it an appetising appearance, or want to add a little extra flavour and colour to the dish – for example, when making a stew – then seal the meat first.
- With dishes cooked for very long periods – for example, daubes – searing the meat is irrelevant.

TEMPERATURE CONTROL: SIMMERING

General faults with recipes of this type are that not enough attention is given to controlling the heat and recommended cooking temperatures tend to be too high. This is because there is a misconception that for meat to cook properly the liquid must boil, or at very least simmer. In fact, the opposite applies. The quickest way to produce a tough casserole or stew is to let the liquid boil. To achieve tender meat, you need to have a little more patience and cook it as gently as possible. This means the liquid must barely move and the only visible signs you should see are wisps of steam. This applies whether you are cooking a braise on top of the stove or in the oven. Electric slow-cookers demonstrate this perfectly. All work by heating meat through to simmering point, 94–98°C/200–208°F, but no hotter, and letting it cook for anything up to 8 hours. The old Hay Box cookery method, where the dish was heated first then left to cook overnight in a sealed box stuffed with hay to act as an insulator, and the slow oven in Aga cookers are two other examples.

In practice, what temperature you can get away with depends on how tender the meat is. This is why, for example, a pot-roast can be cooked at higher temperatures. Remember, too, that the meat takes time to heat through to the same temperature as the surrounding liquid. This also effectively gives the cook two choices:

■ **Cook braised meat dishes for conventional times:** this is quicker but there is less leeway. You run the risk of overshooting and it is more difficult to judge exactly when the meat becomes tender.

■ **Cook the same dish at a very low temperature:** the dish will take 2–3 times longer to cook but will not spoil, and tenderness and succulence are guaranteed.

Do whatever is convenient at the time and depending on whether you are the kind of cook who prefers fixed temperatures and cooking times or who is happy to let dishes tick away slowly and look after themselves.

A few more hints:

■ Irrespective of the starting cooking temperature, once the meat and liquid have become hot and the dish shows signs of simmering, be prepared to lower the temperature.

■ Liquid heats up at a faster rate and will bubble more furiously in a tightly sealed pot; by adjusting the lid to leave a tiny gap, this can be quickly corrected as and when necessary.

■ If cooking in the oven, you can either start the meat in a moderate oven and turn it down once the food is thoroughly hot or put it into a very low oven and cook it at this temperature throughout. In this case, allow an extra 30 minutes or so for the food to become hot.

■ The tougher the meat, the longer and slower it should be cooked. As a general rule, turn down the oven to the lowest temperature – anything from 200–275°C/100–140°F/Gas Mark $\frac{1}{4}$–1 – which produces the gentlest simmer: the liquid should merely 'smile'. Check and adjust the temperature as necessary.

■ If a small amount of liquid is used, the dish can go straight into the oven. If a large amount is used, heat gently first on top of the stove.

■ Dishes in which the meat sits on a bed of vegetables and is not surrounded by liquid will be cooked by the steam and are less affected. Here, however, you need to watch very carefully that the liquid – and meat – do not dry up, so reducing the temperature is a wise precaution.

■ Meat begins to lose moisture and starts to cook at around 38°C/100°F, and is well cooked at 71°C/160°F. At 75°C/165°F all possible bugs have been destroyed. Both are well below the temperature of water when it starts to simmer (93°C/200°F) or boils (100°C/212°F) – that is, it is perfectly safe to cook meat as gently as you can.

Ingredients and Flavourings for Braises

Vegetables, aromatics, different liquids and garnishes will add extra flavour to the dish. You do not need to use many or to use large quantities.

Vegetables

These can be divided into two groups: those which flavour the dish and those which are an integral part of it.

Flavouring vegetables are usually chopped finely. Unless they form part of the sauce – see Italian-style Braise, p 240 – they are generally discarded before serving. Pour the sauce through a sieve, pressing the vegetable debris hard against the sides to extract all the moisture.

- The best flavouring vegetables are onions, garlic, leeks, carrots, celery, celeriac and tomatoes. Tomatoes add sweetness and moisture and dissolve to form a sauce.
- Do not use potatoes (they break up and produce a murky sauce) or green vegetables as flavouring agents, especially brassicas, which do not stand up well to long cooking.
- Red peppers add sweetness and colour to a braised meat dish; in long-cooked dishes they may soften completely and amalgamate to help form a sauce.

When the vegetables are to be part of the dish, choose either firm ones or ones that are pleasant to eat when very soft. They should be left whole or cut into sizeable chunks.

- Because the vegetables have already been cooked for so long, meat and vegetable dishes do not reheat as well as meat and sauce dishes; they are best suited to moderately tender cuts of meat which can be cooked in $1-2\frac{1}{2}$ hours.
- All flavouring vegetables listed above are good. Other suitable root vegetables are parsnip and swede.
- Potatoes are excellent but do not reheat well.

- Other good vegetables include broad beans, fennel and aubergines. White cabbage is excellent with pork dishes.
- Soaked, dried beans – for example, white beans and chickpeas – make excellent additions.

Aromatics

The most useful are:

- Herbs – bay, rosemary, sage, thyme, parsley, tarragon, basil. A sprig or two will be sufficient. Remove soft-textured herbs – for example, basil, parsley, tarragon – before serving.
- Spices – apart from paprika and cayenne, which are bought ready-ground, whole spices are better. If you want to make a spiced braise (as opposed to a curry or other ethnic dish), use a spice paste such as harissa.
- Whole spices – peppercorns, juniper berries, caraway, fennel, cumin and coriander seeds, cloves, cinnamon sticks, anise, allspice.

Other flavouring ingredients

There are not many of these, but they are very useful:

- anchovies: 1–2 anchovy fillets will add piquancy to beef, lamb, veal and chicken braises.
- bacon: excellent for beef, veal and chicken braises. Cut into dice; if very salty, blanch first.
- orange zest: especially for French daubes but

suitable for all meats. Bitter (Seville) or sweet oranges can be used. A small strip is sufficient.

■ dried fruit: add sweetness. To prevent them from disintegrating in dishes which require very lengthy cooking, add towards the end or as a garnish.

■ dried mushrooms: a few pieces of these will contribute a concentrated meaty flavour to the sauce. Useful when no stock is available or to add extra flavour generally. Best suited to beef, veal and chicken.

■ mustard: for pork and beef dishes. Used in specific dishes – for example, beef carbonade. Can also be stirred in at the end, thickening and flavouring the sauce.

■ olives and preserved lemons: these are better added towards the end. They also make good garnishes.

Liquids

You can use a variety of liquids, or a combination of several:

■ Meat stock – produces a richer sauce, though is not essential.

■ Milk – this can be used to cook pork or veal and produces a sweet- flavoured dish; the sauce develops a curdled, grainy effect, but this is usual.

■ Tomatoes, *Sugocasa*/passata, sieved canned tomatoes – very useful and always successful.

■ Water – this is fine. The vegetables and meat will flavour the sauce sufficiently.

■ Wine, cider and ale/stout – these lend their own characteristic flavour to a dish.

■ Wine vinegar, brandy, port, sherry, vermouth – these are used in small quantities (up to, say, 5 tablespoons) and can be substituted for wine, etc.

Any alcohol present will evaporate during lengthy cooking. For this reason it is not necessary to boil wine or other alcohol first, or to flame brandy.

Thickeners

Sauces can be thickened or not, as you prefer. Thickeners are not needed for those braises that are intended to produce a small amount of well-flavoured sauce. Here the flavouring vegetables give body to the sauce or the meat is removed and the sauce finished by skimming off the fat and reducing further.

If you want a thickened sauce, you can:

■ Dust the meat with flour, then shake off the excess and brown the meat. The flour will thicken the liquid during cooking.

■ Thicken the sauce before serving, using any of the thickeners listed on p 35.

Garnishes

These add contrast and texture. They should be cooked separately and added last, just before you serve the dish. Some examples are:

■ Capers/olives/chopped preserved lemons.

■ Caramelised baby onions (p 245), carrots or baby turnips.

■ Diced fried bread (croutons) or rounds of baked bread (croutes).

■ Dried fruit: soaked prunes, dried apricots, dried pears, muscatel raisins.

■ Herbs – chopped parsley or chives, shredded basil, chopped coriander or tarragon, as appropriate to the style of the dish. A mixture of finely chopped parsley, garlic and lemon zest (gremolata) is excellent with braised beef, veal, oxtail and chicken.

■ Fried mushrooms.

POT-ROAST CHICKEN

Pot-roasting is the easiest way to produce a moist, full-flavoured chicken. Once cooked, it will keep perfectly for 30–45 minutes in the turned-off oven. The carcass can be made into stock to give you chicken soup, while any left-over chicken is superb cold.

If there are only 2 to feed, save the cooked thighs to make a stir-fry for another meal or to serve cold with salad and baked potatoes.

■ You can use a wide selection of vegetables. Those which work well are root vegetables, celery, broad beans and Mediterranean vegetables like aubergines, peppers, fennel and tomatoes.

■ You can also use a wide selection of flavourings, such as rosemary, thyme, basil, tarragon, bay leaves; lemon and orange zest, fennel and coriander seeds; green peppercorns and saffron. If making a Mediterranean-style pot roast, olives can be added 15 minutes before the end.

■ Whole unpeeled garlic cloves, cooked in their skins, will flavour a chicken or pork pot-roast in a gentle way. To eat, squeeze the pulp out of the skins and spread over the meat.

The following recipe gives the general idea.

Chicken Bonne Femme

SERVES 4

| 1.5kg/3½lb free-range chicken |
| 4–6 medium parsnips |
| 4 large carrots |
| 4 leeks, trimmed and washed |
| 8–12 whole unpeeled cloves garlic (optional) |
| 16 smallish waxy potatoes, peeled |
| 1 wine glass dry white wine (about 100ml/ 3½fl oz) |
| 2 bay leaves |
| 1 sprig of thyme, or lemon thyme if available |
| chopped parsley to finish |

Wash out the insides of the chicken with water and remove any fat in the cavity. You will need to keep all the vegetables big for this dish: cut the parsnips and carrots in half, or into sizeable chunks as appropriate, and cut the leeks into half or thirds.

Arrange the parsnips, carrots, leeks and garlic, if using, with the bay leaves and herbs in the bottom of a heavy, ovenproof casserole. Sit the chicken snugly on top, then tuck in the potatoes around the sides. Pour in the wine and enough water to cover the vegetables by about half their depth; if you have no wine, use extra water.

Bring to simmering point on top of the stove, then cover tightly and cook in a moderate oven, around 325–350°F/170–180°C/Gas Mark 3–4, for around 1¼ hours, or until the chicken is cooked: test the thighs – the juices will be clear. Check half-way through that the liquid is no more than gently simmering, adjusting the heat accordingly.

Remove the chicken, tipping the juices from the cavity back into the pot. The simplest way to do this is to stick a carving fork into the cavity and lift the chicken. Blot up any excess fat from the cooking juices with kitchen paper.

Serve the chicken on a board and carve at the table, with the vegetables and their juices in a separate dish scattered with parsley.

POT-ROAST PORK

Pot-roasting is an admirable way to cook most joints of pork, small or large, fatty or lean. The guidelines are the same as those for chicken. The meat can be cooked in advance and reheated later. Instead of browning the pork first, I find it better to remove the lid towards the end of cooking and let the pork and vegetables brown naturally; or if reheating the meat, stand it on a trivet and heat through in a hot oven until well browned.

Pork produces a reasonable amount of natural juices: boil down if necessary, then pour around the vegetables or serve in a separate jug.

There are various ways to flavour pot-roast pork:

■ For a simple pot-roast, set the meat on a mixture of chopped carrots, onions and celery.

■ Other vegetables that complement pork are root vegetables, tomatoes, fennel, garlic, peppers, potatoes, broad beans and cabbage.

■ Flavourings that complement pork are fennel seeds, garlic, sage, rosemary, oregano, lemon thyme, and lemon and orange zest. Oriental flavourings are particularly good with pot-roast pork. The meat can be cooked with water, dry white wine or cider.

■ The pork can be stuffed with dried prunes or apricots, or with savoury breadcrumb stuffings, mixing a few tablespoons of breadcrumbs with herbs/spices as above. Untie the joint, spread the stuffing very thinly and retie with string. For a Tuscan flavour, spread the pork with a mixture of chopped garlic, rosemary and fennel seeds or fennel herb.

Pot roast shoulder of pork with fennel, tomatoes and garlic

SERVES 6

| 2kg/4½lb boned and rolled shoulder of pork, tied with string |
| 2 large bulbs of fennel, halved and sliced from top to bottom into thick wedges |
| 570g/1¼lb ripe tomatoes, halved |
| 12–18 whole unpeeled cloves garlic |
| 1 onion, sliced |
| 1 teaspoon fennel seeds |
| 150ml/¼ pint dry white wine or cider |
| finely chopped parsley |

Put the vegetables and fennel seeds into a deep dish that will just take the meat comfortably. Sit the pork on top, then pour in the wine or cider, bring to the boil and cover tightly.

Transfer to a very moderate oven, 170°C/325°F/Gas Mark 3, and cook for around 2½–3 hours. Check after 45 minutes or so, and turn the heat down a notch once the juices start bubbling. When the juices run clear in the centre the meat is done. If you want it to brown, remove the lid and turn up the heat.

Remove the meat and keep warm. Put the vegetables in a shallow serving dish and keep hot. Remove the fat from the juices and boil down to reduce if necessary, or thicken with potato flour.

Carve the meat into thick chunks. Serve with the vegetables, sprinkled generously with parsley, and the juices poured into a jug and handed round separately.

SIMPLE BRAISES

The following selection of dishes can be made with a variety of meats. The quantities provide enough sauce for 2 people and are based on using around 450g/1lb braising meat, or a couple of large chicken legs, or thick pork steaks or chump chops, etc. For meat on the bone, allow 570g/1¼lb weight. For 4 servings, simply double the quantities. You can use dry white wine for all meats and red wine for beef and lamb. All the dishes can be cooked in advance and reheated later.

■ Trim the meat of excess visible fat and choose a heavy ovenproof dish that will just hold the meat and other ingredients comfortably.

■ The dishes can be cooked at any temperature from around 130°C/250°F/Gas Mark ½ to 170°C/325°F/Gas Mark 3. The timings given below are based on cooking the dishes at 140–150°C/275–300°F/Gas Mark 1–2. If cooking at very low temperatures, remember to bring the contents of the dish up to simmering point, then transfer to the oven. Though I find all dishes cook best in the oven, they can also be cooked on top of the stove. Because it is tender, chicken is the most suitable meat.

■ Check the liquid levels during cooking. If the seal is not tight or the meat does not produce much juice, you may need to add a little extra water. When cooking relatively thin pieces of meat, for example, chicken breasts or chops, add enough water to come level with the top of the meat.

■ The amount of liquid produced will vary according to the type of meat and the length of cooking. Pork, for example, generally produces more liquid than beef or lamb. Taste the sauce and reduce or thicken accordingly. Similarly, if the sauce thickens too much during cooking, add a little extra water.

■ Chicken takes the shortest time to cook, pork and lamb around the same time, and beef the longest. This alters from one cut to another.

Italian-style braise

This makes a good midweek supper. Use for lamb, beef, pork, veal and chicken. For cooking notes, see left.

SERVES 2

450–570g/1–1¼lb meat, or 2 large chicken breasts or legs

FOR THE BASE

1 carrot, 1 onion and 1 celery stick, whizzed to a fine hash in a food processor or finely chopped by hand

Plus

150ml/¼ pint dry white wine (or red wine for beef or lamb)

2 tablespoons tomato purée/2 large chopped ripe tomatoes/small can of chopped tomatoes and their juice/150ml/¼ pint tomato sauce, for example *Sugocasa*

bay leaf/sprig of parsley/rosemary/sage/oregano as appropriate

olive oil

1 tablespoon finely chopped parsley, or to taste (optional)

Choose a heavy-based casserole dish that will just take the meat comfortably. Brown the meat on all sides in its own fat, or in a little olive oil if the meat is lean. Remove and set aside. Add the vegetable hash, and soften over a gentle heat, adding a little extra olive oil if necessary, for around 5–7 minutes until the vegetables begin to colour. Stir often and don't let them brown.

Pour in the wine, bring to the boil, then add the rest of the ingredients except the parsley. Season with freshly ground pepper, if liked, and stir. Replace the meat on top. Add extra tomato sauce or water if needed to come about 1.25cm/½ inch up the sides of the meat.

Bring to simmering point, then cover tightly and transfer to the oven. Cook for around 1–2½ hours, or until the meat is tender. Chicken breasts should take around 30–40 minutes, chicken legs around 45 minutes–1 hour. Mop up any fat, scatter with parsley if using, and serve from the same dish, with pasta.

Saffron and almond braise

A delicious creamy braise, excellent for veal or chicken. For cooking notes see the page opposite.

SERVES 2

450g/1lb boned shoulder or breast of veal, or 2 large chicken breasts or legs

FOR THE BASE:

1 carrot, 1 onion and 1 celery stick, whizzed to a fine hash in a food processor or finely chopped by hand

Plus

150ml/$\frac{1}{4}$ pint dry white wine

$\frac{1}{2}$ packet of powdered saffron infused in 1 tablespoon hot water for 30 minutes (see p 26)

30g/1oz ground almonds

1 sprig of rosemary

olive oil or knob of butter

Brown the meat in a heavy-based casserole dish, remove and set aside. Add the vegetable hash and soften in a little olive oil or butter over a gentle heat for around 5–7 minutes until lightly coloured. Add two-thirds of the saffron infusion to the wine, keeping back 1 teaspoon to add later, and pour into the dish. Bring to the boil, stir in the almonds, tuck in the rosemary and replace the meat on top. Add enough water to come a third of the way up the meat. If using chicken breasts add enough to come level with the top of the meat.

Bring to simmering point, then cover tightly, transfer to the oven and cook until the meat is tender. Veal will take 1$\frac{1}{2}$ hours or a little longer, chicken breasts around 30–40 minutes and chicken legs 45 minutes–1 hour.

Remove the meat, keeping it hot in a low oven. Fish out the rosemary and check the consistency and flavour of the sauce, reducing if necessary (veal produces a reasonable amount of liquid). Stir in the rest of the saffron. Arrange the meat on top of the sauce, carving veal first. Serve with plain rice.

Spanish-style red pepper and paprika braise

A sweet braise suitable for lamb, pork, beef or chicken. It is important to use fresh, sweet-tasting paprika, either Spanish or Hungarian. For cooking notes, see the page opposite.

SERVES 2

450–570g/1–1$\frac{1}{4}$lb meat, or 2 large chicken breasts or legs

Plus

1 small red pepper, seeded and cut into short, fairly thick slices

1 large mild onion, finely sliced

1 tablespoon paprika

1 clove garlic, crushed

pinch of cayenne pepper/powdered chilli (optional)

1 tablespoon sherry or red wine vinegar

1 bay leaf

olive oil

Brown the meat in a heavy-based casserole dish and then remove. Add the red pepper and onion and soften for about 5–7 minutes over a gentle heat until coloured, adding a little olive oil if necessary. Stir in the paprika. Return the meat to the dish, turning it over in the mixture, then add the rest of the ingredients. Pour in 150ml/$\frac{1}{4}$ pint of water, or enough to come about 1.25cm/$\frac{1}{2}$ inch up the sides of the meat. Bring to simmering point, then cover tightly and transfer to the oven. Cook for around 1–2$\frac{1}{2}$ hours until the meat is tender. Chicken breasts should take around 30–40 minutes, chicken legs around 45 minutes–1 hour. Mop up the fat and reduce or thicken the sauce if necessary. Serve with rice or boiled or baked potatoes.

Variation 110–170g/4–6oz cooked broad beans can be added to the dish just before serving or when reheating.

Moroccan-style braise

A warm, spicy braise suitable for lamb, beef or chicken. For cooking notes, see p 240.

SERVES 2

450–570g/1–1¼lb meat, or 2 large chicken breasts or legs

Plus

150ml/¼ pint tomato sauce, for example *Sugocasa*; or use chopped canned tomatoes and their juice

1 onion, finely sliced

2 teaspoons harissa paste

5cm/2 inch piece of cinnamon stick

½ teaspoon freshly ground allspice

olive oil

TO FINISH:

black or green olives; ½–1 teaspoon finely diced preserved lemon peel (p 21) (optional)

Brown the meat in its own fat in a heavy-based casserole dish, then remove and set aside. Add the onion to the casserole and soften, adding a little extra olive oil if needed. Add the rest of the ingredients, topping up with water if necessary so that the liquid comes about 1.25cm/½ inch up the sides of the meat. Bring to simmering point. Cover tightly, transfer to the oven and cook until the meat is tender, around 1–2½ hours. Chicken breasts should take around 30–40 minutes, chicken legs 45 minutes–1 hour.

Mop up the fat and check the consistency of the sauce, reducing if necessary. Add a few olives and scatter finely diced preserved lemon peel to taste over the top of the meat before serving. Serve with couscous, boiled potatoes or rice.

Soy-braised pork with star anise

This Chinese-style braise works uncommonly well for belly pork and is excellent reheated. If you like pork rind, which becomes as soft as jelly, leave it on; otherwise, remove most of it and use to enrich other meat dishes in this section, leaving just a strip on to enrich this one. You can also use the method for shoulder or knuckle of pork.

SERVES 4

450–570g/1–1¼lb lean belly pork, in a piece

1 whole star anise

1 thick slice of fresh ginger root (about 7mm/¼ inch)

2 tablespoons dark soy sauce

2 tablespoons tomato purée

1 clove garlic, crushed (optional)

Put the flavouring ingredients in an ovenproof dish which will just take the pork snugly, adding enough water to cover the base by about 1.25cm/½ inch. Sit the pork on top. Cover tightly and cook in a low oven, 140–150°C/275–300°F/Gas Mark 1–2, for 2–3 hours, or until the pork is meltingly tender, turning it half-way through if you remember (don't worry if you don't). Check the pot after 30 minutes or so and reduce the heat if necessary.

Cool, take off the fat, and reheat when required, cutting the pork into thick strips. Serve with Chinese noodles and stir-fried vegetables.

BRAISED AND ROASTED SHOULDER OF LAMB

Shoulder of lamb is a particularly sweet, luscious meat but is inclined to be fatty. This method of cooking – a gentle braise to tenderise the meat, followed by a hot blast in the oven – is the most successful I have ever found. It removes much of the fat and the joint emerges simultaneously meltingly tender and well crisped. Oxtail can be cooked in a similar way with equally good results.

The method is open to endless variation; you can cook the meat on a bed of potatoes or a mixture of onions and quinces, or with dried haricot beans; you can use wine or brandy, or just plain water; you can cook the meat with masses of unpeeled cloves of garlic; you can use thyme instead of rosemary, or spices such as allspice, fennel and coriander seeds, and even turmeric and cumin.

One caveat: shoulder of lamb *must* be served piping hot, straight from the oven and on hot plates – nothing congeals faster or is less appetising than cold lamb fat.

If there are only 2 of you, use half a shoulder of lamb.

Braised and roasted shoulder of lamb with a navarin of summer turnips and carrots

SERVES 4–6

1 whole shoulder of lamb, about 2kg/4½lb, trimmed of all excess visible fat
150ml/¼ pint each dry white wine and water, or use water plus 4–5 tablespoons brandy, or plain water
1 onion, chopped
1 large sprig of rosemary
1 bay leaf
1–2 strips of scrubbed orange zest

TO FINISH:

12–18 baby turnips, scrubbed (allow 675–900g/1½–2lb)
2–3 large carrots, cut into thick triangular wedges, or 12–18 small whole carrots
1 teaspoon sugar

Choose a large casserole dish with a tight-fitting lid that will just take the shoulder of lamb comfortably. Put the onions and flavourings in the bottom and sit the lamb on top. Pour over the liquid and bring to simmering point.

Cover tightly and transfer the casserole to a low oven, 140°C/275°F/Gas Mark 1. Cook until the meat is tender and beginning to shrink away from the bone. Depending on the age and tenderness of the lamb, this will take anything from 1¼–2 hours, or even a little longer.

Turn off the heat and leave the casserole to cool in the oven until later, or the following day.

For the final cooking, remove the joint and, with a small sharp knife, score the skin in a diamond pattern. Set the meat on a trivet or cooling rack over a roasting pan. Cook in a hot oven, 200°C/400°F/Gas Mark 6, for around 50 minutes, or until well browned and crisp – a little longer will not harm.

While the lamb is roasting, remove the fat from the stock and strain into a bowl, squeezing out the juices from the debris. Place the turnips and carrots in a pan with sufficient stock just to cover, put the lid on and simmer gently until tender, around 15–20 minutes. Transfer the vegetables and juices to a gratin dish, sprinkle with the sugar and pop into the oven to brown about 20 minutes before you serve the lamb.

Set the lamb on a serving dish, carving it into thick slices or chunks. Accompany it with the navarin of vegetables, a few new potatoes, and any remaining meat juices; these can be thickened, if you want, with a teaspoon of potato flour mixed with a tablespoon of water, adding it gradually until the sauce is thickened enough.

DAUBE OF BEEF

This is the classic rich wine-based stew of Provence, traditionally cooked for several hours in a sealed earthenware pot, a *daubière*, buried in the embers of the fire.

Shin of beef is perfect for this dish. A greatly undervalued cut, and one of the cheapest, it is very lean and full of flavour. The large amount of connective tissue works in its favour, as long, slow cooking breaks it down to yield a gelatine-rich gravy, the mark of distinction of all French daubes. The dish should be cooked in advance and improves on reheating. You can alter the flavourings and garnish to suit.

SERVES 4

4 large thick or 8 smaller slices of shin of beef, approx 1kg/2–2½lb in weight

300ml/½ pint robust red wine

thin strip of scrubbed orange zest

1 large sprig of thyme

1 split pig's trotter or large piece of pork rind

OPTIONAL FLAVOURINGS:

55g/2oz bacon, cut into small dice

1 onion, sliced

1 clove garlic, crushed

1 tomato, chopped

1 bay leaf

1 sprig of parsley

olive oil

GARNISH – CHOOSE FROM:

fried mushrooms

caramelised onions/carrots

rinsed and stoned black olives

gremolata (p 246)

1 If using bacon, fry in a little olive oil until lightly browned in the casserole dish in which you will be cooking the beef.

2 Put the beef, wine and chosen flavourings into a deep, heavy-based dish (a Le Creuset one is ideal). Add water if necessary just to cover the meat. Bring to simmering point on top of the stove, cover very tightly, then transfer to a very low oven, around 110–130°C/225–250°F/Gas Mark ¼–½.

3 Cook for 3–4 hours, or until the meat is very tender. Leave to cool in the turned-off oven. It can be eaten now but is better for being left another day or so in the fridge.

4 Reheat gently on top of the stove or in the oven. Transfer the meat to a serving dish and keep warm. Strain the sauce and reduce down until well flavoured; thicken slightly if you want to with 1 teaspoon of potato flour mixed with 1 tablespoon of water, added gradually until thick enough.

5 Meanwhile, prepare the garnish.

6 Pour the sauce around the meat. Add the garnish. Serve with a plain potato purée or with pasta.

Variations

▪ You can marinate the meat beforehand in the wine, together with a sliced onion, for 8–24 hours.

▪ You can add a little brandy or marc – about 60ml/2fl oz – with the wine.

▪ You can use half port and half wine, or half wine and half beef stock. If you have some, add 2–3 pieces of dried mushroom to enrich the flavour of the stock.

Simple garnishes for daubes

These can make a 'meat and sauce' stew. All except the mushrooms can be prepared in advance.

Carrots Cut the carrots into neat wedges. Soften in a knob of butter in a covered pan over a gentle heat for about 10 minutes. Remove the lid, sprinkle over 1 teaspoon sugar and continue to cook gently, uncovered, until the carrots have become lightly caramelised, about 10–15 minutes, stirring often. These can be prepared in advance and reheated just before serving. Add at Stage 6. Swill out the juices with a tiny amount of hot water and add this to the sauce.

Shallots/pickling onions Put in a pan, cover with water, bring to the boil and cook for 3–4 minutes. Drain, cool and remove the skins: slice off the root and the onions will pop out easily. They can then be cooked and served in the same way as the carrots. Alternatively, they can be cooked in the oven in a separate dish at Stage 5: sprinkle with 1 teaspoon of sugar and dab with butter. Pour in enough water to cover the base of the dish, cover loosely with aluminium fool and cook until caramelised. Watch they do not burn.

A mixture of shallots and carrots can also be used, but cook each separately.

Mushrooms Fry these in a little butter in a frying pan over a high heat, tossing them around for 3–4 minutes until browned and just cooked. Add to the dish at Stage 6.

Prunes These should be added at Stage 5, giving them time to plump up and heat through. Use the water they soaked in to replace some of the cooking liquid (Stage 2). Prunes and caramelised shallots are an excellent combination.

Ripe tomatoes Skin the tomatoes and dice the flesh. Spoon a little on top of each piece of oxtail just before serving.

Gremolata This mixture of uncooked finely chopped garlic, parsley and lemon zest is the traditional accompaniment to Osso Buco (p 246), but is also excellent for oxtail or shin of beef. Place a little on top of each piece of oxtail and serve the rest in a small bowl.

Osso buco

Although it is more usual to eat this glorious dish only in Italian restaurants, osso buco – braised shin of veal – is easy to make, and usually tastes better home-made. It is best cooked in advance and will keep perfectly for 3–4 days in the fridge; it can be frozen. Shin of veal is not a cheap cut, so choose it with care: pick out thick, even slices with a decent piece of bone marrow in the centre. The better the tomatoes, the better the dish also. Gremolata is the traditional accompaniment and is essential.

SERVES 4

4 large, thick pieces of shin of veal, weighing about 225g/8oz each, to include the central marrow bone
150ml/$\frac{1}{4}$ pint dry white wine
675g/1$\frac{1}{2}$lb ripe, juicy tomatoes, coarsely chopped
150ml/$\frac{1}{4}$ pint chicken or veal stock
1 carrot, sliced in half
1 celery stick
1 sprig of basil
1 teaspoon tomato purée
2 tablespoons olive oil plus knob of butter

THE GREMOLATA:

small bunch of parsley
1 clove garlic, peeled
2–3 thin strips of lemon zest (use an organic lemon if possible)

Heat the olive oil and butter in a wide and reasonably deep dish and brown the veal on both sides over a moderate heat. Arrange the pieces side by side and upright so that the marrow does not fall out during cooking.

Pour in the wine, let it bubble and then add the rest of the ingredients. Bring to simmering point on top of the stove, cover loosely and transfer to a very low oven, 140°C/275°F/Gas Mark 1. Cook until the veal is tender and beginning to part from the bones; this can take anything from 1$\frac{1}{2}$–2$\frac{1}{2}$ hours. A little longer won't matter.

Leave the veal in the turned-off oven. You can eat it now or keep it in the fridge until required.

To finish the dish, make the gremolata. Chop the parsley very finely with the garlic and lemon until it resembles fine speckles. Put in a small dish and reserve.

If the osso buco has been made in advance, reheat gently on top of the stove. Transfer the meat to a clean, heatproof serving dish and keep hot, covered, in a low oven. Remove the seasonings, then sieve the sauce, pressing the debris hard against the side of the sieve to extract all the juice. Taste and reduce over a highish heat if necessary for a few minutes to remove any wateriness and to concentrate the flavour. Check the seasoning. Pour the sauce around the meat. Sprinkle a little gremolata over each piece of meat.

Serve with plain rice or – even better – pasta, handing round the rest of the gremolata.

Variation For a richer sauce, substitute 300ml/$\frac{1}{2}$ pint of home-made concentrated sauce (see p 117) for fresh tomatoes, adding water if necessary to top up the liquid to come level with the veal.

Lamb, leek and barley stew

Barley is an old-fashioned grain that is slowly finding favour again. It acts as a natural thickener and goes especially well with lamb or beef. Amend the recipe by using less meat and you will have a hearty, meaty broth.

SERVES 4

1 kg/2–2$\frac{1}{4}$lb neck chops, trimmed of all visible fat

4 large leeks, trimmed, cleaned and thickly sliced

6–8 largish waxy potatoes, peeled and cut in half

1 large carrot/2 celery sticks/110g/4oz celeriac, peeled and cut into small dice

45g/1$\frac{1}{2}$oz pearl barley

TO FINISH:

2 tablespoons each of chopped parsley and chives

If you can, choose a wide, deep non-stick casserole dish which will take everything comfortably. Otherwise brown the meat in a non-stick frying pan, then transfer to a wide, deep, heatproof casserole, large enough to take it in a single layer. Brown the meat on both sides. Add all the other ingredients and enough water to cover, then bring gently up to simmering point. Skim off any scum, cover, leaving the lid slightly ajar, and transfer to a low oven, around 140–150°C/275–300°F/Gas Mark 1–2. Cook for around 2–2$\frac{1}{2}$ hours, or until the meat is tender and parting from the bone. The stew should merely shimmer: check after about 30 minutes and adjust the oven temperature if necessary. Remove the lid after 1$\frac{1}{2}$ hours or so to let the stew brown on the surface and the liquid concentrate, adjusting the heat upwards slightly if necessary.

Scatter with parsley and chives and serve from the same dish.

■ You need to cook the stew until the meat is very tender and the liquid has reduced by a good half and is well flavoured and slightly thickened. How long this takes will depend on the meat and the size of the pan. Keep checking and tasting, and be prepared to give the stew a little extra cooking time.

■ The stew should not be fatty. If necessary, use kitchen paper to blot up any excess fat from the surface of the liquid.

Lamb stew with parsnips, peas and coriander

This is a variation on the previous recipe. The sweetness of the parsnips complements the sweetness of the lamb, and the coriander seeds lend an aromatic touch without making the stew spicy.

SERVES 4

1 kg/2–2$\frac{1}{4}$lb neck chops, trimmed of all visible fat

4 large parsnips, cut into thick wedges

4 large leeks, trimmed, cleaned and thickly sliced

1 onion, roughly sliced

1 tablespoon whole coriander seeds

TO FINISH:

170–225g/6–8oz cooked peas

Cook as for the previous recipe, browning the onion along with the meat. The sauce will not thicken this time as there is no barley. Cook the peas separately for 1–2 minutes in a little boiling water and add just before serving. Serve with couscous or crusty bread.

A few waxy potatoes could also be added with the rest of ingredients, as before.

Minced Meat

Minced meat is not to be scorned, for it produces some of our best-loved dishes. The quality of any minced meat will depend, obviously, on the meat you start with and on the way that meat is minced. For raw meat the old-fashioned mincer scores over a food processor every time. Food processors are violent creatures and reduce meat to a paste, whereas a mincing machine produces a proper crumbly texture and meat that retains more of its natural juices. In short, one produces ground meat, the other ground-down meat.

If possible, buy a piece of meat and mince it yourself. Otherwise buy the best mince you can afford. Cheap butcher's mince is bad value: it has a high fat content, smells awful as it cooks and tastes sickly. Good-quality minced meat should have some fat (this is necessary for flavour and eating quality). It should smell sweet, look appetising and be moist.

Making your own minced meat

There is no advantage to be had from using best steak for mincing. First, because you need a certain amount of fat in minced meat; and second, because all meat, once minced, becomes tender. You can use any stewing steak, chuck, neck or skirt steak. One possible exception to this is rump steak, which is cut by hand for making deluxe hamburgers. Make sure the meat is free from gristle and any visible connective tissue or fat.

A hand-cranked mincer is easy to use. Cut the meat into small cubes and feed through, using the medium holes.

Using the food processor

The food processor is better suited to mincing cooked meat, but if you have to use it for raw meat, there are ways to minimise the damage:

Chop the meat into small cubes first and process in small batches of about 225g/8oz.

Process the meat in short bursts, for the shortest time possible, using the pulser if the machine has one.

Mincing cooked meat

Trim away skin, excess fat, etc. Cut the meat first into strips, then chop finely with a sharp knife. Alternatively, use a mincer or food processor, but avoid overprocessing, which will turn the meat into shreds or a paste.

HAMBURGERS

If you want a good hamburger, make it yourself. They are best either barbecued or fried. A few tips:

- The leaner the meat, the drier the hamburger, so the more it is inclined to break apart during cooking. A decent hamburger should have around 10 per cent fat. To help bind the mixture, use 1–2 tablespoons of double cream or 1 egg yolk per 225g/8oz meat.
- Hamburgers need to be well seasoned. If adding flavourings, leave the mixture for up to 24 hours to allow them to permeate the meat.
- Hamburgers should be about 2.5cm/1inch thick.
- They need a light hand: mix the ingredients with care and shape the hamburgers gently with cupped hands.
- The fat must be hot when cooking hamburgers. To help prevent them breaking apart, they must be sealed well for about 2–3 minutes until a brown crust has formed. Resist the temptation to turn them over too soon or to keep prodding them.

Home-made hamburgers

SERVES 4

570g/1¼lb best-quality minced beef

2–3 tablespoons double cream or 2 egg yolks
(optional, but include if the meat is very lean)

olive oil, or oil and butter for frying

Mix the ingredients lightly with your hands, seasoning generously with salt and pepper. Form into 4 thick, round patties: shape into balls in cupped hands, then flatten the tops slightly. Try not to compact them too much. If you can, leave them in the fridge for at least 1–2 hours (longer is preferable) to allow the meat and seasonings to meld together.

To cook, either barbecue gently over hot coals or fry in a little hot fat over a gentle–moderate heat for around 10–15 minutes, turning them over half-way through or as necessary. The timing depends on how thick the hamburgers are and how well cooked you like them – the best way to tell if they're ready is to slit one open and sneak a look. If you like them rare, they will need 5–7 minutes only. In both cases, make sure you sear them well on the first side until they form a decent brown crust; don't try and move or turn them before this. Sear the outer rim also. Use a flat, wide spatula or fish slice to turn them – this avoids any risk of them breaking apart – and continue to cook the other side until done to your liking.

Serve in a bun, plain or toasted, with the usual accoutrements – sliced tomato, onions, cos lettuce. If frying, you can swill out the pan with a few tablespoons of water, boiling it up for 1–2 minutes and scraping in the meat residues, and pour over the burgers. Barbecued burgers are fine on their own. Serve on a wooden board with salad and mayonnaise, spiced tomato sauce, fresh tomato salsa, salsa verde or whichever bottled sauce you like best.

Variations While hamburgers need only salt and pepper as seasonings, you can also try some of the following:

- 1–2 teaspoons of anchovy essence, Worcestershire sauce, soy sauce, chilli sauce, toasted chilli flakes
- 1–2 tablespoons of tomato ketchup or tomato purée, mild mustard, grated hard cheese, for example, Cheddar or Parmesan, chopped capers, olives or gherkins, finely chopped parsley or dill, finely chopped or minced red onion, shallot or mild, fresh seeded chillies, toasted chilli flakes, 1–2 crushed and finely chopped cloves of garlic.

Ready-made hamburgers

It is now possible to buy decent ready-made hamburgers. Look for those which are made from chopped steak and look like hunky man-sized patties, or those from organic farm shops. They will need seasoning. If they have been made in a machine (often the case with organic burgers) and look flat, crumble them up, mix with seasonings and egg yolks, etc., and reform into proper hamburgers by hand.

MEAT PATTIES

Meat patties have a different pedigree and character from hamburgers. Smaller, they are shaped into round balls, flat patties or wrapped around skewers like sausages to form kofte or Indian seek kebabs. Often they are padded out with bread or nuts and then briefly kneaded, which gives them a softer, less open texture.

Meatballs can be made from lamb, pork and veal as well as beef. They are often incorporated into stews or served with sauces.

You don't need much meat: 225g/8oz will make 4 respectable seek kebabs and 8 smaller patties. If you are using bread to pad the meat out, go for a good-texture loaf (the quality of the bread makes more difference than you would think). Again, you don't need much: 30g/1oz per 225g/8oz meat, weighed after the crusts have been removed, is about right. Soak in water for 5–10 minutes to soften, then squeeze out and add to the meat. As with hamburgers, it pays to blend the mixture well in advance: up to 48 hours is fine.

The basic formula is:

minced meat

+

a little finely grated onion

+

seasonings

or

minced meat

+

bread

+

a little finely grated onion

+

seasonings

The seasonings are the same as for hamburgers on p 249.

Coriander seek kebabs

SERVES 2

225g/8oz lamb, beef or pork

½ small onion, grated

1 clove garlic, crushed

handful (that is, lots) of chopped coriander

Blitz everything to a smooth paste in the food processor, seasoning with salt to taste. Divide into two and wrap around skewers with your hands to form two fat sausages. Barbecue for about 10–15 minutes, turning until all sides are nicely browned, and serve with pitta bread.

Italian meatballs in tomato and sage sauce

SERVES 4

450g/1lb lean braising steak, trimmed of fat, skin and connective tissue, cubed (allow about 570g/1¼lb before trimming)

55g/2oz Parmesan cheese, freshly grated

2 tablespoons olive oil

FOR THE SAUCE:

400g/14oz can of tomatoes and their juice

3–4 sage leaves

1 clove garlic, crushed

flour for dusting

a little olive oil for frying

Process the meat in batches in a food processor, for a few seconds only, so that it retains a slightly coarse texture. Alternatively, put through the mincer. Add the Parmesan and the olive oil and mix well. Form into 16 equal oval-shaped meatballs, dusting each one lightly with flour.

Heat a little extra olive oil with the sage in a non-stick frying pan and brown the meatballs all over for about 4–5 minutes on a moderate heat. Add the tomatoes and garlic, bring to the boil, cover and cook gently for about 20–25 minutes. Remove the meatballs to a serving dish and boil down the sauce until it is thick. Pour around the meat and serve with pasta or rice.

11

Barbecuing and Char-grilling

Barbecuing food over charcoal is the method *par excellence* for cooking any tender piece of meat or fish and many vegetables whenever the weather is warm enough to sit outside. A very relaxed way of cooking that is just as suited to 2 as 20, it produces food that is intensely appetising. This is because the smoke from the coals enhances the flavour of the food, and while the outside surfaces become crisp and browned the insides always remain moist and succulent, much more so, in fact, than with conventional methods of grilling.

Char-grilling food inside has also become fashionable in restaurants, where they use purpose-built char-grills. At home, a char-grilled effect can be obtained using a simple flat-ridged cast-iron grill, which gives excellent results, even though it does not produce the same barbecued taste. When I refer to char-grilling, this is the method I mean. For full details see p 263.

Barbecuing: the Essentials

EQUIPMENT

All that is necessary for ordinary domestic purposes is a simple, well-made cast-iron barbecue set on feet with a detachable grid or rack and 2 handles at the side so it can be moved easily. Check that the barbecue has notches so that the grid can be positioned nearer or further away from the coals. If you customarily cook for 2–4, a medium-sized barbecue that will accommodate 4 kebabs or 4 steaks is large enough. You will also need:

- Pair of long-handled tongs for moving and turning food.
- Long-handled spatula for placing and lifting food such as bruschetta and hamburgers.
- Stout stainless steel skewers for kebabs. These should be about 30cm/12 inches long. Thin disposable wooden skewers are useful for Thai satays and for shellfish.

- Fish baskets are essential for fish and hold whole fish and fish steaks comfortably.

For serving food, wooden platters are by far the best. Though it may sound strange, barbecued food tastes better eaten from them rather than from plates, plus they have the advantage of not breaking, so they last for ever.

KEYS TO SUCCESS

It doesn't take long to become proficient at barbecuing food; mainly it is a question of judging the intensity of the fire. Always bear in mind that:

■ The art of barbecuing lies in lighting the fire well in advance, using a generous amount of coals, and waiting until they have burnt down and the embers are glowing red and covered with a grey-white powdery ash. It is only then that the heat is of sufficient intensity to begin cooking. It is also important to use good-quality charcoal; cheap charcoal produces inferior fires that are more difficult to light and do not develop the same intensity of heat, or sustain it.

■ Flames caused by fat or oil dripping from the food on to the hot coals and spontaneously igniting ruin the flavour of the food. It is these which give barbecued food a bad name and unpleasant burnt flavour. They also deposit harmful substances on the food. This applies to the smoke from the flames also. Flames are bound to appear from time to time, especially when the coals are very hot. The remedy is to remove the food immediately and wait until the flames have died down before putting it back on the barbecue.

■ Barbecuing is *not* like grilling food and is actually a gentle process. Although the heat from the fire crisps the surface of the food quickly, the food itself cooks slowly and steadily. Meat and fish in particular will cook better on a relatively cool fire that is glowing gently.

■ Because food stays moist and does not spoil, cooking times are never critical. You literally cook the food until it is done to your liking; if it is not done enough, simply put it back and cook a little longer. In this respect barbecuing is easier than most other methods of cooking.

■ A final point that cannot be stressed enough, particularly if you are new to barbecuing. There is understandably a common view that the art of barbecuing lies in getting the fire red hot and in cooking food as quickly as possible. In fact, the reverse is true. The more unhurriedly and leisurely you cook the food the better it will be. This is why the last piece of food you put on the barbecue always tastes the best. Promise.

PREPARING FOOD FOR BARBECUING

Barbecued food requires minimal preparation. Any specific notes are included under the relevant headings for barbecued meat, fish and vegetables. A few tips:

■ It is customary to brush the food with olive oil first to help prevent it sticking to the grids. However, whether or not food is oiled it will stick initially; the same is true if you place it on a hot ridged iron grill pan or into a hot frying pan. Once it has formed a crust, then it no longer sticks and can be moved around and turned over.

■ Marinating lean dry meat or fish such as tenderloin of pork or tuna beforehand in a little olive oil for a few minutes (or longer if convenient) benefits them by providing some fat to moisten and help them cook. Although you can if you want, this is not necessary for other types of meat which have enough fat of their own, or for whole fish or chicken, which are protected by their skin.

■ You can season food either before or after cooking. Because barbecued food has a rich taste. I prefer to season afterwards, but this is a matter of personal preference. An exception to this is whole fish. The salt becomes impregnated into the skin and enhances its flavour.

HOW TO BARBECUE

1. Lighting the fire

Since not all of us have been boy scouts, I will pass on the advice given to me by a well-seasoned barbecuer about how to light a fire. Use a solid firelighter. Light the fire 30–40 minutes before you want to start cooking the food.

Arrange a heap of coals in the bottom of the barbecue; use the smaller pieces, setting aside large pieces for the top. Make a well in the centre and put the firelighter in the bottom.

Light the firelighter and, using your large pieces of coal, build an igloo-shaped dome or pyramid on top, enclosing the firelighter and leaving an air space. Leave the fire undisturbed for 30 minutes.

Note that once the fire is ready you do not need to add any extra coals. This is why it is important to use a sufficient amount to begin with.

2. Cooking the food

Once ready, the fire retains its heat well and food can be successfully cooked over it for $1-1\frac{1}{2}$ hours, although obviously the fire will gradually diminish in strength during this time. It will take another hour or so to cool down completely. Remember that the position of the grid may need adjusting, depending on the intensity of the fire.

1 Heat the fire well in advance. Once the coals have formed a white surface ash, spread them out to make a flattish bed, 5cm/2 inches thick, to ensure even distribution of heat under the grid.
2 Place the grid on the barbecue, arranging it so that it lies about 5cm/2 inches above the hot coals. Place the prepared food on the hot grid.
3 Cook the food, turning it and moving it nearer the edge or closer to the centre of the fire as necessary. The second *any* flames appear, remove the food and wait until they have died down.
4 If the heat is very intense and the food seems to be cooking too quickly, lift the grid to a higher notch; if it seems to be cooking too slowly, lower it by a notch.
5 Woody aromatic herbs – rosemary, bay, thyme, sage – thrown on to the grid give off wonderful aromas and will perfume meat or fish. You can also lay meat or fish on a bed of herbs: this forms a protective crust as well as flavouring the outside of the food.

Browning: a general caution

Although barbecuing and char-grilling are healthy methods of cooking, it is only fair to point out that browning meat or fish creates tiny amounts of potentially hazardous carcinogenic compounds. This also applies to any method where meat or fish is cooked using high heat, such as grilling, pan-frying or roasting. The darker the browning and the higher the heat used to sear the food, the greater the potential amount of harmful compounds formed.

For this reason it is not a good idea to brown or char-grill the food too much, nor to let it come into contact with the flames at any time, as these deposit additional carcinogenic compounds. Another sensible precaution is to cut away any heavily browned or charred pieces and not eat them.

Vegetables are not affected in this way, and do not form potentially harmful compounds when cooked using intense heat, but the cautionary remarks about flames do apply.

MARINADES AND MARINATING

Marinades are a common feature of barbecued recipes. My own feeling is that, with a few honourable exceptions such as sweet and sour barbecued spare ribs, enhancing the food in a superficial way – for example, laying it on a bed of aromatic herbs, or interlacing kebabs with fresh bay leaves – adds a delightful aroma and fragrance while anything that radically alters the taste of food is best left alone. Barbecued food tastes so sensational on its own it needs nothing extra. In this respect, marinades are not necess-ary for any meat or fish that is decent enough to barbecue and will detract from their natural flavour.

If you want to use marinades, or like to try them from time to time to add variety to your barbecued food, by all means do so. Marinating food in olive oil will help to make it more moist but will not change its flavour; the olive oil can be flavoured with herbs, spices, chilli flakes or citrus zest at the whim of the cook and will flavour the surface of the food only.

Yoghurt marinades alters the taste and texture of chicken and lamb. Spice pastes are useful, if you like them, for kebabs, satays or for rubbing on the skin of chicken. Avoid commercial mari-nades or lurid-looking pre-prepared kebabs and make up your own from a reliable brand of spice paste or appropriate sauces.

Although recipes often stipulate a marinating time, this is rarely critical and food can be mari-nated for longer or shorter as convenient. If you are using olive oil flavoured with spices, etc., either to moisten food or as an external season-ing, it doesn't matter whether you add it to the food just before cooking or 2–4 hours in advance. If you are using a marinade to change the flavour or texture of food, the longer it is marinated, the greater the effect. Allow 4–24 hours.

Brushing food with marinades during cook-ing is not necessarily a good idea and can create its own problems, such as oil dripping on the coals and causing flames, while liquid marinades dampen the fire and produce steam. If you use a liquid marinade, wipe food dry before you barbecue it. Marinades that contain sugar burn easily, and need specially careful cooking.

For further notes on meat marinades, p 217.

MEAT

Meat is the ideal food to barbecue. Whatever kind of meat it is, the tastes are complementary to barbecuing, bringing out the best of the natural flavour of meat. The caveat is that only tender cuts of meat are suitable; despite what books say, anything less will be disappointingly tough. The exceptions are sausages, kebabs, patties and burgers made from minced meat – though again quality matters. Not even a barbecue can make cheap sausages and second-grade butcher's mince taste worth eating.

Meat needs no preparation other than trimming away any excess fat. If you like, nick the edges of chops and steaks to prevent them from curling up. It is usual to brush the surfaces with olive oil. When making kebabs, cut the meat into even-sized cubes, about 2.5cm/1 inch, and do not squash them together too tightly. To ensure each cube of meat is uniformly tender, try and cut them from a single muscle. For more information on this, see p 214.

Finally, don't worry if the weather changes. Pour a little olive oil over both sides of the meat to seal the surfaces, preventing exposure to the air, put on a plate, cover with clingfilm and keep in the fridge. Any red meat treated this way will keep well for 4–5 days. Pork and veal can be kept for 2–3 days. Chicken should not be kept more than 1–2 days, but should be frozen instead.

CHOICE CUTS

The following cuts of meat are all suitable for barbecuing. Average cooking times are based on a fire of moderate intensity. In all cases actual cooking times will depend on the thickness of the meat and the intensity of the fire. For How to Tell When Your Meat is Done, see p 257.

Beef

Only good quality beef should be used for barbecuing. Avoid frying steak or similar second-grade steaks.

Sirloin, rump and T-bone beef steak The classic meat for barbecuing and difficult to beat. They need to be thick: a generous 1.25–2cm/ $\frac{1}{2}$ – $\frac{3}{4}$ inch. Serve with aïoli (best) or mustard, and plain or barbecued potatoes.
Average cooking time: 5–15 minutes.

Fillet of beef Surprisingly good, despite its leanness. Slice thickly, 1.25–2.5cm/$\frac{1}{2}$–1 inch, and moisten with olive oil on both sides. It needs a pat of savoury butter, for example, anchovy or crushed green peppercorn butter, or aïoli to finish it off. Serve with potatoes.
Average cooking time: 5–15 minutes.

Lamb

Lamb is a favourite meat for barbecuing in all Mediterranean countries. The leanest joints are best. Shoulder of lamb is often suggested, though I do not recommend it, because being a fatty joint it needs more careful cooking and can lead to problems with flames. If you do use it for kebabs, make sure the meat is thoroughly trimmed of all fat and connective tissue.

Leg of lamb steaks Almost as good as beef steaks. Marinate in olive oil with a squeeze of lemon juice, plus oregano, thyme or rosemary, first if you want, though plain lamb steaks are equally good. Lay sprigs of rosemary or thyme on the barbecue first and lay the lamb on top for extra aroma. Serve with rice.
Average cooking time: 5–15 minutes for pink meat.

Lamb kebabs A favourite classic. The best are made with leg of lamb, threaded on to large skewers and interlaced with wedges of onion, separated into individual layers, and fresh bay leaves. Place all three in a bowl and moisten well with olive oil, mixing with your fingers before threading on the skewers. For extra aroma, lay sprigs of rosemary on the barbecue first and place the lamb on top. Serve with rice or hot pitta bread.

Average cooking time: 10–20 minutes.

Lamb chops Any lean kind, but cut off all surplus fat.

Average cooking time: 10–15 minutes.

Pork

All pork is tender enough to be barbecued. Because much modern pork is bland, it particularly benefits from cooking on a bed of herbs, or from rubbing into the surface crushed spices such as peppercorns and fennel seeds. Marinate dry lean cuts, including lean pork chops, in olive oil first.

Pork chops Need to be thick and juicy. Cook them on a bed of rosemary, thyme or sage leaves. Spare rib chops have more fat and therefore more flavour.

Average cooking time: 10–20 minutes.

Pork kebabs These can be made from leg or shoulder. Tenderloin of pork, though very lean, is invariably bland. If you use it for kebabs alternate with pieces of bacon. For a fruity version, thread with slices of fresh pineapple. Also try rolling the meat in fennel seeds and threading the cubes with wedges of onion and sage leaves; or rub with Indian or Southeast Asian pastes mixed with a little olive oil. Serve with rice.

Average cooking time: 15–25 minutes.

Pork spare ribs Delicious the traditional way coated with a thick, sweet-sour paste. You can also use hoisin sauce mixed with a little olive oil and spiked with extra ginger, garlic and orange juice. They should be cooked slowly and carefully; watch they do not char too much.

Average cooking time: 30 minutes.

Veal

Vastly underrated and excellent cooked on the barbecue. It is, however, the most expensive meat to buy, so select carefully.

Loin chops Superb, better than beef or anything else. Buy them on the bone (like a T-bone steak). Cook plain or on a bed of sage leaves. Serve with barbecued potatoes or polenta, or rice.

Average cooking time: 10–20 minutes.

Veal kebabs These can be made from shoulder of veal. Spice and oriental flavoured pastes and marinades apart, treat and cook as for pork kebabs.

Average cooking time: 15–25 minutes.

Chicken

Chicken should be cooked with its skin as this bastes it and dramatically improves its flavour. There is no need to oil the skin first. Chicken should also be cooked slowly – the slower the better for legs and wings.

Breast As well as improving the taste, the skin acts as a pocket into which you can stuff chopped herbs, pesto, etc. Or rub it with punchy spiced mixtures, Tandoori pastes and Creole seasoning. Chicken fat has a low melting point and bursts into flame easily – watch out for this. Buy breasts on the bone, which again acts as a protective shield and helps keep the meat juicy.

Average cooking time: 20–35 minutes.

Legs and wings Both are superb cooked on the barbecue. Cook them long and slow until the skin is very crisp.

Average cooking time: 25–45 minutes.

Minced lamb kebabs (seek kebabs)

These can be made from the trimmings of shoulder or leg meat used for kebabs or from lean breast meat, and make excellent starters to serve with pittas. Season well, adding a little finely chopped onion and a spot of oil to moisten the meat while it cooks. You can also flavour them with chopped garlic, dried mint, cumin and fresh and dried coriander. Make well in advance if you can, up to 24 hours ahead, for the flavours to permeate the meat. Using your hands, form into thin sausages around skewers. See Coriander Seek Kebabs, p 250.

Average cooking time: 10–15 minutes.

Sausages

Everybody's favourite. Buy the best. Do not prick. Cook steadily, turning frequently. Serve with aïoli and pittas.

Average cooking time: 20–30 minutes.

Hamburgers and meat patties

Hamburgers are uncommonly good on the barbecue, and can be made from beef, lamb, veal or pork (p 249). Small patties are made in the same way. Serve with salsa or mayonnaise.

Average cooking time: 10–15 minutes for small patties, 15–25 minutes for large hamburgers.

How to tell when meat is done

The following remarks, specifically for barbecued steak, apply to other similar pieces of tender meat cooked on the barbecue or char-grilled on a flat-ridged cast-iron grill. These include lamb steaks and tenderloin of pork.

Whether you like steak rare, pink or well done, suggested cooking times should only ever be taken as a guide. This is because cooking times depend on the thickness of the meat, but also, critically, on the intensity of the heat of the barbecue. A better way is to learn when meat is ready by sight and feel. This is the method professional cooks use.

The feel The simplest and most direct way to judge how well cooked meat is is to press it with your finger: the more the meat yields, the rarer it is. A rare steak will feel soft to the touch, almost as if you were pressing your finger into raw meat with a crust on it (which is what it is). A medium steak will feel springy; anything beyond this is well done and will feel progressively hard to the touch.

The juices The colour of the beads of juice that collect on the surface of the meat after it has been seared on one side and then turned over tell you approximately how well cooked it is. This is one of the reasons why it is not a good idea to turn over the steak for a second time (you lose the beading of juices). As a rule of thumb:

- red beads indicate meat is rare;
- pink beads indicate meat is medium;
- clear juices indicate meat is well done.

FISH

The same general principles apply to barbecuing fish as they do meat, the only difference being that fish should be cooked more gently. Oily fish such as sardines are the exception. To prevent them from being greasy, these should be cooked over a brisk heat close to the coals until well crisped. As with meat, be prepared to adjust the level of the grid as necessary. Apart from descaling and scoring the skin of whole fish, no preparation is necessary.

- Cook fish on the highest notch away from the heat source. Should flames arise, move the fish away until they have died down.
- If you have some, lay the fish on branches of rosemary, fennel or dill. These can be laid in fish baskets and the fish placed on top as shown, or placed on the grid direct. You can also stuff the cavities with herbs if you like.
- Score whole round/torpedo-shaped fish across the back, using diagonal cuts, and cook until the skin, which protects the flesh, is crisp and the flesh just parts from the bone.

- Small oily fish like sardines do not need scoring. They can be placed on the grid direct or threaded on to skewers as shown below.

- If you need to crisp the skin further, sizzle the fish when it is almost done by moving the grid closer to the coals and letting the skin crisp on both sides.
- Soak the barbecue grid and fish baskets in water to dislodge any fish skin, and clean thoroughly afterwards to remove any fishy taints.

Salting fish

Salt enhances the flavour of fish cooked on the barbecue and is specially good for the skin: use coarsely ground sea salt, sprinkling it liberally over the surface. Oily fish like sardines can be buried in a layer of coarse salt for 1–2 hours, or longer if it suits, before being barbecued: this counters the oiliness of the fish and dries the skin, which helps it to crisp. Brush off and discard the salt before you cook the fish. Any small whole fish in the Mediterranean category on p 181 can be treated in this way.

WHICH FISH TO BARBECUE?

Thin fillets apart, it is difficult to think of any fish that you cannot barbecue successfully. As with meat, cooking times vary according to the thickness of the fish and the intensity of the heat.

Whole fish

Any small- or medium-sized whole fish, from the mundane to the exotic, is good on the barbecue. The skin protects the flesh and becomes deliciously crisp; the thicker the skin, the better. Mediterranean fish, with sweet flesh and oval shapes, such as mullet, bream or snapper, and exotic fish like tilapia are perfect. Oily fish need watching as the oil is inclined to drop on to the coals and will flame easily.

Average cooking time: 5–10 minutes for thin, small fish; 10–25 minutes for flat whole fish or medium round fish; 20–30 minutes for salmon tails.

Fish steaks

Salmon, cod, hake, halibut, tuna, swordfish. Skate wings are also good – sandwich them between two flattened fish baskets. Dry meaty fish like tuna and swordfish benefit from marinating in olive oil and lemon juice. They can also be studded with anchovy fillets or slivers of garlic pressed into the flesh with the point of a knife. For a bit of bite, brush white fish steaks with chilli-laced olive oil; or sandwich them in the fish basket between sprigs of rosemary, fennel, dill or oregano.

Average cooking time: 10–20 minutes.

Shellfish

Large prawns and scallops are especially good on the barbecue. Cook prawns in their shells, threaded on skewers, until the shells are crisp, and serve with aïoli. Thread scallops on skewers. Cut squid into squares and crisscross one side with a knife. Paint both sides with olive oil and cook very briefly.

Average cooking time: squid and scallops, 1–3 minutes; prawns 3–5 minutes.

Fish kebabs

Choose firm, meaty fish such as monkfish or tuna. Marinate in olive oil and the finely grated zest and juice of lemon, lime or orange. White fish with firm flesh and large flakes, such as cod, are also suitable. These can be rubbed with Thai or Indian spice pastes mixed with olive oil; or with garlic, ginger, spring onion and soy sauce mixtures; or with chilli, garlic, lemon grass, crumbled kaffir lime and olive oil.

Thread the fish on to skewers with thick wedges of cucumber / green, red or yellow pepper / red onion / mushrooms / cherry tomatoes / sage leaves / bay leaves as appropriate. Bacon is another excellent addition to fish kebabs and goes well with scallops, monkfish and white fish.

Average cooking time: 7–15 minutes.

Barbecued salmon steaks with tarragon

My favourite way of cooking salmon on the barbecue. Lay sprigs of tarragon thickly across both sides of each steak, arrange in a fish basket and barbecue for 5–7 minutes each side. Serve with cucumber raita or tomato salsa and rice.

Sardines with fennel seeds

Barbecued sardines need just a couple of minutes each side. A lovely variation is to sprinkle them liberally with fennel seeds (put some in the cavities also) and clamp them in fish baskets lined with fennel fronds.

Barbecued tilapia with lemon slices and bay leaves

Make 5–6 diagonal slashes down both sides of the fish. Cut a lemon into thin slices, then cut each slice into half and mix with 1 teaspoon of ground cloves – use your fingers and make sure each slice is dusted with spice. Insert a slice of spiced lemon and a fresh bay leaf into each split. Beat the juice of $\frac{1}{2}$ lemon with $\frac{1}{2}$ teaspoon of salt and enough olive oil to make a small amount of thick vinaigrette, then pour over the fish, making sure it gets into the flesh on both sides. Leave it the fridge for up to 6 hours until needed. Barbecue in the usual way. Serve with wedges of lemon.

Slivers of garlic or pieces of dried chilli soaked in hot water to soften can also be slipped into the slits. Serve with a chilli-laced fresh tomato salsa.

This lovely dish can be made in winter using a normal grill. Place the prepared fish in a shallow dish, pour the vinaigrette over and leave until needed. Turn the fish just before you cook it, so that both sides are well moistened. Cook in the dish.

Thai-style barbecued squid

This is an idea from the Carved Angel restaurant in Dartmouth. Cut the prepared squid into smallish squares. Marinate it in olive oil for a couple of hours with shredded red chilli. Thread on small wooden skewers and cook on a hot barbecue for not more than a minute each side until the flesh just turns white. Season with salt and serve immediately, scattered with a little chopped coriander.

SAUCES FOR BARBECUED FISH

Cucumber raita

Peel and coarsely grate a cucumber. Sprinkle lightly with salt, leave for 5–10 minutes, then squeeze out the moisture with your hands. Stir in half a carton of thick plain Greek yoghurt, or to taste. Season with a splash of wine vinegar and add 1 teaspoon of finely chopped dill, tarragon or chives; alternatively, season with a dash of Tabasco sauce. Serves 4–6.

Fresh tomato salsa

Allow 1–2 chopped ripe tomatoes per person. Put into a bowl. Next, for piquancy, add, to taste, a selection from chopped fennel, capers, olives, anchovies, gherkin, spring onions, preserved chopped lemon peel, green chilli and celery. Add a little finely chopped basil, tarragon, mint, parsley or fennel tops, and finish with a splash of wine vinegar and enough fruity olive oil to make a thick sauce.

See also Caribe Salsa (p 95), Salsa Verde and other salsas (pp 70–3), Aïoli, (p 262), Spanish Hazelnut and Pepper Sauce (p 186) and Pestos (pp 65–9).

VEGETABLES

Barbecued vegetables are easy. At home, they tend to be cooked first, as an appetiser before the meat or fish. A brief resumé of the best to use is set out below. The same principles apply as for meat or fish. In all cases, lubricate the vegetables lightly with olive oil first.

Asparagus

This is better blanched first until *al dente*, then finished off on the barbecue. Cook gently for 5–10 minutes, turning once. Do not let it char too much.

Aubergine, fennel and red onion

Cut into thick slices and barbecue until just soft, 5–15 minutes. For ideas for barbecued and chargrilled aubergine, see p 88.

Chillies

Choose large mild chillies. Barbecue whole, turning frequently, for 5–10 minutes until softened. Remove the seeds before eating.

Corn on the cob

One of the best vegetables to barbecue. You do not need to soak the husks in water beforehand. Pull off the brown tassle and cook for 15–25 minutes until the outside leaves are well charred. Remove the husks and eat the corn with melted butter.

Courgettes

Small courgettes can be barbecued whole; larger ones can be sliced in half or cut into wedges. Cook gently until soft. They do not take long, around 5–10 minutes depending on their thickness.

Garlic

Rub whole heads of garlic with olive oil and berbecue slowly, around 45 minutes, until soft, turning them frequently. Or you can blanch them first, which shortens the cooking time and makes them milder.

Mangetout

Choose large ones and barbecue whole for 2–5 minutes so that they remain *al dente*.

Mushrooms

Large open-capped mushrooms are best. Oil well, place cap-side down and cook until soft and the juices are beginning to ooze out, around 5–10 minutes. Serve with aïoli. Or spread a cooked stuffing on to the mushrooms first. Small whole mushrooms are best for vegetable kebabs.

Small onions

Barbecue gently in their skins for around 30 minutes, until they become completely soft; the slower they cook the sweeter they become. Squeeze the pulp out of the skins and serve with steak, pork chops or leg of lamb steaks. If you prefer, they can be blanched in boiling water for 1–2 minutes first.

Red/yellow/green peppers

Slice in half, remove the seeds and barbecue, skin-side down, for 10–15 minutes. Serve with olive oil drizzled over the top.

Potatoes

Another winner. These accompany most barbecues at my home and are excellent. The potatoes can be cooked in advance.

1 Boil large potatoes in their skins until just cooked. When cool enough to handle, remove the skins and cut the potatoes into thick slices. Pour a small amount of olive oil on to a large plate. Arrange the potatoes in a single layer, turning them so that each side is coated with the oil. Leave until you want to cook them. Barbecue gently for around 15–20 minutes until the outsides are crisp and golden, turning them over half-way through.
2 Boil small potatoes in their skins until just cooked; thread on skewers, season with coarse salt and coarsely ground pepper and barbecue for around 5–10 minutes until the skins are crisp, turning frequently.

Tomatoes

Barbecue whole or sliced in half, laying the tomatoes skin-side down. They do not take long, around 5 minutes. Cook until the skins are charred and the tomatoes heated through. Serve with olive oil. See also bruschetta, p 262.

Vegetable kebabs

The knack is to choose a colourful mixture, blanching hard vegetables such as cauliflower, baby onions and carrots for 2–3 minutes first. Cut the vegetables into chunky pieces or cubes, put in a bowl with a little olive oil and herbs of your choice, adding chopped garlic, chopped fresh chilli or toasted chilli flakes, if you like. Mix well and thread on skewers, interlacing the vegetables with bay leaves. For vegetarians, add cubes of tofu, marinating these first either in the same marinade as the vegetables or with soy sauce and ginger. Or spread the tofu with a paste of your choice. Cook gently, turning frequently, for around 10–15 minutes.

Bruschetta on the barbecue

This has achieved such ritual status in my home that no barbecue would be complete without it. Good bread, gutsy olive oil and ripe, tasty tomatoes are a must.

PER PERSON

1 thick slice of country-style bread
1 large, ripe tomato, cut in half
$\frac{1}{2}$ clove garlic
fruity olive oil

Put the tomato skin-side down on the barbecue and cook until softened. Toast the bread on one side only (this can take just seconds). Rub the toasted side with the cut clove of garlic and moisten with olive oil. Skin the tomato and place on the bread, crushing it lightly with a fork so it covers the slice. Moisten with a dribble more olive oil. Using a spatula, carefully put back on the barbecue, untoasted side down. Cook until the underside is brown. Eat immediately, dressed with extra olive oil and seasoned if you wish.

Barbecued polenta

See p 143.

Aïoli: a few tips

The pure version opposite is the one I have settled on as best. Some recipes call for a few drops of lemon juice, which you can add if you like. Remember, too, that the more garlic you add, the more oil you will need for the aïoli to become sufficiently thick. Should it curdle, start again with a fresh egg yolk, beating in the curdled aïoli a teaspoon at a time until well blended, then proceed as before.

Aïoli

A bowl of thick, golden aïoli – the garlic mayonnaise of Provence – turns any meal into a summer feast. It is the best accompaniment for barbecued steak, sausages, fish and shellfish and just about any char-grilled vegetables. It can be spread on croutes and floated on thin fish broths; it is marvellous with boiled potatoes or stirred into cooked broad beans, fennel or cauliflower florets.

Aïoli is only worth making with fresh garlic. You also need a pungent, good quality fruity olive oil. The quantity given below makes a fair amount. At home, I make half this quantity with one egg yolk and this is ample for two. Any remaining stores well for up to a week covered with clingfilm in the fridge.

Aïoli is made in the same way as ordinary mayonnaise. Two things are important. Make sure eggs and olive oil are at room temperature; and pound the garlic until it is absolutely smooth – adding chopped garlic to mayonnaise does not produce anything like such good results.

up to 300ml/$\frac{1}{2}$ pint fruity extra-virgin olive oil
2 very fresh free-range egg yolks (the deeper the colour of the yolk, the more golden the aïoli)
4–6 fresh, fat cloves garlic
$\frac{1}{4}$–$\frac{1}{2}$ teaspoon salt, or to taste

Using a pestle and mortar, pound the garlic to a creamy pulp with most of the salt. Stir in the egg yolks, beating well. Add the oil, drop by drop at first, beating it well after each addition with a wooden spoon to make sure it is thoroughly amalgamated. Once it starts to thicken, this means the emulsion has formed and the oil can now safely be added in a slow trickle, again beating well. Add the oil until the aïoli is thick and stiff enough to stick to the spoon. Taste, add extra salt if needed and cover with clingfilm until required.

Char-grilling

Char-grilling is a great way to cook any prime piece of meat – and polenta – and is well suited to certain fish and vegetables.

You need a heavy, flat, ridged cast-iron grill, which you use like a frying pan on top of the stove. There are various brands. Choose one like the Le Creuset grillomat, made from cast iron with a black matt enamel finish to prevent it from rusting, and it should last a lifetime. They come in various shapes – round, square, oblong – and sizes. If you intend char-grilling vegetables or fish, a large oblong griddle is the best all-purpose shape. Ideally, it is preferable to have one for fish and one for meat and vegetables, though this is not absolutely essential, and you can (I do) use the same grill for all three.

The benefits of a cast-iron grill are that: once heated, it retains its heat and cooks food at a steady consistent heat, emulating the kind of heat effect you get on a charcoal barbecue. The ridges, meanwhile, give the food an appetising charcoal-grilled effect with brown streaks, which enhances its flavour.

The ridges also raise the food slightly; this means it does not sit in its juices. The air space between the ridges creates steam and seems to give the food 'breathing space'.

Pre-heating

The grill should always be heated through before you start to cook. This should be done over a moderate–moderately high heat so that it can heat up evenly, and will take 2–3 minutes.

To test whether it is hot enough, splash a few drops of water on the surface: they should sizzle violently and instantly evaporate. Alternatively, hold your hand about 2.5cm/1 inch over the grill: if it feels hot it is ready.

An overheated grill will burn food and fat; should this happen, remove from the heat and allow it to cool for 1–2 minutes.

COOKING ON A RIDGED CAST-IRON GRILL

As with barbecued food, there is a misconception that to char-grill food effectively the grill must be searing hot and the food must be cooked at an intense heat. This is *not* true. The grill should be hot enough to act like a branding iron when the food is first placed on it, so that the food has char-brown streaks. Thereafter it should be cooked over a gentle heat. If you continue to cook the food at an intense heat, it will burn, dry up and cook unevenly.

Exactly how you cook the food varies slightly whether meat, fish or vegetables, and according to the texture and thickness. It is important to realise, too, that although char-grilling gives a similar appearance to barbecuing, the heat source is very different and char-grilled food cooks much more quickly, just as if you were using any other heavy-based frying pan.

A cast-iron ridged grill is *not* non-stick. Food will stick to it initially, but once a crust has formed it can be moved or turned over. If the food still sticks when you come to turn it, leave it a little longer.

Adding chopped herbs and spices

Though these can be used as flavour enhancers they are not entirely successful. They burn quickly, and will probably get picked off and left on the plate. If you would like to try them it is better to use tough-leaved herbs such as rosemary, sage, thyme or oregano (soft, tender herbs are not suitable) and whole or coarsely ground spices. Sprinkle over food as it cooks, or pat on to meat or the skin of fish direct.

MEAT

Only choose tender cuts of meat, and make sure they are of even thickness. Bring to room temperature before cooking.

■ Cooking times are brief, measured in minutes. You need to give the meat your undivided attention while cooking. Less rather than more is the rule: as with barbecued meat, you can always correct it if it is undercooked.

■ How you cook the meat depends on its thickness. The thicker it is, the more gently it should be cooked after the initial searing. The ideal thickness for steaks or lean slices of meat is 1.25–2cm/$\frac{1}{2}$–$\frac{3}{4}$ inch.

Very thin slices of meat should be cooked over a high heat and will take only around 1 minute each side.

Thick slices of meat, more than 1.25cm/$\frac{1}{2}$ inch thick, should be sealed over a high heat, then cooked over a low heat. Cooking times are around the same as for pan-frying or barbecuing. Lamb, beef and pork will usually take 5–10 minutes and chicken breasts 10–15 minutes.

1 Rub both sides lightly with olive oil.
2 Pre-heat the grill over a moderately high heat until hot, about 2–3 minutes.
3 Slap the meat on the grill at an angle, so that it lies across the ridges. Sear for about 1 minute. For a criss-cross effect, rotate the meat through an angle of 45 or 90 degrees after 30 seconds. Turn over and sear the other side over a high heat for another 30–60 seconds.
4 Turn the heat down to low and continue to cook until beads of juice are showing on the surface, or the meat is cooked to your liking. Do not turn the meat again during this time.
5 Transfer the meat to a hot serving dish and let it rest a couple of minutes before serving.

FISH

Cooking fish on a cast-iron grill is trickier than cooking meat or vegetables. The flesh is softer, more delicate and usually uneven in thickness. Nor is fish as easy to turn over as meat. Char-grilling is best suited to flat whole fish, escalopes of salmon, steaks from meaty fish such as tuna and swordfish, and squid and scallops. Small whole fish such as red mullet can be cooked successfully, though you may need to (try to) turn them 2–3 times to make sure they cook evenly.

Other than scoring, whole fish need no preparation. If the tail or fins do not fit neatly, cut these off with a pair of kitchen scissors. A nice variation for thick fish is to insert thin slices of lemon or orange or bay leaves into the scored flesh.

More so than with meat, once the fish has been seared it is important to cook it gently. Indeed, it is better to turn up the heat at the end to complete the cooking and/or crisp the skin a little more than to have the heat too hot to begin with. Note that thin escalopes, squid and scallops are exceptions and should be cooked briefly over high heat for 30–60 seconds each side.

The method for fish steaks and whole fish is:

1 Score whole flat fish or round/oval fish in the usual way as described on p 174. Paint lightly on both sides with olive oil. Season the skins of whole fish with salt.
2 Pre-heat the grill over a moderately high heat for 2–3 minutes until hot, then lay on the fish. Let it cook for 2–3 minutes, then turn over carefully using a fish slice.
3 Turn down the heat to very low and continue to cook until just done – check the centre of the thickest part with the point of a sharp knife, turning fat torpedo-shaped fish over again if necessary.
4 Serve immediately.

VEGETABLES

Vegetables are the easiest food to char-grill, though not all are suited to this method of cooking. The best are aubergines, courgettes, fennel, red onions, peppers, mushrooms and mangetout. You can also char-grill slices of cooked potato. Thin slices of carrot, parsnip and celeriac are surprisingly good, too.

The same basic principles apply: the idea is not to burn the vegetables but to brown them. The only difference is that they should be cooked at a steady heat throughout. This is because they contain more moisture than meat or fish, and start to sweat easily and become flabby. It doesn't matter if you overcook them.

The general method is:

1 Prepare as for grilled vegetables (on p 86), slicing them thinly. Paint lightly on both sides with olive oil.

2 Pre-heat the grill over a moderately high heat until hot, about 2–3 minutes. Lay the vegetables on top in a single layer. Let them sear for 1–2 minutes, until the underneath becomes streaked with brown and a crust has formed.

3 Turn the vegetables over and continue cooking until just soft – that is, when the point of a sharp knife slides in easily, around 2–4 minutes depending on the vegetable.

4 Serve with olive oil, tomato sauce, pestos, etc.

■ If the vegetables do not move easily when you try to turn them, leave them a little longer. They should cook briskly, as if they were being fried. Adjust the heat accordingly.

Italian-style char-grilled marinated aubergines and courgettes

This produces one of the most delicious ways to eat char-grilled vegetables. You need to slice them ultra-thin. A ridged grill is best but you can also use a heavy frying pan. You may need to experiment a couple of times until you get them right, but thereafter this method quickly becomes second nature. Do them in batches and serve in a large dish with wedges of grilled or roasted red peppers. Thin slices of parsnips, carrots or celeriac can be treated in the same way.

Choose small or medium courgettes and small aubergines, allowing one medium courgette and one aubergine as a first course or side-dish for 2. Slice them from top to bottom as thinly as you can, about 3mm/$\frac{1}{8}$ inch thick. Paint lightly on both sides with olive oil. Cook on a pre-heated ridged grill or in a heavy frying pan as above. Courgette slices will need about 1 minute each side and should be barely cooked; aubergines slices will need a little longer and should be soft in the centre.

Arrange in a serving dish, stacking the slices in overlapping layers. Season with salt, scatter over a little thyme, chopped rosemary, oregano or parsley, and drench with olive oil; ideally they should be covered with olive oil but you can use less.

Cover with clingfilm and leave to marinate for a few hours before serving. Serve at room temperature. They will keep for 2–3 days in the fridge.

Variation Scatter the vegetables with finely chopped preserved lemon peel or a pinch of toasted chilli flakes.

For ideas for char-grilled aubergines, see p 88.

12

Woks and Stir-fry Cookery

Woks and stir-fry cookery suit modern lifestyles and modern ideas on healthy eating so supremely well, it is a wonder we have ever managed without them. The key to making the most of this simple utensil and easy method of cooking is not to confine wok cookery to Chinese or Southeast Asian food, or to think that stir-fried food has to be authentic, or even necessarily taste 'oriental'. Western ingredients work just as well in a stir-fry as Asian ingredients. Stir-frying is primarily a technique of cooking small pieces of tender food quickly. It does not require specific recipes. Though a wok is ideal, it is not mandatory. As long as you do not overcrowd the pan, you can stir-fry just as successfully in a large frying pan or a saucepan.

There is nothing strange about a wok. A masterpiece of simplicity and functional design, it is as perfect and as versatile a cooking vessel as you can get. Though it is primarily used for stir-frying, you can literally cook anything in it, including bacon and eggs if you want.

WHAT MAKES A WOK UNIQUE

What makes a wok unique is its shape and size. Being curved, it collects ingredients and liquid at the bottom; being capacious, it gives you lots of room for manoeuvre. The combination of the two means it handles small or large quantities with equal ease. It also means that apart from stir-frying you can, in fact, steam, poach, braise or do just about anything in it – including using it as a home-smoker, to boil water or just to cook chops in if you want. To give you an idea of the versatility of a wok, some of the ways you can use it include:

- to cook and toss pasta or Chinese dried noodles;
- to blanch vegetables;
- to cook fish stews and chowders;
- to cook mussels;
- as a deep-fat fryer;
- to poach fruit;
- to make tomato sauces;
- to make small quantities of jams and preserves.

CHOOSING A WOK

Design features are paramount. What you want is a single-handled wok with a deep bowl and a base which suits your cooker. Single-handled woks enable you to toss the food with one hand while stirring with the other. Two-handled woks are specifically for steaming or deep-frying rather than stir-frying.

Thereafter it depends on your heat source, how often you are likely to stir-fry, and whether or not you prefer to stir-fry in the traditional Chinese way. There are essentially three options:
1 Traditional round-bottomed carbon-steel Chinese woks are only suited to cooking on gas.
2 If you cook on an electric or solid-fuel cooker, you'll need a wok with a slightly flattened base. This shape is not ideal, but it is a necessary compromise for the wok to be stable. Generally speaking, heavier-based woks are better than thin-based ones, which develop hot spots and therefore burn food easily.
3 To stir-fry in the traditional Chinese way, you need a traditional Chinese wok. To stir-fry any other way, you can use any other kind of wok or capacious pan.

■ Never buy a small wok, even if you only cook for one or two. However small the quantity of ingredients, a larger wok is much easier to use. The standard recommended size is 35cm/14 inches in diameter.

■ Some woks are heavier than others; pick the wok up and see if it feels comfortable to shake and toss easily.

■ A domed lid is invaluable and can be bought separately. So can simple steaming racks or trivets which sit in the bottom of the wok.

Which material?

Though woks themselves are a model of design, the materials of which they are made are not. Which to choose depends, again, on your heat source, how much you are likely to use your wok and whether you prefer the traditional Chinese method of stir-frying or not.

Carbon steel woks Most traditional Chinese woks are made out of thin carbon steel. Chinese cooks would use no other. They are cheap to buy, can be heated up over a fierce heat, are an excellent conductor of heat and are very durable. Because the heat travels quickly and evenly up the sides of the wok, it provides the largest possible surface area to cook food quickly. If you cook on gas and want to stir-fry the traditional Chinese way, this is the wok you should buy. Its disadvantages are that it rusts easily and needs meticulous looking after, especially if you only use it occasionally. Also, acid in the form of vinegar or lemon juice reacts with the steel and taints the food slightly.

Non-stick woks These are a Western invention. Being non-stick, they are easy to use and easy to clean. Their major disadvantage is that the non-stick coating burns easily. For this reason it is not worth buying cheap non-stick woks; invest in a more expensive kind with a heavier base and a bonded non-stick coating. For this reason, too, they are not suited to the traditional Chinese method of stir-fry, but are excellent for other kinds of stir-fry.

Enamel woks An enamel wok is used by South-east Asian cooks and is suitable for stir-frying over moderate heat. The sides burn if the heat is too high, making it less suitable for the Chinese method of stir-fry.

Cleaning and storing a wok

Traditional carbon-steel woks develop a blackish patina which, as Chinese cooks will tell you, gives a wok its satin-smooth surface and 'grip'. To protect this, as soon as you've finished cooking, wash the wok in hot water with a soft brush. Do not use soap. For stubborn bits of food, use rough salt as an abrasive (a non-scratch scourer is OK, too). Dry thoroughly, putting it back on a low heat to drive off any remaining moisture. Finally, if you use a wok less than once a week (or keep it in a damp atmosphere), rub a little oil over the surface with a piece of kitchen paper; this will protect it from rusting. Before using, wash off the oil first. This is especially important if you use the wok infrequently, as the film of oil goes rancid quite quickly.

A traditional carbon steel wok needs seasoning before you use it for the first time. Scrub it thoroughly in hot water to remove the protective oil. Dry, place over a low heat until hot, then rub all over with a wad of kitchen paper dipped in a little vegetable oil until the paper becomes black. Repeat using fresh oiled kitchen paper until the paper stays clean. Should the wok become rusty in future, scrub off the rust, then repeat the seasoning process before using.

Other types of wok need no special cleaning, just washing with hot soapy water in the usual way, followed by thorough drying; alternatively, see the manufacturer's instructions.

Woks take up room. The most convenient way to store them is to hang them on the wall, or keep them on top of a cupboard, where they inevitably collect dust (this is where a lid comes in handy). The other good place to store them is on the floor under a work table. Rinse them first before using.

Other essential implements

Wok cookery comes with its own *batterie de cuisine* of metal scrapers, spoons, drainers and bamboo-type brushes for cleaning. None of these is necessary, though all are nice to have. Their main advantage is that they enable large amounts of food to be scooped and tossed in one go. A fish slice or large skimmer serves almost as well. If, like me, you can't abide the sound of metal scraping metal, use a wooden spatula. Chopsticks are handy for moving small amounts of food around or for separating pieces of food. A simple trivet for steaming is also useful. A Chinese cleaver for chopping gives me the shudders, though I know many cooks who use nothing else.

Stir-fry Cookery

Stir-frying is a modern cook's dream: the method is simple to master, it requires small amounts of ingredients, making it one of the cheapest meals to produce, and it is remarkably versatile. Indeed, for making impromptu meals out of virtually nothing, I know of no other method which yields such tasty results. The secret is to divorce stir-frying from its roots. If you think of it as a method of cooking first and an oriental meal second, then it will automatically become a way of life.

A stir-fry meal does not have to be a gastronomic *tour de force*. The simplest – and often most successful – stir-fries are composed of a base of Chinese noodles, topped with a few stir-fried vegetables, with perhaps some strips of meat. A separate dish of Soy-braised Pork with Star Anise, which can be cooked in advance (p 242), or Shredded Sesame Omelette (p 279) would be excellent. Though perhaps I should not say so, experience has also taught that a mixed stir-fry of Western vegetables is nicer than one using solely Chinese greens.

There are one or two caveats here. Though stir-frying is a fast way of cooking, it is not a fast way of preparing dinner. The preparation – cutting and dicing ingredients, mixing up sauces, etc. – takes a fair bit of time. Allow for this when calculating how many dishes to serve or what cook. The best advice is not to be too ambitious. Keep it down to one or two dishes, and things will work out fine.

Secondly, despite the impression often given in cookery books, trying to create an 'authentic' stir-fry at home is, frankly, difficult. It is impossible to re-create the kind of heat used in the kitchens of a Chinese restaurant, or to master the dexterity of Oriental cooks, who can toss a panful of stir-fry with the flick of a wrist. Anyone who has been brought up with a particular cuisine has a native understanding and different 'taste-bank' experience from those of us who come to it, as it were, second-hand, and we should not expect too much of ourselves. This in no way means that stir-frying at home is second best, rather that it is different. The results are just as good, and can often be better, because the stir-fry is made to your taste.

GAS V. ELECTRIC

There is a common view that gas is by far the best heat for stir-frying. It provides instant heat, can be adjusted in a flash, and the flames envelop the base of the wok, giving heat where it counts. However, though true in the general sense, because of the way that gas hobs are designed some traditional round-bottomed woks cockle and often need a wok stand, which sits on the grid over the flame, to remain stable. This means the wok is raised above the heat and the heat is dissipated more. If this is the case, use the largest gas jet you have to stir-fry; or remove the hob grid and set the wok stand directly over the jet. Aluminium wok stands can be bought cheaply. They are useful for storing woks also.

Electric hobs work quite well but do not have the flexibility of heat control, which makes for harder work and poorer results. For electric hobs you will need a flat-bottomed wok. They suit a stir-fry cooked over a moderate heat better. If you become a devotee of wok cookery but are stuck with electric or a less than ideal gas hob, you can invest in a purpose-built (expensive) gas wok hob, which runs on mains and Calor Gas.

WHAT IS STIR-FRY?

Stir-frying consists of briefly cooking tender meat, fish or vegetables in a little oil or fat over a brisk heat in a wok or roomy pan. The average cooking time is 2–5 minutes. The distinguishing characteristics are:

- Ingredients for stir-fries are always cut up into strips or bite-sized pieces. Because the food is cooked swiftly, stir-frying is only suitable for tender cuts of meat.
- Unlike in Western dishes, meat and fish often assume the role of flavouring ingredients. This means you need far less meat or fish in a stir-fry, which is bulked out with strips of crisp vegetables to add colour and texture.
- Once in the pan, the ingredients are stirred about constantly. Hence the name 'stir-fry'.
- Stir-frying follows a set order: aromatics first, ingredients second, sauce last.

Successful stir-frying in turn depends on:

- The quantity of food – Don't try and stir-fry too much food in one go. All the food must come into direct contact with the heat, otherwise it ends up being steamed rather than stir-fried.
- Correct cutting – This enables each piece of food to cook quickly. The aim is to expose as much surface area as possible. This is achieved by cutting the ingredients into slanting or diagonal slices, or into thin strips.
- Gauging the right heat.
- Movement – Keep stirring the ingredients and shaking the pan.

The basics of stir-fry

Organisation Stir-frying has to work like clockwork. For this to happen smoothly, all the ingredients need to be prepared in advance, with sauces pre-mixed, bottled ingredients at hand and everything easily accessible – that is, next to the stove. It also pays to be logical: arrange the flavourings around a plate, so you can slip them into the wok in an orderly progression, and have all the vegetables which are to be cooked together in a plastic bowl so they can be tipped in in one go.

Quantity The pan or wok should never be more than a third full; any more and the ingredients will steam rather than stir-fry. You also run the risk of ending up with half your stir-fry on the floor.

Heat You do not necessarily have to use a blistering heat to stir-fry effectively. The reason why the Chinese stir-fry over intense heat is historical rather than culinary. In other parts of Southeast Asia stir-frying is conducted at a more gentle pace, using a moderate to hot heat. What this means in practice is that you have a choice: if you find Chinese stir-fry too frenetic, you can opt for the more gentle Southeast Asian style or even go for something in between.

Timing There is a misconception that each ingredient in a stir-fry has to be cooked for a precise number of seconds or minutes, and that stir-frying needs to be timed with a stop-watch. This is not true. While this is a rapid means of cooking, the vegetables can be cooked to the degree of doneness you like, be it crisp or soft.

Serving stir-fries Nothing is worse than dried-up noodles or a limp stir-fry. Unlike with other methods of cooking, stir-fried food really does need to be served immediately it is ready, while the food is as fresh, colourful and crisp as can be.

HOW TO STIR-FRY

The two methods that follow illustrate the extremes of how to stir-fry. The essential difference between them is the intensity of the heat. What they both show, though, is that the method and technique rather than the ferocity of the heat are the most important aspects of stir-fry to grasp. For general stir-fries, a good compromise is somewhere in between.

Chinese stir-fry

This is the most familiar style of stir-fry. Everything is done at great speed and the food is cooked over the highest heat you can manage, using a traditional Chinese wok.

A successful Chinese stir-fry produces food with a concentrated flavour, brought about by a combination of two factors: first, the surface moisture is driven off very quickly; and secondly, the food is cooked so quickly that its internal moisture does not have time to seep out. To achieve this you need enough room in the pan for all the pieces of food to come in contact with the side of the wok.

Remember that heating woks in a domestic kitchen can be more of a hit-and-miss affair than is generally recognised. You need to take account of your particular heat source and how your wok heats up, and work around this as best you can.

The basic cooking method is:

1 Set the wok over a moderate heat. Rub the inside surface with kitchen paper dipped in a little vegetable oil. This 'seasons' the wok, sealing the surface, and improves the grip. Continue to heat over a high heat for another minute or so until very hot. Add 1–2 tablespoons of oil and swirl it around.

2 Immediately after the oil has been added, add the aromatics – ginger, garlic, chilli, spring onion. Cook for a few seconds, stirring constantly.

3 Keeping the heat high, add the rest of the ingredients. Let them sear for a few moments, then toss, shake or stir constantly for 1–3 minutes until barely cooked.

4 Add seasoning of soy or any other sauce. Stir well to coat and serve.

Comments

- The higher the heat and the thinner the wok, the more quickly the food will cook.
- How 'charred' you make the stir-fry is a matter of individual preference. If the food is charring or burning too quickly, remove the wok momentarily from the heat.
- If you are using a non-traditional, heavy-based wok, you will need to adapt the method slightly to accommodate the thickness of the pan. Here, use a high but not ferocious heat, and settle for a crisp but not heavily browned stir-fry.

Gentle stir-fry

Here, as Southeast Asian cookery expert Sri Owen explained, the cooking is done over a less intense heat. The wok is generally not heated first; instead the oil is put in and both are heated together until hot enough for the food to sizzle when added. Vegetables are also cooked slightly longer – until they are just soft. This is achieved by putting the lid on the wok for the final 1–2 minutes, so that the vegetables steam rather than fry. Otherwise, everything remains the same.

1 Set the wok over a moderate heat, adding 1–2 tablespoons of oil. When the oil is hot, add the aromatics, stirring constantly for 30–60 seconds.

2 Add the meat/fish/vegetables. Stir-fry over a moderate to high heat until just cooked, adjusting the heat as necessary so that the food fries briskly.

3 Add seasoning and a little sauce, or chopped fresh tomatoes.

4 If cooking vegetables, put the lid on and cook for a further 1–2 minutes until they are just soft.

5 Add any fresh herbs and serve.

A FEW PRACTICAL TIPS ON INGREDIENTS

Meat and fish

Stir-frying is suitable only for tender strips of lean meat and poultry, for firm fish such as monkfish and squid, and for shellfish such as scallops and prawns. Tough meat, soft-fleshed fish, which breaks up too easily, and oily fish are not suitable.

- Semi-frozen meat and poultry can be sliced into thin strips very easily using a sharp knife. By the time you come to cook the stir-fry they will have thawed.
- Meat can be used to flavour any stir-fry successfully. Fish is more limited and should be used in specific recipes with vegetables such as mangetout and red peppers.
- Both meat and fish need the briefest of cooking: 1–3 minutes. Longer will toughen meat and overcook fish.
- The simplest way to ensure meat and fish do not overcook is to stir-fry them first, then keep them on a hot plate while you cook the vegetables. Either return them to the pan and toss with the vegetables, or arrange the vegetables on a hot serving dish and place the slices of meat or fish on top.
- You need far less meat or fish than in a conventional Western meal. For a main course, 55–110g/2–4oz per person is ample; 30–55g/1–2oz per person goes a long way and is sufficient to give a 'meaty' feel to a dish.
- Leftover cooked meat is excellent in stir-fries and can be fried first or tossed with the vegetables; or moistened with a little sauce and reheated separately.

Vegetables

Many vegetables are suitable for stir-frying. Although it is better to prepare them just before you start the stir-fry, they can be prepared in advance and kept in a sealed box in the fridge.

Good ones include:

bean sprouts	celery	peppers
broccoli	courgettes	spinach
cabbage	leeks	spring onions
cabbage, Chinese	mangetout	sweetcorn
carrots	mushrooms	watercress
cauliflower	peas, frozen	

- Leafy vegetables wilt down to nothing, so you will need a fair quantity if you want them to form a significant part of the stir-fry. Because of the volume, these stir-fry much better in a wok. They are usually shredded, thickly or finely. An easy way to do this is to take a big handful in one hand and snip them with kitchen scissors a bunch at a time. Other vegetables, in contrast, once diced, bulk up alarmingly; you need small amounts of these, and they can be stir-fried successfully in a frying pan.
- The easy way to stir-fry vegetables is *not* to worry that some may take slightly longer than others, but to cook everything together, tossing the vegetables constantly by a combination of stirring and shaking the pan to and fro vigorously until thoroughly hot, about 1–2 minutes. This effectively produces a crisp, hot 'salad', and works every time.
- If you prefer slightly softer vegetables, add 2–3 tablespoons of stock or water, or water with a dash of soy. This produces an immediate jet of steam, which completes the cooking. Clamping on the lid and turning down the heat to low has the same effect; cook for 1–2 minutes longer.
- Adding a few sweet-tasting vegetables will lift any stir-fry and make it immediately appetising. Good ones to use are diced/strips of red pepper, frozen peas, a little grated carrot and chopped fresh tomatoes (added at the last minute).

- Hard vegetables such as cauliflower florets or French beans are best blanched briefly first.
- Because they soften easily and have a milder fresh flavour, spring onions or shredded leeks are better than onions to use for stir-fries.
- Chinese vegetables that have a crisp midrib should be shredded or sliced and added with the other vegetables.

Fresh herbs

Fresh herbs are not a feature of Chinese stir-fries, but they are often used in Thai cooking, make a pleasant change and work nicely in most stir-fries. The best herbs to use are coriander, chives, mint, basil and lemon thyme. Add them just before serving.

Nuts

Nuts are a delicious addition to stir-fries. Keep a packet or two in the storecupboard.

- Mild, milky nuts are best. Choose from cashew nuts, pine kernels, macadamia nuts and flaked almonds.
- Nuts can be used to bulk out any vegetable or meat-based stir-fry. A small handful, 15–30g/$\frac{1}{2}$–1oz, is sufficient for a stir-fry supper for two. They can either be added when you cook the stir-fry or tossed in at the end.
- Flaked almonds are good toasted and scattered over the top of the stir-fry just before serving.

Cutting ingredients for stir-fries

The aim is to cut ingredients so that they can all be cooked in approximately the same amount of time. Meat and fish are cut across the grain. Some of the cuts most commonly used are:

Slices The ingredients are cut into very thin slices, 3–7mm/$\frac{1}{8}$–$\frac{1}{4}$ inch thick, and about 5cm/2 inches long, either straight or on the diagonal, which exposes a greater surface area. To make julienne or matchstick slices, stack the thin slices on top of each other and cut down the length to form matchsticks. Use for meat, fish and hard vegetables like carrots, celery and mooli radish, and for softer vegetables like courgettes, runner beans, mangetout, spring onions and leeks.

Slices of vegetables, for example, mushrooms, carrots, celery, cauliflower and broccoli florets, may also be cut crossways into thin rounds or cross sections.

Dices This is achieved by stacking slices on top of each other and dicing into tiny cubes. Used for hard vegetables and onions. French beans are cut into short lengths.

Shreds This is used for cabbages and other leafy greens, rolling loose leaves into a tight cigar first. Shred across with a serrated knife into thick or thin ribbons.

Wedges Cucumber, carrots, and radish can be cut into V-shaped wedges by cutting the vegetable from top to bottom into quarters or sixths, then slicing each segment across into thick or thin wedges. Asparagus and celery can be cut into triangular wedges by making a diagonal cut across the stem, then making a second diagonal cut the other way to form a V.

Essential Flavourings

The great thing about stir-frying is that the number of flavouring ingredients you need is very small. Everything else comes out of a bottle. And you don't need very many. Oriental shops and supermarkets have a wide range to choose from.

The main flavouring ingredients are as follows:

Fresh aromatics	Spices	Bottles
fresh chillies	5-spice powder	chilli sauce
garlic	star anise	hoisin sauce
ginger		oyster sauce
spring onions		plum sauce
		rice vinegar
		sesame seed oil
		soy sauce

For Thai and Southeast Asian flavourings see pp 276–7; for notes on individual flavourings see pp 280–1.

Oils and fats

A number of oils and fats are suitable for stir-frying. Sesame seed oil and butter are not; both have low smoke points and burn too easily.

Grapeseed and groundnut (peanut) oil These are the two best general-purpose oils for stir-frying. Both are flavourless. Grapeseed has the higher smoke point (230°C) and is the better of the two.

Olive oil Olive oil has the same smoke point as groundnut oil (210°C) and is also suitable for stir-frying. It does impart its own flavour, though generally this is scarcely noticeable. Use a mild-flavoured olive oil.

Poultry fat Though they have lower smoke points and therefore should not be heated as much, chicken and duck fat add extra flavour to stir-fries. Use them mixed with a little oil.

If you have some, chicken or duck skin can be cooked gently in the wok to release its fat, which can then be used for the stir-frying. Finish crisping the skin under the grill or in the oven if necessary and serve broken into pieces scattered over the stir-fry, or in a separate bowl as a tasty accompaniment.

Pork and bacon fat These also add flavour to stir-fries. They have higher smoke points than poultry fat, but not as high as oils. You need very little oil or fat to stir-fry well, just enough to coat the sides of the wok or pan. This usually works out to 1–2 tablespoons; if the food looks too dry or is sticking, add a little extra.

The oil should be hot enough for the food to sizzle as soon as it is added to the wok or pan, but preferably not smoking. You can disregard instructions that tell you to heat the pan, then wait for the oil to heat up. If you heat the wok or pan first, the oil or fat will automatically be hot enough the second it is added and swirled around.

Seasonings

Salt You won't need to add salt to any kind of oriental-flavoured stir-fry; every bottled oriental sauce and condiment has plenty.

Pepper White rather than black pepper is preferred in China and is used less than in the West. Freshly ground black pepper is more a feature of Thai and Indonesian food. Neither is obligatory; use if you like it or as you see fit.

Sugar Sugar is a standard seasoning in Thai food. A little sugar brings out the flavour of stir-fried vegetables – a useful tip to know. Use about $\frac{1}{2}$ teaspoon, sprinkled on when you stir-fry the vegetables.

EASY WAYS TO FLAVOUR STIR-FRIES

Standard sauces

One of the reasons oriental stir-frying is so easy for a domestic cook is that the same few ingredients are used repeatedly to produce the 'sauce'. All you have to do is change them about a bit. A basic standard formula for Chinese-style stir-fries is:

2 tablespoons soy sauce +
1 tablespoon sherry +
1 teaspoon cornflour +
1 teaspoon sugar.

Mix them together, then add to the stir-fried vegetables, stirring until well coated. Check the seasoning and add extra soy as needed. Serve.

Using this basic formula, you can ring the changes to produce different flavours. Some examples are:

- Substitute the sherry with plum sauce or hoisin sauce diluted with 1–2 tablespoons of water.
- Add a few drops of chilli sauce.
- Substitute soy and/or sesame seed oil for oyster or teriyaki sauce.

The cornflour in the mix thickens on contact with the heat and helps to soak up extra moisture from the vegetables. If you are using a dry stir-fry mixture, you will need to add a little chicken stock or water to the basic formula. Alternatively, for dry mixtures, you can leave the cornflour out, substituting a dollop of thick hoisin or plum sauce, which will act as a thickener.

Pastes and bottled sauces

These can also be spiked with additional flavourings to produce instant sauces. Some examples are:

Thai curry paste Mix 1–2 teaspoons of Thai curry paste with 5–6 tablespoons of coconut milk, or 1 teaspoon of honey and 2–3 tablespoons of soy sauce.

Hoisin sauce Mix 2 tablespoons of hoisin sauce with 1 teaspoon of finely grated ginger, a little sherry and soy sauce to taste.

Plum sauce Mix 2 tablespoons of plum sauce with a good pinch of 5-spice powder, 1 tablespoon of tomato purée, and soy or teriyaki sauce to taste.

In each case, stir-fry the meat, add the mixture and cook briefly until the flavours have melded. If you are using cooked meat, pour the mixture over it, and reheat under the grill or in the oven until thoroughly hot and the edges of the meat are beginning to catch.

As a general guideline, spike strong, salty-based sauces with honey/sugar or a sweet sauce, and vice versa. Ginger, garlic, chilli and spices can be added at whim.

Paste Hoisin; oyster sauce; peanut sauce; plum sauce; Thai.

Liquid Chicken stock; coconut milk; sherry; soy sauce(s); water.

Flavourings Chilli (fresh/sauce/flakes/oil); garlic; grated ginger; sesame seeds/oil; nam pla/fish sauce.

Sweetener Honey; sugar.

Other easy ways to flavour stir-fries

- Use one of the various soy sauces or chilli sauces, shaking a few drops over the stir-fry just before serving.
- Depending on the quantity of food, dilute 1–3 tablespoons of bottled sauce with water or sherry to a thick pouring consistency. Pour over the cooked stir-fry, toss and serve. Perk up with a dash of chilli, sesame-seed oil, rice wine, soy sauce or 5-spice powder.
- A tip from one of the best cooks I know: have the bottled sauces on the table and let everyone season their own stir-fry.

THAI STIR-FRY

Thai food is a subtle and tantalising mixture of sweet, sour, spicy and nutty flavours, with the accent on simplicity and freshness. Easy to make at home, Thai stir-fry differs from Chinese in three respects. First, it uses a different, more fragrant, group of flavourings; secondly, it uses curry pastes and coconut milk to produce a range of stir-fried curried dishes; and thirdly, it uses sugar as a seasoning, and nam pla and Thai soy sauce, rather than dark Chinese soy. Otherwise the technique is the same. Glutinous rice or Thai fragrant (Jasmine) rice are served with Thai food, though Chinese dried noodles go well.

Essential flavourings

These are the ingredients commonly used in Thai cooking. The ones marked with an asterisk are the most distinctive and stamp 'Thai' on any simple stir-fry. Remember that though fresh chillies feature in virtually every dish, Thai food is not necessarily hot. It is, however, always fragrant.

basil	kaffir limes*
chilli-basil sauce	lemon grass*
chillies*	nam pla (fish sauce)
coconut milk*	oyster sauce
coriander	satay (peanut sauce)*
garlic	Thai curry pastes*
ginger	Thai soy sauce
kaffir lime leaves*	

QUICK CHECKLIST

Coconut cream and coconut milk

The convenient kind comes in packets (cream) and tins (milk). Coconut cream is so hard because it is extremely high in saturated fats. This is not to say don't use it, but just to remind you that if you think butter is unhealthy, or cannot eat it for medical reasons, coconut cream is worse, and so it would be wise to steer clear of it or use it in small quantities. To make coconut milk, dilute coconut cream with enough hot water to give you a smooth sauce of the thickness you require. As a general guide, 30g/1oz coconut cream will give a dish a perceptible coconut flavour:

30g/1oz coconut cream

+

2 tablespoons of boiling water

= thick sauce;

30g/1oz coconut cream

+

4 tablespoons of boiling water

= thin sauce.

Though convenient, coconut milk made from coconut cream has a slightly flat flavour. By comparison, fresh coconut milk – not to be confused with the sweet, watery liquid inside the coconut – has a lovely fresh, sweet flavour. To make this, you need a fresh coconut and the patience to hack out the white flesh. The rest is easy. Whiz the pieces of coconut in a food processor until finely chopped. Pour boiling water over the mush and squeeze out through a sieve, collecting the thick coconut milk in a bowl. The grated coconut can be stored in a freezer for up to 12 months. It can be used instead of desiccated coconut, and has a better and sweeter flavour.

Galingal

Similar to ginger in flavour and appearance but has a thinner skin and a pinkish tinge. It is used in Thai cooking. As it it not generally available, fresh ginger may be substituted.

Kaffir lime leaves

Wonderful bright-green shiny leaves with an exotic, spicy, slightly bitter lime scent and flavour. They are available in packets from ethnic shops or mixed in packets with lemon grass and Thai chillies from supermarkets. Shred finely with a knife or snip with scissors. One will perfume a whole dish. They do not stay fresh for long but dry out naturally in a warm kitchen. Use like bay leaves, crumbling them in the same way. If you want to keep their bright green freshness, pop them in the freezer instead.

Lemon grass

Long, slender stalks with an intense lemon-citrus flavour similar to lemon verbena. They keep 2–3 weeks in the salad drawer of the fridge; otherwise freeze.

The outside layers are tough. They should be peeled off and used to flavour stocks, soups, coconut milk, etc. The tender inner core is the part used in a stir-fry, to flavour rice, crab cakes, etc. Shred finely or grate on a hand-grater.

Mint and basil

Thai mint and basil are stronger and more med-icinal than the sweet mint and basil Europeans are familiar with. Available from Thai shops; otherwise use whichever mint or basil you have.

Nam pla

This fish sauce made from fermented anchovies is a remarkably good seasoning, and nothing like as fishy as it sounds. A few drops heighten the flavour and add an indefinable (and most agreeable) salty piquancy to dishes. Nuoc nam is the same thing from Vietnam. They are available from Chinese supermarkets and Asian stores.

Thai soy sauce

A light and piquant soy sauce, more akin to a flavoursome stock. This is my favourite soy sauce, especially for fish. Available from Chinese and Thai supermarkets and shops.

Thai yellow, red and green curry paste

These can be bought in tins, packets or fresh from Thai supermarkets and keep for ages. The yellow (mild) is bearable; the red (mild) curry paste is hot; the green (hot) curry paste is searing hot. They are different in style from Indian curry pastes, being a mixture of garlic, chilli, spices, nam pla and herbs such as coriander and lemon grass. Apart from in Thai-style curries, they can be used as fragrant pastes to flavour rice, potatoes, soups, fish, etc.

Simple Thai fragrant stir-fry

This is a basic recipe which you can use for a variety of vegetables, and which you can adapt to include meat or fish. Choose at least 2–3 from the following: broccoli florets, carrot, cauliflower florets, celery, French beans, mangetout, mushrooms, a few frozen peas, red or yellow pepper, baby sweetcorn (tinned ones are fine).

SERVES 2–4

340–450g/12oz–1lb mixed chosen vegetables

Plus

1 clove garlic, chopped

1 mild red chilli, seeded and shredded

1 dessertspoon chopped lemon grass

1 kaffir lime leaf, finely shredded (snip with scissors)

2–4 tablespoons chicken stock or water

2 tablespoons nam pla

1 dessertspoon sugar

fresh basil or coriander to finish

grapeseed or peanut oil for frying

Have all the vegetables cut or sliced into bite-sized pieces; blanch carrot/broccoli/cauliflower for 1 minute just to soften. Heat 1–2 tablespoons of oil in a wok. Add the garlic, stir for 30 seconds, then tip in the rest of the vegetables and aromatics. Toss over high heat for a minute or so. Add the chicken stock or water, nam pla and sugar. Toss again for another minute or so, check the seasoning and serve sprinkled with fresh herbs.

Variations Add 170–225g/6–8oz prawns, chicken pieces or strips of tender pork to this basic mix. Add with the garlic and stir-fry until the surfaces have turned opaque.

For a spicy version, omit the garlic and chilli, but add 2 teaspoons of Thai curry paste, frying it first with the oil before adding the meat or vegetables. For a creamier flavour, stir in coconut cream to taste just before serving.

Stir-fried squid, roasted red pepper and coriander

This colourful recipe illustrates how to use a wok for pasta dishes. It works well with mixed seafood – adding a few cooked mussels or prawns, for example – and with any firm fish such as monkfish.

SERVES 2

170–225g/6–8oz prepared squid, cut into bite-sized strips approx. 1.25cm/$\frac{1}{2}$ inch wide × 5cm/2 inches long (include the chopped tentacles)

170–225g/6–8oz dried Chinese noodles or Italian pasta

1 large red pepper, roasted, covered with olive oil and cut into strips (see p 103)

1 tablespoon each chopped coriander and chives

olive oil

Rinse the squid, dry briefly on kitchen paper, then put on a plate – don't leave it on the paper as it will stick – and toss in a little olive oil. This can be done in advance and the squid left in the fridge until needed. Cook the noodles or pasta in a wok half-full of boiling salted water until *al dente*. Drain, toss with a little extra oil in a large, oiled, hot serving dish, cover and pop in a low oven to keep warm. Dry the wok. Heat over a high heat, add 1 tablespoon olive oil, swirl, then add the squid. Stir-fry for about 1 minute until the squid is just opaque. Add the red pepper, and its oil, tossing to heat through. Season lightly if you want, then lightly mix into the pasta together with the herbs; or mix in the wok. Serve immediately on hot plates, with extra olive oil.

Variations You can add more or fewer herbs as you wish; use chopped parsley instead of coriander; flavour the oil with a crushed clove of garlic or dried chilli; add a few tablespoons of fish stock or white wine with the red pepper.

Stir-fried chicken with corn, red pepper and ginger

SERVES 2

225g/8oz cooked chicken, cut into strips

$\frac{1}{2}$ red pepper, seeded and diced

4 baby corn, sliced into nuggets

1 green chilli, seeded and finely sliced

1 dessertspoon chopped thyme

1 teaspoon finely chopped fresh ginger root

1–2 tablespoons vegetable oil

TO SERVE

110–170g/4–6oz Chinese dried noodles or Thai fragrant rice, freshly cooked

4–5 tablespoons chicken stock

Thai soy sauce (or nam pla if not available)

Heat a non-stick heavy frying pan. Add the oil, swirl it around and then tip in all the ingredients. Stir-fry over a brisk heat for 4–5 minutes until the chicken is browned.

Arrange the noodles or rice in a heated serving dish. Moisten with hot chicken stock and season with Thai soy sauce. Top with the chicken mixture and serve immediately.

Variation Add a kaffir lime leaf, cut into strips if fresh or crumbled if dried, and stir-fry with the chicken and vegetables.

Fried 'seaweed'

Remove the thick midribs from about 225g/8oz dark spring green cabbage leaves and roll into a tight cigar. Shred into fine strands using a serrated knife, separating the coils out lightly with your fingers. Heat 2.5–5cm/1–2 inches of oil in a wok or large pan and deep-fry small handfuls at a time: they will sizzle immediately. Cook for barely a minute until the foam subsides and the strands become translucent. Scoop out, drain very well and spread the glistening crispy strands on kitchen paper. Pile into a dish and season with salt. Serve with stir-fries or scatter over salads.

Shredded sesame omelette

A favourite standby – good to accompany any stir-fry meal. You can make it with one egg or several.

To serve 2, beat a couple of eggs with 2–3 tablespoons of sesame seeds. Heat a little oil in a non-stick frying pan. Keeping the heat fairly high, pour in enough mixture to cover the base and cook until the bottom is light brown and the omelette has set but is still moist on the surface. Lift one edge and pour in a tablespoon of sherry; it will sizzle violently, flavouring the omelette. Roll up like a Swiss roll and cut into strips. Repeat with the rest of the mixture and keep hot in the oven – this crisps the edges – while you make the stir-fry. Serve in a separate bowl or scattered over stir-fried vegetables and noodles. It's also good with stir-fried rice and to pad out strips of stir-fried chicken or beef. The sherry can be left out or you can add a little minced spring onion to the beaten eggs.

Any-time stir-fry

This is the basic method I follow at home to produce stir-fry suppers. You do not need to buy food especially for this kind of stir-fry; build it around whatever you happen to have.

Have everything ready by the stove; sauces mixed, rice or noodles cooked, Shredded Sesame Omelette (above) cut into strips keeping hot in the oven, and hot plates waiting. Transfer the noodles or rice to a hot shallow serving dish and keep warm, covered if necessary, lightly tossing the noodles first in oil to prevent them from sticking.

Heat the wok or pan and cook the stir-fry. Tip the stir-fry over a waiting bed of noodles or rice. Season/drizzle over the sauce/scatter with herbs, and serve immediately, with the Shredded Sesame Omelette as a side dish or scattered over the top of the stir-fry.

Core flavourings

This is a list of the core flavourings you will come across most frequently in recipes for Chinese and Southeast Asian stir-fries. The other major stir-fry cuisine, Japanese, is slightly more esoteric and less well known, and is not included here.

	Chinese	Southeast Asian
Flavourings	black beans	basil
	chilli	chilli
	5-spice powder	coconut cream/
	garlic	milk
	ginger	curry paste
	rice vinegar	galangal/ginger
	rice wine	garlic
	sesame seed oil	kaffir lime
	sesame seeds	lemon grass
	spring onions	mint
	star anise	onions
Bottled sauces	chilli sauce	chilli sauce
	hoisin	chilli and basil
	plum sauce	sauce
	oyster sauce	nam pla
	soy	satay sauce
		Thai soy

QUICK CHECKLIST

Black beans

These are salted and fermented soy beans. Said to predate soy sauce, they have a similar flavour but are far more pungent. Used as a seasoning for meat, fish and vegetables, they have a soft texture and are easily chopped or mashed. They keep indefinitely.

Bean sprouts

Should be fresh – alabaster white and very crunchy-looking. Any which look in the least bit slimy or have a hint of brown to them are too old.

Chilli sauce

A bottle of chilli sauce is an admirable thing to have and it keeps indefinitely. It is convenient to use and is a more than handy substitute for fresh chillies. Every nation which has taken chilli to its heart has its own variation, all awesomely hot. Because you need so little, it doesn't matter much which you use. Oriental chilli sauces tend to be hot, sweet and garlicky, and can be used by the teaspoon. All others – Jamaican hot pepper sauce, Tabasco, etc. – should be used by the drop.

Chinese dried noodles

A must for instant stir-fries. Though made from the same ingredients as pasta – either flour and water or flour, eggs and water – these taste entirely different. For some equally unfathomable reason, you can eat fewer noodles than pasta: one sheet is ample for one, one packet (225g/8oz) ample for four. All brands seem to be the same and all supermarkets stock them. Medium-thick ones are suited for most stir-fries.

To cook them, put them in a pan of boiling water, cover, remove from the heat and leave for 4–5 minutes. If overcooked, they become as pappy as commercial white bread. To prevent them from sticking, drain under running water or toss in a little oil seasoned, if you like, with a few drops of sesame seed oil. To reheat, toss in the pan with the stir-fried vegetables or dunk into boiling water.

Other oriental noodles The two other common types are rice noodles and Japanese buckwheat noodles, soba. On the principle that everything should be tried once, have a go. Rice noodles have a peculiar jelly-like texture and taste of virtually nothing. Buckwheat noodles taste of buckwheat.

5-spice powder

An aromatic ground spice mixture commonly containing star anise, fennel, cinnamon, cloves and either ginger or Sichuan pepper. It is used to season meats and in marinades. Good to add to dressings, too. A pinch is enough.

Hoisin sauce

Another soy-bean-based sauce and one of the most useful to have. Thick, dark red, sweet and garlicky, it is used for barbecued meat, pork spare ribs and dipping sauces.

Rice vinegar

Vinegar made from rice, it is slightly sweeter, milder and less acidic than wine vinegar. It adds sharpness rather than acidity.

Rice wine

A colourless or yellow wine used as a beverage and in cooking. Pale dry sherry can be substituted. Not to be confused with Japanese rice wine, mirin, which is sweet, thick and viscous.

Sesame seed oil

Not as useful as you might think. There are two types: light, which is flavourless and not worth buying, and dark. Dark sesame seed oil is made from roasted sesame seeds and is generally so strong that a few drops will overpower any other flavour and dominate the dish. Use with caution. It has a low smoking point and burns very easily.

Sesame seeds

Cheap and nutty, these must be toasted first to bring out their flavour. Put them in a small pan and set over a moderate heat until the seeds begin to pop. They are used to coat strips of meat and to make sesame prawns, and are good with stir-fried greens, beans, cauliflower and carrots. See Shredded Sesame Omelette, p 279.

Shiitake mushrooms

Now available fresh and dried. Dried, they have a strong, pronounced flavour and a chewy texture. They are not to everybody's taste, including mine, but can be used in meat, fish and vegetable dishes. Proceed as with other dried mushrooms, rehydrating them first. The stalks are very tough and should be cut off. See also Sea Bass under Wraps, p 195.

Soy sauce

This is as readily available these days as HP sauce. A bottle with a small aperture so you can shake the soy sauce out and season food directly is more useful than one with an ordinary cap. There are two types: light and dark. Light soy is thinner and tends to be used for general cooking purposes, while dark soy is sweeter, thicker and the one used as a dipping sauce; it doesn't really matter which you use.

There are, in fact, a group of sauces made from fermented soy beans. Chinese soy sauce is strong, powerful and salty. Japanese soy sauce, shoyu, is sweeter, lighter and more refined. Japanese tamari sauce, made from fermented soy beans and sweet rice wine, mirin, is akin to Bovril and has a richer, more rounded flavour, while teriyaki sauce, made from soy sauce, mirin and ginger, is mellow, sweet and gingery. Thai soy sauce is delicious enough to eat on its own. All can be used to season stir-fries and can be substituted for each other if push comes to shove.

Star anise

A dark, mysterious, star-shaped spice with a potent aniseed-cum-liquorice flavour. Used in meat marinades (spare ribs, slow-cooked pork dishes, crispy duck), it is the predominant flavour in 5-spice powder. Either use whole or grind in a coffee-grinder. The longer it cooks in a dish, the stronger the flavour. One packet will last for ever. In Europe it has become a new-wave spice, used with fish, pulses, beef and desserts.

UK Suppliers

The following mail-order companies may be useful for UK readers.

Dried chillies A comprehensive range of Mexican dried chillies, and toasted chilli flakes, can be ordered from The Cool Chile Company, PO Box 5702, London W10 6WE. Tel: 0973 311714.

Saffron Mancha saffron, first category, can be ordered direct from Amber Food, Kingarth, Fernleigh Road, Wadebridge, Cornwall PL27 7AZ. Tel: 01208 815309.

Spices A full range of spices can be ordered direct from Fox's Spices, Masons Road Industrial Estate, Stratford upon Avon, Warwickshire CV37 9NF. Tel: 01789 266420.

Salt Brittany sea salt, and a full range of peppercorns, vinegars etc., can be ordered direct from Morel Brothers, Cobbett & Son, Unit 1, 50 Sulivan Road, London SW6 3DX. Tel: 0171 384 3345.

In addition, the Sainsbury Special Selection, found in selected Sainsbury's stores, stocks many items including saffron, spices, risotto rice, specialist vinegars and oils.

Organic produce Details of the Home Delivery Basket Scheme for organic fruit and vegetables, which operates nationwide, can be obtained from The Soil Association, 86 Colston Street, Bristol BS1 5BB. Tel: 0117 9290661. The Fresh Food Company in London. Tel: 0181 969 0351, and The Organic Marketing Company in Hereford. Tel: 01531 640819, also operate home delivery schemes.

Real or organic meat The Real Meat Company offers an overnight express service, Real Meat Express, and a full advisory service. Their address is 31 Deverill Road Trading Estate, Sutton Veny, Warminster, Wiltshire BA12 9BZ. Tel: 01985 840436.

Two suppliers of organic meat offering a comprehensive mail service are:
Graig Farm Meat, Graig Farm, Dolau, Llandrindod Wells, Powys LD1 5TL. Tel: 01597 851 655.
Heal Farm, Kings Nympton, Umberleigh, Devon EX37 9TB. Tel: 01769 574341.
Michael Richards, 21 London Road, Calne, Wiltshire SN11 0AA. Tel: 01249 812362, is a Real Meat specialist butcher.

Q Guild butchers A full list of these can be obtained from PO Box 44 Winterhill House, Snowdon Drive, Milton Keynes MK6 1AX.

Specialist food producers Many of these operate mail-order services or can be visited direct. The best reference guide to small food producers and shops currently available is Henrietta Green's *Food Lovers' Guide to Britain*, published annually by BBC Books.

Acknowledgements

Many people have contributed in different ways to this book; my profound thanks to all. In particular, I owe a special debt to the following:

For the fish chapter, Rick Stein and the Seafood Restaurant, Padstow, and Chris Ramus of Ramus Seafoods, Harrogate. The Seafood Restaurant and Rick Stein's own book, *English Seafood Cookery*, are constant sources of inspiration and I should like to acknowledge their influence on the recipes in the fish chapter.

For the chapter on meat, special thanks to Richard Guy of the Real Meat Company, Warminster, Mike Richards, real meat butcher in Calne, and Ian Rowland of the British Industrial Biological Research Association. The staff at The Meat and Livestock Commission were enormously patient and of great help; in particular I should like to express my gratitude and appreciation to Clare Greenstreet and Chris Warkup. My thanks also to Sue Eddleston of Russell Hobbs, the home economists at Stoves, and Paul Vickers of The Castle Hotel, Taunton.

For general cookery, I am indebted to Willi Elsener, executive chef at the Dorchester, Shaun Hill, and friend and colleague Sybil Kapoor, whose help and sunny optimism brightened many a dull day. My warm thanks to all three.

Along the way, Sue Ashworth of the Butter Council, Frances Bissell, Shirley Bond, Charles Carey, Richard Cawley, Anna Del Conte, Clarissa Dickson-Wright, Ann Dolamore, Rose Elliot, the Fresh Fruit Information Bureau, Professor Kurti, Elizabeth Lambert Ortiz, Tony Muir of the Soil Association, Hugh Roberts of Fiskars, Claudia Roden, Sue Style, potato expert Alan Wilson and Jane Whichello of British Gas all answered pleas for help, for which many grateful thanks. A special mention for Roz Denny who arrived with a carload of rice, the ever helpful and considerate Sri and Roger Owen, John Humphries who gave immeasurable help on saffron, Dodie Miller for the same on chillies and Sonia Stevenson.

For the unsung heroine of this book, my editor, Louise Haines, my heartfelt and affectionate gratitude for never flinching at my ideas, for her gentle good sense and daily doses of encouragement when the going got tough. For Christabel Gairdner for keeping cheerful and sane under a barrage of phone calls and mountain of photostats. For Rick, as ever, my love for continuing to smooth my brow and still allowing me to be impossibly selfish.

Finally, as the song says, everybody needs somebody to lean on. For Joanna and Nigel, my everlasting thanks.

I would like to thank the following for their permission to reprint previously published material. Alan Davidson for quoting material from his book, *Seafood*, published by Mitchell Beazley; Drew Smith of *Taste* magazine for some of the material used in the chart on cooking polenta; Frances Bissell for the roasting chart, taken from *Real Meat*, published by Chatto and Windus; the Meat and Livestock Commission for the cooking chart, published in their booklet, *Cooking British Meat*.

For permission to include their recipes, I would like to thank the following: Frances Bissell, Shaun Hill, Geraldene Holt, Simon Hopkinson, Madhur Jaffrey, Pierre Koffmann, Alastair Little, Claudia Roden and Colin Spencer. Recipe credits are acknowledged on the relevant pages.

Select Bibliography

General

Christian, Glynn, *The New Delicatessen Food Handbook*, Good Food Retailing Publications, 1993

McGee, Harold, *On Food and Cooking, The Science and Lore of the Kitchen*, Unwin Hyman, 1988

McGee, Harold, *The Curious Cook*, HarperCollins, 1992

Olney, Richard (ed.), *The Good Cook Series*, Time-Life Books, 1979–82

Slater, Nigel, *Real Fast Food*, Michael Joseph, 1992

Slater, Nigel, *The 30-Minute Cook*, Michael Joseph, 1994

Fish

Davidson, Alan, *Mediterranean Seafood*, Penguin, 1987

Davidson, Alan, *North Atlantic Seafood*, Penguin, 1980

Davidson, Alan, *Seafood*, Mitchell Beazley, 1989

Grigson, Jane, *Fish Cookery* (new edition), Penguin, 1993

Stein, Rick, *English Seafood Cookery*, Penguin, 1988

Food suppliers

Gear, Alan and Jackie, and Mabey, David (eds), *Thorsons Organic Consumer Guide*, Thorsons, 1990

Green, Henrietta, *Food Lovers' Guide to Britain*, BBC Books, 1995

Meat

Bissell, Frances, *The Real Meat Cookbook*, Chatto and Windus, 1993

Grigson, Jane, *Charcuterie and French Pork Cookery*, Penguin, 1981

Olive oil, seasonings, spices and herbs

Cost, Bruce, *Food from the Far East*, Century, 1990

Dolamore, Ann, *A Buyer's Guide to Olive Oil*, Grub Street, 1995

Forbes, Leslie, *Recipes from the Indian Spice Trail*, BBC Books, 1994

Grigson, Sophie, *Ingredients Book*, Pyramid Books, 1991

Holt, Geraldene, *Complete Book of Herbs*, Conran Octopus, 1991

Humphries, John, *The Saffron Companion*, Grub Street, 1995

McVicar, Jekka, *Jekka's Complete Herb Book*, Kyle Cathie, 1994

Norman, Jill, *The Complete Book of Spices*, Dorling Kindersley, 1990

Ortiz, Elizabeth Lambert, *The Encyclopedia of Herbs, Spices and Flavourings*, Dorling Kindersley, 1992

Pasta

Del Conte, Anna, *La Pasta*, Pavilion, 1993

Del Conte, Anna, *Pasta Perfect*, Conran Octopus, 1991

Hazan, Giuliano, *The Classic Pasta Cookbook*, Dorling Kindersley, 1993

Rice, grains and dried pulses

Del Conte, Anna, *I Risotti*, Pavilion, 1993

Elliot, Rose, *The Bean Book*, Thorsons, 1994

Fletcher, Janet, *Grain Gastronomy*, Aris Books, 1988

Madison, Deborah, *The Savoury Way*, Bantam Press, 1990

Owen, Sri, *The Rice Book*, Doubleday, 1993

Vegetables

Bareham, Lindsey, *In Praise of the Potato*, Michael Joseph, 1994

Brown, Lynda, *The Cook's Garden*, Vermilion, 1992

Grigson, Jane, *Jane Grigson's Vegetable Book*, Penguin, 1980

Grigson, Sophie, *Eat Your Greens*, BBC Books, 1992

Spencer, Colin, *Vegetable Pleasures*, Fourth Estate, 1992

Vergé, Roger, *Roger Vergé's Vegetables*, Mitchell Beazley, 1994

Index